National Trust Guide

San Francisco

Other National Trust City Guides:

THE NATIONAL TRUST GUIDE TO NEW ORLEANS
Roulhac Toledano

THE NATIONAL TRUST GUIDE TO SAVANNAH
Roulhac Toledano

THE NATIONAL TRUST GUIDE TO SANTA FE
Richard Harris

THE NATIONAL TRUST GUIDE TO SEATTLE
Walt Crowley

National Trust Guide
San Francisco

America's Guide for Architecture
and History Travelers

PETER BOOTH WILEY

PRESERVATION
PRESS

John Wiley & Sons, Inc.
New York • Chichester • Weinheim • Brisbane • Singapore • Toronto

Published by John Wiley & Sons, Inc.

Published simultaneously in Canada.

Library of Congress Cataloging-in-Publication Data:

Wiley, Peter Booth.
    National trust guide—San Francisco : America's guide for architecture and history travelers / by Peter Booth Wiley.
        p. cm.
    Includes index.
    ISBN 0-471-19120-5 (pbk.)
        1. Historic buildings—California—San Francisco—Guidebooks. 2. San Francisco (Calif.)—Guidebooks. 3. Architecture—California—San Francisco—Guidebooks. 4. San Francisco (Calif.)—Buildings, structures, etc.—Guidebooks. I. Title.

F869.S343 W55 2000
917.94'610454—dc21   00-043267

*This book is dedicated to
my beloved wife Valerie*

SAN FRANCISCO WALKING TOURS

San Francisco offers numerous walking tours, many of them free. Here are some of them:

Barbary Coast Trail, a self-guided 3.8 mile walking tour of historic sites, museums, and landmark buildings—775-1111
California Historical Society—357-1848 ext. 15
City Guides, neighborhood and theme walks with trained guides—557-4266
The Castro—550-8110
Chinatown—788-8388, 986-1822, 982-8839
Golden Gate Park, McLaren Park, and Stem Grove—263-0991
Grace Cathedral Tour—749-6348
Haight-Ashbury—221-8442,775-6773
Historic San Francisco Post Office and Courthouse—556-9945
History, food, and cultural tours led by local columnist—397-8530
Jewish Landmarks—921-0461
Mission District Murals—285-2287
National Aids Memorial Grove—750-8340
Nob Hill and the Financial District—(650) 851-1123
North Beach, history, food, and culture—397-8530, (800) 820-2220
Performing Arts Center (Symphony, Opera, and Herbst Theatre)—552-8338.
Arts Commission docent tours of City Hall—554-6139, www.thecity.sfsu.edu/sfac/
San Francisco Heritage, Pacific Heights walks—441-3000
San Francisco Then and Now—931-4021
Tours of the City specializing in sites mentioned in Armistead Maupin's *Tales of the City*—734-2986. www.ToursoftheCity.com
Victorian Home Walks, historical homes in Pacific Heights and Cow Hollow — 252-9485

Contents

Preface

Though a small city with a population of approximately 850,000, San Francisco has long enjoyed a reputation as one of the country's premier tourist attractions. Its magnificent natural setting, fine restaurants, museums, and tourist attractions, such as Golden Gate Park and Fisherman's Wharf, combine with a peculiar kind of cultured libertinism to make a heady combination for any visitor looking for an entertaining time.

An appreciation of the city's colorful history and its diverse architectural traditions can substantially enrich a visitor's experience. An essential part of the city's appeal is the ambience created by its architecture, most notably in the Victorian neighborhoods of the Western Addition, Mission District, Haight-Ashbury, and Pacific Heights. San Francisco has other striking architectural features: Its Civic Center—a cluster of government buildings centered on a restored city hall whose dome reaches higher than the capitol in Washington—is the finest and most complete example of municipal buildings in the French neoclassical style anywhere in the country. Downtown San Francisco boasts an extensive collection of graceful lowrise office buildings erected between 1889 and 1920. Even though every longtime San Franciscan experiences a sense of violation when the current skyline is juxtaposed with the skyline of the 1940s, some of the skyscrapers thrown up during the Manhattanization of the downtown financial district between 1955 and 1986, most notably the Transamerica Pyramid, are signature buildings in their own right.

Then there are the architectural features that have drawn the attention of history and architecture buffs. They include, among many others, the remnants of the gold rush city clustered in the Jackson Square Historical District on the border between Downtown and Telegraph Hill; the buildings designed by anti-Victorian rebels such as Willis Polk; the experiments with innovative forms of modern and postmodern architecture, particularly South of Market; and the new departures in the development of low-income housing epitomized by the Delancey Street complex for drug addicts and ex-convicts on the Embarcadero south of the Bay Bridge.

Because I will describe the city in terms of the relationship between geography, history, urban design, and architecture, the book is an invitation

San Francisco skyline in 1958. *San Francisco Public Library.*

to use your imagination. It will help you see not only the buildings as they are today, but also to imagine how the city has changed since the arrival of the Spanish in 1769. You will be like an archeologist working your way downward layer by layer — in some cases virtually into the muck and sand underlying much of the city. In the end you should come away with a better understanding of how the city came to be the endlessly fascinating place it is.

This book is written for an audience with varying degrees of knowledge about architecture. For this reason I have written a summary history of San Francisco's architecture (Chapter Eight) while trying to minimize the use of architectural terminology as much as possible. It is important, however, to be familiar with some terms and with a number of styles, schools, and traditions that had a significant impact on the architecture of San Francisco.

Even the greatest architectural innovators, such as Frank Lloyd Wright studied and borrowed from other styles. In a sense, architecture is a language; its practitioners use its grammar and vocabulary, either comfortable within its traditions or eager to reshape them into something new. For the client, architecture is a different matter. Architects may want to see themselves as artists; ultimately it is the clients who call the shots. A client may know a great deal about architecture, or very little for that matter. But clients turn to architects to express their ideas about how their homes, office buildings or other structures should look. In this way clients tell us about how they view their place in the urban landscape. In their silence, the resulting structures speak volumes about the city's history and the way its citizens have viewed themselves over time.

San Francisco skyline in 1999. The Ferry Building (left of center) is dwarfed by a wall of high rises.
Peter Booth Wiley.

The growth of conflict over historic buildings, high-rise construction, urban congestion, low-income housing, and many aspects of urban design has encouraged nonprofessionals to learn about and formulate opinions about architectural matters. I hope that this book will encourage people, wherever they live, to look at their built environment and decide what they do and do not like about it.

HOW TO USE THIS BOOK

Part I comprises seven introductory chapters covering the geographical transformation of the city and its history. Part II offers maps and descriptions of suggested walking tours to help you find architectural and historic sites, museums, bookstores, and a few historic restaurants and bars. Do not rely on these maps alone. Go to a bookstore or a large drugstore and buy a good map of the city. You will need it. This is a book to guide you through San Francisco—by auto, on foot, by public transportation, or even from your armchair. I recommend public transportation and foot travel. You can see a lot more when you are not driving. The Municipal Railway covers the entire city—though it is not the most efficient system—with buses, trolleys, cable cars, and even a collection of historic trolleys, which run up and down Market Street and along the Embarcadero to Fisherman's Wharf. You will be pleased to discover that street signs include a number—00, 100, 200, etc.— which provides a guide to building numbers on the block with an arrow pointing in the direction of the ascending numbers.

The development of San Francisco radiated outward from the small cluster of shacks and adobes on the eastern bay shore known as Yerba Buena, which was founded in 1834. The earliest neighborhoods, such as Telegraph Hill, Chinatown, and South of Market, were the closest to the first beachfront community. I have arranged the walking tours so that you can visit these neighborhoods roughly in the order of their historical development, starting with the remnants of the gold rush city adjacent to today's downtown financial district. Once you have completed the tours of Downtown and its proximate neighbors (Chapters 9 to 14), the next group of tours (Chapters 15 to 21) take you to more residential neighborhoods (Russian Hill, Nob Hill, Pacific Heights, the Western Addition, the Mission, Haight-Ashbury, the Marina, Cow Hollow, and the western suburbs) as they fan out from Downtown.

Once you have reached a district or neighborhood, the only way to see its buildings is on foot. So this is a guide for walkers—in some instances where the terrain in this hilly city is steep, for hearty walkers. There is one exception. A walking tour of the western suburbs would require too much time. In Chapter 21, I have listed some of the most significant houses and attractions in the western suburbs. Given the distance between the houses, it would be best to visit them by car.

This book does not pretend to be a guide to San Francisco's wonderful restaurants. I mention restaurants that are either historic or give you a sense of the history of a neighborhood. If you are a gourmand, you may not find these to be the finest restaurants in the city.

I assume that even with this book, you may want additional information about the city. The resources included in the bibliography at the end of the book can be helpful. If you want to peruse an excellent collection of books on the city, visit the San Francisco History Room on the sixth floor of the New Main Library in the Civic Center (100 Larkin Street). While you are there, find the computer terminal on the same floor and take a look at *Shaping San Francisco*, a multimedia presentation of the history of the city. In addition, I have mentioned a number of bookstores that offer books on architecture or local history. I have also included a list of walking tours offered by various organizations.

Acknowledgments

I would like to thank Jan Cigliano for starting both this project and my education about preservation architecture. Mike Berline convinced me to go ahead when he told me it would be a privilege to write this book. My editor, Amanda Miller, combined patience, a firm hand, and enthusiastic support during the writing while Valerie Peterson launched our marketing effort. My son, Nate Wiley, did some of the original research while his brother, Beau, contributed his photographic skills. Mimi Manning was my able research assistant. Pauli Rose and Mike Pincus critiqued early drafts of some of the chapters while Ruth Mills exercised her considerable editing skills by forcing me to cut where I had not been able to cut before. Elizabeth Goldstein and Courtney Damkroger from the National Trust's Western Regional office offered early advice while Don Andreini provided access to San Francisco Heritage's files. The following architects and their employees provided interviews, illustrations, or other information: Robert Cole, Susie Colliver, Linda Crouse, Diane Filippi, Kevin Hart, Lucia Howard, Charlie Kreidler, Rebecca Schnier, Richard Schluemer, Linda Sobuta, R.K. Stewart, and Graham Wyatt. I interviewed community and preservation activists Buck Bagot, David Bahlman, Laura Culbertson, John Elberling, Linda Jo Fitz, G. Bland Platt, Toby Levine, Chandler McCoy, Charles Hall Page, Norman Rolfe, Douglas Shoemaker, Oba T'shaka, J. Gordon Turnbull, and Dee Dee Workman. Others interviewed: Joel Bashevkin, Donald Brown, Eric Elsesser, Susan Brandt-Hawley, Jean Kortum, Michael McCone, Vincent Sancimino, and Helen Sause. I would also like to thank Emily Wolff and Scott Shields from the California Historical Society, Gary Kurutz of the California State Library, Richard Dillon of the California State Preservation Office, Waverly Lowell from the College of Environmental Design at the University of California Berkeley, and Pat Akre, Selby Collins, Susan Goldstein, Amy Holloway, and Faun McInnis from the San Francisco Public Library. Numerous local historians were helpful including Malcolm Barker, Sara Holmes Boutelle, Joseph Blum, Gray Brechin, Jeffrey Burns, Chester Hartman, John McCosker, Joe Pecora, William Kostura, Nancy Leigh Olmsted, Jerry Schimmel, and Masha Zakheim. I would also like to thank Jeff Berger, Barbara Berman, Dale Carlson, Alicia Champion, Nancy Chan, Samara Diapoulos, William Dick, Mary Gentry, Donna Gouse, John Graham, James Haas, Beverly Hennessey, Ellen Huppert, Angela Jackson, James Lawrence, Clarence Lee, Janice Levy, Lupe' Machuca, John Martini, Nancy Morita, Jane Morrison, Alan Nichols, Ira Nowinski, Vicky Powers, Michelle Ragland-Dilworth, Richard Rutlinger, Gary Schilling, Victoria Shelton, Phil Skidmore, David Styles, Jim Swanson, Barbara Traisman, Kristy Van Koughnet, Norman Walsh, Nancy Weston and Myra and Nate Berkowitz and Brian Tench, owners of the historic Grant Building, who provided me with a comfortable place to work.

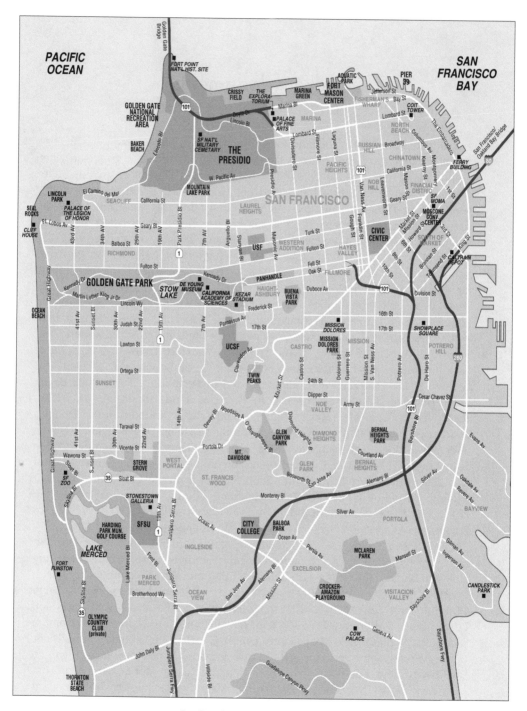

San Francisco and its neighborhoods.

PART I

San Francisco: A History

1

A Beautiful City in the Wrong Place

San Francisco derives its world-renowned beauty most of all from its natural setting. Ironically, the beauty comes from the "unnatural" act of building a city on extensively altered terrain.

There is no better way to appreciate San Francisco than a visit to high ground. Try the top of Telegraph Hill at the foot of Coit Tower, the bar at the top of the Mark Hopkins Hotel on Nob Hill, or, higher still, the Carnelian Room at the top of the Bank of America building at Kearny and California Streets. Here on a clear day (fog is always a problem in San Francisco) you can see the full, spectacular panorama of the city and its environs. For your next introductory visit try the National Maritime Museum in Aquatic Park at the north end of Van Ness Avenue, which offers an exhibit on the history of the city.

AN ALTERED LANDSCAPE

You can begin to imagine a completely different place, for many of what appear to be natural features in San Francisco are actually the work of humans. Before the arrival of Europeans, San Francisco was a wild and beautiful, but forbidding, place—a windswept and fog-shrouded headland with barren sand dunes, high, rocky outcrops, and thickets of stunted trees and underbrush growing in its protected lowlands. East of the Golden Gate Bridge along the shoreline, sandy beaches and mud flats alternated with

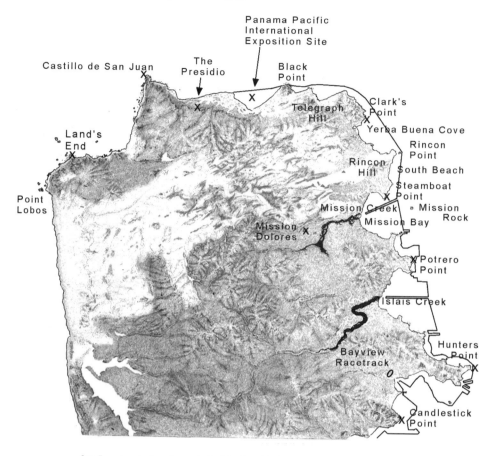

San Francisco before the arrival of the Spanish in the 1770s indicating the modern waterfront. The light areas were sand dunes. *Nancy Morita/Jim Swanson.*

coves, creeks, and marshy inlets that left several headlands jutting into the bay. It is hard to imagine the surfeit of wildlife—enormous flocks of birds, abundant fish and shellfish, wolves, grizzly bears, mountain lions—that populated these shores.

There are signs of prehistoric human habitation in San Francisco. The native population was soon overwhelmed by the Spanish, who arrived in 1775. The newcomers built the Presidio, the Mission, and a small settlement on the shores of Yerba Buena Cove where the beach ran along what today is Montgomery Street. The gold rush brought massive and rapid development after 1849. But even with the beginning of urbanization, General Persifer Smith, the commander of the U.S. military forces in California in 1849, concluded that "San Francisco is in no way fitted for commercial or military purposes." There was little solid, level ground to build on. Most of what would become the city was either steep hillsides, rolling sand dunes, or marshy ground. There were scant local supplies of water and firewood. The bay was one of the great natural harbors of the world, but because of tidal mud flats, it was impossible to approach the shore near the village of San Francisco except in a shallow-draft boat. In its first decade many of the city's leaders were convinced that there would be a great metropolis on the bay, but in a better location.

THE GOLD RUSH CREATES A CITY

With the pell-mell influx of gold seekers, San Francisco became the West's first "instant city," growing up the sides of Nob Hill and Telegraph Hill from the first civic center, which was Portsmouth Square on the eastern edge of Chinatown. To build a city, there had to be level land, and the city's founders went about reclamation in a chaotic fashion. Finger piers were built out over the mud flats to provide deep-water berths for the ships that brought the argonauts and their supplies. The spaces between the piers were linked by rickety catwalks and then filled by carving away at the foot of Telegraph Hill and leveling the 80-foot-high dunes that ran east and west along what later became Market Street.

In 1868 work began on a bulkhead, which was backfilled, thus eliminating Yerba Buena Cove by 1910. The new shoreline ran in a straight line from Telegraph Hill to Rincon Hill where the Bay Bridge touched down. Today, between Telegraph Hill and the Bay Bridge east of Montgomery Street, almost all of the downtown office buildings, constructed over the remains of dozens of gold rush–era ships, are embedded in landfill.

Yerba Buena Cove in 1847. The size of the hills is exaggerated, but this lithograph gives a sense of the size of the village of Yerba Buena and its barren surroundings. *Bancroft Library.*

The Second Street Cut (1869). When Second Street was extended south, Rincon Hill *(to the left),* the city's first fashionable neighborhood, went into decline. *California Historical Society.*

The Mission Plank Road (1856). One block south of today's Civic Center, this early road to the Mission Dolores ran through sand dunes. *San Francisco Public Library.*

In the early 1850s, Henry Meiggs, one of the great scoundrels of the city's boom and bust years, built a road along the eastern shoreline of Telegraph Hill to North Beach and then a 1,600-foot wharf at the foot of Powell Street. Later came a bulkhead and backfill. Land was reclaimed east of Black Point for construction of a lead smelter and a woolen mill. After the city's large fishing fleet was moved from the eastern side of Telegraph Hill to the foot of Taylor Street in 1900, a seawall and new piers were built over the next three years to house its operations at what would become known as Fisherman's Wharf.

RINCON HILL AND MISSION BAY

Rincon Hill, hidden today by the west end of the Bay Bridge, was the city's first fashionable neighborhood. Its decline set in when Second Street was run through a deep cut to South Beach in 1885 and its large, ornate homes were isolated from downtown. The final insult came in 1936 when the top of the hill was leveled for the huge concrete piers anchoring the western end of the Bay Bridge.

South of Rincon Point the coastline curved westward into Mission Bay, a marshy tidal inlet almost a mile across that was navigable by flat-bottom scows up to piers just east of the Mission Dolores at approximately Nineteenth and Folsom Streets. The Arroyo de los Dolores near the Mission drained into Mission Bay from the west; to the north its tidal marshes extended to Mission Street and to the south to Twentieth and Harrison Streets. The plank roads that ran through the dunes from the waterfront westward along Mission and Folsom Streets in the 1850s were occasionally threatened by high tides, and when an attempt was made to drive 40-foot piles for a bridge at Mission and Seventh Streets, the first two disappeared into the mud. This terrain with its islands of peat also proved dangerous to foraging livestock. Occasionally a cow or goat would simply drop from sight. This area is subject to dangerous liquefaction during a major earthquake, and one can still see, for example, that buildings are continuing to settle into the fill by noting the uneven rooflines of buildings along Folsom Street between Seventh and Eighth or on Harrison between Sixth and Seventh. At the entrance to the bay was Mission Rock (now the site of the Mission Rock Resort at 817 China Basin). Because of the deep water surrounding this cluster of rocks, it became the site of a shipping terminal and home to oyster pirates, who lived in a jumble of shacks along the beach.

South Beach, south of Rincon Hill, was reclaimed and extended in the 1860s, 1870s, and 1880s to make level ground for shipyards, lumberyards, a gas company, and piers and repair shops for the Pacific Mail Steamship Company, the New York–based company that dominated transportation across the Isthmus of Panama, up the West Coast, and westward to Asia.

Starting in 1862, a railroad causeway with a drawbridge was pushed across Mission Bay following what is now Third Street. Gradually Mission Bay was filled, leaving only Mission Creek, which is crossed by bridges at Third and Fourth Streets. After the 1906 earthquake and fire more than 10 million cubic yards of rubble were dumped here. Some of it was moved by horses, 15,000 of which, it was said, were worked to death cleaning up the city. Steam engines moved the rest along rails laid southward from downtown to unfilled parts of Mission Bay. The last of the reclamation took place after World War II when the Mission Rock Terminal was built at Pier 50.

AN INDUSTRIAL CENTER

Potrero Point marked the southern end of Mission Bay. During the first decades of the city's history, Potrero Point became its largest industrial district. Operations that began as modest, improvised blacksmith shops in an area known as Tar Flat near First and Folsom Streets were moved, starting in 1867, to impressive brick factories located on reclaimed land at Potrero Point. As a result, the 100-foot-high headland, which extended most of the way to today's waterline, was gradually carved away while the tidelands and salt marshes around the point were filled to accommodate shipbuilding and repair facilities, a rope walk, iron factories, a gasworks, and a sugar refinery (see illustration on page 46).

South of Potrero Point, the marshy inlet shaped by Islais Creek was for many years a barrier to the southward development of the city. The creek was crossed by the railroad to the Bay View Racetrack, and a road—now Bayshore Boulevard—was built along the eastern flank of Bernal Heights in 1880. But large-scale reclamation did not begin until after the Chamber of Commerce described the area as "an eyesore and a cesspool" in 1925. Land both north and south of the creek was then reclaimed, leading to the construction, in the 1950s and 1960s, of new piers and storage areas that would permit the use of shipping containers.

THE LAST FRONTIER

Hunter's Point was an early target of land speculators, who bought 2,445 acres hoping to develop a residential neighborhood. However, the area's isolation ultimately worked against them. Businessman William Ralston built a drydock there in 1868, large enough to berth all but the *Great Western*, then the world's largest ship. A second drydock, also the world's largest—it could berth a battleship—was constructed in 1903. During World War II the Navy

Looking west from the top of Russian Hill toward the Presidio and the Golden Gate in 1863. The Presidio Road, which ran over Russian Hill near present-day Union Street, originally connected the Presidio and the village of Yerba Buena. Tall dunes outline the beach in the deep cove to the left of the center of the picture. James Fair filled the cove to make space for new factories. *Courtesy of the California State Library.*

took over, converting the ship repair facilities into the Hunter's Point Naval Shipyard. More drydocks were built, and the fill from leveling a 170-foot hill at the end of the point was used to reclaim the marshlands in Candlestick Cove to the southwest. This final cove on the southern border of the city was filled to provide land for housing shipyard workers during the war. Reclamation continued when the city chose the area for a baseball stadium for the Giants after they moved to San Francisco in 1958. To the east of the stadium a new headland was fashioned from fill and turned into a park.

Major alterations to the shoreline were also made along the beaches, coves, and tidal inlets between the Golden Gate Bridge and Aquatic Park. Directly under the Golden Gate Bridge, the headlands where the crude Spanish fort known as the Castillo de San Juan stood were chopped away to near sea level to accommodate a massive brick coastal fort completed in 1861, just in time not to see action during the Civil War. In the 1880s, James Fair, one of the "Silver Kings" whose fortune came from the mines of Virginia City, Nevada, built a bulkhead along the beach and turned the shoreline of what is now the Marina District into an industrial district with a distillery, a gasworks, a factory for iron parts and wire, another that fabricated small ships, railroad cars, and pipe, and a hotel with a shooting gallery and other amusements. A pier was built at the foot of Fillmore Street to load dairy products from the farms of Cow Hollow (near Union Street).

In 1910 the city chose this site for a world's fair, the Panama Pacific International Exposition, to mark the opening of the Panama Canal and celebrate the reconstruction of San Francisco after the earthquake. Additional land was reclaimed for the fairgrounds. After the fair all of its buildings, with the exception of the Palace of Fine Arts, were razed and the area became a new residential district.

The filling in of the waterfront represented the most significant change in the urban landscape. The advent of the cable car and, later, the gasoline engine probably saved the tops of many of the city's numerous hills from the levelers. Some of them, like Telegraph Hill and Bernal Heights, were assaulted by quarry owners, landfill crews and highway developers, but by the early twentieth century the city's hilltops were deemed worthy of preservation either as desirable places to live or part of plans to preserve them for parks and open space.

COVERING THE DUNES

Up until the time of the 1906 earthquake the development of new neighborhoods was confined almost entirely to that part of the city east of Twin Peaks and north of Bernal Heights. Period photographs show a few homes scattered in wonderfully bucolic settings such as Glen Canyon or the dunes west of Twin Peaks. The rest was dunes. This wilderness was first tamed by the creation of Golden Gate Park, which was fashioned to look like a natural woodland. The dunes proved only a minor problem when the city's streetcar system was finally extended into the western part of the city. In 1918 a tunnel was drilled under Twin Peaks for the Municipal Railway, opening up new areas on the western side of the city to real estate developers, and in the next few decades the dunes disappeared beneath whole new neighborhoods.

Even as late as 1902 much of the western half of the city was undeveloped sand dunes. The band of trees is Golden Gate Park, which was planted by city gardeners. Note the Cliff House and Adolph Sutro's home in the background. *California Historical Society.*

This apartment building in the Marina District collapsed in the 1989 earthquake. *San Francisco Public Library.*

THE RING OF FIRE

Located on the eastern edge of the Ring of Fire, which encircles the Pacific Basin, San Francisco sits just to the east of the San Andreas Fault. Here the seaward tectonic plate is inching northward while the inland plate heads south. This is earthquake country, evidenced by seismic events in 1857, 1865, 1868, 1906, and 1989. Much of the city is built on fill and, as we have seen, can thus be highly unstable in an earthquake. A handful of builders responded to the 1868 quake, which killed six people, by introducing new ways of dealing with structural instability. After 1906 the city imposed new structural regulations, many of which were blithely ignored in the rush to rebuild. The city remained highly vulnerable to quakes, as was demonstrated in 1989, which in many neighborhoods was due to the way the landscape was shaped for urban development. In 1989 the Marina, the residential neighborhood built on the landfill for the Panama Pacific Exposition, was badly shaken. Several buildings collapsed, others were severely damaged, and three people died in a burning building. A swath of destruction was also noted in the downtown area—again, where there had been extensive landfill.

2

Before the
Gold Rush

B
efore the Spanish arrived in 1775, the California coast between
Monterey and the San Francisco peninsula was the site of one of the
densest populations of native peoples north of Mexico. Even then
there were only an estimated 10,000 people divided into autonomous
tribelets of 200 to 400 people living in intermarried families. Called
Costanoans by anthropologists, their descendants in the Bay Area call themselves Ohlones. They were hunters and gatherers, living in villages of round
reed houses. Their food forays took them into the interior valleys in summer
and fall. After gathering seeds and roots, they torched the grass, leaving naturally fertilized parklike meadows. During the rainy season, which extends
roughly from December to May, the Ohlone returned to their villages. It was
an abundant and, for the most part, harmonious life.

The arrival of the Spanish brought an end to a way of life that stretched
back for thousands of years. At the peak of their empire in the sixteenth century, the Spanish were the dominant power in the Pacific. The first Spanish
expedition sent north along the coast of California was searching for the
fabled Northwest Passage thought to connect the Atlantic and Pacific. Later
Spanish expeditions explored the coast looking for a port of refuge for
galleons sailing from the Philippines to Mexico.

The only challenge to the presence of Spanish ships in the Pacific during
the sixteenth and seventeenth centuries came from the British, specifically
the piratical raids of Sir Francis Drake and Thomas Cavendish. In 1579, Drake

anchored and careened the 80-foot *Golden Hind*, deeply laden with booty, north of San Francisco, probably under a high bluff east of Point Reyes. Drake claimed the surrounding country in the name of Queen Elizabeth. In the eighteenth century, with growing signs of British and Russian interest in California, the Spanish undertook to reassert their claims to Alta California through the creation of permanent settlements centered on a series of missions, pueblos (towns), and presidios (forts) stretching north from San Diego.

LA MISION DE SAN FRANCISCO DE ASIS (MISSION DOLORES)

Somehow, over two and a half centuries of exploration, the Spanish missed the entrance to San Francisco Bay until it was discovered by Captain Gaspar de Portola in 1769. Six years later Lieutenant Juan Manuel de Ayala spent 44 days exploring and mapping this large body of water, naming many of its principal features such as Angel Island, Sausalito, and Alcatraz.

In 1776, Captain Juan Agustin Bautista de Anza led a small party of soldiers, accompanied by Pedro Font, a Franciscan brother, up the peninsula from Monterey looking for a site for a new mission and presidio. After camping next to Mountain Lake (in Mountain Lake Park, see map on page XIV). Anza picked a place for a presidio on a headland overlooking the Golden Gate now known as Fort Point. Three days later he and Font explored the arroyos and meadows east of Twin Peaks, where they found a stream emerging from a canyon into a small lagoon that emptied into Mission Bay. They called the canyon Arroyo de los Dolores because it was Friday of Sorrows, the Friday before Palm Sunday. Because of its water supply and ample fertile ground, Font pronounced the location suitable for a mission. Three months later the first settlers arrived in a party of 193 people. On October 9, 1776, Father Francisco Palou dedicated the Mission of San Francisco de Asis, named after the patron saint of Palou's order; it is better known as Mission Dolores.

THE PADRES AND THE OHLONE

The Ohlone were initially drawn to the mission, reacting with fear and fascination. With their guns, metal implements, and ships that dwarfed the Indians' reed canoes, the Spanish could only be some kind of gods or perhaps, as the Coastal Miwoks thought when they encountered Drake, men returning from the land of the dead. The first converts, from a nearby village on the shores of Mission Bay, visited the mission in large numbers. Problems,

Native Californians at the Mission Dolores (1816). *Bancroft Library.*

however, developed quickly. Within weeks of the Spanish arrival, a native was shot by a soldier after some of the villagers were accused of theft, firing arrows too close to the soldiers, and attempting to kiss a soldier's wife.

Nevertheless, the Spaniards systematically converted the Indian population, starting on the peninsula and then crossing the bay and the Golden Gate to find new recruits. At the height of its development in 1805 the mission community of padres, converts, settlers, and guards from the Presidio numbered 1,163.

Whatever its appeal to the natives, mission life turned out to be fundamentally unsettling and ultimately disastrous. The padres believed in hard work and strict discipline, including the use of stocks and the lash, leading the president of the California missions to warn at one point against "going to extremes." Various Europeans who visited the missions remarked on the dejected demeanor of the native converts. Yet it was disease, not excessive discipline, that proved the undoing of the native converts. The Europeans brought measles, syphilis, smallpox, tuberculosis, and other diseases that ran through the native population in recurring epidemics, the highest mortality rates being among women and children. At times infant mortality rates were appalling: Of 38 children born at the Mission Dolores in 1796 and 1797, only two lived until their tenth birthday. Proselytizing campaigns, military forays to return runaways, and, ultimately, disease virtually obliterated village life in the Bay Area. Of the 72,000 Indians who converted, only 18,000 survived. By the time of the secularization of the missions in 1833, "all tribal lands within 40 miles to the north of San Francisco Bay and 80 miles to the east were empty of villages," according to historian Randall Milliken.[1]

THE PRESIDIO

In contrast to the Mission with its large, active, if tragically conflicted community, the Presidio proved to be little more than a military joke. Established in 1776 as the northernmost outpost of the Spanish empire in North America, its 70-year history of obvious neglect under Spanish, and then Mexican, rule proved ultimately to be a temptation to land-hungry interlopers, particularly the Americans.

When José Joaquin Moraga arrived in June 1776 with a party of settlers, he moved the site of the Presidio from that chosen by de Anza overlooking the Golden Gate to level ground about a mile southeast near a cove sheltered by Fort Point. This area, like the rest of the western half of the peninsula, was largely windswept sand dunes relieved by occasional stands of scrub oaks and thick brush. Moraga's party of some 15 soldiers immediately set about constructing a chapel and some crude shelters within a three-sided square palisade.

Like the Mission, the Presidio went through stages of construction and decay. From time to time the commandant or some other official would draw up plans for a walled compound that were not particularly elaborate, but more extensive and durable than that already existing. Neither the Spanish nor their Mexican successors, however, were ever willing to finance the construction and equipping of a real military outpost. The original palisade and buildings, some made of adobe, some nothing more than crude huts, were completely destroyed by storms within four years. Over time all of the original buildings were replaced with stronger structures made with wood, adobe, and stone.

In the 1780s, Spain's long-standing rivalry with England flared up, partly over competition for the fur trade in the Pacific Northwest. As a result the Spanish commenced construction of a fort, the Castillo de San Joaquin, where they mounted a coastal battery overlooking the Golden Gate on the point originally selected by de Anza for the Presidio. In 1792, Captain George Vancouver sailed through the Golden Gate looking for a town. Instead, he found the Presidio, which by then was a compound about 300 yards square surrounded on three sides by walls 14 feet high and 5 feet wide on a base made of redwood timbers, packed earth, and sod. Built along the inside of the compound walls were quarters for approximately 20 soldiers, a small but neat chapel, the commandant's two-room adobe, and a variety of other buildings, all with packed earth floors. These structures featured open windows with no glass. Vancouver noted the beginnings of the grandly named Castillo and 11 dismounted cannons lying nearby. The Presidio's commandant could manage only a one-gun salute for the British. Vancouver concluded that the Presidio could be easily destroyed by cannon fire and that the Spanish had decided to leave this enormous and inviting port essentially unprotected.

The Spaniards responded to the arrival of the British by intensifying their work on the Castillo, which was dedicated in 1794. The result was "a more permanent work consisting of 10-feet-thick embrasures on the seaward side of adobe faced with brick and mortar."[2] Within five years, the Castillo was in a state of collapse, caused by the erosion of the sandy soil beneath the fort and the dissolution of its walls and structures in the rain.

Ironically, 1799 marked the arrival in the bay of the first American ship, the armed merchantman *Eliza* from Boston, and the beginning of a small but steady flow of British, French, Russian, and American visitors. In 1809, the Russians began work on a settlement, which became Fort Ross (an American corruption of *Rus*), to the north near Bodega Bay for the collection of sea otter and seal skins. The Americans came originally looking for a site for a whaling station, but returned in greater force to trade with the missions and Californio ranchers for cowhides, which they shipped to the shoe factories of New England. The presence of so many aggressive foreigners, often aboard heavily armed ships, naturally made the Spanish nervous about their real intentions. And so they again pleaded with the authorities in Mexico City to strengthen the Presidio.

The Castillo was rebuilt and some extra troops were dispatched from Mexico, but with the beginning of Mexican rule in 1821 the Presidio began its final decline. Troops were released from duty because they could not be paid or properly supplied. In 1834, Mariano Guadalupe Vallejo, the Presidio commandant, a major landowner and the most influential Californio leader in the north, moved the garrison to Sonoma, leaving the crumbling facility in the hands of a caretaker.

Some of the ex-soldiers and their families remained in the area, however, and visitors in the 1820s reported a number of houses, some of them built by Russians, scattered around the Presidio. Part of the attraction of the area was the water emerging from El Polin Spring. According to local lore the spring enhanced women's fertility, and one woman with 20 children was cited as proof.

YERBA BUENA

Others preferred to live at the pueblo of Yerba Buena, which was established in 1834 on the eastern bayshore and named for a plant that was brewed for tea. With the growth of trade, Yerba Buena Cove became the best location for transferring cargo, most of it brought up the bay by launch from the missions of San Jose and Santa Clara to the ships anchored in deep water off the mud flats. William Richardson, a deserter from a British ship who married the Presidio commandant's daughter, built the first permanent structure in the newly founded village of Yerba Buena in 1835 when he was appointed port captain by the provincial governor. In *Two Years Before the Mast,* his classic account of the California hide trade, Richard Henry Dana, who visited Yerba Buena in the same year, described Richardson's abode as "a shanty of rough boards."

Overwhelmed by the majestic bay, Dana called Yerba Buena "the best anchoring-grounds in the whole western coast of America" and predicted that the area would become "a place of great importance."[3] Steve Richardson, the port captain's son, was less sanguine. In later years he recalled that "Yerba Buena was a dismal thing to look on in those early days. The beach was right enough, but to the westward stretched a wildnerness of desolation, forbidding sand dunes, often shifting their positions overnight." The persistent winds carried "an almost incredible burden of both fine and coarse sand that got into clothes, eyes, nose, mouth...penetrating the innermost recesses of a household." Yerba Buena, in short, "had a reputation for unhealthfulness, not entirely undeserved."[4]

CALIFORNIOS AND YANKEES

The abandonment of the Presidio coincided with the secularization of the California missions. With Indian labor, the padres had created the most productive farms in California, and the missions initially dominated the trade in hides, tallow, and grain, becoming what one historian described as "veritable general stores." The padres controlled the best lands, whereas only a handful of Hispanic soldiers, ex-soldiers, and settlers, known as Californios, were granted grazing rights but without permission to actually own land. All of this changed with the departure of the Spanish and the passage of Mexican laws in the 1820s permitting Californios to buy land. With the ability to buy land, the Californios cast covetous eyes on the missions' farms and extensive grazing lands. In 1833 the missions were secularized, and the Californio ranchers pounced on the spoils. Between that time and the end of Mexican rule, approximately ten million acres, or 10 percent of all the land in California, passed into private hands. Perhaps a third of this land came into the hands of non-Hispanic, particularly American and British, settlers. With secularization, most of the Indian converts living at Mission Dolores left to work on the ranchos or settle elsewhere. The Mission became a parish church at the center of a small village.

The Mission Dolores in 1856, when the structure in the center was a roadhouse and the area in front of the Mission was a popular spot for horse races and bull and bear fights. *San Francisco Public Library.*

Thus, the Californios emerged as the dominant class. Some of the more astute or romantic of the young American hide traders married into Californio families, facilitating their control of California's foreign trade and the ability to acquire their own ranchos. Despite Spain's ban on trading with foreigners, illegal trade began under the Spanish and grew apace once Mexico opened California to commerce. California became a succulent fruit, ripe for plucking. The British, the French, and the Americans all hatched schemes to seize the state, but it was the Americans who went to war with Mexico in 1846 and stole a land whose potential wealth neither the Spanish nor the Mexicans were able to protect or realize.

Inspired by the presence of Lieutenant John Fremont and a party of well-armed adventurers, in 1846 a group of Americans settlers launched the Bear Flag rebellion with the intention of setting up an independent republic à la Texas that would then join the United States. After some inconsequential skirmishing near Sonoma, on July 1, 1846, Fremont and his party, which included Kit Carson and 20 Delaware Indians, borrowed a launch from a ship anchored at Sausalito and crossed over to the Castillo at Fort Point, where they spiked its guns and raised the American flag over the abandoned Presidio. By early 1847, all of California had fallen into American hands.

The Californios, who were forced to surrender to the Americans, would eventually lose almost all their lands either by sale or at the hands of American lawyers. The heritage they left inspired popular Anglo writers and numerous architects a half century later—when the realities of Californio life had disappeared into the haze of romance. The Presidio was meant to protect the northern frontier of Mexico and its wealthy silver mines. It was now a forlorn ruin, and nothing remains from this period but four cannon and a section of wall that can be seen inside the Commandante's headquarters.

Early Architecture

At the time of the so-called conquest, Yerba Buena was a village of some 500 people, half of them newly arrived Mormons hoping to establish a colony somewhere nearby. There were two hotels, numerous shops and small businesses, even a schoolhouse. William Richardson had built a large adobe known as La Casa Grande at the corner of what is now Grant and Clay Streets. At the Presidio and the Mission, however, adobe construction had proven itself unsuitable to San Francisco's rainy climate. Sam Brannan's house was more typical of an architectural style that would become significant in California. The leader of a Mormon expedition that arrived by sea, Brannan started the first newspaper in San Francisco and established himself as a wealthy land speculator. His house was built of heavy timbers sawn from redwood logs north of San Francisco and constructed with mortise and tenon joints. Its lines were derived from a tradition that extended from the houses of Massachusetts Bay Colony to the modern Cape Cod bungalow.

The home of Samuel Brannan, emigrant leader, newspaper publisher, and land speculator, was typical of the numerous New England–style houses built in the city immediately before and after the gold rush. *Annals of San Francisco.*

The Mexican Customs House in the village of Yerba Buena (early 1850s). *Annals of San Francisco.*

Even the Mission came under Yankee influence. When the parish house was added in the early 1850s, it featured a shingled roof, green shutters, and a fan window over the doorway, the hallmarks of the New England style. The preponderance of this style of housing is not surprising, given that most pre–gold rush American immigrants came from New England and the Middle Atlantic states.

The future city's street pattern was laid out by the Swiss surveyor Jean-Jacques Vioget in 1837. Vioget marked off a central Spanish style plaza, the site of the Mexican customs house, which later became Portsmouth Square and the center of the new community on the bay. In a second survey in 1847, Jaspar O'Farrell added Market Street to the city plan and extended its grid out into the bay, where new "water lots" could be created with fill. There remained the problem of the prospective city's name. There was talk of building another city inland—to be called New York of the Pacific—and the founders of Benicia on the Sacramento River, then called Francisca, were eager to turn that port into central California's entrepôt. In a preemptive strike, some nervous Yerba Buenans quickly renamed the city San Francisco in January 1847.

3

City of Gold, City of Silver

When Richard Henry Dana returned to San Francisco in 1859, he was overwhelmed by what he saw. Before him was a city of more than 50,000 people,

> with its storehouses, towers and steeples; its court-houses, theatres, and hospitals; its daily journals; its well-filled learned professions; its fortresses and light-houses; its wharves and harbor, with their thousand-ton clipper ships, more in number than London or Liverpool sheltered that day, itself one of the capitals of the American Republic, and the sole emporium of a new world, the awakened Pacific.[5]

What had taken eastern cities a century or more to accomplish, San Francisco had achieved in the space of a single decade.

CITY OF GOLD

And, of course, gold—a nugget discovered in a mill race in the Sierra Nevada foothills in 1848—was the driving force behind this astounding transformation. Gold was the catalyst for the greatest migration in the history of the Republic and its most unique chapter in city building. Between 1849, when the first argonauts began to arrive, and 1854 some 300,000 people, mostly male and mostly young, made the trip by sea or by land to California. They

The San Francisco waterfront in 1851, packed with ships whose crews had abandoned them for the gold fields. The curved roof in the center of the picture is on a corrugated iron building. The flat-roofed curved structure above it is the ship *Niantic*, which was hoisted onto the piers and served as a jail, warehouse, and hotel. *California Historical Society.*

came from all corners of the globe: China, Australia, Peru, and France; Hawaii, Germany, Ireland, and Italy, drawn by the heady promise of quick wealth.

The lure of the diggings created a frenzied, carnival atmosphere in the burgeoning village. Within two years there were 779 ships lying abandoned in Yerba Buena Cove. People were on the move—coming and going—off to the diggings in the spring when the rain and snow stopped, back to the city as winter set in. Others came, however, to mine the gold that lined the miners' pockets. And there was plenty of it. In the first six years of the gold rush, prospectors brought in some $300 million in gold.

In short order, the city became a supply depot and watering hole for an itinerant population. It looked most of all, diarists said, like a chaotic and poorly kept military camp. To accommodate the onslaught, every manner of building was thrown up—tents, canvas-lined brush shelters, crude frames covered with cowhides, more conventional frame structures, some with canvas walls and ceilings—and they sprawled up the sides of Telegraph and Nob Hills. Dozens of wood frame houses were brought in pieces in the holds of ships, and corrugated iron buildings were imported from England and China. The city's first speculative housing development consisted of 50 houses brought from Boston and set up south of Market Street in 1850. Abandoned ships were commandeered to serve as warehouses, boarding houses, hotels, and even a jail, and their deck cabins were moved ashore to serve as houses.

As money poured in from the gold fields, ornate hotels were built to accommodate the free-spending miners, and a wide variety of eateries, French and Chinese restaurants, English style chophouses, German beer halls, and street stalls, provided food. Among the flashiest structures were the gambling houses (known as "hells") and saloons, some of them remarkably ornate. The brothels soon followed: With few local women available, prostitutes flocked to the city from Mexico, Panama, and the ports along the west coast of Latin America.

There were also more refined types of entertainment. One of the city's most notorious saloons featured five Mexican musicians playing harps, guitars, and a flute. Troupes of visiting actors presented popular melodramas, contemporary plays, and Shakespeare. There was a French theater and a circus, and the city fell in love with opera; in 1851 a traveling company staged Bellini's *La somnambula*, the city's first complete operatic production.

The town became a literary mecca: There were no more colorful subjects for the writer than the early history of San Francisco. The city heralded its fine bookstores and boasted that it supported more newspapers in more languages than London. Four libraries were opened, and more books were published in San Francisco in the 1850s than in all other cities west of the Mississippi.

French influences far outweighed the number of French nationals in San Francisco. French style became a mainstay of the city's wildly polyglot culture and would continue its impact well into the twentieth century: French fash-

Early San Francisco architecture. The ship *Niantic* (c. 1850), now buried at Clay and Sansome Streets, converted into a hotel. *California State Library.*

ion, French interior and exterior design, French theater, cuisine, and elegant shops, and even French manners. The City of Paris, one of the city's most famous department stores, opened near Portsmouth Square in 1850, named by its founder Emile Verdier after the ship he sailed to the city loaded with silks, lace, hats, dresses, linens, champagne, and wine.

THE MOST CURIOUS BABEL OF A PLACE

The city was a constant carnival. The streets and public places were crowded with young men who had no other space in which to spend their idle hours. There were long-haired Americans in broad-brimmed hats, red flannel shirts, and high boots, often with a red silk scarf worn around the waist; Californios in serapes, woven sashes, silver buttons down their pantlegs; an occasional turbanned Turk; Fiji Islanders; elegantly dressed Frenchmen; portly Brits in suits and waistcoats; Malays armed with the deadly kris; even a tattooed Maori or two. It was, a local newspaper reported, "the most curious Babel of a place imaginable."

When the unpaved streets turned into mud holes in the rainy weather, San Francisco was named "the wading city," with one newspaper reporting on street conditions under the headline "Marine Intelligence." During the dry season, dust and sand got into everything. The streets were strewn with litter, tin cans, and broken bottles. To the delight of the growing rat population, garbage was dumped along Market Street and in Washington Square while the plank sidewalks and piers were a danger to walk on. Between 1850 and 1856 an estimated 57 people died in street accidents, mainly by falling through poorly constructed piers.

WHARVES AND WATER LOTS

Level ground was quickly taken up as the city radiated outward from the area around Portsmouth Square. Houses, shacks, and tents pushed up the sides of Telegraph and Nob Hills and through the notch between Telegraph and Russian Hills, then over the dunes to the south, into Happy and Pleasant Valleys, and up the sides of Rincon Hill. The race soon began to push piers out into the bay, both to create level land and to reach out over the mud flats into deeper water so that ships could be brought alongside for easier unloading. The east-west streets, starting with Broadway, Commercial, and Pacific were extended eastward over the mud flats. In the process many abandoned ships were surrounded by pilings and incorporated into the piers. Others were dismantled for their lumber and fittings or simply disappeared into the mud flats, to be used as the underpinnings of new water lots. The piers were linked with crosswalks, and then men with wheelbarrows and, later, with a steam engine known as the "Irish Paddy" or "Vaporific Patrick" attacked the hillsides and sand dunes, gradually filling in the bay.

The competition to build wharves was bitter, punctuated on occasion by gunfire: Ownership of a wharf meant not only control of trade, but access to water lots. Yet in this fast-buck environment none of the wharf owners was willing to invest in a sound structure unless guaranteed a 50-year monopoly controlling the waterfront. So the wharves decayed and often collapsed, taking buildings with them, while the fill used in the new water lots oozed into the bay, silting up the piers. Finally, in frustration, the state took control of the waterfront and began work on a permanent bulkhead in 1867.

With wooden construction, oil lamps, and canvas walls and ceilings, fire was a constant danger. The central part of San Francisco witnessed six major fires in the span of 18 months, beginning with a fire that burned 50 buildings in December 1849. In 1850 the city barred wooden buildings from the downtown area around Portsmouth Square. Construction had to be of brick, stone, or iron. But both brick and iron proved dangerous. The brick buildings, according to one eyewitness, "crumbled together with incredible rapidity, whilst [the iron houses] got red-hot, then white-hot and fell together like cardhouses," subjecting those who sought refuge inside to a most horrible death.

THE BEGINNINGS OF ORDER

Amid the turmoil of everyday life, the city gradually took on a semblance of order. The first city charter was passed in 1850. City Hall was established in Portsmouth Square, first in the Jenny Lind Theatre, later in its own building. The first streets were paved, and sidewalks were laid. The Portsmouth Square area was lit with coal gas lamps. Battery Street was extended north to Clark's Point to provide access to the warehouses built where there was deep water closer to shore. Parallel plank roads were built through the sandy marshlands along Mission and Folsom Streets, and another road ran west on Pacific Street over the flank of Russian Hill to the Presidio. Horse-drawn omnibuses provided the first transportation, carrying passengers to South Park, the Mission, North Beach, and the Presidio. Fire companies were organized, the rudiments of a police force were formed, and a garbage barge was launched.

With the end of the most devastating fires, distinct downtown districts started to coalesce. Warehouses were built at Clark's Point, where they serviced the graceful clipper ships. Passenger steamers docked at the Broadway Pier. Wholesalers moved eastward with the waterfront, and retail outlets moved westward toward Market and Stockton. Commission merchants gathered on California Street, produce dealers on Clay, lawyers on Montgomery, clothing and dry goods merchants on Sacramento. Chinatown grew up around Sacramento and DuPont Streets (now Grant Avenue), and the red light district was centered in the eight blocks between Clay, Broadway, Kearny, and Stockton, where a committee appointed by the city's aldermen found 100 houses of prostitution. Land was set aside for parks and public schools. Forges, machine shops, the gasworks, and other industry clustered in Happy Valley south of Market and along the northern waterfront. Lower-income people lived in these areas, particularly in Happy Valley, soon known as Tar Flats; those who were better off moved up the hillsides, into the valley between Russian and Telegraph Hills, or westward, where new residential construction reached Larkin Street (in the present Civic Center) by 1857. More families arrived, but the city was still dominated by single men. Hence, hotels and boarding houses continued to accommodate a large part of the population.

VIGILANTES

In its first decade the city was plagued with corruption and lawlessness. The city's treasury was filled by selling off public property. Then politicians stole the funds, while prominent citizens, such as Samuel Brannan, neglected to pay their taxes. The volunteer police force was ineffective. Squatters fought each other and the rightful owners over building lots. Heavy drinking contributed to gun fights and stabbings. The locals were well-armed, and the ante-bellum code duello was very much in effect. Shanghaiing of sailors was common. And arson, a particularly frightening crime in a tinderbox city, was epidemic.

After a suspicious fire in May 1851 leveled 18 blocks in the heart of the city, some of its leading citizens took it upon themselves to form a Committee of Vigilance. Four men were lynched. A second committee was formed in 1856 after Charles Cora, a wealthy gambler, shot a United States marshall who had insulted his wife—one of the city's most notorious madams—and James Casey, a supervisor and ballot box stuffer, shot crusading newspaper editor James King of Williams. Cora and Casey went to the gallows. Some thought that the Vigilantes were not interested solely in law and order, but were out to weaken the political machine controlled by David Broderick, the son of an Irish bricklayer, raised in a New York City slum. Broderick would die in a duel with Judge David Terry three years later.

LOST NEIGHBORHOODS:
SOUTH PARK AND RINCON HILL

With their sweeping view of downtown and the bay, South Park and Rincon Hill were San Francisco's first fashionable neighborhoods. South Park was the brainchild of George Gordon Cummings, an Englishman who came to San

South Park, San Francisco's first planned development, was the brainchild of George Gordon in the early 1850s. The buildings burned after the 1906 earthquake, and only the park remains. *San Francisco Public Library.*

Francisco with a new name, George Gordon, and a shady past. Gordon arrived as the head of a gold-mining association, whose members paid a fee and were promised transportation, good food, and mining equipment. The association quickly broke up amid loud complaints about the quantity and quality of the food and the length of the voyage. Gordon meanwhile had used association funds to buy lumber in Nicaragua, which he sold for a healthy profit when he made port. In addition to the lumber business, he went into wharf construction and imported prefabricated houses, including the Abner Phelps house (see page 320).

Gordon bought 12 acres south of Market Street, proposing an enclosed community of "ornamental grounds and building lots on the plan of the London Squares, Ovals or Crescents, or of St. John's Park or Union Square in New York, and equally elegant." The architect was George Goddard, Esq., "late architect of Lord Holland...who laid out that magnificent addition to the West End of London, known as the Holland Park Estate." [6] South Park's appeal was to the city's nouveaux riches. The attached houses, the first of which was built in 1855, were designed in what architectural historian Harold Kirker called "the severe English Roman style" and were built of stuccoed brick. With few exceptions, they had the same floor plan: dining room, kitchen, and servants quarters on the basement floor, parlors on the first, and five bedrooms on the second. A stable and coachman's quarters occupied a separate building in the rear.

Rincon Hill, the neighborhood surrounding South Park, attracted wealthy individuals looking for home sites in the early 1850s. Two bankers and an industrialist built the first three houses on Rincon Hill before 1854. Soon after, Henry Halleck, builder of the Montgomery Block (see page 149) and later chief of staff of the Union Army in the Civil War, put up a house. The houses were in a variety of styles, ranging from Gothic to Second Empire and Italianate, with many manifestations of the ever-popular bay window. Many were substantial in size and featured elaborate formal gardens. The list of residents reads like a Who's Who of San Francisco business leaders of the city's first three decades: Sam Brannan; Peter Donahue, founder of the Union Iron Works and San Francisco Gas Company; Irving Murray Scott, manager and later owner of the Union Iron Works; Andrew Hallidie, inventor of the cable car; William Tecumseh Sherman, banker and Civil War general; John Parrott, builder of Parrott's Granite Block on Montgomery Street and at one time the wealthiest man in California; Asbury Harpending, real estate speculator and associate of William Ralston; historian and publisher Hubert Howe Bancroft; Charles Lux and Henry Miller of the Miller-Lux land company; U.S. Senator William Gwin; Hearst business associates James Ben Ali Haggin and Lloyd Tevis, who also was president of the Wells Fargo & Company; Robert Woodward, developer of Woodward's Gardens; and David Colton, political fixer for the men who built the western section of the trancontinental railroad.

Rincon Hill, where stately homes, such as Mrs. Peter Donahue's, were built in the 1850s and 1860s, was the city's first fashionable neighborhood. Mrs. Donahue was the wife of one of the city's first industrialists. *California Historical Society.*

Rincon Hill's decline can be dated from the completion of the Second Street Cut in 1869 (see page 6). To improve wagon transportation to the Pacific Mail Steamship Company docks on the south side of Rincon Point, Second Street was cut through the south side of Rincon Hill and a wooden bridge was built over the cut. Some of the houses nearest the cut were damaged. Others were moved. Many of the residents sold their houses at a loss and left. The fashionable shopping district along Second Street was ruined, and draymen preferred other routes to the Pacific Docks and warehouses. Meanwhile, the cut became a hangout for young toughs, who stoned Chinese cart drivers as they moved back and forth between the piers and Chinatown, a perverse sport known as "Rocking the Chinks." The cut's new name became "Apache Pass."

In 1892, Robert Louis Stevenson described Rincon Hill as "a new slum, a place of precarious sandy cliffs, deep sandy cuttings, solitary ancient houses and butt ends of streets." The curtain fell on the final act soon after the earthquake of 1906. Rincon Hill turned out to be stable ground, and little damage was done to its buildings. But within days a mighty holocaust swept through, leveling both Rincon Hill and South Park. Rincon Hill was humbled further when it was lowered and leveled for the western end of the Bay Bridge. Today all that remains of these two lost neighborhoods is oval-shaped South Park, which runs between Second and Third Streets south of Bryant.

THE COMSTOCK LODE: VIRGINIA CITY

By 1853 the most readily accessible sources of gold were played out, and San Francisco's artificial economy slid into a recession from which it did not recover until 1859, when a strange substance was discovered in the modest gold deposits being worked in the Washoe Mountains east of the Sierra Nevada. When it was found that the bluish, sticky mineral gumming up two prospectors' equipment was in fact silver sulfurets, the news quickly reached San Francisco and the rush was on. The lode was named for Henry Comstock, a quick-thinking loudmouth, who told the two Irishmen who discovered the first deposit that they were trespassing on his claim. And the city itself was named for an amiable drunk called Old Virginny.

Soon a rough camp of tents and shacks sprang up on the steep slopes, where new arrivals dug shallow pits like so many exuberant puppies. However, mining was now the work of bigger dogs. The days of pick-and-shovel mining were over. It took men who could muster capital to sink shafts deep enough into the hillside, top them with head frames to raise and lower the mechanical lifts that carried workers down and up and brought ore to the surface, to install the huge pumps to force air below, and to build the quartz mills to grind the ore and reduce it to bullion.

Virginia City mushroomed virtually on top of the Comstock mines after vast silver deposits were discovered in 1853. The Gould and Curry Mine shown here was a case study in wasteful investment, inefficient extraction of ore, and endless litigation. *California Historical Society.*

Like some rank, composted weed, Virginia City seemed to grow literally out of the mines. Describing the city in 1862, Mark Twain, who worked as a reporter for *The Territorial Enterprise,* wrote that Virginia City

> roosted royally up the steep side of Moutain Davidson, seven thousand two hundred feet above the level of the sea, and in the clear Nevada atmosphere was visible from a distance of fifty miles! It claimed a population of fifteen thousand to eighteen thousand, and all day long half of this army swarmed the streets like the bees and the other half swarmed among the drifts and tunnels of the "Comstock," hundreds of feet down in the earth directly under those same streets. Often we felt our chairs jar, and heard the faint boom of a blast down in the bowels of the earth under the office.[7]

Shacks gave way to wood frame houses, and they in turn, after the usual fires, were replaced by brick and stone buildings. Hotels were built, saloons and boarding houses opened, bordellos plied their trade. There were shootings and knife fights. It was San Francisco all over again, but this time in a desert climate miles from a decent source of timber, water, and the supplies needed for a major city.

Almost all of the wealth generated by the Comstock Lode, some $375 million in silver and gold, passed through San Francisco, not only making the names and fortunes of the Bonanza Kings—Flood, Fair, McKay, and O'Brien—and of William Ralston, George Hearst, William Sharon, and a motley crew of merchants, stock speculators, and lawyers, but also changing the very face of the city. The two Irishmen who discovered the lode fared poorly. Patrick McLaughlin, who sold his interest in the Ophir Mine for $3,500, died after years of wandering from job to job as a cook. Peter O'Reilly held out for a time, ultimately receiving $50,000 for his interest. He built a hotel in Virginia City but soon lost everything speculating in mining stocks. "Spirits" told him to run a tunnel into the Sierras, where he would find a richer vein. "However, the spirits talked so much about caverns of gold and silver," wrote Mark Twain's friend Dan De Quille, "that he became insane and was sent to a private asylum at Woodbridge, California, where he soon died."[8]

Henry Comstock made $11,000 on his false claim and then wandered the West talking big, boasting that he owned the Virginia City mines, even the city itself, until he blew his brains out in Bozeman, Montana.

Virginia City, three blocks of honky-tonk saloons and a few grand buildings surrounded by a lunar landscape with mounds and mounds of mine tailings, is well worth a visit. It is a five-hour drive east of San Francisco via Interstate 80 and U.S. Route 50 through Carson City, Nevada, which has an excellent museum.

The first phase of the Comstock boom was dominated by William Ralston. Ralston arrived as the captain of a steamer owned by Cornelius Vanderbilt. In an era of corporate mining, he became a banker, not a miner, an investor in a wide range of enterprises, a man who dreamed of San Francisco as a great metropolis at the center of an economy that included

Empire builder William Ralston founded the Bank of California (on the right) at the corner of California and Sansome as the centerpiece of his business empire. Looking up California Street in the 1880s. Note the spire of St. Mary's Catholic Church on the right up California Street. Gray Brechin.

manufacturing and agriculture as well as mining. His was an era of high finance. Banks, particularly the Bank of California, and later its rival and usurper, the Bank of Nevada, dominated the economic scene, and more money was made from speculation at the city's three stock exchanges than in the mines themselves. A half billion dollars changed hands in 1876 alone. Through the Bank of California, Ralston not only bought into and took over numerous Virginia City mines, he also gained control of the companies providing goods and services such as water, rail transportation, and timber.

Ralston continued his extravagant ways despite signs of a possible downturn when in 1864 Virginia City miners hit 500 feet and paused, owing to the problems caused by hot water in the mines. In 1869 recession set in, intensified by the completion of the transcontinental railroad. Long sought by San Franciscans as the key to their economic independence, the railroad in fact brought a flood of cheap goods into the city, undermining the local economy. Businesses failed, unemployment grew, and a general sense of malaise and ill will, much of it directed at the Chinese who competed for jobs, settled over the city.

Ultimately, Ralston was outflanked by James Flood, William O'Brien, James Fair, and John McKay, the so-called Bonanza Kings. Flood and O'Brien were saloonkeepers and sometime stockbrokers; Fair and McKay their mine superintendents. After accumulating stock in two Virginia City mines, in 1873 they hit the Big Bonanza, an enormous pocket or silver ore that produced $100 million in its first five years. Challenged for control of the Comstock, Ralston continued to spend recklessly on various enterprises, including work on the Palace Hotel, which became the largest building west of the Mississippi. In August 1875 the battle between the Bonanza Kings and Ralston triggered a run on the Bank of California, which led to the closing of the bank and a near riot. Ralston, forced by his board of directors to resign and turn over all his assets to pay his debts, mysteriously drowned while taking his daily swim in the bay.

Ralston, like many of his fellow parvenus, built his mansion on Nob Hill, the fashionable neighborhood that replaced Rincon Hill. The crest of the hill, however, was commanded by his rivals James Fair and James Flood, along with San Francisco's newest set of millionaires, the railroad magnates known as the Big Four and their factotum, David Colton. Charles Crocker, Mark Hopkins, Collis Huntington, and Leland Stanford were all merchants of modest means who had set up in Sacramento to supply the mines. As backers of a scheme to build a transcontinental railroad, they discovered a novel source of wealth—the public treasury—and new ways to exploit public lands. In all, the federal government turned over 10,000,000 acres of public land to the Central Pacific (later the Southern Pacific) as an incentive for the Big Four to build a line from Oakland to Promontory Point, Utah, where the Central

William Ralston built the Palace Hotel in 1875, the largest building west of the Mississippi. Lotta's Fountain, in the foreground, was restored in 1999. *California Historical Society.*

Pacific linked up with the Union Pacific coming from Chicago. For a time the Big Four monopolized western transportation, and having found that politics was the way to new-found wealth, through the Southern Pacific secured a grip on state politics that was not relaxed until well into the twentieth century.

CLASS WAR–RACE WAR

By 1870, San Francisco's population had reached 150,000. According to one newspaper account, there were 122 San Franciscans who controlled approximately $146 million in local capital. At the top of the list with $10 million was Leland Stanford, who would head the Southern Pacific for 28 years and serve as both governor and a United States senator. In 1868 in a prescient essay, "What the Railroad Will Bring Us," Henry George, the radical economist, who had settled in San Francisco, said of the city that he saw "a new era opening before us." It would be based on great concentrations of wealth, class differentiation, "less personal independence among the many, and the greater power of the few."[9] The city's first two decades had indeed been an era of independence and the self-made man. But with the concentration of wealth and power in the hands of a new elite, upward mobility appeared limited and the number of unemployed grew rapidly.

Despite the ups and downs of the mining economy, the early 1870s witnessed the greatest increase in the population since the first years of the gold rush. Tens of thousands of people poured into the city by land and sea, only to find their economic prospects circumscribed. Although the myth of the quick buck still prevailed, it was easy to find a scapegoat—the Chinese—to explain why the pickings were no longer easy. The first Chinese had arrived in Yerba Buena as early as 1838. Merchants and traders, they had come from areas near the southern Chinese port city of Canton. Chinese in large numbers began to arrive on their way to the diggings in 1852. At the diggings, the Chinese were quickly pushed out of the best claims, and discriminatory legislation directed at Chinese miners was passed in 1855. The number of Chinese increased dramatically when Charles Crocker began to import coolies, known as "Crocker's pets," to work on the railroad. Others worked in the wheat fields and on the enormous task of draining and constructing levies in the inland delta between the Sacramento and San Joaquin Rivers, which created some of the richest farmland in California. When farmers shifted to fruit crops, the Chinese, who were skilled farmers in their own right, provided the labor. Others took jobs in San Francisco, where they held half the manufacturing jobs by 1870. White male workers might make between $2.25 and $5.00 a day and white child laborers $1.00; the Chinese were paid $.90. Confined to Chinatown, 10,000 men lived there in squalid boarding houses.

As unemployment grew, agitators harangued crowds of whites gathered at the sandlots adjacent to the new city hall under construction near Market and Eighth Streets. The city's politicians responded sympathetically, closing the Chinese public school and banning Chinese students from attending other public schools. Basket poles were ruled illegal, boarding houses were required to provide 500 square feet per person, and the city's first zoning ordinance banned Chinese laundries in certain parts of the city.

The temporary closure of the Bank of California in 1875 was followed by recession. Two years later the campaign against the Chinese led once again to violence. During an anti-Chinese rally shots were fired into a crowd of several thousand gathered at the sandlots. Part of the mob set out to burn Chinatown, attacking Chinese along the way. Another group headed for the Pacific Mail Steamship Company docks at Steamboat Point, the principal disembarkation point for newly arriving Chinese. A three-day battle ensued as the mob tried to burn the Pacific Mail facility.

Irishman Denis Kearney, drayman and fiery orator, assumed leadership of the anti-Chinese agitators. His message, couched in violent language, was a simple one: Smash the monopolies controlled by the Nob Hill millionaires and run the Chinese out of town. In 1878, Kearney and his associates formed the Workingmen's Party of California and catapulted to power at the state and local levels. San Francisco seemed to teeter on the brink. Some business leaders, eager to revive the vigilance committee, saw anarchy stalking in the wings.

STREETCARS AND VICTORIANS

In city politics, the awarding (really, the selling off) of franchises for streetcar lines and water and gas services for new neighborhoods proved to be a profitable undertaking for politicians, and this was at the heart of the process that drove real estate speculation and shaped the new city. Streetcar lines were literally the harbingers of new development. Consider Hayes Valley and Van Ness Avenue, for example. When Thomas Hayes was county clerk from 1853 to 1856, he bought 160 acres in Hayes Valley west of Van Ness and received a franchise to build a railway line through the sand hills on Market

The first cable car heads up Clay Street in 1873 with its inventor, Andrew Hallidie, seated on the left. *California Historical Society.*

Street. Hayes gave Mayor T. C. Van Ness a block on what would become Van Ness Avenue. Van Ness obligingly built a home, helping to anchor further development. By the 1860s new streetcar lines ran into the Mission District and the Western Addition, by 1870 reaching Lone Mountain where the University of San Francisco campus sits today. In 1873 Andrew Hallidie, a manufacturer of wire cable used in the mines, successfully ran the first cable car up Clay Street to the top of Nob Hill. The cable car further enhanced Nob Hill's reputation as *the* place to live.

The new state constitution, ratified in 1879 at the urging of the Workingmen's Party, placed restrictions on the granting of franchises. To avoid those restrictions, every railway company in San Francisco petitioned the Board of Supervisors for 50-year extensions of their franchises to take effect before the ratification of the constitution. The extensions, once passed, laid the groundwork for the creation of an informal streetcar trust, the Market Street Railway Company, controlled by members of the Big Four and their allies.

New housing to accommodate the rapid increases in population during the 1860s and, particularly, the 1870s sprang up along streetcar lines in the Mission District and the Western Addition. Thus began the era of Victorian cottages, row houses, and detached homes that are among the most appealing features of today's San Francisco. The new Victorians held out the promise of modern, lavishly decorated homes for a large portion of the population. Historian Theodore Hittell wrote in 1878 that the city "at the same time [had] fewer paupers, more land-owners, and more comfort in the homes of the multitude." Ronald Delahanty, author of *In the Victorian Style,* noted that "the San Francisco Victorian was essentially *modern.* The key to understanding it lies not in its obvious façade but in its invisible plumbing. It was born of a fascination with two things: new technologies and the architectural styles of the past. In how it was built, sold, financed, and served (by streetcars, municipal sewers, running water, gas, electricity, even telephones), the San Francisco Victorian row house was radically new, not old-fashioned." The contractors installed "up-to-date bathrooms with reliable utilities and porcelain fixtures. These advances made possible tremendous improvements in health, hygiene, and individual privacy." [10]

Homestead and savings and loan associations played an important role in the construction of Victorians. The homestead associations were joint stock companies into which members paid an initial fee of from 10 to 100 dollars, followed by monthly payments. The companies—there were 170 of them at one point—bought up large tracts of land, which were sold to the members. Each new lot owner then hired a contractor to build his or her home. Many of the savings and loans, such as the Hibernia Savings & Loan Society, were established to provide low-interest loans for the city's ethnic communities, in this case the Irish.

During this period the city was linked to its new suburbs. In the 1850s a railroad line was laid west of the San Bruno Mountains from San Mateo County to downtown San Francisco, leading to construction in Palo Alto a decade later. The East Bay was connected to the city by ferry lines that were owned by the Southern Pacific (SP).

Public transportation changed San Francisco from a walking city, in which residences and businesses were in close proximity, to a city in which streetcars linked the downtown to new residential neighborhoods in the Western Addition and Mission. The families of the business elite could live in the new suburbs and commute to the city. The families of professionals and well-paid skilled workers could aspire to a house or an apartment in the new neighborhoods in the Western Addition and the Mission. Despite the growth of new neighborhoods, much of the city remained undeveloped. There were still farms in the Mission and beyond, only occasional houses in the Haight, and sand dunes beyond the point where O'Farrell reached Van Ness. The western half of the city beyond Twin Peaks remained a sandy wasteland.

Contemporary observers noted the impact of the expansion of the city on street life. In the inner city, many single men and families still lived in boarding houses or hotels or in apartments above retail shops. Walking on Montgomery, Market, and Second Streets was a popular form of nighttime or weekend entertainment. For those who wanted open space, there were a number of private resorts: Woodward's Garden at Mission and Duboce, the Willows nearby, and the Hayes Valley Pavilion plus race tracks in the Bay View district and the Mission. The Lone Mountain Cemetery was a popular gathering place, as was the Mechanics Pavilion at Market and Eighth, and a visit to the Cliff House at Land's End to see the seals, with stops at various roadhouses along the way to have a drink, was a must.

In time a new attitude toward public space developed: Citizens looked to the city rather than individual entrepreneurs to provide public facilities. In a city shaped by real estate speculators, little consideration was given at first to public space. Two park sites were set aside in 1850 for Union Square and Washington Square. Early historians noted: "There seems to be no provision for a public park—the true 'lungs' of a large city. The existing Plaza, or Portsmouth Square, and two or three other diminutive squares, seem the only breathing holes intended for the future population of hundreds of thousands. This is a strange mistake." [11] When the Western Addition was mapped in 1855 and 1856, provisions were made for the inclusion of nine parks and a hospital. In 1865, with the newspapers agitating for a major public park, the city hired noted landscape designer Frederick Law Olmsted to draw up plans for an extensive park system that would run from the Mission along Van Ness Avenue to the northern waterfront. Olmsted's plan was quickly abandoned in favor of creating a thousand-acre park that would run from the Western

Addition to the ocean through the sandhills in the western part of the city. Construction on Golden Gate Park began in 1871.

Despite the city's enormous wealth, there were few public amenities besides a public hospital, a home for merchant seamen, an almshouse, and a public school system that poorly served the citizenry. The few museums that existed were at private parks and featured bad reproductions of European artwork. The first public library opened in 1879. Although one newspaper called for "a very large edifice" to be supported with a $250,000 budget, the library actually opened in a rented second-floor auditorium. The supervisors appropriated $24,000, but the mayor sequestered the funds and the library's backers had to borrow money to buy books and furniture for the opening.

CULTURAL CRAVINGS

Early San Franciscans were devoted to all forms of culture, high and low. The opera remained popular, as did minstrel shows, Shakespearean tragedy, Irish melodrama, and vaudeville. Historian John Young listed 19 theaters operating in the 1860s, most of them on or near Montgomery Street.

The city retained its lively literary atmosphere, and a number of its writers from this era — Henry George, Bret Harte, Joaquin Miller, John Muir, and Mark Twain among them — gained national stature. Many of the city's writers apprenticed or found work at San Francisco, Sacramento, and Virginia City newspapers, while journals such as the *Californian*, the *Golden Era,* and the *Overland Monthly* provided outlets for their more literary endeavors. The *Golden Era,* one of the best of the early publications, was founded in 1852 by 21-year-old J. Macdonough Foard and 19-year-old Rollin Daggett. Daggett sold subscriptions to miners, traveling from one camp to another. Later, under "Colonel" Joe Lawrence in the 1860s, the *Golden Era* office on Montgomery Street (see page 149) became San Francisco's literary headquarters, home to Harte, Twain, Ina Coolbrith, Charles Warren Stoddard, Prentice Mulford, Ned Buntline — the master of the dime Western novel — and lesser lights. The *Era's* office was "the most grandly carpeted and gorgeously furnished that I have ever seen." [12] Another virtue: It was less than a block away from the Montgomery Block with its cheap restaurants and popular saloons.

By the end of the 1870s, San Francisco boasted some of the features of a modern city. Electric lights were introduced at the centennial celebration on July 4, 1876, when four floodlights were trained on Van Ness Avenue from the roof of St. Ignatius College. Two years later the *Chronicle's* newsroom was lit, dimly as it turned out, with new electric light bulbs. The first telephones were installed in the same year.

The decade of the 1870s was a harbinger of a very different era in San Francisco history. Production at the Comstock lode was declining, and there would be no more bonanzas. The days of boom and bust brought on by the mining economy were over. Amid their incredible indulgences, capitalists such as William Ralston had made some sound investments in agriculture and industry, and these would provide the basis for the city's emergence as a manufacturing center and commercial entrepôt whose fate was tied to what Richard Henry Dana had called "the awakened Pacific." The 1870s pointed toward other aspects of the future: the growth of class conflict and the emergence of a militant labor movement, the steady swing of the political pendulum between corruption and reform, and a new sense of civic pride that would demand more elaborate public amenities and even urban planning.

4

Urban Ambitions

When William Tecumseh Sherman's employers decided to shut down their San Francisco bank in 1857, Sherman wrote to one of them, "This city was supposed to be marching forward at a giant stride toward its sure destination as the Great Pacific City. It is now pretty well demonstrated that we calculated a *little* too fast, that San Francisco, though destined at some future time to a high position, has to pass through toil & trouble & misfortune before she attains that end." [13]

Gold and silver mining had generated enormous wealth, turning San Francisco into a fabled city. The city had also passed through more than its fair share of toil, trouble, and misfortune brought on by, among other things, the instability of the mining industry, the dislocations that attended the completion of the transcontinental railroad, class and race conflict, and the excesses of its self-made millionaires. By the beginning of the 1880s the city was entering a period of relative stability during which it would fulfill its destiny as the dominant and, for a time, only major urban center on the American shores of the Great Pacific Lake.

Opposite: The Call Building (c. 1904), once regarded as San Francisco's finest office building. John Spreckels bought the *Call* in 1895, making it a voice for reform and a rival of Michael de Young's *Chronicle*. The Chronicle Building is on the left. *San Francisco Public Library.*

GIANTS OF COMMERCE

San Francisco's progress can be measured by its lessening dependency on the riches of the mining frontier and its growth as a center for commerce, finance, and manufacturing. As a port the city ranked just below Boston, New York, and New Orleans. San Francisco virtually dominated coastal commerce from Panama to Alaska. The city's economy was shaped by a group of aspiring businessmen, many of them European immigrants. There were Frenchmen, Italians, Irishmen, Scots, and Germans, both Christians and Jews. They built an industrial economy and a vast system of trade networks that extended throughout the American West and into the Pacific Basin, virtually colonizing new territories, such as Hawaii and Alaska.

Isaac Friedlander, the so-called Wheat King, became fabulously wealthy as a middleman and speculator, buying wheat and flour and moving them via ships that he chartered. To be invited to one of the famous 17-course dinners at Friedlander's home in South Park or, later, at his Bryant Street mansion meant that one had arrived socially. For a time wheat was like gold. California's munificent farmland produced bumper crops on multithousand-acre ranches. The grain and flour trade brought hundreds of "Down-Easters," Maine-built square-riggers as fast as the famous China Clippers, into port. Soon shippers were using iron-hulled sailing vessels, similar to the *Balclutha,* which is tied up and open to the public at the National Maritime Museum's Hyde Street Pier. The wheat trade began its decline in the 1870s, and by the 1890s there were signs of a definite shift by California farmers away from grains to specialty fruit and vegetable crops.

With no money, Claus Spreckels, a German-born 17-year-old, made his way to San Francisco during the gold rush. After opening a brewery, he built a sugar refinery on the waterfront at Union and Battery Streets, moving it later to Potrero Point. In the 1870s, Spreckels traveled to Hawaii and used his advanced knowledge of a treaty between Hawaii and the United States to gain control of half the island's sugar crop. By 1882, Spreckels and his partner controlled almost all of the crop. With his sons, John and Adolph, he established the Oceanic Steamship Company to transport his sugar cane to San Francisco.

In 1884 a long-lasting feud between the Spreckels family and the de Young family, owners of the *Chronicle,* began when Adolph Spreckels shot and wounded Michael de Young after de Young accused Spreckel's father of enslaving the employees of his sugar plantation. De Young survived, unlike his brother Charles, who was shot and killed five years earlier by the outraged son of another subject of the *Chronicle*'s go-for-the-jugular journalism. In 1895, the Spreckels institutionalizd the rivalry, buying the *Call* and moving into a new skyscraper on Market Street just across from the *Chronicle.* A third newspaper, the *Examiner,* was bought by George Hearst, one of the West's canniest prospectors, the owner of millions of acres spread from Mexico to Montana, and a U.S. senator. Hearst's son, William Randolph, would make the *Examiner* the foundation for the country's mightiest media empire before World War II, becoming a pioneering yellow journalist and a Democratic Party kingmaker along the way.

Lewis Gerstle, a Bavarian Jewish itinerant peddler, arrived in San Francisco in 1848, where he sold apples before moving to Sacramento. In Sacramento, Gerstle became partners with Louis Sloss, another Jewish immigrant from Bavaria, who was selling livestock, harnesses, and wagons out of a tent. Gerstle and Sloss married sisters and became patriarchs of a series of intricately intermarried families that included the Haases, Lilienthals, Fleisshackers, Koshlands, Branstens (originally Brandenstein), and Sterns— all associated with major San Francisco businesses and a long tradition of philanthropy. In 1867, Gerstle, Sloss, and their partners formed the Alaska Commercial Company, which quickly gained control of the islands off Alaska where seals bred, and for a time monopolized trade with Alaska and dominated the territory's political affairs.

The forays of San Francisco's empire builders were a fitting prelude to the country's first experiments with colonialism. Indeed, the entire history of California since 1846 had been an exercise in imposing American laws and customs on earlier inhabitants while wresting the best resources from their grasp. So, naturally, the annexation of Hawaii and the invasion and seizure of the Philippines in 1898 were greeted in San Francisco as foreshadowing the city's ascendancy to heights perhaps even greater than New York's.

THE CITY'S MANUFACTURING CENTER

San Franciscans' far-flung commercial empires appeared to be built on a solid manufacturing base. Metal manufacturing and shipbuilding were emerging as major industries, as were meat packing, clothing and shoe manufacturing, canning, brewing, and sugar production. The city's importance as a manufacturing center was symbolized by the launching of the USS *Charleston,* the first heavy warship built on the West Coast, at the Union Iron Works in 1886.

Irishman James Donahue founded the Union Iron Works near the beach in Yerba Buena Cove in 1849 as a primitive blacksmith shop housed in an adobe shack roofed with sails. He and his brothers, Michael and Peter, moved their forge to a tent nearby, where they built a furnace from the smokestack of a steamship. Their first customers were steamship companies seeking repair work. Peter soon took control of the company and moved it to the new manufacturing district at Potrero Point. There the Union Iron Works built pumps, railroad engines, and other heavy equipment for the mines of California and

The Union Iron Works, the cover story in *Scientific American* (July 2, 1892), at the foot of Potrero Hill was capable of building battleships. *San Francisco Public Library.*

the Comstock lode. With this company at the center of a series of family enterprises that included the city's first gasworks and a streetcar line, James and Peter became wealthy men with homes on Rincon Hill.

In 1865, Irving Murray Scott and a number of partners bought the Union Iron Works from Donahue, and just as production at the Comstock began its final decline in the 1880s, Scott invested heavily in a shipyard capable of building large ships. The *Charleston* was the first of nine warships built at the facility. The Union Iron Works, according to local historian Joseph Blum, led the West Coast shipbuilding business, launching 76 ships before being sold to Bethlehem Steel in 1906.

Levi Strauss, another German Jewish immigrant, who also began life in the new world as an itinerant peddler, followed his sister and brother-in-law to San Francisco. According to legend, Strauss came to San Francisco in 1853, where he went to work with his brother-in-law, David Stern. With him Strauss brought a small amount of canvas cloth, which he hoped to sell for tenting. Instead he found that the miners wanted durable pants, which he sewed himself. Levi's soon became a standard part of a miner's outfit, and Strauss, his brother, and his brother-in-law became the millionaire owners of Levi Strauss and Company. In the 1920s control of the company passed to the Haas and Koshland families, who were already intermarried with the Strausses and the Sterns.

Business leaders, such as the Donahues, Irving Scott, William Ralston, and Claus Spreckels, formed the nucleus of a new manufacturing center at Potrero Point, while James Fair financed a manufacturing complex along the waterfront where Marina Green now lies. But San Francisco, it was said, lacked certain attributes considered essential to making it a great manufacturing center: a ready supply of coal and iron ore, a transportation system that could move raw materials and finished products at reasonable rates, and a steady source of cheap labor. When local supplies were exhausted, colliers brought coal from Australia and British Columbia. Iron ore came from the Mojave desert. Local businessmen paid a heavy price for the Southern Pacific's near stranglehold on land and water transportation, and increasingly San Francisco's workers were willing to challenge their employers over wage levels and the right to bargain collectively.

THE WATERFRONT

In a city whose economy was organized around its shipping industry, sailors were at the forefront of efforts to organize unions in the late nineteenth century, which is little wonder because sailors were condemned to a status closer to that of the peon than of the so-called free worker. Hours were long, sleep irregular, conditions dangerous, the food barely edible, and many sea captains and their mates were the worst sorts of tyrants. Sailors were bound to their ships by law. If they deserted, they could be returned by force, and the courts condoned the violence visited upon sailors as a suitable way to maintain discipline.

Most of the visiting sailors lived in boarding houses located near the docks at the foot of Vallejo, Broadway, Pacific, and Jackson Streets or near Mission and Howard just south of Market. These boarding houses served as headquarters for crimps, who engaged in a vicious hiring practice known as "shanghaiing." Crimps were paid a fee to deliver sailors, usually after drugging them, to captains looking for crews to man their ships. The city's most notori-

The Bells of Shandon, a sailors' boarding house and scene of more than one shanghaiing, on Howard near Steuart (c. 1912). The city's fabled waterfront was a dangerous and dilapidated place. *San Francisco Maritime National Historical Park.*

ous crimp was James "Shanghai" Kelly, who operated several boarding houses at different times near the Broadway pier. His specialty was plying his customers with a mixture of schnapps, beer, and drugs. With three ships requiring crews, Kelly once gave a birthday party for himself aboard a paddle wheel steamer. Having gotten the revelers sufficiently drunk, he took them outside the Golden Gate and turned them over to their new masters.

Conditions in the boarding houses themselves were grim. Some were little more, or in one case less, than shacks. In 1910 one sailor-turned-sea-captain described a boarding house on Steuart Street known as Scab Johnny's. Scab Johnny had a unique way of accommodating the overflow of guests:

> He walked down the sidewalk scanning chalk marks and then leaned over and lifted a couple of boards. Underneath...there were a couple of feet of clearance under the board sidewalk...a whole row of straw mattresses, side by side, their confines defined by chalk marks on the planks above...It was quite a sight to look down that sidewalk in a morning, seeing planks tipped up and heads appearing like so many Lazaruses.[14]

The vicissitudes of the sailor's life led to the formation in 1885 of the Coast Seamen's Union, which merged with the Sailors' Union of the Pacific (SUP) in 1891, a mainstay of the city's increasingly powerful labor movement.

The sailors, encouraged by reporters and reformers sympathetic to their plight, responded with strikes, support for pro-labor candidates, and an occasional satchel of dynamite. Sailors ultimately won the same rights as other adult working people. In 1902, the SUP signed its first contract. Shanghaiing was finally and effectively banned by federal law in 1915.

The Coast Seamen's Union was not the city's first. Union activity began with the gold rush and was encouraged by recurring shortages of labor. In 1886, 10,000 union workers marched in the city's first Labor Day parade. The first permanent Building Trades Council—five others had come and gone—was formed by construction workers in 1896. The San Francisco Labor Council was formed two years later, with the SUP as its largest affiliate, and longshoremen organized the International Longshoremen's Association in 1892.

Denis Kearny's agitation and the rise of the Workingmen's Party issued in a period of limited reforms, which were swept aside by the rise of Christopher Buckley, the "Blind Boss," in the 1880s. The son of an Irish stonemason, Buckley was a skillful organizer who turned his job as a saloonkeeper into a lucrative career as a politician. In a community that was still overwhelmingly male, the saloon, along with the parish hall and the firehouse, was one of the centers of political life, and Buckley, the head of the Democratic machine, was a master at mobilizing the dead, the foreign-born crews of visiting ships, and a host of repeaters to vote on election day. Fashionably dressed and with an intelligent demeanor, Buckley, though blind, could quote from memory long passages from the Bible, Homer, Shakespeare, Thucydides, and Gibbon. "I placed a stiff value on my services and always rated myself a high-priced man," Buckley recalled. "It was surprising to see how universal was the desire among men of substance, firms and corporations, to get on the right side of politics." [15] Buckley's power waxed and waned and was then eclipsed in 1896 when he left the city for a convenient vacation during a grand jury investigation.

CITY POLITICS AND URBAN PLANNING

In the 1890s, San Francisco entered a reform era that would shape the city well into the twentieth century. Despite the enormous wealth displayed with great ostentation in the mansions of Van Ness Avenue and Nob Hill and the hotels of Market Street, much of the city and its public institutions were in deplorable shape. Boss politics had turned the school system into a nepotistic employment agency, and school construction had failed to keep pace with the growth in population. There were only the rudiments of a library system. Many streets lacked pavement, and raw sewage routinely poured into the bay, collecting beneath the piers at low tide and adding offensive odors to the acrid smoke produced by the coal-consuming factories along the waterfront. The almshouse, jail, and city hospital were so deeply in debt that merchants refused to deliver food for the inmates and patients or hay for the horses that drew the wagons and ambulances.

The new City Hall, under construction since 1871, epitomized both the corruption of city politics and the outmoded nature of the city's finances. The dollar limit—meaning no more than a dollar of taxes for every $100 of assessed value in real estate—was the basic axiom of city politics no matter one's political affiliation. By reducing the size of the city treasury, reformers hoped to keep politicians' hands out of the till, but they also produced a budget incapable of funding the needs of a modern city. The construction of City Hall was prolonged and its cost ran into the millions because of the supervisors' unwillingness to do more than fund it on a short-term basis. Every year or so a new appropriation was made. The usual payoffs for contracts exchanged hands, and work resumed. Besides adding immeasurably to its ugliness—it was dubbed "the city hall ruin"—this practice ensured that shoddy work would be done.

The corruptibility of local politicians fostered disillusionment with both parties. Thus, when Adolph Sutro, a wealthy mining engineer, was asked to run for mayor on the ticket of the new national Populist Party in 1894, he won

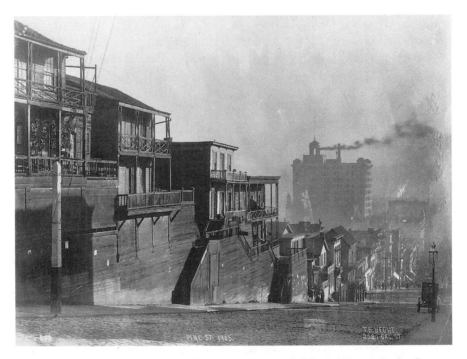

Looking east down Pine Street in 1905, the Merchants Exchange Building belching smoke. San Francisco before 1906 was filled with run-down wooden housing and often wrapped in smog generated by its industries. *Bancroft Library.*

City Hall, built over a 20-year period, became a symbol of political corruption and a monument to bad architecture. Note the Pioneer Monument in front. City Hall was destroyed in 1906. *San Francisco Public Library.*

handily without even campaigning. Born into a well-to-do Prussian family, Sutro immigrated to New York, where he caught gold fever. Once in San Francisco he became a store owner and tobacconist and then set out for the Comstock lode, where he opened a stamp mill employing an ore extraction technique of his own invention.

From his first visit Sutro recognized that the Washoe mines, which were plagued by enormous heat at depths below 500 feet, could be accessed, drained, and ventilated by a tunnel passing beneath them. Accordingly, he drew up plans to bore a 3-mile tunnel below Virginia City that would connect to the mines 1,600 feet below the city. However, he was prevented from financing his scheme by William Ralston and the Bank of California. Ralston feared Sutro's plan would turn Viriginia City into a ghost town by shifting milling operations to the mouth of his tunnel some miles away. Sutro turned to Europe for finance, but by the time the tunnel finally opened, the value of production on the Comstock had fallen to less than $2 million a year.

Sutro got out just in time. He sold his stock in the tunnel company for $900,000 in 1880 and invested in prime real estate in downtown San Francisco and the western part of the city, buying up approximately 1 of every 12 acres in the city, including Point Lobos and Land's End. Sutro bought a modest home on the cliff overlooking the Cliff House at Point Lobos, laid out elaborate gardens, and then bought the Cliff House itself. When the Cliff House burned, he built a new and more spectacular one and then an elaborate bath, museum, and aquarium on the beach nearby, all of which he opened to the public.

Sutro's successful 1894 mayoral campaign was helped by the fact that he was not only well known and well liked, but had good populist credentials. He supported the labor movement and women's suffrage and had taken on the Ralston Ring and the Southern Pacific. Despite his good intentions, however, Sutro's contributions to the city as mayor, beyond the construction of the city's most popular resort, were neglible. According to his biographers, in failing health at the end of his term, Sutro sadly concluded, "What have I accomplished as Mayor? Very little." He went on to say, "The Mayor is little more than a figure-head." [16] And that was the crux of the matter. The efforts of a single individual, no matter how willful and magnanimous, could not overcome the structural problems embedded in the city's vigilante era charter.

It would take an intellectual with a broader grasp of urban problems and close ties to the city's business class to play a leading role in restructuring city government. James Duvall Phelan was born and bred to this challenge. The son of a wealthy Irish-American merchant and banker, Phelan was educated at Saint Ignatius College (later the University of San Francisco), began law studies at Hastings College, and then continued his education with a grand tour of Europe. There he studied urban problems while writing on the subject for the *Examiner.* Phelan was impressed by two cities in particular: Glasgow, where public ownership of the utilities (as opposed to control by private monopolies) was so profitable, he claimed, that citizens escaped taxation; and Paris, where the Baron Georges-Eugene Haussmann had carried out an ambitious construction program that made the city a model of urban planning. Back in San Francisco, Phelan took over his father's banking and real estate interests, making him one of the wealthiest men in town.

THE CITY BEAUTIFUL

Another phenomenon that influenced Phelan's views about architecture and urban planning was the ersatz metropolis constructed in Chicago for the exposition organized to commemorate the 400th anniversary of Christopher Columbus's arrival in the Western world. As vice president of California's World Fair Commission and manager of California's exhibit at the 1893 Columbian Exposition, Phelan was exposed to the work of Chicago architect Daniel Burnham, chief of construction, and the group of talented architects whom he had gathered around him. These architects, a number of whom were educated at the École des Beaux-Arts in Paris, became advocates of the City Beautiful movement, an effort to produce a planned and unified approach to the redesign of major cities and the construction of monumental public buildings in the neoclassical style to fit within that design. Burnham and his ideas, as we will see, would have a major impact on the shape of San Francisco.

Phelan was a clubman and a joiner, and the organizations he joined often came under his leadership. San Francisco's first politician to identify himself as a progressive, Phelan was convinced that the city needed home rule, a strong mayor, civil service reform, public utilities, strict supervision of franchises and contracts, and the ability to raise funds to pay for needed public amenities.

For Phelan, the status quo not only meant continued corruption and a shabby city, it could bring something worse: the threat of revolution. He had witnessed the rise of the labor movement and understood the role of anarchists and socialists in its development. To circumvent working class radicalism, Phelan worked closely with conservative labor leaders. Besides labor unions, the other new ingredient in San Francisco's electoral stew was the neighborhood improvement club. Such organizations focused on very local issues, such as sewer lines, street cleaning, and the paving of streets. In 1893 clubs from the Richmond District, the Western Addition, the Mission, and South of Market formed a citywide organization, the Federation of Improvement Clubs, which Phelan served for a time as president. Elected mayor in 1896, Phelan campaigned successfully for a new charter. Then, armed with new powers, including the ability to raise funds through the sale of bonds, he was reelected for a third time in 1899. Phelan went right to work proposing bond measures for a new sewer system, main library, hospital, 17 schools, and two parks. Ironically, given his work to create a business-labor-neighborhood alliance on behalf of urban reform, Phelan's career as mayor came to an end in 1901, during the biggest outburst of labor militancy before the general strike of 1934.

PARIS OF THE PACIFIC

Having decided to leave office before the 1901 strike, Phelan continued his efforts to reform his beloved city. He was both expansive and anxious about the fate of San Francisco. He continued to argue: "[Because] cities are the repositories of everything that science and art and invention have done for mankind...we must make them fit for a free and enlightened people." The Spanish-American War, staged in large part from the Presidio, marked the advent of American imperialism in the Pacific Basin, which had a significant impact on San Francisco commerce. Plans were being laid for a canal across the Isthmus of Panama, and local merchant Reuben Brooks Hale called for a world exposition in San Francisco in 1915 to mark its opening.

But there were other ominous signs: San Francisco manufacturing had peaked, and local manufacturers had begun to relocate to other parts of the Bay Area. The rise of unionism could only deter further investments. And although San Francisco's population was larger than that of Los Angeles, Portland, and Seattle combined, these cities were destined to become rivals. San Francisco "is and must be the chief outlet into the Pacific of the trade of the American continent," Phelan asserted. San Franciscans were also beginning to eye the tourist and convention trades. San Francisco, however, lacked attractions such as museums, grand boulevards, and parks other than Golden Gate Park, which was still under construction, and its idiosyncratic museum, founded by Michael de Young in 1895.

At the beginning of the century, the city was once again growing at a rapid pace and changing in its appearance. In 1891, de Young had hired Burnham and Root to build the city's first skyscraper, a 10-story, steel-framed structure at the corner of Third and Montgomery (see illustration on page 165). Seven years later Claus Spreckels went 8 stories higher with a new building for the *Call*. Farther west along Market Street, the Floods were putting up a 600-room office building, and the St. Francis Hotel was being built in Union Square and the Fairmount atop Nob Hill. The first apartment building in the city had been constructed in the 1880s, and by 1900 there were 3,300 such buildings, adding immeasurably to the congestion and population density in the eastern half of the city. The first automobiles, odd-looking machines maneuvering around the streetcars and horse-drawn vehicles, appeared on Market Street.

South of Market was more of a slum than ever. Shabby dives and boarding houses lined the waterfront, and the Tenderloin north of Market and east of City Hall was now competing with the Barbary Coast near the waterfront in the business of providing women, and in one instance men, for sale. Despite its robust growth, the city lacked beauty, lamented the manager of the St. Francis, who beseeched civic leaders to form a committee to make San Francisco "beautiful and enticing as a place for tourists and for residence... to make San Francisco to Americans what Paris is to Europeans." [17]

Yet even with its shabbiness, San Francisco held tremendous appeal for all sorts of travelers. Great performers, such as actress Sarah Bernhardt and operatic tenor Enrico Caruso, fell in love with the city. Audiences were enthusiastic, the hotels were luxurious, and the food and drink were world class and abundant. The renowned photographer Arnold Genthe, who opened his first studio here before moving to New York, noted that San Francisco had retained much of the color and prodigality of the days of forty-nine, pleasantly tempered by the native culture which had come to California out of Spain. Saloons offered a wide array of free food, their counters "piled with crisp French bread, platters of cold meats and cracked crab, and different kinds of cheese." For 50 cents one could buy a five-course meal with wine at many of the city's restaurants. For those with more elaborate tastes, there were French restaurants, such as the Poodle Dog, Marchand's, the Pup, and Delmonico's, "where on Sunday evening," according to Genthe, "all of San Francisco, so to speak, came for family dinners."[18] On the upper floors were private rooms, accessible via a private entrance, where men could entertain their lovers or pursue assignations with prostitutes.

Despite the city's lack of cultural amenities, its literary life flourished under the influence of a new generation of Bay Area writers, including Gertrude Atherton, Mary Austen, Ambrose Bierce, Jack London, Frank Norris, and Kathleen Norris. Beginning with her fictional account of the rise and fall of the Gordon family of South Park fame, Atherton wrote nine novels describing San Francisco and California over eight decades. Tart-tongued and cynical, Ambrose Bierce settled in San Francisco after fighting and suffering a wound for the Union in the Civil War. Bierce's writings epitomized the slash-and-burn style of local journalists in the face of the city's corruption and pretensions. Of San Francisco he wrote, "It is a moral penal colony. It is the worst of all the Sodom and Gomorrahs in our modern world.... It is the paradise of ignorance, anarchy, and general yellowness.... It needs more than all else a steady trade wind of grape-shot."

Inspired by realist writers such as William Dean Howells and Emile Zola, Frank Norris was eager to capture the peculiarities of San Francisco: the grim routine of a murderous dentist living on Polk Street *(McTeague)*, the delights of the city's self-conscious bohemia *(Blix)*, or the dangers of its demimonde *(Vandover and the Brute)*. Norris began an ambitious trilogy about the grain trade by chronicling the epic struggles between the Southern Pacific and the San Joaquin Valley farmers *(The Octopus)*, but died at 32 before completing it.

Jack London liked to see himself as one of the crown princes of the Bay Area Bohemia. Born into a family facing straitened circumstances, he grew up semieducated on the Oakland waterfront. A committed socialist *and* a believer in Anglo-Saxon purity *and* an astute critic of racism, London hit the road in 1894. With an army of unemployed men, he marched on Washington, ended up in a Pennsylvania jail, and followed the siren call of gold to the Klondike. Once published, London wrote at a furious pace and produced two novels a year, including *Call of the Wild* and *Sea Wolf,* until he died of drink and self-medication at the age of 39.

The Bay Area's new artists communities were self-conscious in their bohemianism, forming cliques, salons, and an artists' colony in Carmel. Some experimented with utopian communities, others with drugs, and many with new sexual arrangements. Some worshiped nature or tried to get close to the Native American experience while others, young and old, burned out and killed themselves. In this atmosphere, Willis Polk launched the *Architectural News* in 1890 to attack Victorian architecture and promote the work of a new generation of architects while writing a critical column about architecture in a literary publication.

THE BURNHAM PLAN

At the Bohemian Club, the city's premier cultural gathering place, civic leaders such as Phelan mixed readily with Bohemians—Genthe and London, among others. They were all part of the larger effort to imagine a new world in an innovative environment. Phelan was drawn to the idea of remaking the city in a modern image, but paid homage to the great cities of Europe, particularly Paris. Asked by the San Francisco Art Association to draft a comprehensive plan for the beautification of the city, Phelan hired Daniel Burnham to do the work. Burnham visited Italy's hill towns to search for ideas and then set up shop in San Francisco in 1904 in a specially constructed cottage on the east side of Twin Peaks with a panoramic view of the city designed by Willis Polk.

Working with Polk and Edward Bennett, Burnham drew up an ambitious plan that he estimated would take 50 years to implement. To begin with, Burnham decided to modify, but not fully disrupt, the orthagonal grid system by which the city was platted in rectangular blocks that ignored the city's hilly topography. His study of European cities, Burnham argued, showed that they were laid out in concentric rings with public buildings (governmental, educational, and cultural) arrayed around a civic center. Burnham's plan called for a series of diagonal boulevards that would cut across the orthagonal grid and meet at new plazas. In certain areas, new streets would follow the curvature of the terrain.

The civic center was to be located at the intersection of Market and Van Ness, and this intersection would be linked to Golden Gate Park by extending the Panhandle to the civic center, where it would turn into a new boulevard running southeasterly to the Pacific Mail Steamship docks. There would be an opera house to the north on Van Ness, a railroad station to the south, a library on the Panhandle Extension, and adequate space for museums, a convention center, a technical school, and other buildings. A waterfront boulevard would circle the city, and a subway would be built under Market Street. New streets would curve up the side of Telegraph Hill past Roman villas and commercial structures to a hilltop park with a monument. Ashbury Heights would feature an amphitheater and sports fields with a grand view of the Golden Gate. On the west side of Twin Peaks there would be a new park at least twice the size of Golden Gate Park and an Athenaeum modeled after Hadrian's Villa with a colossal statue of Athena facing the sea. New parks were scattered throughout the city, including one along today's Cesar Chavez Street that would resemble the Bois de Boulogne of Paris. Burnham was particularly eager to maintain all undeveloped hilltops in their natural state.

Although it was called a plan, Burnham's 1905 report was more a visionary statement, written at a time when American city planning was still in gestation. Burnham made no assessment of the plan's economic impact, nor did

Telegraph Hill as visualized in the Burham Report of 1905. The Report called for a hilltop park and monument, with streets winding up the hillside, lined with Roman style villas and commercial buildings. *San Francisco Public Library.*

he recommend specific measures beyond calling for the establishment of a uniform cornice height for buildings in the business district and the establishment of an art commission. Burnham's plan must have been breathtaking in its impact: He was proposing an essentially low-rise city filled with neo-classical structures, parks, and open space. Despite its vastness and the implicit challenge to the established order, which had been based on the grid pattern and real estate speculation, Burnham's work was greeted with great enthusiasm by the press and the business community. There was little opposition at first; that would come only after a series of unforeseen events had reshaped the city.

5

Phoenix Rising

At 5:13 A.M. on Tuesday morning, April 18, 1906, an earthquake roared through the city like a hundred freight trains traveling at rocket speed. The streets heaved and pitched. In a great cloud of dust, bricks poured into the streets while façades pulled away and columns tumbled. Several buildings constructed on fill were sucked into the ground; others collapsed or toppled against each other. At first San Franciscans seemed to be in a state of shock. According to Arnold Genthe, there was very little panic. He went to his neighbors, and they all decided to go the St. Francis for breakfast! "Near the entrance we saw Enrico Caruso [he had performed the night before] with a fur coat over his pajamas, smoking a cigarette and muttering, "'Ell of a place! 'Ell of a place!" [19]

Before San Franciscans could gather their thoughts, the fires began. Ignited in kitchens and by broken electric wires and gas mains, they flowed together into fire storms that swept through the northeast quadrant of the city. The residents streamed out of the city, many thronging the Ferry Building to escape. To stop the fires from moving westward, buildings along Market, Kearny, and Eighth Streets were dynamited. Again and again there were attempts to create a barrier against the flames, but throughout Wednesday and Thursday fire fighters and troops from the Presidio were forced to abandon one fire line after another. One fire was burning into the Mission District; another was racing along a mile-wide front toward the Western Addition.

A decision was made to create an enormous firebreak along Van Ness Avenue by dynamiting and setting backfires. As mansions, shops, and churches were systematically torched and blown up, from south to north along Van Ness, the fire ran ahead of the destruction in what seemed like a willful attempt to out-flank the fire fighters. After one last round of dynamiting in the area of Gough and Sutter, the fire was brought to a halt, as it was in the Mission District with the use of the same techniques. By Saturday morning little remained but smoldering ruins. The earthquake and fire had left 3,000 people dead; anoth-er 250,000 people out of a population of 400,000 had lost their homes. Four-and-a-half square miles of the city were leveled, with 28,000 buildings destroyed and only 303 structures left standing.

There were pockets of buildings that survived: around Jackson Street between Montgomery and Sansome, in the warehouse district at the foot of Telegraph Hill, and on top of Russian and Telegraph Hills. Among the notable buildings that remained were the U.S. Customs House on Battery, the Montgomery Block, the Ferry Building at the foot of Market Street, the U.S. Mint at Fifth and Mission, and the new U.S. post office and courthouse at Seventh and Mission. Numerous commercial structures—the Fairmount and St. Francis hotels, the Chronicle, Call, Mills, and Merchants Exchange buildings—were gutted by the fire, but their frames and façades remained intact, fire-scarred and empty-windowed, a testimony to the strength of steel used in the

Powell Street and Nob Hill after the 1906 earthquake and fire. The destruction was staggering. The St. Francis Hotel on the left and the Fairmount Hotel behind it on top of Nob Hill were rebuilt. *San Francisco Public Library.*

modern skyscraper and the use of bond iron, a reinforcing technique, in the newer buildings.

Homeless citizens moved into tents, and then into relief shacks in encampments in city parks and open spaces, or simply abandoned the city. Former mayor James Duvall Phelan wired architect Daniel Burnham in Chicago, "Come at once! This is a magnificent opportunity for beautifying San Francisco, and I believe that the property owners will gladly cooperate, now that their personal improvements have been swept away."

Phelan was sadly wrong. In fact, the city, once he had left the mayor's office, was again wallowing in the ugly muck of boss rule. The new boss was Abraham Ruef, lawyer, fixer, and Republican party operative. His minion was Eugene Schmitz, the handsome head of the Musicians Union, who had been elected mayor of the Union Labor Party in 1901. (The Union Labor Party had been the result of the rise of labor militancy after the violent and successful strikes of 1901.)

Behind the scenes, deal making and bribe taking were the order of the day, and Ruef, working out of his offices at the corner of Kearny and California Streets and at the Pup, a French restaurant on Stockton, called the shots. Ruef was offered retainers to facilitate everything from railway franchises to prize fight permits, while he and Schmitz collected payoffs from bordello owners and the proprietors of French restaurants. The Pacific States Telephone and Telegraph Company (later Pacific Bell) was eager to protect its telephone monopoly. The newly formed Pacific Gas and Electric Company (PG&E) had to go before the city's supervisors to seek a rate increase. The Parkside Realty Company, headed by William Crocker, needed a trolley car franchise to provide transportation for a 400-acre development planned for the West Sunset. United Railroads, the company formed by an Eastern syndicate to buy out the Market Street Railway Company, needed to convert its collection of traction systems (horse, cable, steam, and overhead trolley) to a more efficient overhead trolley system.

In November 1906, after an investigation backed by Phelan and Rudolph Spreckels, Ruef and Schmitz were indicted for extorting $10,000 from French restaurant owners. The graft investigation and trials went on during four years of nasty infighting. Ruef served four years and seven months in San Quentin. In 1907, Schmitz was convicted and went to jail briefly. Schmitz, forced to vacate his office, was replaced by reform advocate Edward Robeson Taylor, doctor, poet, lawyer, newspaperman, and friend of Phelan's. In 1909, Patrick "Pinhead" McCarthy, head of the Building Trades Council, was elected mayor on the Union Labor Party ticket. McCarthy eagerly sought an alliance with the city's business leaders on an agreement that the graft prosecutions should be wound down. Although 12 executives from PG&E, Pacific Telegraph, and United Railroads and the lawyer representing the Parkside Realty Company were indicted, their charges were eventually dismissed.

THE BURNHAM CONUNDRUM

San Franciscans went to work with tremendous energy and unanimity on the massive job of rebuilding their beloved city. The most intense period of reconstruction lasted until 1909, during which 27 major commercial buildings were restored, another 114 were built, and 19,000 wooden frame buildings went up. In 1908, when the city revived plans to hold a world's fair to mark the opening of the Panama Canal and celebrate the revival of the city, $4 million were pledged in 1 hour and 45 minutes.

Soon after the earthquake, Mayor Schmitz declared that in rebuilding the city the Burnham Plan "should be the ideal for which we strive." However, in the rush to rebuild the city, the plan was brushed aside. Although Phelan played a major role in reconstruction, he and his associates, including Willis Polk and John Galen Howard, head of the architecture department at the University of California, came to be known as "the dreamers." Michael de Young led the downtown business interests' attack on the new Burnham Plan, calling for leadership from "hard-headed businessmen," not "artists or professional beautifiers." "The crying need of San Francisco today," the *Chronicle* editorialized, "is not more parks and boulevards; it is business."

Burnham, in a sense, was responsible for both the urge to build fast and build "up" and the desire to create a European low-rise city of parks, monuments, and spacious boulevards. Burnham had designed the city's first skyscraper *and* written the city's first plan. From the perspective of a century later the Burnham conundrum—whether to be Paris on the Pacific Rim or Wall Street West—still shadows the city.

Over time, elements of the Burnham Plan were realized, starting with the construction of the Beaux-Arts civic center, and changes in the cityscape are still being implemented, particularly along the waterfront, that are very much in its spirit. The de Young, Palace of Fine Arts, and Steinhardt museums were built. A new opera house went up across from City Hall in the 1930s, and a new symphony hall was built in the same area in the 1970s. A park and monument were created on top of Telegraph Hill. Aquatic Park and Marina Green were built along the waterfront. Significant amounts of hilltop open space were protected, and the Presidio, not by plan but by the happenstance of the military base closure movement in the post–Cold War years, is becoming the huge park in the western part of the city envisioned by Burnham. A subway was built beneath Market Street. The new suburbs in hilly areas in the western part of the city, such as St. Francis Woods and Forest Hill, were built with streets following the contours of the terrain.

Ironically, what Burnham, Phelan, and even Polk considered thoroughly modern architecturally—such as the Civic Center and the new buildings downtown—was quickly becoming stylistically passé. The Civic Center with its imperial pretensions harked back to classical Rome and nineteenth-century Paris. Downtown architects favored the Chicago-style architecture introduced to San Francisco by Burnham 20 years earlier. They did offer some new applications of traditional materials, such as greater use of glass and terra-cotta, which had proved fire-resistant, and, of course, new engineering lessons were learned from the earthquake. Across the country architecture in general was stuck in the middle ground between neoclassicism and the modern, with the first truly innovative modern architecture coming from Frank Lloyd Wright, as exemplified by his prairie homes and first office buildings. Polk seemed capable of innovation. He had designed some of the city's first shingled houses, which broke with Victorian traditions and pointed toward the future, as did his glass-fronted Hallidie Building, which is both startlingly modern and one of a kind. But Polk and his peers, with few exceptions, remained more wedded to the past than directed toward the future.

NEW CONSTRUCTION BEGINS

In 1911 the cream of the city's business elite recruited James Rolph Jr. to run for mayor. The son of immigrants, "Sunny Jim" was proud of his rise from newsboy to owner of a shipping firm and a bank. Rolph's personality would dominate city politics until he went to the statehouse in 1931. Florid faced, immaculately dressed right down to his trademark cowboy boots, and fond of his red Stutz Bearcat, Rolph was the perfect mayor for a city that during the Roaring Twenties was still wild and wide open. He maintained what his friend Sally Stanford, the city's most famous madam, called a "Caucasian geisha house" on Sanchez Street and once threw a four-day party, complete with jazz band, on a Pullman train, which hauled his friends back and forth to Eureka for the launching of one of his ships.

During Rolph's long reign, the city fulfilled many of the ambitions spelled out by progressive reformers. To provide convention space during the Panama Pacific International Exposition (PPIE), construction began on the Civic Center with a new auditorium, which was completed in 1915, the same year as the new City Hall. The Main Library followed two years later. Rolph began the conversion of the city's streetcar system to a publicly owned transportation system, opened the western half of the city to real estate developers by digging a tunnel beneath Twin Peaks, and oversaw completion of the Hetch Hetchy project, which brought water from the Sierra Nevada to San Francisco. Rolph, however, had problems with the bottle, a chronic San Francisco malady. By the late 1920s, he was appearing more often in public visibly drunk and conducting his affairs with young starlets more openly. He was elected governor in 1930, but the office was beyond his fading capabilities. He died in the last year of his first term.

"It was a great town," a retired police officer told reporter Jerry Flamm. "Everyone made a buck. The gamblers had to pay off. The whorehouses had to keep clean girls. If you welshed on a bet, they'd close your gambling joint. If you had a bad girl in a whorehouse that tried to roll somebody, she got fired. It was a great town."[20]

It was a great town for everyone but union labor and the city's small Asian communities. After a round of bitter strikes along the waterfront in 1919, the city's business elite—the Bank of America, Wells Fargo, Pacific Telephone and Telegraph, PG&E, the Southern Pacific, and others—organized to break the back of the militant labor movement. During the 1920s, San Francisco, once regarded as the strongest union town in America, became one of the cities where the nationwide attack on unions was most successful.

Union labor and its progressive allies, urged on by Senator Phelan, could claim one dubious victory. Early labor leaders had played a major role in barring Chinese immigrants and enshrining restrictions on Chinese workers in the state constitution of 1879. By the turn of the century, Japanese were coming to California, replacing the Chinese as a source of cheap labor, many soon proving to be successful farmers in their own right. Others settled on Rincon Hill, in Chinatown, and in the Western Addition. These new immigrants were rewarded with the same treatment as the Chinese, culminating in the termination of Japanese immigration in 1924.

SAN FRANCISCO MODERNE

Progressivism, with all its contradictions, left a planning legacy that would affect the city for the rest of the century. Pressure for a planning commission increased when the organizers of the PPIE faced the problem of what to do with the enormous ersatz city built in the Marina. Planning advocates hoped to use a plan for the new community in the Marina as the beginning of a citywide plan. In response, Rolph appointed the first planning commission in 1917. Rather than offering plans, however, the commission focused on the city's new zoning laws as a way to protect property values. De facto planning continued as it had since the earliest days of the city; the construction of the transportation system, now in public hands but still at the service of real estate developers, determined the pace and shape of development.

In this context, Department of Public Works chief Michael O'Shaughnessy, the imperious Irish-born champion of new tunnels, boulevards, and streetcar lines, became "a sort of city planner ex officio." Then there was the type of planning inspired by James Duvall Phelan's work with Daniel Burnham: planning as the private preserve of reform-minded civic leaders. Thus the planning section of the Commonwealth Club, an organization formed in 1903 to debate issues of public concern, became one of the city's most important planning bodies before World War II. Here, for example, discussions were held about the need for an airport, built in the 1930s, and a regional transportation system, a major preoccupation after World War II.

By 1931, the city looked significantly different from the one Rolph had inherited in 1911. San Franciscans could justifiably claim that the new Civic Center was the most striking and harmonious assemblage of public buildings in the country after the nation's capital. During the 1920s there was a commercial construction boom. New office towers went up in the financial district and along Market Street, medical buildings and apartment buildings, many of them for women who were moving into secretarial work, near Union Square. There were also new posh apartment complexes on Nob Hill, Russian Hill, and in Pacific Heights. Laid out before the war, subsequent years witnessed the construction of the city's first "suburbs," elaborate developments such as Sea Cliff, St. Francis Wood, and Forest Hill.

The city's first high-rise skyline, built before the earthquake and modest by present standards, had featured office buildings that were monuments to the personal fortunes accumulated by nineteenth-century San Franciscans. The postearthquake skyline became home to the new corporate San Francisco as many of the city's and the West's largest companies—the Southern Pacific, Standard Oil of California, the Bank of America, PG&E, the Matson Steamship Company, and Pacific Telephone and Telegraph—built new headquarters in the period between the earthquake and the Depression. With the city tilting steadily toward being a financial and service center for the regional and Pacific Rim economies, these new structures would house the growing ranks of white-collar workers.

Many of the new office buildings were in the Chicago style. Others were modeled after the new skyscrapers being built in New York and the Windy City. But the downtown building boom of the 1920s also featured some architectural departures. Most striking were two buildings by Timothy Pflueger. The first was a new office building for Pacific Telephone and Telegraph (later Pacific Bell) in 1925 on New Montgomery Street (see illustration on page 135). At 26 stories, the building dominated the skyline and was the city's first modern, stepped-back office tower. Pflueger's other triumph was the Medical Arts Building on Sutter Street. Here he emphasized verticality through the use of curved bays, decorated above and below the windows with Mayan designs in terra-cotta. Fittingly, Pflueger and other architects influenced by Deco styles saved their most flamboyant designs for movie houses, such as the Castro Theatre, a monument to the new medium dazzling the country.

THE GENERAL STRIKE

San Francisco's construction boom tapered off precipitously after the 1929 stock market crash, and the economy slid downward toward the abyss. Because of its high level of employment in service jobs, the city was not as badly hit as others. All of the banks remained open, and most white-collar employees stayed on the job with reduced hours and wages. The waterfront remained active though half the longshoremen were unemployed: In 1933 7,000 ships tied up at city piers. Still, by 1932 one out of four workers was unemployed.

Casual labor on the piers attracted a particularly tough type of itinerant males. Many of them lived in cheap boarding houses along the waterfront, patronizing its saloons and bordellos. But with the falloff in jobs, men slept in doorways, parks, sheds, under bridges, anywhere they could throw down their bedrolls. The dockworkers toiled under a system organized by waterfront employers when they broke the unions in the 1920s. "We were hired off the streets like a bunch of sheep, standing there from 6 o'clock in the morning, all kinds of weather," Harry Bridges, the Australian who would become the head of the longshoremen's union, told a government hearing in 1934.[21] For the laborers, there was a lack of steady work; moreover, the gang bosses increased the size of loads and the pace of work while wages fell.

In 1933, when the Roosevelt administration legalized collective bargaining, dockworkers rushed to join the East Coast longshoremen's union. After a brief strike, the shipping companies eliminated wage cuts while preparing secretly to smash the union, using violence if necessary. When the longshoremen went out again the next year, the shipping companies closed down the waterfront, hired strikebreakers, and took on the strikers in a series of increasingly violent confrontations. In the midst of one of the pitched battles that swirled along the waterfront, a police officer emerged from a car at the corner of Mission and Steuart Streets and shot three strikers, killing two of them. San Franciscans went into a state of shock, and when the Teamsters went out in solidarity, the city was shut down by a general strike. The longshoremen emerged from the strike with a new contract and a new union, the International Longshore and Warehouse Union. San Francisco was once again at the forefront of the national labor movement.

NEW DEAL LEGACIES

Despite the economic woes and class conflict brought to San Francisco by the Depression, programs funded for the most part by Roosevelt's New Deal would have a significant impact on the city's infrastructure. At the same time, plans were devised, if not implemented, that would redefine San Francisco's relationship to the larger Bay Area. Some of the projects, such as the War Memorial complex, which includes the Opera House, had been funded before the Depression. These buildings and a new federal building completed in 1936 were the last neoclassical structures to go up in the Civic Center.

Even after the collapse of the economy, San Francisco voters showed a willingness to fund public works projects through support of new bond issues. Four branch libraries, two financed entirely with federal funds, and 12 schools went up, and passenger piers along the waterfront were renovated. The Works Progress Administration (WPA) funded most of the construction of the San Francisco Zoo, as well as Aquatic Park, with its distinctive modern building shaped like a ship, on the waterfront at the northern end of Van Ness. The building would become the National Maritime Museum. Federal largesse built the Oakland Bay bridge, and New Deal programs paid for the creation of Treasure Island, an island fashioned from landfill north of Yerba Buena, for the Golden Gate International Exposition, a world's fair that celebrated the opening of the Golden Gate and Bay Bridges.

The federal government also funded public housing, another first for San Francisco. Using WPA field workers, the city conducted a survey of housing and found that even though San Francisco was "comparatively free from crowded and obvious slum areas," 28 percent of the city's dwelling units were substandard. A third of these lacked private toilets and bathing facilities. Substandard housing was concentrated in Chinatown, South of Market, and in the center of the Western Addition. Starting in 1939 with the Holly Court project in the Mission District, the city completed four housing projects accommodating 1,741 families by 1942. At that point plans for more projects were put on hold while emergency housing for war workers was begun. Featuring simple concrete and wood frame construction, these one- and two-story structures were modest but appealing by later standards in public housing.

Valencia Gardens, one of the projects, was designed by William Wurster, who had made his reputation by designing rustic homes in the California ranch vernacular, such as the Gregory farmhouse (see page 137), for well-to-do patrons. Wurster was influenced by the work of Catherine Bauer, whom he would eventually marry. Bauer had been introduced to modern architecture while living in Paris in the 1920s. In 1934 she published *Modern Housing*, which *Architectural Forum* described as having the same relationship to architecture that *Blackstone*, the great British legal classic, has to law. Bauer lauded European modernism but encouraged Americans to develop their own style. She was particularly interested in public housing, which, she argued, could be built with "innumerable variations, affecting both method and form, which

The western span of the Oakland Bay Bridge from Yerba Buena Island to Rincon Hill. *San Francisco Public Library.*

are due to local requirements, habits, limitations or desires."[22] Ultimately, Bauer concluded, support for public housing would require significant political changes. She helped to bring about these changes, becoming one of the principal organizers of the Labor Housing Conference, which led to the passage of the U.S. Housing Act of 1937.

THE BRIDGES AND THE TYRANNY OF THE AUTOMOBILE: A TASTE OF THE FUTURE

The most significant and magnificent structures built during the Great Depression were the Oakland Bay and Golden Gate Bridges. The Oakland Bay Bridge, funded by the federal government, was the first to be completed, in 1936. The Golden Gate Bridge, financed by the sale of bonds, opened the next year. The new bridges provided quicker access to areas outside the city previously reached only by ferry. A railway line was added to the lower deck

The Golden Gate Bridge with Fort Point in the foreground. *San Francisco Public Library.*

of the Bay Bridge, but in 1958 it succumbed to the demand for more space for automobiles. San Francisco was fast becoming a commuter city, and the groundwork had been laid for the new suburbs that would spring up around it after World War II.

As soon as the bridges were completed, there was a noticeable increase in automobile traffic, and trolley service on Market Street slowed appreciably. City officials and a study funded by the WPA suggested two contradictory approaches to the problems of congestion: Build a rapid transit system or a network of elevated highways that would permit traffic to flow around congested areas at speeds estimated at 40 miles per hour. The proposed rapid transit would service downtown, the Mission, and western areas of the city. Voters, however, turned down a rapid transit bond measure in 1937. Both rapid transit, in the form of the Bay Area Rapid Transit System (BART), *and* a freeway system would be developed in the postwar years, setting off epic battles that would shape the very way San Franciscans saw their beloved city.

ART AND ARCHITECTURE

The years between 1906 and the Depression marked the institutionalization of high culture in the city. The opera company was founded in 1911, the symphony in 1923, and the ballet in 1933. Generally speaking, however, these two decades were marked by a kind of cultural lassitude. "When I came to San Francisco in 1927," wrote Kenneth Rexroth in *An Autobiographical Novel*, "it was the worst city in America for a writer.... The city was so ridden with native son-ism that it was literally impossible to get anywhere in the professions, let alone the arts." Rexroth described cultural life as "dependent upon a small group of interrelated Jewish families....San Francisco was still in the grip of the Jack London, Frank Norris, George Sterling tradition."[23]

In his search for artistic comraderie, Rexroth found a couple of young painters, Gertrude Atherton and Ralph Stackpole. Stackpole, a scultpor and painter with a house on Telegraph Hill and a studio on Montgomery Street, was at the center of a group of artists and architects whose most memorable achievements were the Stock Exchange Club and Coit Tower and its murals. Rexroth failed to mention William Saroyan, who drew intimate portraits of San Franciscans in his first book of short stories, *The Daring Young Man on the Flying Trapeze* (1934), and his play, *The Time of Your Life* (1939), which described the clientele at Izzy Gomez's saloon on Pacific Street.

The Stock Exchange Club (now the City Club), described on pages 168–169, was part of a larger complex designed by Timothy Pflueger. With a mural by Diego Rivera, it was a successful integration of architectural, interior, and craft design. Using Asian and Mayan design motifs, Pflueger was one of the first San Franciscans to look beyond Europe to Asia and Latin America for artistic inspiration. When he was once asked, "Why the use of Asian themes?" he responded, "It's too damn bad we didn't have the Oriental influence on the coast instead of the European." Of course, the "Oriental influence" was right at their doorstep, but cultured San Franciscans, beyond their interest in Japanese gardens, were not in a receptive frame of mind.

Something of a renaissance in the San Francisco art world was inspired by a public arts program funded by the Roosevelt adminstration, particularly among supporters who were influenced by the murals of the three great Mexican painters Rivera, José Clemente Orozco, and David Siqueiros.

In San Francisco control over federal funding for the arts passed into the hands of the city's elite, specifically a committee headed by Walter Heil, director of the de Young Museum, who was advised by prominent citizens such as Templeton Crocker, Mrs. Oscar Sutro, Arthur Brown Jr., designer of City Hall and the Opera House, and Mrs. Lewis Hobart, wife of the designer of Grace Cathedral and the Bohemian Club. The city had recently made a commitment to build a tower in a park on the top of Telegraph Hill, and the tower was judged a suitable location for a display of public murals. Simultaneously,

Stackpole, painters Bernard Zakheim and Maynard Dixon, and sculptor Beniamino Bufano were petitioning Edward Bruce, a Treasury Department employee, to fund a federal arts project in San Francisco. The two groups ended up working together, much to the regret of the project's elite supporters.

Almost all California artists followed the general guidelines offered by Washington for both the Public Works Art Project and the later and better-known Federal Arts Project: They painted or sculpted representational works that ignored the realities of the Depression and evoked a mythic past when America was doing just fine, thank you. Not so with certain San Franciscans. Immersed in a long-standing radical tradition and the highly charged political atmosphere that led to the general strike, Victor Arnautoff, John Langley Howard (the son of the first head of the architecture school at the University of California–Berkeley), Clifford Wright, and Bernard Zakheim, all of whom had worked with Rivera, touched on political themes in their murals. When the *Chronicle* got hold of the story, the resulting brouhaha led to the closing of the tower while the artists were still at work. The most original works of the project, Anton Refrigier's murals in the former Rincon Annex Post Office at Mission and Steuart Streets, were not completed until 1943. But they too raised a storm of protest and were censored because of their uncompromising look at California history (the grim experience of the forty-niners who came cross-country, vigilante activities, abusive treatment of the Chinese, and the general strike).

With the end of public arts funding during World War II, Rivera, who painted murals for the San Francisco Art Institute and the Treasure Island World's Fair, became a footnote in San Francisco arts history—until the 1960s. Then a whole new generation of mural painters, many of them Hispanic, again drew inspiration from his works, making the Mission District a national center of mural painting. These young artists would take part in the new cultural wars over the spending and control of funds—this time city funds—for public art.

6

The Pacific Rim
Metropolis

For San Franciscans, World War II was a karmic event that would have a profound impact not only on the shape of the city, but also on its very people. The city's civic leaders would renew their campaign to make the city a major Pacific Rim metropolis. In the process, the racial barriers to Asian immigration, which contributed mightily to the war with Japan, would be swept away and the city would become a great multicultural metropolis with a significant Asian population.

With the Roosevelt administration pushing rearmament, the San Francisco economy, stimulated by military contracts, was already showing signs of a dramatic turnaround as early as 1940. While the United States poured troops and materiel into the great naval battles and island-hopping campaigns in the South Pacific, San Francisco, as administrative headquarters for the Army's Western Defense Command and Fourth Army and the Navy's Western Sea Frontier and Twelfth Naval District, became the most important forward staging area on the American mainland. For two decades before the war, the Bay Area's shipyards had remained largely idle. During the war it became the largest ship construction complex ever known, and the number of Bay Area shipyard workers rose to 244,000. With most war production taking place outside the city, San Francisco became a "dormitory metropolis," which put extraordinary pressure on its housing stock and public facilities.

The federal government responded by suspending construction of public housing and shifting resources quickly to the construction of housing for military personnel and civilian defense workers. The results were impressive. At Hunter's Point and on fill in Candlestick Cove, facilities for 35,000 people were thrown up almost overnight. Ultimately, the pressure on housing pushed the city beyond its capacity to respond; thousands of people were turned away from the War Housing Center.

ONCE AGAIN A CITY OF IMMIGRANTS

The war brought marked changes to the city's population mix, prefiguring the remarkably diverse city of the end of the century. Originally an immigrant city, by the end of the nineteenth century San Francisco was known for its large number of foreign-born residents. In the first four decades of the twentieth century, the city, despite small Asian, Latino, and African-American populations, had become overwhelmingly white as the number of foreign-born declined. That would soon change. Among the 200,000 who came to the city during World War II were 27,000 blacks, most of them fleeing the racism and limited prospects offered them in Arkansas, Texas, and Louisiana. Some moved into temporary housing in Hunter's Point, and others settled into homes in the Western Addition, which had been conveniently vacated when their Japanese-American occupants were shipped off to concentration camps.

After a campaign of racial provocation inspired by General John DeWitt, Army commander at the Presidio, and inflamed by the Hearst press, President Roosevelt in 1942 ordered that most of California's 94,000 Japanese-Americans be loaded onto special trains and shipped to camps in six Western states. Not surprisingly, the evacuation had a very unsettling effect on the city's Japanese population. After the war many returned to their old neighborhoods, mostly in the Western Addition, to find their homes and businesses in the hands of new owners and with no recourse but to accept the situation. Some moved westward into the Richmond District; others left the city for good. Although Japan Town, as we will see, became a prime target for urban renewal, the Japanese-American population of the city remained small in relation to other nonwhite immigrants.

The Chinese population, in contrast, grew steadily until the 1970s, when growth accelerated. Chinatown remained the preferred neighborhood of entry for poor immigrants, many of whom worked in sweatshops both in that area and south of Market. Second-generation families and wealthy immigrants peopled a new Chinatown along Clement Street in the Richmond District, and by 1990 there were signs of a third Chinatown emerging on the Sunset side of Golden Gate Park.

Although smaller in number, the Filipino population also grew during the postwar years. The original Manila Town—a community of single males who worked seasonally in the fields or took unskilled service jobs in places such as San Francisco's hotels—was located within three blocks of the intersection of Jackson and Kearny Streets in Chinatown. A second family-based Filipino community formed south of Market in the 1950s. Over time Daly City, just south of San Francisco, became the major Filipino enclave, even electing a Filipino mayor in 1995.

The city's latest Asian arrivals are Vietnamese and Cambodian. The first Vietnamese were often members of elite groups allied to the United States; they came to this country after the fall of Saigon in 1975. During the next five years they were followed by thousands of boat people and members of Cambodian hill tribes, such as the Khao and the Hmong. These new Asian arrivals moved, for the most part, into the Tenderloin, transforming this tough, seedy district north of Market Street between the Civic Center and Union Square into a flourishing community.

Hispanics, of course, were San Francisco's first immigrants, settling at Mission Dolores and the Presidio. With the collapse of the mission system, the abandonment of the Presidio, and the usurpation of Hispanic land rights by Americans after their conquest, the small remaining Hispanic community shifted its base to the Latin Quarter near Columbus and Broadway. By the end of the century many Mexicans and Central Americans were following the shipping lanes north—established in part by local coffee companies—to take jobs as laborers in canneries and wholesale produce businesses along the waterfront. Other Mexicans came to California as farmworkers before moving into the city. Because wartime employers recruited heavily in Central America as well as the South, Central Americans began to outnumber Mexicans. Latinos at first moved into the north Mission, an area of factories and breweries mixed with low-cost apartments. The rapid growth of Latino population in the 1960s accelerated with the influx of people fleeing the conflicts in El Salvador and Nicaragua in the 1970s and 1980s.

There was also dramatic movement by whites, both in and out of the city. So-called white flight to the suburbs led to a drop in the city's population from a wartime high of 850,000 to 617,000 in 1980. Simultaneously, the city attracted many young whites either because of the opportunities offered or the atmosphere of tolerance. The first wave of whites consisted of servicemen who had passed through the city during World War II and either stayed or returned later. As early as the 1950s numerous whites, often students or young Bohemians, began moving into established neighborhoods such as the Haight-Ashbury, North Beach, Potrero Hill, and the Mission. They proved to be the forerunners of the huge Hippie influx that peopled the Haight after the "Summer of Love" in 1967 and the massive arrival of gays and lesbians following the Stonewall Riots in New York in 1969. Polk Street, or Polk Gulch, and the Castro District became the centers of the gay community.

Two groups of foreigners, the Irish and the Russians, have continued to contribute to the city's diversity. Many Irish people live in the Sunset District, where the Irish Cultural Center is located, and Russians tend to cluster in the Richmond District. White in-migration reflected significant changes in the nature of the city's work force. Technological changes in cargo handling led to the almost total decline of the port, and urban renewal South of Market and in Hunter's Point pushed out many blue-collar workers. San Francisco was becoming even more markedly white-collar as young whites began to gentrify formerly blue-collar neighborhoods.

By 1996, San Francisco, in ethnic terms, was barely recognizable as compared with the San Francisco of 1940. The number of whites had fallen to 39 percent, the Asian and Pacific Island population had grown to 34 percent, Latinos to 16 percent, and the black population remained at 11 percent. San Francisco, a generation earlier overwhelmingly white, was now a multiracial city with a white minority population. Despite the change in the city's racial composition, it would take innumerable political skirmishes for the city's latest arrivals to gain a political voice commensurate with their growing numbers.

After the war San Francisco became more than ever a city of neighborhoods, each with its own distinctive physical terrain, its shifting ethnic mix, its shopping district, restaurants, and Catholic parish. Having disrupted family ties to come here, many new San Franciscans seemed to compensate by developing strong attachments to the larger community, whether defined by turf, ethnicity, or gender. As the city's business elite began to carry out their plans to rebuild the city in the image of New York, their vision of San Francisco inevitably clashed with the new San Franciscans' urge to recreate and protect village life in an urban environment. It was the complex interplay between what came to be called "Manhattanization," the quest for ethnic and gender-based political power, and village resistance that shaped San Francisco's politics for the rest of the century.

THE OLD POLITICS:
PUBLIC AND PRIVATE POWER

Shipping magnate Roger Lapham was elected mayor in 1943. A relative newcomer, he had led the fight against Harry Bridges and the dockworkers and, in the process, had become reconciled to a permanent role for the unions along the waterfront. Lapham led the effort to revitalize the city, particularly the downtown, to make San Francisco "the gateway to all the lands and peoples of the great Pacific Basin." But he was leading a city that was unsure of its future and dependent on a crumbling infrastructure neglected during the Depression and pushed beyond capacity during the war. One of Lapham's primary goals was the reconstruction and extension of the city's transportation system, beginning with the purchase of the deteriorating Market Street Railway, the last privately owned piece of the mass transit system, and the construction of a subway system.

Lapham's successful effort to purchase the Market Street Railway triggered a recall movement that allied working-class areas of the city with conservative neighborhood groups, mostly from the western part of the city. The movement was led by Henry Budde, publisher of the *San Francisco Progress*, a newspaper devoted strictly to neighborhood news. Budde and his associates charged that Lapham ran the city in a "dictatorial manner" and was discriminating "against the neighborhoods in favor of downtown." Lapham defeated the recall and retired after one term.

What Henry Budde and some of his followers were objecting to when they challenged Lapham for being "a rich man who didn't give a damn about the concerns of ordinary people" was a form of private sector governance that was beginning to solidify during the Lapham regime and would ultimately reshape Downtown and the so-called blighted neighborhoods such as the Western Addition and South of Market.[24] Wartime necessity—dealing with Bay Area problems such as housing and the location of new industries —led to some tentative efforts at planning. At the same time, the city's most powerful business leaders began to focus their own planning efforts on the city's economy and its place in the regional and global marketplaces.

In 1944, the Bank of America, the American Trust Company, Standard Oil of California, Pacific Gas and Electric, US Steel, and the Bechtel Corporation pledged $10,000 each to fund the operation of the Bay Area Council. San Francisco business leaders, despite their fears of an economic downturn, saw themselves at the beginning of a potentially expansive era that would make some of their companies into global players and would strengthen San Francisco's position as a major Pacific Rim metropolis. Standard Oil of California (SOCAL) was the city's first company to become a global force. SOCAL had begun life as part of the Rockefeller empire, then became independent when the U.S. Justice Department forced John D. Rockefeller to break up his giant oil trust in 1911. By 1919, SOCAL was the largest single oil producer in the United States. In 1932, after signing agreements with the royal families in Bahrain and Saudi Arabia to develop their enormous oil reserves, SOCAL struck the first significant oil deposit in the Arab world.

In stature and power A. P. Giannini's Bank of America was equal to SOCAL. Although Montgomery Street bankers originally dismissed the Bank of Italy (the forerunner to the Bank of America) as a "dago bank" serving North Beach's "foreign colony," Giannini was building up his assets by serving the state's 35,000 immigrant farmers. In October 1945, Giannini proudly announced that the Bank of America had overtaken New York's Chase Manhattan Bank, long associated with the Rockefeller family, to become the largest bank in the world.

Another large San Francisco–based business was Bechtel, a family-owned engineering and construction firm. In the 1930s, Bechtel formed a partnership with five other Western construction firms. The Six Companies, named for the organization that controlled Chinatown, built the massive Hoover and Grand Coulee Dams, projects that provided the water for the postwar expansion of Western agribusiness and the continuing development of some of the West's largest cities. During the war, Bechtel and the Oakland-based Kaiser Industries, the two Bay Area members of the Six Companies partnership, went into the shipbuilding business. Bechtel operated Marinship in Sausalito and Henry Kaiser started the world's largest shipyard in Richmond. In the postwar years Bechtel became one of the world's largest construction companies, with contracts to build important infrastructure projects in countries such as Saudi Arabia. Understandably, the concerns of these economic giants were vastly different from those of the anti-Lapham neighborhood groups who spoke of the need for stoplights, street cleaning, and police service.

A CORPORATE HEADQUARTERS CITY

In 1945 the Bay Area Council (BAC) joined the Chamber of Commerce and the Downtown Association to become part of a network of interlocking and overlapping corporate-sponsored organizations. This group took on what business leaders saw as the city's most pressing problems, namely, the lack of a regional transportation system and the need to expand the downtown business district, to clear blighted areas, and to return control of the port and its valuable real estate to city control. Behind all of these initiatives was the desire to secure San Francisco's position as a corporate headquarters city.

The Bay Area Rapid Transit System (BART) was the BAC's first significant undertaking. Headed by executives from the Bank of America and Kaiser, the BAC's BART campaign placed a bond measure on the ballot in 1961. Funds for the bond campaign were provided by another private-sector organization, the secretive Blyth-Zellerbach Committee, formed in 1956 by Charles Blyth, a prominent stockbroker and director of computer maker Hewlett-Packard, and J. D. Zellerbach, the head of the Crown-Zellerbach paper and timber company. BART's final engineering report was written by Bechtel, and Bechtel built the system with former Six Companies partner Morrison-Knudson. BART turned out not to be the urban mass transit system first envisioned by Daniel Burnham and spelled out in greater detail by city planners in the 1930s. It is primarily a regional railway designed to take commuters to and from the new headquarters city. Meanwhile Muni, the city's vast mass transit system, deteriorated as San Francisco business leaders fought attempts to increase taxes to pay for improved Muni service.

BART was a case study of how the city's small business elite did things after World War II, until the political response triggered by events like its construction brought new political forces into play. San Francisco in the postwar years still functioned in many ways like a small town. The city's corporate leaders knew each other well. They dined at the same restaurants, sat in adjoining boxes at the opera, symphony, and ballet, lived in the same wealthy neighborhoods and suburbs, and belonged to the same clubs. Further, the boards of the city's major corporations were tightly interlocked, as tightly as the corporations were interlocked with organizations like the BAC.

True, the city did have a Department of City Planning presided over by a Planning Commission appointed by the mayor. But Planning could not keep pace with the plans of the business leaders. Once redevelopment of poor neighborhoods got under way, the Planning Department was simply overwhelmed by the magnitude of the changes wrought. As discussed later, at times private developers came to a cash-starved Planning Department seeking endorsement of their plans with offers of donations. But even more significant, a new city bureaucracy—the Redevelopment Agency—was formed once federal funding for urban renewal started flowing into the city. With its enhanced powers, ready access to federal funds, and close ties to the city's real estate developers, the Redevelopment Agency ran roughshod over City Planning.

FIRST SIGNS OF PRESERVATIONISM: SAVING THE CABLE CARS

After the city had established the Municipal Railway system in 1912, there was a systematic effort to replace cable cars—which, after all, dawdled along at a mere 9.5 miles per hour—with faster electric, then gasoline and diesel, vehicles. In 1942, the Clay Street line, the first built by cable car inventor Andrew Hallidie, carried its last passenger. It was replaced by diesel buses, but Nob Hill proved to be too steep for the new vehicles; at times passengers had to get off and walk. In 1947, Mayor Lapham informed the Board of Supervisors that it was time to get rid of the old system of cable cars: "They are outmoded, dangerous, and lose too much money." The newspapers were outraged but resigned.

Not the citizenry. Opposition to Lapham's plan was organized by Friedel Klussmann, a Telegraph Hill resident who was president of the San Francisco Federation of Arts. She and a group of associates, known as the "Ladies,"

Friedel Klussmann, one of the city's first preservationists, led the fight to save the cable cars in the 1940s and 1950s. *San Francisco Public Library.*

formed San Francisco Beautiful in 1947. Given the system's status as one of the city's premier tourist attractions, it was easy for the Ladies to mobilize support from women who caught the eye of the media, including Eleanor Roosevelt and actress Katherine Cornell, who told the press she "would not care to return to San Francisco if the cable cars were not there." Lapham sought to parody the backwardness of the Ladies' effort by riding down Market Street in the type of horse-drawn trolley used in the nineteenth century. One citizen's response: "It would be a good thing to have these charming horse cars back, as well as the cable cars." [25]

In 1947 the Ladies rounded up more than 55,000 signatures to put a charter amendment protecting the Powell Street Line on the ballot. Meanwhile, cable car ridership declined and the cable cars themselves deteriorated. In 1961 a local advertising executive suggested selling billboard space on the sides of cable cars as a way to cut the costs of the system. The city jumped at the idea, and the cable cars became associated in the minds of American TV watchers with the jingle "Rice-A-Roni, the San Francisco Treat" and the opening scenes of the TV show *The Streets of San Francisco.* Ultimately, the system was protected from further closures when the U.S. Department of the Interior declared the cable cars a national landmark.

THE FREEWAY REVOLT

While BART was on the drawing board, civic leaders recommitted themselves to the automobile instead of the Muni system, with enormous consequences for the city. In 1954, the Department of Public Works, backed by the Chamber of Commerce, announced plans for a $355 million freeway project that would take 20 years to complete. The proposed system would connect two freeways coming north up the Peninsula (today's Interstates 101 and 280) to the Golden Gate and Bay Bridges. It also featured several crosstown arteries and an extension that would follow the waterfront north from the Bay Bridge along the Embarcadero and then west to the Golden Gate. After Mario Ciampi, a local architect, began work on the design of the first phase of the project, a two-deck monster that would run from the Bay Bridge to Broadway in North Beach, it became apparent that the freeway would wall off the waterfront from downtown, throwing up a barrier between the historic Ferry Building and the end of Market Street.

Opposition surfaced, albeit in a gentlemanly manner. The San Francisco office of the architectural firm Skidmore Owings Merrill suggested moving the freeway westward so as to at least create space for a park and plaza in front of the Ferry Building. No, the freeway juggernaut was rolling, and nothing could or should be done to slow it down. During the late 1950s work was completed on the Embarcadero Freeway; the James Lick, which connected the Bay Bridge to Interstate 101; the Southern Freeway (Interstate 280), which crossed 101 heading for another connection either to the Bay Bridge or to a proposed "second crossing" of the bay; and the Central Freeway, which split off from the James Lick and headed north toward the Golden Gate Bridge.

However, when plans for a Western Freeway surfaced, serious opposition began. Without being specific about its route, the state proposed running Interstate 280 north through Golden Gate Park to a connection with the Golden Gate Bridge. A second arm would turn eastward through a corner of the park and down the Panhandle to meet with Interstate 101 in a concrete reprise of James Duvall Phelan's beloved plan to extend the Panhandle to the Civic Center. Public meetings to discuss the freeway were packed with hundreds of angry home owners eager to know exactly where the freeway was going and how many homes would be condemned. At the urging of neighborhood activists, the Board of Supervisors voted against the proposed freeway. Warning that the city could lose more than $100 million in future freeway funding, Mayor George Christopher, who was elected in 1955, vetoed the resolution. Unaccustomed to opposition that was both strong and persistent, state and local officials with support from the Chamber of Commerce presented new plans to complete the city's freeway system to the supervisors in 1958. They were again turned down in early 1959 in what was billed as the Freeway Revolt.

The Embarcadero Freeway being completed in 1958. A design disaster, it became a concrete wall cutting off views along the waterfront. "X" marks the site of the Produce Market. *San Francisco Public Library.*

Opponents of the freeway were making a strong statement about the city's aesthetic. In an era when freeway proposals went through with little opposition, San Francisco distinguished itself nationally—and undoubtedly added to its reputation for peculiarity—by opposing the freeway juggernaut. The city was left with some strange structures: three elevated freeways that ended in off-ramps while the main arteries terminated abruptly, leaving reinforcing steel sticking out into the air. As early as 1961, State Senator Phillip Burton, the enfant terrible of San Francisco politics and soon to be its most powerful politician, introduced the first legislation that called for funding for the demolition as well as the construction of freeways. In the ensuing years, there were a number of unsuccessful efforts to "recall" the Embarcadero Freeway at the ballot box. In time, nature took its course. Both the Central and Embarcadero freeways were so weakened by the Loma Prieta earthquake of 1989 that they had to be torn down. The Embarcadero Freeway was demolished, opening up the waterfront to become the magnificent public esplanade it is today, and the final section of the Central Freeway is scheduled to be demolished as of the year 2000.

For the most part, the resulting Freeway Revolt was a genteel insurrection against an ethic of uglification. One supervisor thought to exploit the class nature of the revolt by suggesting that the Western Freeway be rerouted through the working-class Mission District. When freeway construction was finally brought to a halt, it was by activists from the city's more comfortable neighborhoods such as Telegraph Hill, Russian Hill, the Inner Sunset, and Pacific Heights.

There was one other small foreshadowing of future conflict. In 1961, the Southern Pacific began construction on the Fontana Apartments, two towers at the northern end of Van Ness Avenue adjacent to Aquatic Park. Russian Hill residents had unsuccessfully opposed the construction, which blocked their spectacular views of the Golden Gate. Under pressure from irate citizens, the Board of Supervisors limited the height of new buildings in the area to 40 feet.

THE REDEVELOPMENT BULLDOZER

Redevelopment of the city's poorer neighborhoods fit hand in glove with freeway construction as part of the larger scheme to build a new San Francisco. With redevelopment, the assault on low-income neighborhoods was massive and blatant, and it would eventually mobilize citizens in these neighborhoods on the eastern side of the city and create new alliances, not always cordial, between the city's more genteel rebels and inner-city activists. Together, and sometimes apart, they would shape a new political dynamic while ultimately limiting the downtown business community's plans to transform the city skyline.

The city's business community was faced with the physical reality of San Francisco. It was a peninsula with a downtown business district nestled against the waterfront and hemmed in by residential neighborhoods on Telegraph and Nob Hills. To the west of downtown along Market Street, there was only limited space for expansion, given the presence of the city's premier shopping district in the area around Union Square. The logical direction for expansion for new office buildings was toward South of Market where shabby neighborhoods of rundown apartment buildings, aging single-residence hotels, and a few houses mixed with light industry and warehouses. Market Street, according to the Board of Supervisors, was the city's "Great Divide," "a physical and psychological barrier to orderly development South of Market."

There was one exception to this situation: Right in the heart of downtown, between Sacramento and Broadway, stood the 51-acre wholesale Produce Market. The original Colombo Market built by Italians in 1876 had become the center of the wholesale produce industry by the 1880s. Rebuilt after 1906, the Produce Market was a collection of warehouses, loading docks, and an occasional apartment building. In the postwar years, to city officials and real estate magnates the Produce Market meant traffic congestion, poor sanitary conditions, low taxes, and very valuable real estate. The Produce Market was to become the Golden Gateway Redevelopment Project.

The Produce Market and the Western Addition became the city's first candidates for redevelopment. The fight over the Western Addition is described in Chapter 17. Urban renewal was officially ushered in by federal law in 1949. The Redevelopment Agency, set up the year before, soon became known as a superagency, a governmental entity with extensive powers such as condemnation, financing, and the creation of special tax districts that could be used on behalf of real estate developers to tear down and rebuild so-called blighted neighborhoods. With powers that no public planning agency had ever enjoyed, the Redevelopment Agency became the bulldozer that cleared the path for the city's influential developers. The problem with San Francisco was that although it had its share of poor people and rundown neighborhoods, particularly after the influx of new populations during the war, it was not really like larger cities where vast slums covered whole neighborhoods. For redevelopment, a neighborhood had to be declared "blighted," but in one proposed area only a quarter of the structures were considered seriously substandard. A good portion of the city's poorest housing stock, particularly in the Western Addition, comprised elegant Victorians gone to seed.

Redevelopment got off to a slow start under Mayors Elmer Robinson and George Christopher. By 1955 only one major office building, the West Coast headquarters of the Equitable Life Assurance Company, had been built downtown and one major corporation, the Fireman's Fund Insurance Company, had moved out of downtown to a modern building in the western part of the city. Robinson, an ineffective leader, seemed indifferent to the Redevelopment Agency, which became a sinecure for political hacks.

THE GOLDEN GATEWAY PROJECT

In 1955 Christopher defeated Robinson to become mayor. Christopher was a self-made businessman. The son of poor Greek immigrants who ran a lunch counter south of Market, he bought a milk distribution business during the Depression and built it into a dairy empire. As mayor, Christopher began to query the Planning Commission on a regular basis about the status of redevelopment plans, including the Golden Gateway Project. Although he was a wealthy businessman, Christopher came from South of Market and was not privy to the inner councils of the city's business elite.

In his first term Christopher met with William Zeckendorff, head of Webb and Knapp, a huge New York real estate firm, and protégé of the Rockefellers. Zeckendorff wanted to become the developer for the Golden Gateway Project. Zeckendorff, according to Roger Lapham Jr., the former mayor's son and Christopher's new head of the Planning Commission, offered to give the Planning Department $250,000 in exchange for "a free hand in the development area." Zeckendorff had the backing of Joseph Alioto, the brilliant young attorney who was president of Redevelopment Board. Christopher at first went along with the offer. The Planning Department was outraged, and Lapham felt he had to support his department chief. But, more important, the Blyth-Zellerbach Committee did not want an Eastern interloper taking over the city's most important development project. Describing themselves as "just a group of fellows devoted to San Francisco," the Blyth-Zellerbach committee countered with the first of two gifts of $25,000 for an "objective" study of the alternative plans for the Produce Market. Christopher changed his mind, and Zeckendorff was replaced by a local partnership, Perini-San Francisco Associates, as the developer for the Golden Gateway.[26]

The conflict over the Golden Gateway inspired Christopher to revamp the San Francisco Redevelopment Agency (SFRA). In 1959 he hired M. Justin Herman and gave him carte blanche to run the agency as he saw fit. As the federal administrator who oversaw urban renewal in the Western states, Herman had been a frequent critic of San Francisco redevelopment. Herman quickly reorganized the agency, accelerated property acquisition in the Western Addition and in a new area, Diamond Heights, and carved out new redevelopment zones in Hunter's Point, Chinatown, and South of Market, where there were plans to build a convention center. In short order Herman gained a reputation as a combative wheeler-dealer. "SFRA soon became a powerful force," wrote Chester Hartman in *The Transformation of San Francisco*, "with a staff of several hundred (compared with 60 in the pre-Herman era), a battery of consultants, close working relations with the mayor's office, and control over eight renewal projects and tens of millions of federal subsidies."[27]

Construction on the first phase of the Golden Gateway began in 1959 and was completed in 1964. It was an ambitious project, the largest undertaken since the construction of the Civic Center. It was also something strikingly new for San Francisco, a modernist essay in the spirit of the International Style, which was defined by the work of European architects, such as Le Corbusier, Walter Gropius, and Mies van der Rohe. Skidmore Owings Merrill's (SOM) general plan called for residential and commercial towers and townhouses in a park and plaza setting. Connected by footbridges, the plazas were to be one level above the street, creating a pedestrian environment apart from the automobile. The distribution of buildings over eight blocks offered a contrast to the older downtown where there was almost no open space and buildings stood in rank shoulder to shoulder. The city's leading architectural firms, SOM, Wurster, Bernardi and Emmons, Anshen & Allen, and DeMars and Reay worked on Phase I. In the next phase, completed in the 1980s, John Portman Jr. designed the Hyatt Regency at the junction of California and Market Streets and the Embarcadero Center, four office towers just south of

Manhattanization. The Transamerica Pyramid with the Bank of America Building on the right. On the left is Embarcadero Center One, built in the second phase of the Golden Gate Redevelopment Project. *Jan Cigliano.*

the Golden Gateway project. In the final phase, completed in 1982, Fisher Friedman Associates built additional residential buildings north of the Golden Gateway Apartments around Sidney Walton Park.

The construction of Phase I of the Golden Gateway marked the beginning of what the Chamber of Commerce called the "Big Build." An increasing number of new high rises were going up downtown. SOM designed a striking building for the Zellerbach family's timber and paper company on Market Street and a regional office that was in some ways more innovative, though less appealing, on California Street for Boston's John Hancock Insurance, both built in 1959. In retrospect these buildings and the Golden Gateway towers, though taller than the Chicago style skyline, seem of modest proportions next to the huge boxes that went up soon after them.

THE NEW POLITICS:
SIGNS OF THE RAINBOW

In 1955, Ben Swig, owner of the Fairmount Hotel and a major real estate developer, boasted, "The whole San Francisco skyline is going to change.... We are going to become a second New York." San Francisco real estate developers pressed on with their plans to build more office towers and megaprojects downtown and along the waterfront, and Justin Herman targeted the Western Addition for accelerated redevelopment. The neighborhood had never recovered from the overcrowding caused by the influx of black workers during World War II. Once the war was over, job opportunities were circumscribed, and blacks were barred from living in all but a small number of the city's neighborhoods and one of the city's housing projects. "Job discriminating based on color," wrote Thomas Fleming, managing editor of the *Sun Reporter,* an African-American weekly, "is, in my opinion, more vicious in the city of San Francisco than it is in parts of the South." [28] By 1960, the Redevelopment Agency had forced 3,700 families out of their homes.

This onslaught sparked opposition in the Western Addition as the fight agains redevelopment became part of the larger civil rights struggle in San Francisco. Civil rights, both in the Asian and black communities, were pursued by a group of young Democrats led by Phillip Burton. Burton was a complex figure, who liked to say that he admired "people whose balls roar when they see injustice," but could also be rude, boorish, and downright crude. Joined later by his brother John, George Moscone, and Willie Brown, Burton set out to build an electoral base in Chinatown and the Western Addition, communities that had heretofore been quiescent. Brown had come to San Francisco from Texas in 1951 at the age of 17, following in the path of his uncle, who ran an illegal gambling operation in the Western Addition.

Brown worked as a shoeshine boy and a lookout for his uncle's gambling operation before going to San Francisco State University. There he became friends with John Burton and later with John's best friend, George Moscone. As a member of the National Association for the Advancement of Colored People, Brown became a leader in campaigns for open housing and jobs for blacks. "[Phillip] Burton took the New Deal coalition of Franklin Roosevelt," wrote John Jacobs, his biographer, "and extended it beyond what anyone thought imaginable."[29] Over time, Burton and company would broaden their progressive coalition, bringing together voters from the black, Asian, and Latino communities with middle-class activists, gays, lesbians, environmentalists, and downtown height-limit advocates. Their impact on the shape of the city would be profound.

By 1963, when John Shelley was elected as the first Democratic mayor since James Duvall Phelan, opposition forces had slowed the redevelopment effort. Shelley, a labor leader and congressman from South of Market, was closely aligned with the Democratic Party's largely Irish establishment, but he had been elected with the backing of young Turks like the supporters of Phillip Burton. At his inauguration Shelley announced, "I intend to plan San Francisco's future with a heart as well as a bulldozer."

THE GROWTH MACHINE IN HIGH GEAR

By this time, Justin Herman had carved out seven redevelopment zones, incorporating 20 percent of the city's housing, and the SFRA was proposing to clear and rebuild in all but one of them. Shelley, like some of his union allies, was initially critical of redevelopment. But by the time he began to consider reelection in 1966, he had changed his tune. He supported redevelopment in the Mission District even when the Board of Supervisors opposed it and vetoed another vote against the Agency's plans to build a convention center South of Market, known as the Yerba Buena Center.

Shelley's inability to keep redevelopment on track led to the formation of a "dump Shelley" movement in 1967 by the supporters of redevelopment. The ringleaders were a group of downtown businessmen, including Joseph Alioto, former head of the SFRA and would-be mayor, Vernon Kaufman, a clothing manufacturer, Cyril Magnin, a department store owner who had ambitious plans for the waterfront, and Ben Swig, hotelier, real estate magnate, and initiator of the plan for the Yerba Buena Center. Within two weeks of their meeting to discuss finding a replacement for Shelley, Shelley suddenly announced that he would not be running for mayor again. Alioto quickly announced his candidacy, and in one of the fabled episodes in San Francisco's checkered political history, Swig raised $203,500 for Alioto in 45 minutes at a meeting at the Fairmount Hotel.

When Alioto won, he was something of an unknown outside North Beach and the business community. A wealthy and successful antitrust lawyer with a particularly aggressive and talkative style, he was the son of an Italian fish merchant who had opened one of the first shops on Fisherman's Wharf. Alioto was a cultured man, an omnivorous reader and opera lover, who could recite long passages from Dante and the Brownings. The mayor spoke of fashioning "a sort of New Deal coalition of labor and minorities, plus flag-waving Italians." Unabashed in his support for the growth machine, Alioto argued that San Francisco must either grow — preferably upward, but any direction would do — or die. He was so enthusiastic that he even supported the construction of apartment towers in Golden Gate Park. Accordingly, the mayor moved quickly to signal his support for the Redevelopment Agency, lavishly praising the work of Justin Herman, whom many black leaders had hoped Alioto would get rid of.

More than two dozen high rises, including the city's largest building, the 52-story Bank of America building (778 feet) at the corner of California and Kearny, were either already under construction or on the drawing boards when Alioto took office. The first major fight over downtown development began in January 1969, when the Transamerica Corporation, once A. P. Giannini's holding company and now a multibillion dollar global conglomerate, proposed constructing a 1,000-foot-tall pyramid on the site of the old Montgomery Block building. To reduce view obstruction and permit more light to reach the street, William Pereira designed the building with a base that tapered to a point. Pereira's pyramid was opposed by the Planning Department and the Telegraph Hill Dwellers Association. City zoning called for a 65-foot height limit in the area. With this in mind, the Planning Department, which was headed by Shelley appointee Allan Jacobs, was trying to establish height and bulk guidelines that would ensure that new structures would be compatible with buildings in the adjacent neighborhoods of Jackson Square, Chinatown, North Beach, and Telegraph Hill.

Transamerica waited until the very last minute to inform Jacobs about its plans and then launched a major public relations campaign, which included hiring Hippies to picket, carrying signs that read, "Artists for the Pyramid." After Jacobs met with Alioto, who was well informed about the project, Jacobs left "with a sinking feeling that the issue was already decided."[30] It was. In Alioto's fantasy San Francisco was a European city, and the Pyramid had become the Eiffel Tower. Transamerica was willing to make some modifications in the height and bulk of the building, but left the height at 853 feet. Meanwhile, Alioto lobbied the Planning Commission in support of the building, and it was finally approved by a narrow vote.

MORE NEW POLITICS:
URBAN CONSERVATION

The fight over the Transamerica Pyramid marked another significant transition in San Francisco politics. The SFRA's willful destruction of the Western Addition, its efforts to push poor people out of South of Market (see Chapter 7), and its targeting of other neighborhoods, such as the Mission, for the same treatment spawned an array of citizens organizations that dedicated themselves to protecting the urban landscape and the integrity of the city's distinct neighborhoods.

One result was an effort to build an organized preservation campaign. This began in 1962 when a group of architects, architectural historians, and writers asked the Junior League to conduct a survey of historic buildings in San Francisco, San Mateo, and Marin Counties. Then John Shelley, during his 1964 mayoral campaign, pointed out that although numerous American cities had landmark preservation boards that protected their architectural heritage, San Francisco, despite its rich architectural heritage, had none. The Landmarks Preservation Advisory Board was established by the supervisors in 1967. A year earlier, the idea of an urban, as opposed to a nature-oriented, environmentalism was enshrined in the National Historic Preservation Act. The law provided for a way to evaluate and list historic buildings and districts that would be helpful to local preservation boards.

In 1968, the Junior League published *Here Today: San Francisco's Architectural Heritage* with text by Roger Olmsted and T. H. Watkins and photographs by Morley Baer. In urging San Franciscans to resist the further decimation of the city's architectural heritage, Olmsted noted that it was "not enough to preserve a few monuments or 'historic buildings.'" He went on to say, "The double-decker freeway running in front of the Ferry Building symbolizes the bankruptcy of this traditional approach, as does the wholesale destruction of a large part of the old Western Addition in the name of 'Redevelopment.'"[31] *Here Today* was successful beyond the Junior League's wildest dreams.

In 1971 architect Charles Hall Page and attorney Harry Miller formed the Foundation for the Preservation of San Francisco's Architectural Heritage to provide a citizens' counterpart to the Landmarks Board. The Board "provided a stick that told people what they could or could not do if a building was designated," explained Page, "but we did not have a carrot. We wanted to become the carrot to the stick."[32] Page had been impressed by other well-known preservation organizations, specifically those in Annapolis, Maryland; Charleston, South Carolina; and Savannah, Georgia. Page suggested that Heritage, as it came to be known, start on a positive note. Accordingly, Heritage arranged to purchase and move 14 Western Addition Victorians to sites farther west in the city. In 1974 members of the Haas and Lilienthal families donated a family home at 2007 Franklin Street to serve as the fledgling organization's headquarters.

In the Mission District and South of Market, other new organizations were taking on the preservation issue from a very different perspective. Residents of both neighborhoods had watched the desecration of the Western Addition and concluded that they were faced with the same prospect. Following the SFRA proposal for redevelopment of Mission Street as part of the construction of BART in 1966, Mission residents formed the Mission Council on Redevelopment. In 1967, after the Council packed the supervisors' chambers, the proposal was turned down by one vote.

A year later, when Alioto announced that he was seeking Model Cities funding for the Mission, the Mission Coalition was formed to bring together dozens of local organizations to ensure citizen input in the program. The Mission Coalition (MCO) also set out to organize around a number of community issues—economic development, housing rehabilitation, low-income housing, education, neighborhood planning. Membership was broad-based, and leadership was popularly elected. Among the new organizations inspired by the MCO was the Mission Housing Development Corporation (MHDC), formed in 1971 to campaign for low-cost housing. After an unsuccessful campaign to build a small number of low-cost units, the MHDC undertook to write a plan with federal funding for general improvement in the neighborhood, including the construction of housing. The plan was completed in 1974.

Simultaneously, Toby Levine, a junior high school teacher, Judy Bowman, a public housing tenant, and Judith Lynch Waldhorn, who later coauthored *The Victorian Legacy* with Sally Woodbridge, formed the Victorian Alliance. The Alliance emphasized preservation of older housing while opposing what the founders called "misguided improvements," such as the stripping away of exterior finish work, the replacement of wooden windows with aluminum, and the use of asbestos shingling to cover the original channeled redwood siding. The Victorian Alliance's preservation objective was to increase home ownership among low-income people. Of course, this was nothing new. Numerous Victorians, both apartment buildings and cottages, had been originally built to broaden the social base of home ownership in San Francisco. The Victorian Alliance fought the redlining of the Mission District by mortgage companies and helped secure low-interest loans to increase home ownership. (Redlining is the practice, now illegal, of denying loans in areas inhabited by low-income people and people of color).

The opponents of redevelopment in the Mission and South of Market were turning San Francisco's traditional planning process on its head. Since the days of James Duvall Phelan, planning had been initiated by private elite organizations. In the postwar years the Planning Department had found itself reacting to these private plans, and the SFRA, working on behalf of the city's biggest developers, became the de facto planning agency. Under Allan

Jacobs, the Planning Department, although ceding control of the larger rede-velopment projects, began to push for more limited efforts at home rehabili-tation and neighborhood beautification. To this end, Jacobs and his planners found themselves working with citizens who, with the help of federal funding, organized neighborhood groups, such as the MCO and the MHDC, and came forward with their own plans.

Starting in the neighborhoods, architecture and urban design were becoming irreversibly politicized as new constitutencies fought their way into the process. These new constituencies turned to the ballot initiative or refer-endum as their chosen instrument of change. As electoral campaigns grew increasingly expensive, supervisors became dependent on downtown inter-ests for funding. Initiatives were often a different matter. Even when organiz-ers of initiative campaigns found themselves outspent by large margins, they could still win.

The incredible burst of activity that took place in the late 1960s and early 1970s added a range of new organizations and agendas to the political equa-tion, rewritten by politicians such as the Burton brothers, Willie Brown, and George Moscone. At times some of these organizations worked together—to limit high rises *and* promote construction of low-income housing, for exam-ple. At other times they contributed to what sociologists call hyperpluralism, the fragmentation that takes place in a complex social movement that appears to share the same goals but cannot find a common agenda.

The opponents of the Transamerica Pyramid looked at the proliferation of organizations and campaigns trying to establish some degree of citizens' con-trol over the transformations of the urban landscape and decided that they needed yet another organization. When it became apparent that the Pyramid would be built, the Telegraph Hill Dwellers contacted organizations, such as the Sierra Club and the Planning and Conservation League, and individuals who had fought against freeways or redevelopment or who had worked to establish the 40-foot height limit on the northern waterfront. The result was San Francisco Tomorrow, a citywide organization that would bring people together irrespective of their political affiliation to protect the urban environment.

THE ALIOTO WATER LOTS AND THE ANTI-HIGH-RISE INITIATIVES

San Francisco Tomorrow would meet its first challenge in the Alioto adminis-tration's plans for the waterfront. Soon after taking office, Alioto prevailed upon the state to return control of the waterfront to the city. Alioto knew that the port's days as a shipping facility were numbered. In the 1950s shipping companies had begun to introduce containers, large trailer-truck-sized boxes in which cargo was packed. The containers were removed from ships by cranes and stacked along the waterfront awaiting loading on trucks. Container ports required large amounts of open space adjacent to the piers, and San Francisco, with its downtown and the freeway encroaching on the piers, lacked space. Containers did not, however, require large numbers of longshoremen. At first the International Longshore and Warehouse Union (ILWU) resisted containerization. But in 1960 the ILWU gave in to the inevitable and cut a deal with the shipping companies that ensured the disappearance of almost all longshoremen from the city's northern waterfront. The 1960 contract permitted the introduction of containers in exchange for incentives for early retirement and pay for a guaranteed work week for those still working. It marked the beginning of the end for a working waterfront. As shipping companies fled the port for Oakland, they left the city's most valuable real estate in the hands of Joseph Alioto's Port Commission.

While the Board of Supervisors removed itself from the review process for waterfront development, the Port Commission began to advertise "prime waterfront property in San Francisco now available for commercial development." Much of this property was, of course, publicly owned, though now under control of Alioto and his cronies. It was the old fight over who would control the "water lots" created in the nineteenth century.

Since 1959, Alioto backer Cyril Magnin, head of the Port Commission, had been floating a waterfront development scheme known as Embarcadero City, a project to be located just south of the Bay Bridge. Magnin's plan included office space, a hotel, and a cruise ship passenger terminal. Soon after Alioto was elected, he and Magnin went to New York to solicit Fortune 500 firms to build their western headquarters in San Francisco. United States Steel responded with a proposal to build a 550-foot office tower on the waterfront between Howard and Folsom Streets as part of Magnin's Embarcadero City. Plans were drawn up by SOM. The US Steel tower would be 80 feet taller than the west tower of the Bay Bridge.

San Francisco Tomorrow quickly jumped into the fray, urged on by Charles McCabe and Herb Caen, two widely read columnists for the *Chronicle*. Caen wrote of trading "the God-given beauties of San Francisco for a mess of blottage" and then joined actor Paul Newman, a sometime resident of the city, in a protest march against the building. US Steel at first considered scaling its tower down to 125 feet, but then abandoned the project as economically unfeasible.

The unions, particularly the Building Trades Council, supported US Steel. "Eight hundred guys are sitting in our hiring hall waiting for work," a union official told the *San Francisco Bay Guardian*, with a logic that was hard to argue with, "...and conservationists are screaming about the US Steel project blocking the view. View? How many working people have a view?"[33]

After the supervisors voted down the US Steel plan, developers proceeded with caution when making proposals for projects along the waterfront. Not so with the downtown: Here activists and the Planning Department were vying unsuccessfully to establish control over the building boom. Planning was working on guidelines that would govern height, bulk, color, and views, while maverick businessman Alvin Duskin was campaigning in 1971 for an initiative measure that would limit the height of downtown buildings to 72 feet, lower than most of the Chicago style buildings put up around the turn of the century. The Planning Department's draft of its Urban Design Plan (UDP) called for a 40-foot limit in most residential areas. The UDP, trying to encourage a skyline patterned after the contours of the hills, called for smaller buildings at the foots of hills and tall buildings on top. The height limit downtown ranged from 300 to 700 feet. There was obviously a wide gap between Duskin's plan and the UDP's. The Planning Commission, not surprisingly, began to show more interest in the UDP height limits as publicity about the Duskin height-limit measure grew.

The weekly *Bay Guardian* was the source of much of this publicity. Bruce Brugmann and Jean Dibble had started the paper in 1964 as an alternative weekly committed to investigating the uses and abuses of power in the city. The *Guardian* proved to be a refreshing antidote to the two dailies, whose deference to the established ways of getting things done was notorious. Besides opposing high rises, *Guardian* reporters hammered away at the idea that the downtown community was a consumer of services, such as public transportation, disproportionately paid for by average San Franciscans rather than the corporate community.

The downtown business community poured hundreds of thousands of dollars into the campaign against the Duskin initiative, which lost, gaining only 38 percent of the vote. Duskin immediately put a second measure on the ballot for the next year, calling for a 40-foot limit throughout the city and 160 feet downtown. After 1971 the business community, in the person of Walter Haas, chairman of Levi Strauss, appeared to soften its stance and approached Jacobs about participating in the formulation of height controls. The Duskin initiative lost again, but now support for the measure had grown to 43 percent. An analysis of the vote showed that the measure had actually gained a majority in wealthy liberal areas such as Pacific Heights and Russian, Telegraph, and Nob Hills while losing in working-class and conservative middle-class neighborhoods.

THE MOSCONE INTERREGNUM

In 1975, George Moscone narrowly won a hotly contested campaign for mayor in a runoff. Swept into office by a broad coalition of unions, minority groups, neighborhood groups, urban conservationists, and, for the first time, the city's gay and lesbian movement, his election was celebrated as a grand victory for the new politics.

The brief Moscone years were heady if disturbing times in San Francisco. It was as if the peasants who had spent years clamoring at the gates had suddenly won access to the royal palace. In the election Moscone promised to halt Manhattanization, build low-income housing, and expand the city's job base while protecting the rights of all San Franciscans.

During his campaign Moscone had limited donations to $100, thereby precluding the possibility of significant contributions from the business community. He further antagonized the growth machine by appointing slow growth advocates to the SFRA Board and the Planning Commission. The critics of the growth machine were in the minority, and in a 1978 letter to the *Chronicle* Moscone insisted that he was not "antigrowth": "Since 1976, when my Planning Commission took over, not a single *major* project has been turned down. Indeed, 11 have been approved." [34] In fact, high-rise construction continued at roughly the same pace in the second half of the decade as in the first. "I've seen six mayors pretty closely," San Francisco Tomorrow activist Jack Morrison told Chester Hartman, "and have yet to see one who can stand up under the pressures of the real estate developers." [35]

Moscone did not live long enough to indicate how he would manage the political forces his campaign had unleashed. Ultimately, he was a victim of the bitter conflict that divided the old from the new San Francisco. On November 27, 1978, Dan White, who had resigned from the Board of Supervisors, bypassed the metal detectors at City Hall by entering through a basement window. He went to the mayor's office and shot Moscone, then sought out gay supervisor Harvey Milk and shot him too.

DIANNE: THE DOWNTOWN MAYOR

With the support of Willie Brown, Dianne Feinstein rallied the votes needed from her fellow supervisors to replace Moscone. A self-avowed centrist, she moved quickly to undo any damage that Moscone's leftist inclinations might have encouraged. City politics, however, would never be the same. The changes emanating from the neighborhoods that put Moscone in the mayor's office and his grave could not be reversed. The rainbow may have lacked grace and symmetry, but all the varied colors, sometimes shimmering in disarray, would remain in place.

Urged on by corporate leaders, Feinstein was particularly eager to demonstrate that she could rev up the growth machine before she faced her first popular election as mayor in 1979. She was assisted by her new husband, Richard Blum, a successful financier, described by the *Examiner* as "her ambassador to The City's corporate community." In February the *Chronicle* published an account of a meeting between the new mayor and representatives of the Southern Pacific, Bank of America, Foremost-McKesson, Wells Fargo, Crocker Bank, Macy's, and Transamerica. One corporate chairman "lectured Feinstein sternly," saying, "If it's going to be a headquarters city, some consideration must be given to the headquarters companies—to not let groups that are contributing little or nothing to the headquarters concept have the final say." Specifically, the mayor's hosts wanted to discuss Crocker's proposal to build a high rise at the corner of Post and Kearny that was 200 feet beyond the existing height limit. The mayor agreed to allow the building to exceed the limit. Money from downtown poured into her campaign coffers, and Feinstein narrowly won the election. But the corporate community was also contemplating a new role for itself in the planning process.

To clear the way for the growth machine, the mayor removed Moscone appointees from both the SFRA and the Planning Commission and then cleaned out the Landmarks Board. In the next six years the construction crane became the city's official bird, while structures equivalent to 37 Transamerica Pyramids were built downtown. The days of unrestricted construction of high rises were numbered, however. The city faced a very different economic environment, for one thing. In 1978 California voters had passed Proposition 13, which, although presented as a tax break for home owners, was also a massive tax break for corporate landowners. The impact on the city's budget was immediate. For downtown this meant that the city was hard pressed to provide the kinds of services, particularly public transportation, essential for the functioning of a headquarters city. A second problem was that the city was becoming overbuilt. These were the go-go Reagan years, and Congress had created tax incentives that encouraged financial institutions, many of them corrupt savings and loans, to pour money into commercial real estate in which the possibility of profits was enhanced by tax subsidies even when buildings were vacant. In 1986, Congress reversed field, reducing tax shelters for real estate investors. As a result, lenders began to require preleasing of new office space.

Despite their latest defeat, the anti-high-rise forces, led by San Francisco Tomorrow and San Franciscans for Reasonable Growth, had strengthened and broadened their coalition after the defeat of another height limiting initiative in 1979. They agreed, however, to postpone further action while the mayor and her allies engaged in another round of privately funded planning. While the Blyth-Zellerbach Committee worked on a plan to involve city officials and corporate executives in the development of "business strategic planning concepts modified to recognize the unique aspects of planning for a city," the Chamber of Commerce and a number of other downtown groups financed a Planning Department environmental impact report (EIR) that would assess the effect of various growth control scenarios on jobs, housing, transportation, and the environment. The corporate community was making a final bid to retain control of the planning process, but it backfired. By describing the negative impacts of continued uncontrolled growth of the downtown era, the EIR ended up bolstering the arguments of the anti-high-rise forces.

THE LAST TANGO

The EIR was used to write the Downtown Plan, which was unveiled by the mayor amid tremendous fanfare in August 1983. It was described on the front page of the *New York Times* and hailed by the *Sunday Examiner and Chronicle* as "undoubtedly the most famous urban design document in this nation right now." The plan called for a reduction in building height and bulk, preparation of shadow studies, and more mass transit and banned the "refrigerator row" look, calling for slimmer buildings with variegated tops. Architectural critics noted that the Downtown Plan was an official rejection of the International Style, which had ultimately produced symptoms of elephantiasis in glass and steel.

Allan Temko, the *Chronicle*'s acerbic architectural critic, charged that the plan permitted an "enormous volume of speculative development," but tried to hide the fact "under a kind of postmodern razzle-dazzle that is really cosmetic." Specifically, the plan permitted an additional 24 million square feet of office buildings that would employ 100,000 more office workers, at the same time recommending only 1,000 to 1,500 new units of housing. The plan also called for the establishment of "transfer development rights," which permitted developers to construct taller buildings outside restricted areas. In effect, the Downtown Plan was pushing development south of Market, the only way it could really go.

DOWNTOWN PRESERVATION

The Downtown Plan did little to assuage high rise critics, but it did ensure the protection of 266 historic buildings in the downtown area, all of which had been identified by San Francisco Heritage as worthy of preservation. Heritage had started by focusing on residential structures but soon turned its attention to commercial buildings in the downtown area. In 1974, Heritage campaigned successfully to have the Jessie Street Substation, a Pacific Gas and Electric Company (PG&E) facility designed by Willis Polk, placed on the National Register. Heritage's attention was then drawn to the Union Square area, the heart of the city's shopping district, where two upscale chains, Saks and Nieman Marcus, had announced plans to replace the historic City of

Paris and Fitzhugh buildings with new structures. In the 1971 Urban Design Plan, Union Square had been described as the best example in the city of a well-designed urban space, and the harmonious relationship between the St. Francis, the Fitzhugh, and other newer buildings of the same height had been evoked as an example of appropriate spatial definition. Saks and Nieman Marcus were proposing to cut the heart out of one of the most architecturally significant places in the city—thumbing their noses at the city's preservation process, as both buildings had been nominated for the National Register by the Landmarks Board.

The City of Paris was more than a historic building; it was an institution. Any longtime resident of San Francisco could describe the 60-foot Christmas tree that annually filled the building's four-story rotunda topped by an art glass skylight depicting the ship *La Ville de Paris*. Two French brothers had used the proceeds from the sale of their hosiery mill to stock the ship with dry goods and sailed to San Francisco, arriving in 1850. Their fashionable store moved several times, finally settling as a tenant in a new building constructed by the Spring Valley Water Company in 1896. The design, the work of Clinton Day, was one of the first in the city to be influenced by the neoclassical themes of the 1893 Columbian Exposition in Chicago. Although gutted, the City of Paris was one of 17 downtown buildings to survive the earthquake and fire of 1906. Arthur Brown Jr., of Bakewell and Brown, soon to be famous for the design of City Hall and the Opera House, restored the building in 1908, adding the spectacular rotunda with its art glass by Harry Wile Hopps. The Art Nouveau skylight was a very modern touch, giving a sense of how notions of elegance had evolved in the city. Less spectacular, but nonetheless significant, the Fitzhugh Building was designed by James and Merritt Reid and opened as a medical office building in 1924. Patterned after an Italian palazzo, it was meant to complement the architecture of the St. Francis Hotel.

Despite the collection of 55,000 signatures opposing their destruction and support from 20 civic organizations, the two buildings were demolished. "We went down in flames," recalled Heritage founder Charles Hall Page. "It was a good campaign though. We had good PR. There just wasn't enough public support for it. I don't think there was enough public awareness. The project sponsors just had enough political backing to push it through." Assemblyman Willie Brown represented Nieman Marcus at City Hall.

"I think it became evident to all of us that we lost those battles because there was very little appreciation of downtown architecture," Page went on. "People focused on Victorian houses. People thought they were neat and cute and should be protected. People were not aware that we had some fine commercial buildings downtown."[36] Up until that time only seven buildings in the downtown area had been designated as city landmarks. Heritage quickly set out to change public awareness about downtown architecture. Working with Page's firm, Heritage produced *Splendid Survivors*, a complete

The demolition of the City of Paris department store in 1980 inspired a successful campaign to preserve the city's commercial buildings. *San Francisco Public Library.*

inventory and description of hundreds of buildings on either side of Market Street from the Ferry Building to the Civic Center. The buildings were ranked according to their significance from A (highest importance) to D (Minor or No Importance.) In a significant victory for preservationists, Heritage's recommendations were incorporated into the 1983 Downtown Plan.

HIGH-RISE LIMITS

The process of developing the Downtown Plan had only further enraged anti-high-rise activists. By designating employees working on the downtown EIR as outside consultants, the Planning Department headed off public hearings on its content. So the anti-high-rise forces went back to the ballot once again, and again lost, this time by less than 1 percent of the vote. The anti-high-rise forces were able to chalk up one victory, however. In 1984, Proposition M, which required shadow protection for 70 parks and open spaces, was passed by a wide margin.

After another defeat in 1985 the anti-high-rise forces returned to the ballot box next with an initiative that was essentially a proposal to rewrite the Downtown Plan. The new Proposition M not only called for growth restrictions, but it was also a broad statement about how the progressive coalition viewed the future of the city. The initiative called for neighborhood preservation, including the protection of neighborhood housing and retail outlets, protection and enhancement of low-income housing, maintenance of a mixture of business types—commercial, service, and industrial—landmark and historic building preservation, protection for sunlight and views in parks, and job training for the poor.

As the campaign began, there were signs of shifting political allegiances, which were definitely working to the disadvantage of the downtown business interests. In the past the Chamber of Commerce had led the campaigns against anti-high-rise initiatives. This time the Chamber declined to do so. Showing signs of battle fatigue, the downtown community was divided. At the time, there was excess rental space, and those who had built were less eager for another campaign than those who had not. "Now, because of overbuilding, we don't have downtown jumping in with all that money," an anti-M leader told the *Chronicle*. Organized labor, another key component of the progrowth coalition, was also showing signs of backsliding. High-rise construction had provided thousands of jobs, but as the head of the Labor Council put it, "The blue-collar jobs move out, never to return again." For their part, the anti-high-rise organizers had digested the lessons of numerous defeats and a few small victories. Their polls showed that anti-high-rise sentiment, which had been predominantly an upper and middle-class phenomenon, was spreading to low-income neighborhoods. Even the established press, this time in the form of a four-part investigation of the politics of downtown deal making in the *Examiner*, contributed to the support for the anti-high-rise movement.

On November 4, 1986, Proposition M won by only 5,311 votes. The Downtown Plan made it extremely difficult to destroy what remained of the city's historic commercial districts. Proposition M placed a limit on the amount of square footage that could be built in a year. It also ensured that any new buildings constructed north of Market would have to be stepped back, rather than box-like, and would have to be topped with what architectural critics came to call "funny hats." Proposition M would inspire similar measures in other American cities, including even Los Angeles. But behind these results was the bald fact that Downtown was already largely built up and out.

As early as the 1950s, the growth machine had shifted its attention to South of Market (SOMA) where the prospects for rebuilding a rundown neighborhood excited the city's real estate developers. Here too the growth machine ran into opposition, but at first a very different kind of opposition. The seemingly endless skirmishing over the future of SOMA would raise a whole new series of questions about the nature of the city and its architecture.

7

The City
Moves South

"Old San Francisco," Jack London wrote in his short story "South of the Slot," "was divided by the [cable car] Slot....North of the Slot [on Market Street] were the theatres, hotels, and shopping districts, the banks and the staid, respectable business houses. South of the Slot were the factories, slums, laundries, machine shops, boiler works, and the abodes of the working class." London knew; he was born there. For San Francisco's real estate developers and their allies in the Redevelopment Agency, Market Street was the "Great Divide," "a physical and psychological barrier to the orderly development of South of Market." [37] For these powerful forces, if Downtown was going to expand, it had little choice but to go south, particularly after the last available space there, the Produce Market, was replaced by a massive redevelopment project. In the eyes of the developers, areas once targeted quickly lost their human qualities. They were "blighted," home to winos, derelicts, and assorted unfortunates who stood in the way of progress. South of Market (SOMA) was, in fact, a vital and dynamic if poor community.

SOMA's history reaches back to the days of Happy Valley and Tar Flats when the argonauts pitched their tents along the beach, the area became the city's first industrial neighborhood, and South Park became its first fashionable residential development. After South Park and Rincon Hill lost their luster, SOMA remained a solidly blue-collar neighborhood where single men— sailors, longshoremen, factory workers, and itinerant farmworkers, miners,

103

and loggers—lived in boarding houses and hotels cheek by jowl with small industries and families in modest flats and single-family homes. It was a gateway community through which English, German, Japanese, Irish, Greek, and Filipino immigrants found their way into the city. Houses and apartment buildings, often shabby, lined the neighborhood's numerous alleys, and the main thoroughfares were dotted with hotels, pawn shops, small businesses, bars, and cheap restaurants. By 1950 many of the area's residents, particularly those who found themselves in the path of redevelopment, were single men, often retired, who lived in run-down hotels that had seen better days but were nevertheless capable of being rehabilitated.

THE YERBA BUENA CENTER

SOMA caught Benjamin Harrison Swig's eye soon after he arrived in the city in the 1940s. Before coming to San Francisco, Swig had amassed a fortune as one of the largest real estate developers in the country. Once in the city, he quickly snapped up prize properties, including the Fairmount and St. Francis Hotels and acres of other valuable real estate.

In 1954, Swig announced his "San Francisco Prosperity Plan," the first major effort to push downtown development across the Great Divide. Swig was proposing a six-block development that would include a sports stadium, a convention center, high-rise office buildings, a luxury hotel, a theater-auditorium complex, a shopping mall with moveable sidewalks, a transportation terminal, and parking facilities for 16,000 cars. The problem was that Swig and his associates did not own the real estate. To Swig that seemed an insignificant difficulty. He turned to the Planning Department and asked that the area be declared blighted and subject to purchase by the San Francisco Redevelopment Agency (SFRA) for resale to developers. The Planning Department, however, found that only 10 percent of the structures in two central blocks of the project fit the definition of "blighted," making Swig's plan inconsistent with the urban renewal mandate. Undaunted, Swig donated funds to the Redevelopment Agency to finance planning studies. The Redevelopment Agency returned the donation, but at the urging of Joseph Alioto, the president of its board, agreed to place four of the blocks in a new redevelopment zone.

Swig had a number of powerful opponents, including federal officials, labor unions, and Mayor George Christopher. "Speculative real estate operators…seem to have taken over the planning functions of the city," Labor Council official George Johns wrote in the Council's bulletin in 1965. Noting that redevelopment South of Market would cost the city blue-collar jobs, he went on to question whether "the policy makers of this City have thought of the social and economic effect on over 3,000 single persons, a third of them

aged, who will be displaced in the area without realistic provision for relocation." [38] The answer to Johns's question was, yes, the city's business elite had
thought about the consequences of redevelopment and was ready to press
on. Christopher was an eager supporter of Redevelopment's Golden Gateway
Project north of Market, but not so with South of Market. Swig's plan was halt-
ed, but only temporarily.

Redevelopment director Justin Herman breathed air back into the project in 1961, shifting its focus to the central blocks directly south of Market
between Third, Fourth, and Folsom Streets. Ben Swig had passed the project
on to his son Melvin, who, as part owner of the city's basketball and hockey
franchises, hired Skidmore Owings Merrill to design a convention and sports
complex. When the project was finally announced in 1964, there was little
opposition beyond labor's objections. Two years later federal funding was
made available, and in 1967 the SFRA began to clear the central blocks.
Herman spoke vaguely about "spot clearance" while promising that funding
would be available for replacement housing.

With Ben Swig's ample financial backing, Joseph Alioto took office in
1968, pledging that work on what was now called the Yerba Buena Center
(YBC) would "go forward quickly." Tourism and the convention business were
integral to Alioto's and the growth machine's vision of a new San Francisco.
These two enterprises combined were becoming the city's largest industry. San
Francisco, however, could offer only antiquated and undersized facilities—
the Civic Auditorium and Brooks Hall in the Civic Center—in the increasingly
competitive struggle to secure conventions and sports franchises. Alioto had
successfully yoked the Labor Council to the growth machine with the
promise of union jobs at redevelopment projects and the distribution of seats
on various commissions. Now he set off for Washington, where he was able to
secure additional federal funding for redevelopment in the Western Addition
and South of Market.

In June 1969 a design team delivered plans for the convention center
complex. In the vocabulary of the SFRA, the new complex would be a "protected environment," one that would ensure that "undesirable elements"
would not interfere with sports fans and conventioneers. As a real estate
executive told the *Examiner,* "You certainly can't expect us to erect a 50 million dollar building in an area where dirty old men will be going around
exposing themselves to our secretaries."

THE "DIRTY OLD MEN" FIGHT BACK

By federal law, if the SFRA demolished housing, it had to guarantee that it
would provide housing that charged similar rents, was equally accessible to
public and commercial facilities and places of employment, and was safe,

clean, and sanitary. There were 3,000 single residents and 280 families in the path of the Yerba Buena Center, but according to the plan submitted to the U.S. Department of Housing and Urban Development (HUD) in 1966, the SFRA was proposing to build only 176 units of senior housing.

Federal urban renewal statutes also contained vague language about "citizen participation." South of Market's residents were "represented" by the San Francisco Planning and Urban Renewal Association (SPUR), a creation of the secretive Blyth-Zellerbach Committee. SPUR, though formed to provide for citizen participation in the redevelopment process, was generally regarded at this stage in its history as a front for downtown interests. After Alioto assumed office, the SFRA increased pressure on residents to move out of the area. Once people had moved, new residents were barred, and the old hotels became half empty and frightening. Heat and water were shut off and services were withdrawn. Lobby doors were locked, lavatories closed, and comfortable chairs removed from lobbies. There were also a number of mysterious fires.

In the summer of 1969 local residents organized Tenants and Owners Opposed to Redevelopment (TOOR). SFRA, not surprisingly, stumbled upon a

Radical activist George Woolf helped organize Tenants and Owners Opposed to Redevelopment, forcing the Redevelopment Agency to modify the Yerba Buena project to include low-income housing. *Ira Nowinski.*

group of people with long-established ties to the city's militant labor movement. Among them were George Woolf, a former Communist Party member and first president of the Alaska Cannery Workers' Union, which later affiliated with the International Longshoremen's and Warehousemen's Union (ILWU). The 80-year-old Woolf shared leadership of TOOR with Peter Mendelsohn, a recently retired merchant seaman and former union and Communist Party organizer. "I've lived on this block for 40 years," said Mendelsohn about the neighborhood. "I know everyone here and they know me." TOOR's basic demand was simple and consistent with federal law: replacement housing in the same neighborhood. Although the SFRA declared that the YBC was only the beginning of efforts to clear the rest of South of Market, Justin Herman told a meeting in the mayor's office, "This land is too valuable to permit poor people to park on it."[39]

In November 1969, TOOR asked for injunctive relief in federal court, claiming that neither HUD nor the SFRA had made plans to provide adequate replacement housing. In March 1970, a judge barred all relocation efforts in the Yerba Buena area without a notarized statement of voluntary consent. The SFRA quickly came forward with an offer to provide replacement housing, which would shift low-income housing from other needy applicants to people displaced for the YBC. When presented with the SFRA's proposal, the judge ordered an even more restrictive injunction. In a moment of high drama, Mayor Alioto appointed himself special counsel for the SFRA, and the court appointed former governor Edmund "Pat" Brown a special master charged with reaching agreement in the case.

Meanwhile, TOOR took a significant step. It turned to the University of California's Community Design Center for a housing plan that would provide 2,000 units of new and rehabilitated housing in the immediate area of the YBC. This was preemptive planning, a citizens group proposing to replace the work of public agencies and their developer allies with a people's plan. When Special Master Brown supported the TOOR demand for 2,000 units, the SFRA turned his proposal down, calling instead for Yerba Buena residents to receive priority positions on the list for public housing, a list that was already crowded with families displaced from the Western Addition. Stymied by the two sides' inability to find common ground, the same judge drafted a consent decree, which both sides signed in November 1970. The core of the agreement permitted the SFRA to resume demolition of buildings in the area in exchange for a guarantee to build 1,500 to 1,800 units of housing.

TOOR was not entirely happy with the outcome. Four thousand units were being replaced with 1,500 to 1,800 units, and TOOR held that 2,000 units was the minimum acceptable figure. Nevertheless, TOOR signed the consent decree. Despite the decree, Justin Herman went to his grave in 1971 having told a city official that he had no intention of building the number of units required by the consent decree. The longer the SFRA postponed building replacement housing, the more people would leave the area and the easier it would be for the SFRA to argue that less housing was needed.

THE HERMAN LEGACY: POLITICIZED URBAN DESIGN

In the months before his death in August 1971, Herman found himself on shaky ground. The city's chief administrative officer (CAO) announced that there were possible illegalities and conflicts of interest in the SFRA's financing plans for the YBC, as well as serious design problems. Richard Swig, Melvin's brother, had become a leading critic of the 1969 design for the Yerba Buena Center. He and other representatives of the hotel business opposed the idea of an underground convention hall, arguing that it lacked sufficient unobstructed open space and meeting rooms. Meanwhile, Herman found himself the target of what the *Examiner* called "a political power play" inspired by Alioto and his CAO. Against Herman's wishes, the mayor announced that there would be a new design, a new developer, and a new way of financing the project. Herman was at his apartment in the Golden Gateway project, reportedly writing a memo to the mayor saying he would not go along with the proposed changes, when he died from a heart attack. Herman was 62 years old, and his death was attributed to stress.

Commenting on his career, a U.S. Housing and Urban Development official told the *National Journal,* "Herman could move rapidly on renewal—he was doing what the power structure wanted insofar as the poor and the minorities were concerned....That's why San Francisco has mostly luxury housing and business district projects—that's what white, middle-class planners and businessmen envision as ideal urban renewal."[40] Herman left a contradictory legacy. He oversaw the almost total reconstruction of major parts of the city, but, particularly in the Western Addition, the work was carried out at a steep human price. He cleared the way for two large-scale exercises in planned modernist architecture, the Golden Gateway Redevelopment Project and the collection of buildings that surround St. Mary's Cathedral in the Western Addition. More than anything, Herman politicized the urban design process by inadvertently mobilizing thousands of people to resist redevelopment.

Two years after Herman's death, an agreement was signed in the lobby of the hotel where TOOR had been founded. The agreement called for 1,500 replacement units, while turning three properties over to TOOR and pledging hotel tax funding for new housing. TOOR then transformed itself into the Tenants and Owners Development Corporation (TODCO), a nonprofit that was ready to serve as the developer of three apartment houses to be built on the lots given to TOOR by the city.

MOSCONE TO THE RESCUE

Supporters of the YBC had settled with one major opponent, but had attracted several more. When George Moscone was elected in 1975, he asked for a moratorium on all negotiations on the YBC, which killed the Swigs' plans for a sports arena. As it turned out, Moscone was determined to see the convention center built, and he pushed ahead aggressively. The new YBC plan called for the relocation of the convention center one block south, hotel tax funding for the structure, a mixed-use complex including public gardens and cultural and children's facilities in the block north of the convention center and open space on top of it, preservation of two historic structures, St. Patrick's Church and the Jessie Street Substation, and additional housing, both market rate and low income.

The new YBC plan signaled a major change in the city's attitude toward the involvement of not only low-income people, but also the arts community, in the design and use of government-funded developments. To begin with, the SFRA was no longer a superagency dominating the urban design scene. The SFRA's power was partly based on access to federal funds, and those funds began to be cut in the Nixon years, while the control of significant amounts of money through block grants was shifted to the mayor's office. Moreover, Moscone had been elected with support from the Agency's principal antagonists. Accordingly, he and, later, Mayor Art Agnos pushed the SFRA to accept public participation in its decision-making process and to explore other city needs, such as low-income housing.

As for the arts community, the 1950s and 1960s—identified in the mass media with the Beatnik and the Hippie—had produced a remarkable cultural renaissance and a loose coalition of community arts groups eager to contest developers and elite art institutions over the nature of projects subsidized by the taxpayer. The changes started with the Beats, who had appropriated small amounts of private space—galleries, storefronts, lofts, warehouses, coffeehouses, and old theaters, particularly in North Beach—for their cultural undertakings. Then, during the 1960s, young people poured into the streets and parks for demonstrations, rock concerts, and theatrical performances, appropriating huge amounts of public space for their activities. Two decades of artistic experimentation produced new theater groups, new forms of music, choral groups, arts workshops, galleries, dance troupes, and a wide range of publications. Some were identified with specific neighborhoods. Others, such as the Galeria de la Raza and the Black Writers Workshop, were part of the emergence of the city's minority groups. By the Moscone era, many of these groups had taken their fight to city hall where they argued that the city had a responsibility to fund neighborhood and ethnic arts organizations as well as elite institutions, such as the ballet, the opera, and the symphony. These institutions, the activists pointed out, received government funding, but with their steep ticket prices were hardly accessible to the average San Franciscan.

The YBC was originally conceived as a largely private complex. Although it was heavily subsidized with public funds, the original designers intended to exclude low-income people from the area. Through a committee appointed by Moscone, the grass roots arts community and members of the architectural profession were demanding that both the public and new cultural organizations be given space in the YBC. Thanks to TOOR, low-income housing became part of YBC in the 1970s. In the next two decades, the area would emerge, partly by happenstance, as a major new cultural center and public space for the city. Granted, there would continue to be commercial development and the usual insider wheeling and dealing, but the end result was remarkably different from what Ben Swig dreamed of in 1954.

When construction on the convention center began in 1979, the developers found water just below the sandy soil, which was not surprising to those who knew that much of South of Market was once marshy ground north of Mission Bay. The idea of placing the entire convention center below ground was abandoned, and only the exhibition hall was built in this manner. Moscone Center was rushed to completion, but when it opened in 1981, it quickly became apparent that even with its huge exhibition hall, there was still not enough space for the largest conventions. In 1993 meeting rooms were added on top of the original structure, and a second underground convention hall was built and is now located under Yerba Buena Gardens.

THE TODCO PROJECTS

Ironically, the most significant construction in the immediate area of the Moscone Center in the 1980s was carried out by TODCO. Under Moscone the city released the funds to begin housing construction in 1977, and TODCO hired Robert Herman and Associates (later Herman & Coliver) as its architect. The first part of Woolf House, named after TOOR founder George Woolf, opened in 1979, followed by a second unit in 1982, Dimasalang House in 1980, the Ceatrice Polite in 1984, and Mendelsohn House in 1989 (see illustration on page 232). Sadly, only a handful of the residents of the old hotels moved into the new buildings. By the time Woolf House opened, most of them had died or disappeared.

Having completed the housing construction called for in its 1973 agreement with the SFRA, TODCO pressed on with plans for additional low-income housing in the area west of the YBC and building or remodeling at five more sites. Today a high percentage of TODCO's tenants are elderly people, many with disabilities, but TODCO also provides family housing. The largest group of TODCO tenants is Chinese, followed by Filipinos and African-Americans.

TODCO's facilities offer a full range of social services, including medical care, nutrition programs, and counseling, as well as arts workshops and creative writing classes.

YERBA BUENA GARDENS

With work on the TODCO project and Moscone Center under way, the continuing cat fight between the city, developers, and various citizens groups shifted to the two blocks north of the convention center known as Yerba Buena Gardens. In the early years of the Moscone adminsitration plans were floated under SFRA sponsorship for a kind of "Tivoli Garden" entertainment complex, but the guardians of the sanctity of conventioneers, particularly the city's chief administrative officer, continued to worry that an amusement park might not attract the kind of people who were compatible with dentists from Omaha. So that plan was abandoned, and under Mayor Feinstein a competition was announced for developers to submit a plan for parts of the two-block area. To fulfill its promise to include a public garden and children's and cultural facilities in the project, the SFRA planned to retain control of most of the block between Fourth, Mission, Third, and Howard and the top of the Moscone Center. Six proposals were submitted, two by the huge Canadian developers Cadillac-Fairview and Olympia & York (O&Y).

Of the six, O&Y had the kind of political connections that were de rigeur for a player in big, city-sponsored real estate deals, connections to Dianne Feinstein, Richard Blum (her husband), and then–state assemblyman Willie Brown. Brown saw to it that O&Y was the only developer to be granted the favor of an audience with the mayor. In 1980 O&Y was named developer for Yerba Buena Gardens. Four years later the firm presented its plan, which showed commercial developments centered on gardens running down the center of the block north of Moscone Center, with buildings along Third, Fourth, and Market Streets devoted to commercial and cultural uses. Then, rather than forging ahead, O&Y stalled, ultimately declaring bankruptcy in 1993.

The Marriott Corporation successfully extricated itself from the O&Y debacle to build the first major structure since the Moscone Center, a 40-story hotel at the corner of Fourth and Mission Streets. While the SFRA began negotiations with a number of developers for the O&Y commercial sites, it moved ahead with plans to build the Yerba Buena Cultural Center to the east of the Gardens and a children's entertainment complex on the roof of the Moscone Center. After discussions with dozens of people from the arts world, the SFRA hired James Stewart Polshek to design a theater and Fumihiko Maki to design a gallery. The focus of the new gallery and theater, which opened in 1993, is programming and exhibits that reflect the diversity of the Bay Area. The Children's Center, which opened in 1998, includes the Zeum (a hands-on technology and arts center), a child care center, gardens, a bowling alley, a carousel, and an ice skating rink built to National Hockey League specifications. The Sony Metreon, a commercial entertainment center west of the Gardens, features movie theaters, high-tech shops, numerous restaurants, and entertainment facilities based on the works of children's authors Maurice Sendak *(Where the Wild Things Are)* and David MacCauley *(How Things Work)* (see illustration on page 229).

The SFRA's plans for a cultural complex became a magnet for other city museums. Approaching its 60th year, the Museum of Modern Art (MOMA) was outgrowing its space in the Civic Center and had been included by O&Y in its original plans for the Yerba Buena Gardens.When O&Y defaulted, the SFRA offered space to MOMA on Third Street between Howard and Mission. MOMA was at first reluctant. "South of Market was pretty scary," recalled Helen Sause, SFRA deputy director. "It was a place you did not go. You did your homework before you went down there."[41] But with the maturation of the SFRA's plans for a gallery and theater, MOMA saw that it would be part of a larger cultural complex. The rush was on. The California Historical Society renovated a hardware store on Mission near Third, the Ansel Adams Center for Photography moved to Fourth Street (later Mission near Third), and plans were drawn up for a Jewish Museum and a Mexican Museum. In the end, the Yerba Buena complex retained some of its original features—a convention center, three hotels, and some office space—but the core of the complex, with low-cost housing, six museums, and the Children's Center, reflected the prolonged struggle to reshape Yerba Buena for other than commercial needs.

THE SPORTS ARENA BECOMES A BALLPARK

Having apparently expired at the hands of George Moscone's Yerba Buena advisory committee, the Swigs' plan for a sports arena was temporarily revived by Mayor Art Agnos and then became a new stadium for the San Francisco Giants. In 1958, the New York Giants agreed to vacate the Big Apple on the strength of a promise by Mayor George Christopher to build them a stadium. The arrival of the Giants in San Francisco was a major coup for a city that tended to measure its achievements in comparison to New York. The purchase of land and construction of Candlestick Park (later renamed 3Com Park) on the southern border of the city was the granddaddy of all the sleazy insider deals that marked city-sponsored projects in the postwar years. 3Com, however, turned out to be a dog. Night baseball games took place in a fog-shrouded refrigerator, and the wind could blow so hard there that the umpire had to halt play while the dust clouds settled. In 1970, the Forty-Niners football team abandoned antiquated Kezar Stadium in Golden Gate Park and moved in with the Giants. In 1976, Robert Lurie, a San Francisco real estate investor who was listed as one of the 400 wealthiest men in the country, bought the Giants. After making a substantial contribution to Dianne Feinstein's first mayoral election, Lurie proposed in 1982 that the city either build a new stadium for his team South of Market or put a dome over 3Com Park. Lurie was engaging in the strong-arm tactics used by many sports franchise owners in cities eager to retain major league teams. The ploy went something like this: I may be rich as Croesus, but if you want to keep your major league team, get the citizens, not me, to pay for a new stadium.

The mayor was eager to oblige, but the citizenry, which overwhelmingly opposed paying for the stadium, was less than enthusiastic. The mayor placed a proposition on the November 1987 ballot, but voters turned it down by a vote of 53 to 47 percent.

Feinstein was succeeded by Mayor Art Agnos. Agnos won by a landslide with strong support from environmental and neighborhood organizations. Unable to resist the temptation to become both a master builder and the savior of the Giants, Agnos revived plans for a sports arena and shifted the site to the waterfront near China Basin. The voters rejected this plan too.

Part of the problem with Agnos's proposal was the new location. The site was right in the middle of a newly developing neighborhood along the Embarcadero under the aegis of the Redevelopment Agency. South Beach, which was going up on top of the old Pacific Mail Steamship piers and workshops, featured new housing including some low- and middle-income units, the restoration of old warehouses for commercial use, and a marina. These plans were the product of years of work by a citizens advisory committee. This area "was not a neglected, empty space just waiting to be filled by ambitious politicians pursuing visions of a world-class city grandeur," wrote Richard Edward DeLeon in *Left Coast City.* "It was one of the city's prime growth centers, a source of new housing, a magnet for entrepreneurs, and a model of planned and rational development shaped by citizen participation." [42] But Agnos, the champion of neighborhood rights, had neglected to consult with the advisory committee. With only mixed support among his natural allies, Agnos's stadium initiative failed at the ballot box by 2,000 votes.

Agnos continued to pursue the idea of a sports complex, but was defeated in the next campaign by Frank Jordan, a singularly colorless former police chief with strong ties to the downtown business community and real estate developers. As Agnos vacated the mayor's office, a group of local investors bought the Giants to keep Lurie from selling the team to a Florida syndicate. Working with the new owners, Jordan tried a new version of the old sports complex idea, to be located in the Mission Bay project. When those talks collapsed, the Giants' new owners opted for a privately funded stadium located in South Beach. Although groups opposed to the stadium emphasized the hidden costs to the city (in the tens of millions) and the disruption caused by plunking the stadium down in a new residential neighborhood, the Giants' owners persuaded the South Beach Waterfront Advisory Committee to refrain from taking a stand. In March 1996 the electorate approved the stadium proposal. Pacific Bell Park opened in 2000 and was an instant success (see illustration on page 226).

Jordan would last as mayor for only one term. In 1995 he found himself up against Willie Brown, the former Speaker of the State Assembly and one of the most powerful and skillful politicians in the state. Nonetheless, Jordan did not help his cause when he was persuaded by two shock-jocks to have his picture taken with them naked in the shower, a photo that featured prominently in the campaign.

WILLIE BROWN AND THE MISSION BAY PROJECT

Willie Brown can only be described as a phenomenon, even at 65 a whirlwind of energy. A tasteful dresser who annually refurbishes his wardrobe with expensive European suits, a lover of late-night parties, beautiful women, and fast cars until his eyesight deteriorated, Brown is in some ways a latter-day Sunny Jim Rolph. Whether as lawyer or as politician, and it is often impossible to separate the two, Brown's fingerprints can be found on many of the city's most significant real estate deals.

Even before he took office, Brown, wearing his lawyer's hat, became the advocate for the largest real estate scheme ever proposed for San Francisco, the Southern Pacific Development Company's (SP) 313-acre Mission Bay Project. SP Development proposed building a huge office tower and residential complex—twice the size of downtown—on the water lots that had once been Mission Bay. To facilitate complex negotiations with the city and the state, SP Development and its successor company, the Catellus Corporation, hired Brown and paid him $400,000 between 1982 and 1994.

The Mission Bay Project originated in the days of the giant subsidies and land giveaways that led to the Southern Pacific's virtual control of transportation in northern California and enough political clout to run the state like a private fiefdom. To connect San Francisco to the transcontinental railroad, which terminated in Oakland, a state senate committee in the 1870s proposed selling to the SP, for $100 an acre, 7,000 acres of land that ran from South of Market four miles south to the San Bruno Mountains. The SP planned to use some of the land to develop a railroad terminal that would be connected to the East Bay by a bridge. This proposal raised such a howl of protest in San Francisco that the railroad ended up with 60 acres and a right-of-way heading south out of the city. Over time the SP expanded its holdings in the area to 313 acres and built its headquarters and a railroad terminal on Townsend Street.

To counter SP Development's proposal, the Mission Bay Clearinghouse was formed and offered its own plan designed by architect and well-known affordable housing advocate Tom Jones. Jones emphasized a low-rise skyline, affordable housing, and a measure of public open space. As anti-high-rise sentiment grew, finally culminating in the passage of Proposition M in 1986, the newly merged Santa Fe Pacific Realty Company (later spun off as the Catellus Corporation) offered a scaled-down version of its original plan with less commercial space, more open space, and more housing, a larger percentage of which would be affordable.

The passage of Proposition M fundamentally changed the rules of the development game for the Mission Bay Project. Catellus now had to submit its office building construction plans to the city, hoping that they would become part of an annual allocation of new office space known as the "beauty contest." Catellus opted instead to seek a height-limit exemption at the ballot box in November 1990. The ballot measure was drafted by Willie Brown. In a fascinating twist, the exemption was narrowly defeated in a campaign that was funded in part by Walter Shorenstein, the city's largest real estate owner and the largest single donor to the Democratic Party in the United States. Shorenstein was willing to back his putative antagonists because he feared that Catellus would contribute further to the glut of downtown office space.

Catellus was driven to its knees by the collapse of the city's building boom that began in 1989. Looking for a profitable use for its property, Catellus for a time gave up on office buildings and switched its emphasis to housing and retail space, promising to make 20 percent of its housing affordable. Year by year San Francisco's housing shortage was becoming more severe. Watching the new development in South Beach, Catellus realized that escalating rents could be the key to profitability. Having told the press during his mayoral campaign, "The day after I'm sworn in, I'm going to place a call to the Catellus people," Mayor Brown quickly became the project's biggest booster. However, serious problems remained, including who would make the necessary investment in infrastructure, and how would Catellus, which continued to lose money, turn a profit on the project? Catellus had once offered to pay for all infrastructure investments. It was now looking to the city to pick up the tab. Brown and Catellus engineered an arrangement whereby the Redevelopment Agency would use its bonding powers to pick up the costs for infrastructure improvements, and Catellus announced plans to start construction by building housing and retail facilities on the blocks just north of Mission Channel, the narrow inlet that was all that remained of the old Mission Bay. Still the numbers did not add up for Catellus.

What the project lacked was a major participant to anchor the complex. For a time Catellus had been talking with the University of California–San

Groundbreaking for the Mission Bay Project, the city's largest redevelopment scheme, which will be centered on a University of California medical research campus, took place in 1999. The campus plaza as seen looking west from Third Street. *Machado and Silvetti.*

Francisco (UCSF), one of the nation's premier medical schools, about locating a new campus in the Mission Bay Project. Ironically, Brown had been working with another of his legal clients to short-circuit these plans by moving the new campus to the other side of the Bay. Once elected, Brown changed his tune, and he and Catellus pleaded with UCSF to consider a Mission Bay site. Catellus and Brown found a willing ally in Donald Fisher, founder and chairman of The Gap. Fisher, who was a major donor to UCSF, was instrumental in working out a deal whereby Catellus gave 43 acres to UCSF in exchange for a commitment to locate a new life sciences campus in the heart of the Mission Bay Project. Unnamed wealthy backers of UCSF were reported in the press to be talking about large donations for construction.

The presence of UCSF was a coup of major proportions. In particular, it made it difficult for community groups to oppose the Catellus project. Affordable housing advocates persisted in their negotiations with Catellus, however, finally reaching an agreement that 1,700 of the 6,000 units Catellus planned to build would be affordable. Affordable, according to a Catellus executive, meant pricing units for households that made 70 to 110 percent of San Francisco's median income of $68,600. The UCSF commitment and the agreement with affordable housing advocates added up to a major victory for Catellus. Catellus would receive what amounted to $140 million in subsidies from the SFRA for infrastructure construction. With UCSF in the picture, Catellus planned to develop additional land in the area as office space for biotechnology companies that would feed off UCSF research.

THE FORTY-NINERS FIASCO

Having taken office proclaiming the Mission Bay Project a top priority, Brown soon added to his agenda a new stadium for the Forty-Niners, to be built next to 3Com Park. Once the Giants were clearly on their way out of 3Com, the Forty-Niners feared that they would be stuck with the aging stadium. Unlike the owners of the Giants who paid for the construction of their stadium, Forty-Niners owner Eddie Bartolo Jr., a shopping mall developer, racetrack owner, and aspiring casino operator from Youngstown, Ohio, wanted the city to put $100 million toward a new stadium in the form of a lease revenue bond. When the financial projections for a new stadium did not come out quite right, DeBartolo added a shopping mall and movie theater complex to the project. Tax revenue from the mall would be used to pay the city back, he claimed. The mall, however, was to be located next to the stadium in Bay View-Hunter's Point, one of the city's toughest neighborhoods. Even Forty-Niners president, Carmen Policy, described the mall site as "a less than desirable location." Unfazed, Brown repackaged the stadium-mall proposal as a jobs-creation program for a predominantly black neighborhood where unemployment ran high. There were other problems. The numbers, according to the city's budget analyst, didn't quite add up: The city would lose about $1.5 million a year on the deal. Nevertheless, Brown pleaded with the electorate to trust him and the bond measure went on the ballot for June 1996.

Three months before the election a second measure was added to the ballot. This proposition limited the time permitted for consideration of the stadium-mall proposal by the Planning Commission and raised height limits for the mall to 200 feet, while permitting 150-foot buildings near the mall. With victory at risk, Brown came up with a novel solution: He opened the polls in four housing projects near 3Com Stadium on the weekend before the election. The bond measure passed by 1,500 votes, with support from voters in Bay View-Hunter's Point providing the victory margin.

One complication that Brown had not counted on was the peccadilloes of Eddie DeBartolo. DeBartolo was the subject of a grand jury investigation in Louisiana where he had made a $400,000 payment to former governor Edwin Edwards, allegedly for assistance in securing the last available riverboat gambling license in the state. In October 1998, DeBartolo pleaded guilty to the charge of failing to report an attempt at extortion and agreed to testify against Edwards. Plans for the new stadium were put on hold when DeBartolo was forced to relinquish control of the Niners to his sister in July 1999 but were revived, according to Brown, when DeBartolo and his sister reached an agreement in 2000. With the Forty-Niners' stadium-mall proposal, developers had pushed their plans to the southeastern border of the city. In the process Brown swept aside height limits in the area while running roughshod over the planning process.

THE NEXT FRONTIER

At the beginning of the twenty-first century, San Francisco is blessed with considerable amounts of open space, most of it along the waterfront between Mission Creek and 3Com Park. From the south, the city, even after a century and a half of construction, still has an unfinished look about it. And it is this open space that makes real estate developers salivate. With construction on the UCSF campus under way in 1999, real estate developers are looking farther south to the land east of Interstate 280 between the site of the new campus and Islais Creek. There is already considerable construction in the area, particularly new live-work studios and the transformation of industrial and warehouse buildings into similar arrangements. A new proposal calls for industrial development plus 12,000 units of housing on 130 acres along the waterfront, a project of even greater proportions than Mission Bay. So as the new century begins, the next adventure in urban design is just reaching the drawing boards, and San Franciscans once again face the challenge of trying to maintain control of their urban environment.

THE MIDRISE AND THE 24-HOUR CITY

While developers looked south, the nature of development within SOMA closer to Market Street was changing. High-rise construction began to spill over Market Street into SOMA in the 1970s as new towers went up on the blocks between Market and Mission east of the Yerba Buena Center. Since 1986, new high-rises, to conform to Proposition M, have to be shorter, tapered buildings with sculpted tops and setbacks. The new height regulations also require that buildings must step down at the rate of about 100 feet per block as they move east from Market Street toward the waterfront and south to Mission Bay. The boom years of the 1990s produced a new burst of what architects are calling "midrise construction." There are new office towers on Mission Street, four new towers near the Yerba Buena Gardens, and a new building designed by

Robert Stern for The Gap clothing store chain is under construction on the Embarcadero.

This new urban environment in some ways evokes the past. Yes, there are new hotels and office towers, but other buildings combine commercial with residential space and a significant amount of residential housing is going up, particularly in South Beach. SOMA has become a favored location for new multimedia companies—hence the name Multimedia Gulch. Start-up companies gravitate toward the old warehouses and the numerous buildings that once housed light industry, and the more established companies are putting up new buildings, some of which like Stern's emulate the old brick structures. Intermittently, one finds small architectural gems that suggest the modesty of the early years of modernism. There are more restaurants, more retail amenities, and more open space, particularly along the waterfront in the aftermath of the decline of the port. SOMA south and east of the Yerba Buena Gardens is becoming a "24-hour city," a modern version of the traditional walking city—still plagued, of course, by the automobile.

SOMA's central blocks east and west of Sixth Street are becoming an affordable housing district that combines new construction and rehabilitation of a number of old residence hotels, including a number of TODCO projects. Scattered throughout this area, which was once home to some of the earliest gay bars, are trendy restaurants and night spots. To the southwest around Townsend and Seventh, Showplace Square, established in the 1970s, features a number of old warehouses that have been converted into wholesale showrooms.

The reconstruction of SOMA began very much in the manner of the Manhattanization of Downtown. A big wheel in the growth machine proposed leveling a neighborhood to further an ambitious development scheme. TOOR, however, took on the SFRA and the developers at an early stage in the project, forcing them to make fundamental changes in their plans. The result is a wildly diverse neighborhood that runs the gamut from the new waterfront high rises to the last of the dingy single room occupancy hotels along Sixth Street, from the lofts and cramped offices of the wannabe media tycoons around South Park to the apartments of newly arrived immigrants from China and the Philippines, from sweatshops to artists studios, from furniture showrooms to art galleries, from leather bars to upscale restaurants.

But there is no stasis in this kaleidoscopic world. At the turn of the century, SOMA is threatened by its very success. The relentless pressure on the city's limited housing stock, particularly for low-income people, makes it increasingly expensive to live and work South of Market, or anywhere else in the city for that matter. This trend has been exacerbated by a new real estate dodge known as live-work space. The Planning Commission condoned the conversion of warehouses and other commercial buildings into live-in artist studios. In the realtors' eyes, if you can write a check, you're an artist, and numerous buildings are being converted to expensive live-work spaces. TODCO and the Mission Bay Clearinghouse are giving their best effort to ensure the construction of affordable housing near Yerba Buena and in the Mission Bay Project. But by their own admission, their efforts have fallen dramatically short. Without a major commitment to the construction of affordable housing, the new city spreading south from Market Street will become another exclusive preserve for well-paid professionals. It is quite fitting that after all the Sturm und Drang, after TOOR and TODCO showed neighborhood activists how to assert their own interests when threatened by the growth machine, the new city between Market Street and Potrero Hill should become a series of vital neighborhoods. But the question remains, as with the rest of San Francisco, neighborhoods for whom and for how long?

THE END OF THE HEADQUARTERS CITY?

As the city moves south, the most significant development in its political economy is the decline of San Francisco as a headquarters city. Even this city, once the financial capital of the West, is subject to forces beyond its control. In 1989, the Bay Area Council concluded that San Francisco as "a historical hub in the Bay Area region" seemed to be negatively affected by corporate restructuring. And, indeed, by 1999 the impact was dramatically apparent. Those very companies that played a central role in launching the plans for a headquarters city in the years after World War II were no longer San Francisco companies. The mighty Bank of America—at times the largest bank in the world, whose history was linked to the emergence of one of the city's most important ethnic communities—had been bought by a corporate unknown from North Carolina, and Pacific Bell (PacBell) had become part of SBC Communications headquartered in Texas. Pacific Telephone and Telegraph, Pacific Bell's predecessor, built one of the first modern headquarters office towers, and the Bank of America Building symbolized the explosive growth of corporate San Francisco beginning in the 1960s. The Crocker Bank, a company with a history running back to Charles Crocker of the Big Four, was swallowed up by Wells Fargo, which in turn was ingested by Norwest. And the Southern Pacific, the giant who once held the state in thrall, had been broken up and merged into the Union Pacific. Even the heirs of Charles and Michael de Young fled the city, selling the *Chronicle* to the Hearst Corporation.

There is less need today to build high rises to accommodate corporate headquarters, because San Francisco no longer appeals to corporate bigwigs as a good place to locate. It is easy to blame the decline of the headquarters city on the planning and regulatory climate, but there were other issues that were equally if not more significant—traffic, the lack of adequate public transportation, the cost of living, and, perhaps most of all, the cost of housing. And maybe one of the problems harks back to a simple geographical fact faced by the original city builders: Located at the head of a narrow peninsula, San Francisco may not have been the best place to build the Bay Area's major metropolis.

San Francisco's premier status is also threatened by the emergence of Silicon Valley and San Jose as a second headquarters city to the south, and of Oakland as a city on its way back from a period of near total collapse to the east. San Francisco has its own emergent economy with direct connections to Silicon Valley, but in this start-up environment, young entrepreneurs are more comfortable in converted warehouses than in air-conditioned office towers. Finally, in a curious inversion, San Francisco, as anyone who witnesses the stream of cars heading south on Interstate 101 every morning will testify, has become a bedroom community for Silicon Valley.

The city's built environment clearly mirrors these major shifts in the corporate landscape. At One Market Street, the SP's building was gutted to make way for an atrium and walk-through gallery. The Bank of America long ago sold its building to real estate mogul Walter Shorenstein, and now the number of bank employees in the building is declining as a result of corporate downsizing and the shift of selected operations to other parts of the country. Perhaps most symbolic of San Francisco's loss of status as a headquarters city is Donald Fisher's new Gap Building on the Embarcadero. In the past decade Fisher, The Gap's founder, has emerged as a major power broker in the city. He played a central role in bringing UCSF into the Mission Bay Project, and, as discussed in Chapter 19, he sits on the board of the Presidio Trust, which controls the future of this most precious of all San Francisco landscapes. The Gap's publicist describes the company's new building on the Embarcadero very precisely as "a corporate office building," noting that the company is "headquartered in the Bay Area."[43]

With the decline of San Francisco as a world headquarters city, an era is drawing to a close. But even after more than a century and a half of development, the city remains a work in a progress where a high degree of tolerance, an open political system, and a world of opportunity are attracting new peoples and new ideas about how a city should be built to keep it liveable.

PART II

Neighborhood Walking Tours

8

Prelude: San Francisco Architecture—A Style of its Own

Architectural historian Harold Kirker noted in his seminal study, *California's Architectural Frontier,* that colonialism was the distinguishing characteristic of California's architecture during the nineteenth century. "Each consecutive wave of colonists brought their past with them," he wrote, "and out of it shaped an architecture representative not of conditions on the new frontier but of older and distant societies from which they emigrated."[44] San Francisco's architecture may be distinctive, but despite California's reputation as a daffy hotbed for newfangled ideas, only a small handful of its architects are known for the originality of their work. For the past century and a half the tendency among the city's architects has been to look elsewhere, especially for models for commercial and civic buildings. This inclination reflects one of the underlying cultural peculiarities of the city's elite: The more self-important San Francisco becomes, describing itself, for example, as *The City,* the more its movers and shakers have found it necessary to measure their achievements by someone else's standards, preferably

Joseph Worcester, an amateur architect and Swedenborgian minister, designed two Shingle Style buildings on Russian Hill in 1889, inspiring the architects who founded the First Bay Tradition. *Peter Booth Wiley.*

those of someone to the east. In addition, the presence of the architectural past, the result of San Francisco Heritage and others' campaigns to protect historic buildings, and the eagerness of residents to engage in the architectural review process have created a conservative environment for architectural innovators.

In the late nineteenth and early twentieth century San Francisco looked to Paris as a model of urban planning and civic architecture. Chicago architects defined the office building style for the city's first high rises during the same period. After World War II, when the skyline changed most dramatically, we speak of the "Manhattanization" of the downtown financial district—with the major contribution made by the local office of the Chicago-based firm of Skidmore Owings Merrill. For the past decade the city has been making investments totaling more than $1 billion in cultural and civic structures and entertainment facilities—the Museum of Modern Art, the Yerba Buena Center for the Arts, the New Main Library, and the Pacific Bell baseball stadium. Moreover, renovation of the old main library as an Asian Art Museum is under way, and there are plans to build a Jewish Museum, a Mexican Museum, and even a Grateful Dead Museum. These prize commissions are going not to local architects, but to the so-called stars of the international architectural community.

San Francisco is perhaps most widely known for its large collection of intact and restored Victorians. Here, too, styles were borrowed from the East, often via pattern books filled with floor and façade plans easily copied by a skilled carpenter-builder. Unique to San Francisco, however, were the imaginative use of redwood, the excess of detail and ornamentation, and the abundance of bay windows that could catch the precious sunlight in the fog-shrouded city. *Hittel's Guide* of 1888 noted, "The superior facility for shaping wood, and the abundance of machinery for planing and moulding, has led to the adoption of more architectural ornament here than in any other city."

A number of architects were truly innovative, most prominently Willis Polk, Bernard Maybeck, and William Wurster. Polk, Maybeck, and their peers contributed to what is known as the First Bay Tradition. Wurster is associated with the Second Bay Tradition, derived from his blend of modernism and California vernacular architecture, such as nineteenth-century ranch houses. These architects were not exponents of a style in a programmatic sense, but they designed some striking buildings. Most of Maybeck's and Wurster's, however, were built outside the city and so had only a limited impact on the city's appearance.

The lack of an innovative architectural tradition in San Francisco does not diminish its appeal as one of the most liveable cities. Nor does its history of suffering two major earthquakes, devastating fires, the tyranny of the automobile, the visual blight caused by so-called redevelopment and urban renewal, and the overbuilding of the downtown.

Only one building, La Mision de San Francisco de Asis, or Mission Dolores, survives from the city's Hispanic period. Its design was inspired by religious structures in Spain and Mexico. California's missions engendered a renewed interest in Spanish Colonial architecture in the late nineteenth century, resulting in Mediterranean, Spanish, or Mission Revival designs. Richard Longstreth tells us that Willis Polk and John Galen Howard, the University of California architecture professor and head of the advisory committe for the planning of the Civic Center, were among the first architects to study California's missions in 1887 and 1888. Starting with the Ferry Building in 1903, the various Hispanic revival styles became common in San Francisco with most of the buildings designed just before and after World War I (see page 156).[45]

CLASSICS AND VICTORIANS

Because the 1906 earthquake and fire completely leveled the commercial core and important residential neighborhoods of the city, there are few buildings left from the gold rush period. (The gold rush began in 1849 but was eventually overshadowed, in terms of wealth produced, by the silver that poured from the Comstock lode in the Nevada Territory after its discovery in 1859.) Most of the surviving buildings from this period are concentrated in the Jackson Square Historical District.

Many of the earliest buildings in the city, such as the United States Mint, designed by Alfred Mullett in 1874, were in the Classical Revival style. *San Francisco Public Library.*

Most of the city's first architects, like the largest group of argonauts, came from New England and the Middle Atlantic states, although there were a fair share from Canada, England, and Germany. The Americans favored the Classical Revival, which had been popular in the East since the early days of the Republic. Architects and builders at this time looked to Greece and Rome for inspiration, using the classical orders (Ionic, Doric, and Corinthian) in columns and other elements of ancient architecture to decorate their buildings. Second Empire styles, marked by mansard roofs, scroll-saw brackets, and cast iron fencing along the roofline, were introduced when the French consul built a home near Portsmouth Square. In the 1850s many visitors noted how the residential neighborhoods reminded them of New England because of the prevalence of shingled roofs, white clapboard sidings, and green shutters. The first mansions were a mixture of Classical Revival, Italianate, Gothic, and Second Empire.

After 1853, San Francisco builders were required to use fireproof materials, such as brick, stone, and iron, in the downtown district. Brick and granite, some from China, were the construction materials of choice for commercial buildings. Iron buildings were at first imported. Soon the first ironworks were manufacturing shutters, doors, building façades, columns, and stairways. Yet Kirker estimates that as much as 90 percent of the city was built of wood. This was a direct result of the availability of abundant supplies of redwood, cut first from groves on the peninsula south of San Francisco, in Marin, and later from the enormous stands of timber in Mendocino, Humboldt, and Del Norte counties. It soon became popular to clad and paint wooden buildings to resemble stone. Wood was considered healthier than stone and safer in earthquakes. The introduction of the planing mill, which could mass-produce doors, windows, and an array of wooden ornamentation used on the exterior of Victorian houses, contributed significantly to the ability of contractors and carpenters to move from the construction of houses on a one-off basis to multi-house developments.

As money poured into the city from the Comstock lode, Classical Revival gave way to Victorian styles, which used increasingly elaborate ornamentation and design motifs to dress up everything from workingmen's flats to the mansions of the city's new millionaires.

High Victorian excess led to an inevitable reaction. Willis Polk, in his early years the self-appointed arbiter of San Francisco's architectural taste, described the city's Victorian Western Addition neighborhood in 1893 as "an architectural nightmare conceived in a reign of terror and produced by artistic anarchists." "The proudest boast of our modern householder," he continued, "is that he has all the latest conveniences and he particularly calls attention to the fact that his gables, turrets, bay-windows, and filigree work are entirely original, and that no one has anything like them." [46] Polk was right; these were the glory days of the first generation of nouveaux riches, and they

Italianate mansions and row houses, such as the Parsonage at the corner of Laguna and Haight, were popular from the 1860s to the 1880s. Built on narrow lots, these homes with their high-ceilinged rooms lit by slant-sided bay windows emphasized verticality and elaborate exterior ornamentation, such as brackets under the cornice, pediments atop the windows, and the pipestem colonettes on either side of them. The flat roof on the building on the right is more typical. *Peter Booth Wiley.*

The Westerfeld House, a Stick mansion in Alamo Square. With the Stick Style and a variation known as Eastlake, which were popular in the 1880s, architects squared off bay windows and added more ornamentation. *Peter Booth Wiley.*

The Haas-Lilienthal House at 2007 Franklin, a Queen Anne—a style also popular beginning in the 1880s. Architects emphasized irregular massing and added turrets and towers while experimenting with a variety of ornamental schemes. *The Foundation for San Francisco's Architectural Heritage.*

The architecture of excess, the Mark Hopkins *(right)* and Leland Stanford residences on Nob Hill. Members of the Big Four, Hopkins and Stanford built the western section of the transcontinental railroad. The Hopkins Mansion (1878), with its Gothic exuberance, came to symbolize the conspicuous consumption of the city's self-made millionaires. *San Francisco Public Library.*

wanted homes that showed that they had money, hard-earned or otherwise. Railroad baron Mark Hopkins's house on top of Nob Hill, built in 1878 with its towers, high-peaked gables, and gingerbread trimmings, came to epitomize Victorian excess in a private residence.

ANTI-VICTORIAN REVOLT

Polk and some of his peers—architects such as Bernard Maybeck, Arthur Brown Jr., George Kelham, Albert Pissis, and Julia Morgan—the second generation of San Francisco architects, turned to Chicago, New York, and particularly to designs inspired by Paris's École des Beaux-Arts. After the American Civil War when architectural training consisted for the most part of an apprenticeship, a number of leading American architects traveled to the École to complete their formal education. The École employed a very strict educational approach that began with the study of the great buildings of Greece, Rome, and the Italian Renaissance. The emphasis was on the design of monumental public buildings within this classical tradition. Hence, the description of Beaux-Arts influenced architecture as neoclassical or part of the American Renaissance.

And thus its imitative strain. When one examines San Francisco's famous Beaux-Arts Civic Center, this becomes readily apparent. City Hall, considered a Beaux-Arts masterpiece in the French High Baroque tradition, closely resembles the Hotel des Invalides in Paris, which serves as Napoleon's tomb. The design of the old main library can be traced to Paris's Bibliotheque Ste. Geneviéve via its Boston and Detroit counterparts. And indeed, City Hall

San Francisco's City Hall closely resembles the Hotel des Invalides in Paris. Starting in the 1890s, San Francisco's architects became infatuated with neoclassicism as taught at the École des Beaux-Arts in Paris. *San Francisco Public Library.*

architects Brown and John Bakewell Jr., and Kelham, the library's architect, were all trained at the École, as were Maybeck and Morgan.

In 1893, under the leadership of Chicago's Daniel Burnham, a group of distinguished architects, many of them trained at the École, designed the buildings for Chicago's Columbian Exposition. This was a pivotal moment in American architecture, the beginning of the ascendancy of the neoclassical style and the inspiration for what was known as the City Beautiful movement. For, as architectural historian Thomas Hines wrote in his biography of Burnham, the Columbian Exposition was more than a world's fair, it was "a controlled experiment containing the seeds of a larger urban planning movement."[47] And it was Burnham, first with a plan for completion of the nation's capital, then with a plan for San Francisco, who was at the forefront of this movement.

CHICAGO STYLE

Burnham was also connected to a second formative development in the history of San Francisco architecture, the construction of the city's first skyscrapers in what came to be known as the Chicago style. Increasing land values, the use of the steel frame in large-scale construction, the invention of the elevator, and the formation of the modern corporation inspired America's corporate class to hire architects to build ever taller buildings to house their expanding pool of office workers. A typical Chicago style building in San Francisco stood 10 to 15 stories high. There were numerous variations on the development of the base (large plate glass windows framed by arches or pilasters, for example), the shaft (several floors of office windows, sometimes framed by columns), and the capital (an elaborate cornice or one or two top floors set off by columns or pilasters). Framed in steel, these buildings were clad in brick or terra-cotta, and some were richly ornamented.

Polk and his associates learned in the offices of the great eastern architects, including Burnham and the New York firm of McKim Meade and White, which was the ideological command post of the American Renaissance. For Polk and his peers, neoclassicism offered purity and monumental serenity. For those beginning to tinker with more innovative styles, the Chicago style would produce its own tyranny. Even though he had contributed a building to the Great White City at the Columbian Exposition, Chicago architect Louis Sullivan and his protégé, Frank Lloyd Wright, for example, came to regard the experiment as a catastrophe: It delayed for the years the development of a modern American style.

Polk himself embodied the contradictory directions in which the reaction to Victorian architecture would take the Bay Area's architectural community. As Burnham's local partner, Polk offered his own drawings for a monu-

Chicago-style buildings at the corner of Market, Post, and Montgomery Streets in 1920. *Library of Congress.*

mental civic center in the neoclassical style of his senior associate. Polk also designed a number of Chicago style office buildings in the city's downtown area. But Polk too had his innovative side: He designed the spectacular Hallidie Building at 130 Sutter Street, often described as the country's first glass curtain office building (see page 166).

THE BAY AREA TRADITION

Meanwhile, Polk and a number of his associates, notably Maybeck, Ernest Coxhead, and Albert Schweinfurth, were going off in yet another direction in residential design. Inspired by the English Arts and Crafts movement and by the shingled houses being built in the eastern United States, they were subsequently identified as the founders of what came to be known as the First Bay Tradition. The Arts and Crafts movement drew many of its ideas from the writings of Englishman John Ruskin. Ruskin inveighed against the impact of industrialization and upheld the craft values of the medieval world. Ruskin in turn influenced artists, such as his countryman William Morris, who extolled the virtues of hand-crafted goods and preached a holistic approach to home building. Morris and his peers designed houses, furniture, wallpaper, tapestries, dinnerware—that is, the house and all its furnishings. It is significant that a number of these architects were either the sons of craftsmen (Polk, Maybeck, and Schweinfurth) or craftsmen and carpenters in their own right (Polk and Maybeck).

Polk and his colleagues built a number of shingled houses on Russian Hill and in Pacific Heights, eschewing the external ornamentation of the Victorian era and imparting an air of rusticity. Their interiors featured paneled rooms and intricately designed wainscots, stairwells, fireplaces, and cabinetry, often of native redwood. In addition to favoring the use of native materials, Polk and his peers were inspired by the Spanish missions and California's vernacular architecture, such as barns and ranch houses. Polk's short-lived publication, *Architectual News* (1890–1891), featured the first article on California's missions.

THE MODERNIST REVOLT

While a few San Francisco architects were experimenting with locally derived ideas, Europeans were jettisoning tradition in the name of modernism. The period immediately before and after World War I in Europe—the very time when San Francisco architects were rebuilding the city along the lines of the 30-year-old Chicago Style—marked the formative years of modern architecture. The cultural turmoil before and after World War I inspired numerous architects to call for a complete break with the mimetic aspects of the Classical Revival. European architects, especially German architects associated with the Bauhaus (a German arts school that emphasized the integration of all crafts), produced startling new designs that were sleek, geometrically abstract, and devoid of ornamentation. They drew up plans, frequently not executed because of the struggling economy of the Weimar Republic, for massive skyscrapers sheathed in glass, and numerous experiments were carried out involving the prefabrication and mass production of low-income housing.

Architecture was an integral part of the larger radical revolt against all aspects of European culture, whether in theater, painting, or literature. Practitioners like Le Corbusier saw their designs as emblematic of larger utopian schemes for a planned, socialistic urban society. The modernists aspired to a totally new architecture that fit with and reflected the values of the machine age. The first modern architects freely acknowledged their debt to Frank Lloyd Wright, America's most daringly innovative architect, to ideas about prefabricated homes gleaned from American mail order catalogs, and to the design of such workaday American structures as factories and farm silos.

The 1920s were a period of prosperity in San Francisco, hardly a time of radical innovation. They also marked the second phase in the shaping of a taller skyline that began to overshadow the Chicago-style buildings downtown. San Francisco architects, such as George Kelham and Timothy Pflueger, followed architects in New York and Chicago in designing skyscrapers inspired by Cass Gilbert's Woolworth Building in New York (1910–1913) (at the time the country's tallest skyscraper) and by Eliel Saarinen's entry in a 1922 design competition for a new office building for the *Chicago Tribune*. The new skyscrapers tended to be stepped back vertically, a result of a 1916 New York zoning law passed to increase the amount of sunlight that reached the street. They also featured towers, usually Gothic in style, which were sculpted and, because of their narrowness, facilitated natural air-conditioning.

The one European trend that did reach San Francisco in the 1920s was Art Deco. More a decorative than an architectural style, Deco was influenced by cubist and abstract painting and an interest in ornamental motifs taken from "exotic" locales such as ancient Egyptian, pre-Columbian Mexico, and China. Deco brought an element of the modern to American building design, pushing architects in the direction of longer, cleaner lines and more abstract surfaces. Timothy Pflueger embellished the Pacific Telephone and Telegraph Building, at 26 stories the city's first real skyscraper, with ornamentation drawn from Egypt and China and then topped the building with sleek American eagles. Pflueger also designed one of the city's unique master-pieces, the Medical and Dental Building (1929) at 450 Sutter Street. With its vertical front that eschewed setbacks, 450 Sutter foreshadowed the modernism of the early 1950s. Pflueger's most spectacular work involved the

Two traditions confront each other. Timothy Pflueger's Deco Pacific Bell Building from the 1920s stands behind Mario Botta's neomodern Museum of Modern Art from the 1990s. *Peter Booth Wiley.*

design of early movie houses, such as the Castro Theatre. Not surprisingly, Pflueger was one of the founders of San Francisco's Museum of Modern Art.

Although a handful of American architects sought out the European modernists in the 1920s, it was a show at the New York Museum of Modern Art in 1932 that drew widespread attention to what had transpired across the Atlantic. The show featured the works of, among others, Walter Gropius, Mies van der Rohe, and Le Corbusier, the most commanding figures in the modern movement. (Gropius had helped found the Bauhaus and was its first director; Mies was its director in 1933 when the Nazis shut down the school.) The exhibit traveled to 13 American cities, and an accompanying book, *The International Style: Architecture since 1922*, announced the arrival of what its authors, Henry-Russell Hitchcock and Philip Johnson, claimed would be the new universal style.

The rise of fascism in Europe brought two of the most important masters of modernism, Mies and Gropius, to the United States. Mies came to the Illinois Institute of Technology, where he designed a new campus and became director of the School of Architecture; and Gropius to Harvard, where he was appointed dean of the Graduate School of Design. For San Francisco's architects, commercial and residential commissions were difficult to come by during the Depression. But for engineers, particularly engineers in the West, it was a period of awe-inspiring public works projects. San Francisco's two majestic bridges, the Bay Bridge (1936) and the Golden Gate Bridge (1937), proved to be perfect bookends for the city's growing library of architectural achievements. The Bay Bridge, structurally apparent, bold, and simple, fit well within the modern tradition, and the Golden Gate is one of the great Art Deco masterpieces and the city's best-known structure.

When commercial contracts revived after World War II, Gropius, Mies, and their compatriots began to shape the architectural landscape, not only through their own work but through the work of a new generation of architects whom they trained. The École's approach to the academic training of architects had been the primary influence at American architectural schools from the founding of the first program at Massachusetts Institute of Technology in 1865. With the ascendancy of Mies, Gropius, and their peers, modernism became the new orthodoxy.

BAY MODERN: THE SECOND BAY TRADITION

One design approach that merged readily with the International Style can be said to have emerged in the Bay Area because of the beauty of its landscape. William Wurster was one of the first local architects to approximate some of modernism's architectural principles, but this was only after having designed a number of houses that traced their roots to vernacular architecture, particularly the simple, unadorned ranch house. A native Californian, Wurster was understandably in love with his surroundings. He wanted to design inexpensive, readily built houses out of local materials that would help bring the outdoors in. In time some of Wurster's designs became more minimalist, more abstract, and more in tune with European modernism.

In 1947, Lewis Mumford, noted architectural critic, wrote a column for the *New Yorker* on what he called the Bay Region Style. Two years later the fledgling San Francisco Museum of Art (later the Museum of Modern Art) mounted an exhibit, "Domestic Architecture of the Bay Region." In an essay for the catalog Mumford wrote that the "exhibition repairs a serious omission in the existing histories of American architecture: it establishes the existence of a vigorous tradition of modern building, which took root in California some half a century ago." Mumford went on to say that although the style "was thoroughly modern, it was not tied to the tags and clichés of the so-called International Style: that it made no fetish of the flat roof and did not deliberately avoid projections and overhangs: that it made no effort to symbolize the machine, through a narrow choice of materials and forms: that it had a place for personalities as different as Maybeck and [Gardner] Dailey and Wurster and [Ernest] Kump."[48] Mumford had given a name to a tradition begun by Willis Polk and his colleagues in 1890s.

In another essay, Clarence Mayhew noted both the similarities between the climates of Japan and California and the influence of Japanese architecture on the latest generation of California architects. The interpenetration of California and Asian culture was gradually becoming apparent.[49]

The Gregory farmhouse (1928), an early design by William Wurster, a founder of the Second Bay Tradition whose work had a profound influence on the architecture of the new post–World War II suburbs. *Documents collection, College of Environmental Design, University of California–Berkeley.*

Houses designed by Wurster and other local architects such as Gardner Dailey, Joseph Esherick, and Henry Hill, became the prototypes for the post–World War II tract home and the California ranch house. The impact of these architects' design innovations, when married to prefabrication and other cost-reducing construction methods, was felt across the country…for better or for worse. Drawing on their work, contractors filled the western and southern neighborhoods of San Francisco with tract homes and boxy, colorless apartment buildings with flat roofs during the postwar building boom. However, the finest examples of homes designed in a modern California style were built in wealthy neighborhoods like Pacific Heights, where inviting the outdoors in meant spacious plate glass windows and breathtaking views of the Golden Gate.

THE NEW SKYLINE

European modernism did not have a significant impact on the skyline of major American cities until commercial building revived after World War II. The first modernist skyscrapers, such as Skidmore Owings Merrill's Lever Building and Mies's Seagram Building, both in New York, were striking in their boldness, in the way they stood apart from the skyline built up in the three decades before the Depression. Set back from the street a luxurious and rent-sacrificing 90 feet, the Seagram Building rose straight up 516 feet and was sheathed in pinkish gray glass. Its verticality was emphasized by mullions made of attached I-beams, which had become a kind of Miesian signature emphasizing his fascination with the structural aspects of his work.

Construction of the third generation of San Francisco skyscrapers, the tallest and most controversial, was delayed until the late 1950s. The first modernist buildings were the work of Skidmore Owings Merrill (SOM). This firm's work was influenced by Gropius, Mies, and Le Corbusier. Indeed, some of Mies's best-known protégés joined the firm and shaped its design values. SOM collaborated with Hertzka and Knowles on the city's first post–World War II glass curtain skyscraper on Market Street for the Crown Zellerbach Corporation, which was completed in 1959.

SOM was the first architectural megafirm. It was also the first architectural firm to which New York's Museum of Modern Art devoted an exhibit. Founded in Chicago in 1936, by the 1960s SOM had 18 partners, 700 employees, and branch offices in Portland and San Francisco. What a contrast between the new corporate architect with academic training and the previous generation of largely self-taught practitioners, such as Polk! Polk went to work for his carpenter-builder father at age eight, designed his first building (a schoolhouse in Hope, Arkansas) at fifteen, and apprenticed in various architectural offices while receiving little in the way of formal education.

The Crown Zellerbach Building at Bush and Market by Skidmore Owings Merrill and Hertzka and Knowles, the first International Style building in San Francisco (1959). *San Francisco Public Library.*

SOM, under the leadership of Edward Bassett, went on to design perhaps half of San Francisco's downtown high rises, making a significant contribution to the new skyline. With the awarding of major contracts to firms like SOM, the role of local architectural firms was necessarily diminished, and for the first time it became difficult to identify the distinct role of local architects in shaping the city's built environment.

The setting for a number of San Francisco's modern skyscrapers involved new uses of urban space. In the city's first redevelopment project, Golden Gateway Towers, streets were eliminated and blocks were consolidated to permit large-scale development. Wurster, Emmons & Bernardi worked with landscape designers, such as Lawrence Halprin, to create public and private spaces at and above street level that featured plazas, gardens, and pedestrian bridges connected to adjacent developments. Golden Gateway was very much in the tradition of the International Style, evoking ideas advanced by Le Corbusier.

ARCHITECTURAL REVOLT

In the postwar years San Francisco real estate developers boasted of building a city second to New York, even larger than New York. But when the state announced plans to crisscross, surround, and generally transmogrify the city with new freeways in the 1950s, it triggered the growth of a vigorous preservation effort, which eventually became part of a larger social movement made up of neighborhood activists, environmentalists, supporters of low-income housing, and slow-growth advocates. The "Manhattanization" of the skyline was under way, and a large number of San Franciscans, many of them wealthy and influential in their own right, were not pleased with the results. Michael Corbett wrote, in *Splendid Survivors: San Francisco's Downtown Architectural Heritage,* "In the late 1950s, there began to develop a new city within the old that had little or no relationship to what had been built before....If downtown San Francisco had been invaded by another planet the juxtapositions between the city of 1930 and the post-war city could not be more jarring."[50] The new high rises blocked views from expensive homes and apartment buildings on Telegraph, Russian, and Nob Hills. The more human-scale Chicago style buildings were being demolished to be replaced by concrete and glass towers. The very climate of Downtown was changed by the shadows cast by large buildings and the wind-tunnel effect caused by rows of high rises.

In the neighborhoods, particularly the predominantly African-American Western Addition, the wholesale slaughter of the city's Victorian houses and apartment buildings proceeded in the name of urban renewal or, as some would charge, "Negro removal." Modern architecture was dubbed "the architecture of good intentions" in part because one of the ambitions of modern architects was to provide low-income housing. The American high-rise housing project, also inspired by European experiments with low-cost housing, turned out to be a disaster, more prison block than domicile. In the early 1970s the first large-scale projects in American cities were dynamited; many have followed in their wake, and many more should.

San Francisco was initially fortunate when it came to government-financed low-cost housing. The style of the city's first public housing was inspired more by Wurster, who designed Valencia Gardens in the Mission District in 1943, than by the followers of the European modernists who opted for large apartment towers (see illustration on page 309). San Francisco built only three high-rise towers, and even they were of modest proportions as compared with those in Chicago and New York. (Two of these have been demolished, the most recent in 1998.) The trend, however, was away from public housing to nonprofit housing or private housing whose tenants were supported by federal rent subsidies. The architectural results were, at best, mixed. In the Western Addition, Marquis & Stoller designed Saint Francis Square, a model cooperative housing development, for the International Longshore and Warehouse Union in 1961, and Kwan Henmi designed the Leland Apartments for the Tenants and Owners Development Corporation in 1998, for example. The bulk of the housing built in the Western Addition after the San Francisco Redevelopment Agency leveled the heart of the neighborhood is more typical—block after block of cheap boxes.

As in other American cities, the long and bitter fight over the downtown skyline, which culminated in the passage of height and density restrictions in mid-1980s, ushered postmodernist architecture into San Francisco. Across the country postmodernism (or what some architectural historians have called a second modernism) was a response to a barrage of criticism of the impact of high-rise buildings on city life, such as in Jane Jacobs's classic, *The Death and Life of Great American Cities*. A member of the Bronfman family, which owned Seagram's, approvingly described Mies's Seagram Building in New York as an "ugly beauty" and "terribly severe." Mies's design was both beautiful and severe, though hardly ugly. But all too soon architects—in their rush to build up the American urban skyline and to indulge the grandiose visions of their corporate clients—cast aside aesthetics in favor of sheer size and cost efficiency. As a result, the office districts in major cities came to look like rows of glass and concrete tombstones or shoe boxes tipped up on end. "We tore down the old city and built the new in an impoverished celebration of the Modernist 'city in the park'—without the park," wrote architectural historian Spiro Kostof.[51]

In reaction, postmodernists ranged freely across the fields of history, borrowing from both classical and modern architecture, even reviving the use of ornamentation. Some postmodernists attempted to blend their buildings with the range of styles found in many urban centers. Clearly, the dramatic growth of a preservation ethic encouraged architects to respond with a greater degree of sensitivity to the rest of the built environment. Contextualism became an important concept.

In San Francisco, between 1962 and 1967, William Wurster and his partners, Theodore Bernardi and Don Emmons, completed the transformation of several historic buildings near Fisherman's Wharf, including the Ghiradelli chocolate factory and a nineteenth-century knitting mill, into a retail commercial complex called Ghiradelli Square that became a mainstay of the tourist trade and a model for similar efforts across the country. Modern architects like Wurster and his associates were looking at the prospects of reusing historical buildings rather than replacing them as Wurster's firm had when the

Responding to criticisms of modernism, Charles Moore, working with Clark and Beuttler, tried a more adaptive approach, recapitulating the lines of the Second Empire building (1902) on the left with a new post-modern addition (1964) at 700 Market Street. *Beau Wiley.*

Golden Gateway Towers were built on the site of the city's wholesale produce market. Demonstrating another way to accommodate the past and a neighboring building, Charles Moore, working with a designer from Clark and Beuttler, boldly mimicked a 1902 Renaissance/Baroque structure with a bank building on Market Street in 1964.

THE BAY AREA TRADITION: THE THIRD PHASE

The postmodern sensibility is also associated with the emergence of new styles in residential architecture. David Gebhard has identified what he calls a third phase of the Bay Area tradition in residential design, which he associates with postmodernism and the work of Joseph Esherick, Charles Moore, William Turnbull, and George Homsey, an Esherick partner. Again California vernacular, "especially the wood sheathed outbuildings and barns," is an inspiration, according to Gebhard, but this time "with a renewed pop art appreciation of the constructor/builder's vernacular. In their buildings they tended to turn the horizontal Second Phase buildings on end and to introduce vertical spatial complexity."[52]

There is a visual progression from the early stages of this third phase to renewed interest in early modernism that has inspired many of the residential designs in some areas, such as South of Market. Architect Andrew Batey explained in *New Architecture San Francisco:* "I think [Joseph] Esherick was the turning point, in that he broke down the overt modesty of William Wurster and started playing with the elements." In one striking example, Ace Architects (Lucia Howard and David Weingarten) designed a condominium on Telegraph Hill as "an archeology of the Bay Region style" by blending design elements taken from Maybeck, Polk, Coxhead, Wurster, and Moore (see illustration on page 244).[53]

THE POLITICS OF ARCHITECTURE

The fight for height and density limits downtown also shaped the postmodernist approach, which in a city like San Francisco was inescapably political. The city's Downtown Plan of 1983 protected 251 historic buildings, required developers to set aside property for open space, and banned the refrigerator style building, calling instead for a more sculpted look on the upper floors of buildings. In 1986 another anti-high-rise initiative put more teeth into the master plan, limiting the square footage of office buildings that could be constructed in any one year and calling for citizen approval of exemptions at the ballot box.

Significantly, the attention of many civic leaders turned toward San Francisco, where a model for a new, more participatory form of urban planning was emerging. The presentation of the Downtown Plan in 1983 made the front page of the *New York Times*. Given San Francisco's insecurity in the face of New York's accomplishments, there was a certain irony in the comments of one prominent New York politician, who said the Big Apple could use some "San Francisco-ization."

San Francisco's political style is notoriously liberal and fractious. And no interrelated group of issues has drawn more heat than those of real estate development, architectural design, and historic preservation. Citizens groups fought their way into the privileged relationship between architect and client, and the city was forced to hold "beauty contests" before picking new designs for downtown office buildings.

MOVING SOUTH

As a result of the Downtown Plan and various citizens initiatives, the San Francisco skyline began to take on a new look. From a distance, the financial district appeared like a solid block of high rises, but a closer view revealed that the skyline was gap-toothed, with a mixture of Chicago style buildings, some of the earlier, smaller high rises, and the disproportionately larger buildings that went up starting in the 1970s. To the south of Market, which is the direction in which growth must take place under the Downtown Plan, commercial buildings are stepped down in height and stepped back in their upper stories.

South of Market (SOMA) is the center of the city's biggest construction boom since the remake of Downtown, which ended in the middle 1980s. SOMA has become a playground for the new modernists. Commercial architects have mastered the intricacies of the Downtown Plan, fashioning some attractive "midrise" towers with sculpted tops, an improvement over the first buildings designed under the mandates of the plan. For major cultural statements—the Museum of Modern Art, the Jewish Museum, the Mexican Museum, and the New Main Library (located in the Civic Center)—world-renowned architects such as Mario Botta, Ricardo Legoretta, Renzo Piano, Daniel Libeskind, and James Ingo Freed are being hired. Simultaneously, thousands of units of housing are being constructed, much of it for the young professionals who work in Silicon Valley and Multimedia Gulch, which is cen-

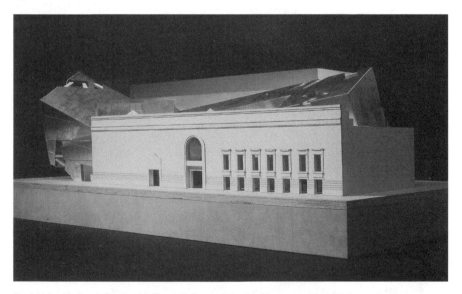

Daniel Libeskind and Gordon H. Chong & Partner's Jewish Museum nested inside an electric power station designed by Willis Polk. *Jerry Ratto.*

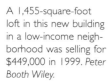

A 1,455-square-foot loft in this new building in a low-income neighborhood was selling for $449,000 in 1999. *Peter Booth Wiley.*

tered in SOMA. In scale and design many of these new buildings—some of them quite far out—evoke the early years of European modernism through the use of new materials, an emphasis on plane surfaces, geometric shapes, and purity of line. Most, however, are cheaply constructed boxes, thrown up to be sold to upwardly mobile professionals at high prices.

One need only walk south from Market Street to realize the extent to which San Francisco is still very much a work in progress. A sizeable amount of acreage south of Market remains either underdeveloped or simply vacant lots. And the city's architectural destiny is still being shaped.

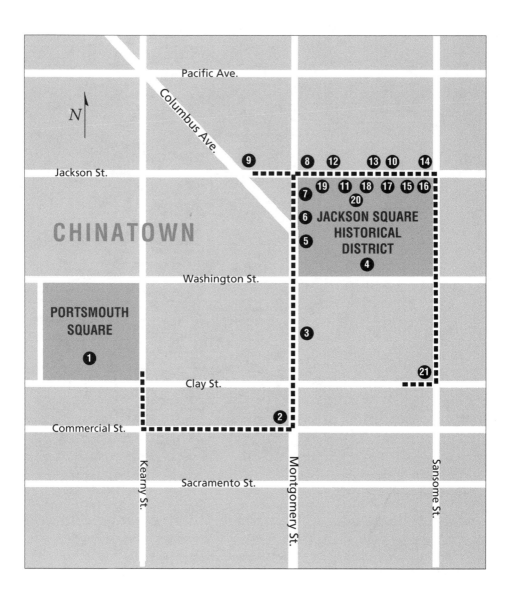

Pacific Ave.

Columbus Ave.

N

Jackson St.

CHINATOWN

Washington St.

PORTSMOUTH
SQUARE

❶

Clay St.

Commercial St.

Kearny St.

Sacramento St.

Montgomery St.

Sansome St.

❾

❽ ⑫ ⑬ ⑩ ⑭

❼ ⑲ ⑪ ⑱ ⑰ ⑮ ⑯

⑳

❻ JACKSON SQUARE
HISTORICAL
❺ DISTRICT

❹

❸

㉑

❷

9

Gold Rush City

A 1½-hour walk on level ground. The tour begins in Portsmouth Square and ends at Sansome and Clay.

ittle remains of the heart of nineteenth-century San Francisco, which covered the blocks between the waterfront, Van Ness Avenue to the west, and Market Street to the south. Almost all of the buildings not torn down and replaced with larger structures were destroyed by the earthquake and fires of 1906. The city's finest commercial and civic buildings, the mansions of Rincon Hill, Nob Hill, and Van Ness Avenue, with an occasional exception, are gone, leaving only a few buildings with which to put together an idea of what early San Francisco looked like.

The only concentration of buildings from the years of the gold and silver booms can be found in the Jackson Square Historical District. But for the best sense of the early city start this tour in **Portsmouth Square** (1). Today the Square is the heart of Chinatown (see Chapter 11). Until the 1870s, it was the center of the city. The beach ran along Montgomery Street, a block to the east, and the city's first main street, the Calle de Fundacion, roughly followed Grant Avenue one block to the west. The adobe Customs House (see

The Jenny Lind Theatre on the east side of Portsmouth Square became City Hall in 1852. The El Dorado to the left was a popular saloon and gambling den. *California Historical Library.*

illustration on page 21) stood on the corner of Clay and Kearny, and the house that William Richardson built to replace his shanty stood at the corner of Clay and Grant. In the heady days of the gold rush the Square, the city's favorite gathering place, was surrounded by hotels, gambling halls, whorehouses, and theaters and was a kind of indoor-outdoor carnival.

The Jenny Lind Theatre was located on Kearny Street on the eastern side of the Square. It was probably designed by Gordon Cummings, a New Yorker who became one of the city's leading architects, and built in 1851 of Australian sandstone. Within a year of its construction, the theater was sold to the city for the enormous sum of $200,000 and refitted for another $100,000 to serve as city hall. To the left of the Jenny Lind stood the El Dorado, one of the city's most popular saloons

and gambling establishments. The El Dorado opened in a tent on land rented for $40,000. The permanent structure featured frescoed ceilings above globed glass chandeliers, an elaborate bar, the requisite female nudes on the wall, an orchestra, and beautiful women serving as dealers and operators of the faro wheels.

From Portsmouth Square walk south on Kearny, cross Clay, and turn east on Commercial Street. At 608 Commercial Street just west of Montgomery is the **Pacific Heritage Museum** (2), housed in the remains of the first United States Branch Mint, which opened in 1854 and was rebuilt as the Subtreasury (1875) when the mint was moved to Fifth and Mission Streets. The first mint stood at the beginning of the Central Wharf. The museum offers a presentation about the history of the site and its buildings and is dedicated to highlighting the artistic, cultural, and economic history of the Pacific Rim. Built into the modern **Bank of Canton** building, it is a fascinating blending of the old and new.

Walk east to Montgomery and turn left. You are now walking along what was the beach at Yerba Buena Cove. A half block to the north on Montgomery Street stands the **Transamerica Pyramid** (3) where the **Montgomery Block** stood before it was torn down in 1959 in an act of wanton destruction. Once the finest office building in the West—Harold Kirker has called it "the most important piece of regional architecture of the mid-fifties"—the Montgomery Block was designed by Cummings in the Italianate style and was built by Henry Halleck, a wealthy pioneer lawyer, with legal fees earned by detaching Californios from their land grants. Halleck went on to command the Union forces in the Civil War. Like a number of buildings constructed on the mud flats, the Monkey

Block, as it came to be known, was built on a raft of redwood logs. The city's first large fireproof building, it also featured innovative structural features designed to minimize damage in earthquakes. The building had a long and colorful history. Newspaper editor James King of Williams was shot by James Casey in front of his office here, and the building then served as one of the headquarters of the Vigilante Committee formed to deal with his murderer. Home of many a stock speculator during the Comstock era, the building eventually housed the studios and apartments of numerous artists, including Mark Twain, Robert Louis Stevenson, Ambrose Bierce, Frank Norris, Kathleen Norris, Joaquin Miller, Jack London, and Kenneth Rexroth. Sun Yat-sen drafted the constitution for the Republic of China in the building, and A. P. Giannini started the Bank of Italy, which grew into the Bank of America, in another office. The Monkey

The Montgomery Block, one of the finest buildings from the 1850s, provided studio space for artists until it was torn down in the 1950s. *San Francisco Public Library.*

Block remained a gathering place for artists into the 1950s, and at least in terms of literature was probably the most historically significant building in the city. The building was also known for its restaurants and saloons, particularly the Bank Exchange, where Pisco Punch was invented.

If you enter the Pyramid from the north side, you will find video screens that are connected to cameras on the top of the building, providing a virtual observation deck, a good way to examine the downtown as if you were on top of the Pyramid. Continuing north on Montgomery, enter the **Jackson Square Historical District** (4). Located near the head of the Central, Pacific, and Broadway wharves, this is what remains of the city's first business district. William Tecumseh Sherman, the Civil War general who headed the San Francisco office of the St. Louis Banking firm of Lucas, Turner & Company, described this part of Jackson Street as "a great thoroughfare to the Clipper wharves all lying north of Pacific. All the miners land at Pacific or Jackson Street wharves so that although we are at the present end of Montgomery, we are at the end nearest the heavy business of the country."

The **Belli Building** (5), 722 Montgomery, was built in 1851 to serve as a tobacco warehouse and then became the Melodeon Theatre. Dancer, singer, and actress Lotta Crabtree, California's first child star, performed here. Melvin Belli, famed local lawyer known as the "King of Torts," bought and restored the building as his law office, which was damaged in the 1989 earthquake and is detiorating while Belli's heirs sue each other. Belli fired a cannon from the roof and raised a "jolly roger" flag every time he won a major lawsuit. This building was constructed on a foundation of redwood logs and fill. You are over the original mud flats, and the tide is said to rise and fall in the elevator shaft. Next door at 728-30 is the

Genella Building (6), built in 1853–1854 for a glass and chinaware business. The city's first Masonic Lodge was organized in the original 1849 building that stood on the site. The **Golden Era** (7) building at 730 housed the famous literary weekly (1852–1893) of the same name (see page 40). The **Lucas Turner Bank Building** (8) at 800 Montgomery was built under Civil War general William Tecumseh Sherman's supervision. All that remained of this building after 1906 was the granite façade on the west side of the first floor. **William K. Stout Architectural Books,** one of the two fine architectural bookstores in the city, is located on the ground floor. Stout is a practicing architect. **Thomas Brothers Maps** (9), an excellent source of maps and guidebooks, is west of Montgomery at 550 Jackson.

Return east on Jackson Street; note the distinct difference between the buildings on the north and south sides of the street, reflecting the movement to more elaborate exteriors on later buildings. In photographs dating from the 1850s, numerous downtown streets had a similar appearance. The early buildings on the north, such as the **Moulinie Building** (10) at 458-60 Jackson, are simple two-story brick structures, elegant, unadorned and almost modern in appearance. The Moulinie Building from the early 1850s was owned by the same French family for a century. On the south side are structures, such as the **Hotaling Building** (11) (1866) at 455 Jackson, that employ brackets, pointed and arched pediments over doors and windows, and pilasters with Corinthian capitals, all features of the increasingly popular Italianate style. The **Solari Building West** (12) (1852) at 472 Jackson was built by a French wine merchant. It served as the French Consulate from 1864 to 1876. The **Solari Building East** (13) at 468-70

From the right, the Belli Building, the Genella Building, and the Golden Era Building on Montgomery Street. *Peter Booth Wiley.*

Jackson was built by Italian merchant Nicholas Larco in 1852 and later housed the French (1860), Spanish (1856–1857) and Chilean (1861–1865) consulates, the Italian Benevolent Society, and *La Parola,* an Italian newspaper. Ina Coolbrith, the poet laureate of California and much admired by Mark Twain and Bret Harte, taught school in this building. She was born Josephine Smith, the niece of the founder of the Mormon church, and arrived in California riding on the same horse with famed African-American mountain man James P. Beckwourth. After an early marriage to an abusive husband, she divorced and moved to San Francisco to write. The **Grogan-Lent-Atherton Building** (14) at 400 Jackson dates from 1859.

On the south side, Domingo Ghiradelli started his chocolate factory at **415-31 Jackson** (15) in 1853 and then constructed a second building at **407 Jackson** (16) in 1860. In 1894, Ghiradelli's sons moved the chocolate

factory to a new building just west of Fisherman's Wharf. The **Medico-Dental Building** (17) at 435 Jackson is built on the hulls of two abandoned ships. Although the building was used as a wine, tobacco, and coffee warehouse, the caducei above the pilasters indicate an unknown connection to the medical profession. In 1866, Anson Parson Hotaling built **455 Jackson** (11) as headquarters for his extensive business interests, which included liquor, real estate, and trade. Its cast iron façade and iron shutters are typical of early fireproof buildings. The **Hotaling Annex East** (18) at 445 Jackson was originally a stable for a hotel. Hotaling took over both this building and the **Hotaling Annex West** (19) (1860) at 463-73 Jackson for warehouse space for his liquor business. The latter was the headquarters for the New Deal Federal Artists and Federal Writers projects in the 1930s. Here a group of writers, including Kenneth Rexroth and Madeline Gleason, compiled *San Francisco, the Bay and Its*

The Hotaling Building. *Peter Booth Wiley.*

Cities, a guidebook, which is still worth reading. A quiet alley running south from Jackson Street is the site of the **Hotaling Stables Building** (20) (c. 1870) at 38-40 Hotaling Place.

As the business district moved south on Montgomery Street, the commercial district around Jackson and Mont-

gomery became a kind of backwater and eventually an adjunct of the North Beach bohemian community. After World War II it revived as the center of a flourishing interior design, furniture, and antique business. Business owners began to restore their buildings, and the area was placed on the National

Register in 1971. Note that the wall of high rises that marks the beginning of Downtown starts with the Golden Gateway Apartments just east of here on Jackson Street. To the north the skyline remains modest.

Walk east on Jackson and turn right on Sansome. At Clay turn right. There is a plaque on the wall near the entrance to Two Transamerica Center on the right, marking the location of the **Niantic** (21) (see illustration on page 25.) The *Niantic* is an excellent example of the adaptive architecture of the gold rush period. Originally a three-masted sailing vessel, she arrived in San Francisco in July, 1849, with 248 passen-gers. Abandoned by her crew, she was beached at what was then the foot of Clay Street and turned into a storage facility, which burned in one of the devastating fires that swept the city in 1851. Her charred hulk disappeared beneath the newly constructed Niantic Hotel and was found beneath 24 feet of mud in 1978 during construction of a new building. The *Niantic* is a reminder that the downtown is built over the bones of the dozens of ships abandoned by their crews when they arrived at the beginning of the gold rush. The National Maritime Museum has identified the remains of at least 42 ships that lie beneath you.

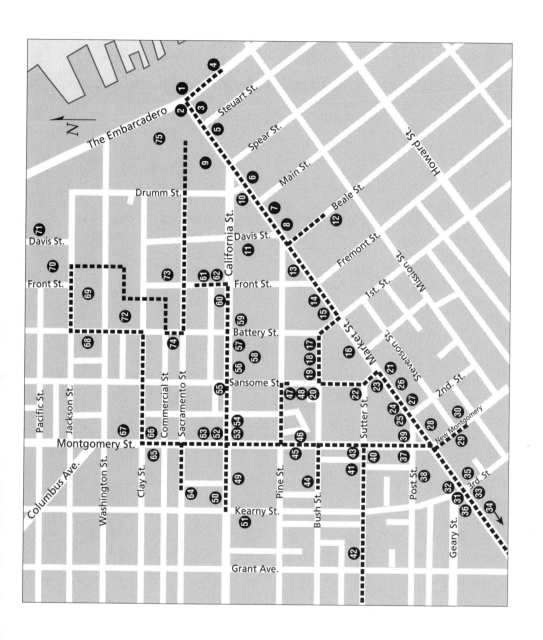

The Embarcadero

Steuart St.

Spear St.

Main St.

Beale St.

Fremont St.

Howard St.

Mission St.

1st. St.

Stevenson St.

2nd. St.

New Montgomery

3rd. St.

Geary St.

Post St.

Bush St.

Kearny St.

Pine St.

Sutter St.

Market St.

Grant Ave.

Montgomery St.

Columbus Ave.

Washington St.

Clay St.

Pacific St.

Jackson St.

Commercial St

Sacramento St

Sansome St.

Battery St.

Front St.

Davis St.

California St.

Drumm St.

Front St.

Davis St.

10

The Downtown/
Financial District

A three-hour walk on level ground. The tour begins at the Ferry Building and returns to the same place.

The downtown skyline is, in essence, a fourth, man-made "hill" located adjacent to Nob, Russian, and Telegraph Hills. The district has three main axes: Market, Montgomery, and California Streets. Start from the Ferry Building, cross the Embarcadero, and you are following the path that tens of thousands of people followed every day to and from work for a time, making the Ferry Building, after Charing Cross Station in London, the second busiest transportation facility in the world. You are also passing under the site of the late, but not lamented, Embarcadero Freeway. Up until the 1960s the piers north and south of here were alive with activity as ships unloaded their cargoes and numerous waterfront bars, hotels, and restaurants, which have all but disappeared, catered to sailors and longshoremen. Walk west on Market Street, and the entire architectural history of Downtown for more than a century lies before you in the first few blocks.

The Ferry Building was the city's principal transit hub before the bridges were built. In the background, Yerba Buena Island before construction of the Oakland Bay Bridge. *San Francisco Public Library.*

Once the structure that was most closely associated with the city, the **Ferry Building** (1) (1903) is one of San Francisco's most important visual landmarks, standing as it does where Market Street meets the Embarcadero. The building was designed in the offices of A. Page Brown by Albert Schweinfurth. Brown was the ringleader of the band of architectural rebels who came to the city in the late 1880s and attacked Victorian excess while searching the classical world for a purer style. A New York architect, Brown worked for McKim, Mead & White before moving to San Francisco, where he employed Schweinfurth and archrebel Willis Polk as his draftsmen. Brown is one of the most important links to two design traditions that would have an impact on San Francisco: the neoclassicism espoused by McKim, Mead & White and Daniel Burnham at Chicago's Columbian Exposition of 1893 and the Arts and Crafts movement inspired by John Ruskin and William Morris. Unfortunately, Brown died in 1896 at the age of 34. The building was completed by Edward Swain. The terminal is patterned after a railroad station designed for the Columbian Exposition. The tower can be traced to the Piazza San Marco in Venice and the twelfth-century Giralda Tower in Seville, Spain. The Ferry Building's steel frame was constructed atop 5,000 Oregon pine piles and a reinforced concrete foundation, which was innovative in its day. The interior features a 656-foot-long grand nave with a terrazzo floor bordered with red marble and walls of creamy, peach-colored Tennessee marble. There are plans to restore the building as a public market and restaurant complex, which are being monitored closely by preservationists because of the possible elimination of the original second floor.

The demolition of the hated Embarcadero Freeway after the 1989 quake gave the city an opportunity to redesign the **Harry Bridges Plaza** (2) in front of the Ferry Building, following a plan by the Roma Design Group (2000). The plaza is named for the city's most famous labor leader (see page 66). Justin Herman Plaza was extended from the north to the south side of Market Street to accommodate a **new music concourse** (3) with a band shell that will house the city organ, which was built for the Panama Pacific International Exposition in 1915. If plans to revive ferry commuting on the Bay come to fruition, the Ferry Building will once again mark an important transportation crossroads.

To the south of the Ferry Building was the **Ferry Station Post Office,** later the **Agricultural Building** (4). Designed in the Mediterranean style by A. A. Pyle of the State Department of Engineering, the building served as the city's central post office from 1915 to 1925. Mail arrived here from across the Bay and was distributed around the city by streetcar. The building was meant to harmonize with the **bulkhead buildings** that were constructed south of the Ferry Building in the Mission Revival style beginning in 1910. Bulkhead buildings north of the Ferry Building were designed in neoclassical style. Most of the bulkhead buildings south of the Ferry Building have either burned or been demolished. More of those to the north have survived.

Irish-born Jasper O'Farrell surveyed **Market Street** in 1847, creating two different street grids with blocks of different sizes on either side of Market Street. San Franciscans have long been preoccupied with the beautification of Market Street. When passengers emerged from the Ferry Building in 1910, they were greeted by a "semi-circle of temporary wooden buildings, topped with hideous signs [that gave] the city an air of crude provincialism and [made] the stranger smile," according to an article in *Architect and Engineer* that called for the beautification of Market Street. The first beautification began six years later, when Market Street was dubbed the Path of Gold. The present streetlights with three globes and relief work on the bases date from that period and were designed by Willis Polk, Arthur Putnam, and Leon Lentelli. The next beautification was completed in the 1970s when the construction of the Bay Area Rapid Transit System (BART) shut the street down for several years. The granite curbs, brick sidewalks, and small plazas along Market Street were designed by Mario Ciampi and Lawrence Halprin, the city's well-known landscape architect. The advertising kiosks and public toilets meant to evoke Paris were added in the 1990s. Market Street and Fisherman's Wharf are served by a **collection of historic streetcars** that the Municipal Railway System has acquired over the past two decades from cities around the world. A working monument to public transportation in less frenzied times, they serve as the perfect connection to the cable car lines at Powell and Market.

As you walk west along the first three blocks of Market Street, the three modestly scaled Chicago style buildings on the left are excellent examples of the first corporate headquarters structures that went up in the period between the 1906 earthquake and the 1929 stock market crash. Towering above them are examples of the high rises built during Manhattanization. **Number One Market Street** (5), one of the first post-1906 corporate headquarters buildings, was designed by Bliss & Faville for the Southern Pacific in 1916. Walter Bliss and William Faville were graduated from the Massachusetts Institute of

Technology, home of the country's first architectural school, and worked for McKim, Mead & White. In 1898 they set up shop in the city, using Bliss's connections to local society to become one of the leading firms serving the well-to-do and the corporate elite. Accomplished if unoriginal architects, they produced some of the finest neoclassical buildings in the city. The Southern Pacific (SP) gutted the Market Street building in 1976 and, with the Del Monte Corporation, constructed two towers on Mission Street, designed by Welton Becket and Associates, that are connected to Market Street by a glazed atrium and gallery. Since then the SP was sold to the Union Pacific and no longer occupies the building, marking the disappearance via corporate merger of the city's most historically notorious corporation. The renovated building is being shared by Del Monte, a historic San Francisco agribusiness giant, and Scient Corporation, a representative of the new "dot com" business world.

Skidmore Owings Merrill's (SOM) **Federal Reserve Building** (6) occupies the south side of the next block on Market Street. The leading practitioner of modernism in the city, the San Francisco office of SOM under chief designer Edward Bassett is thought to have designed close to half of the downtown high rises during Manhattanization. Built in 1982, the Fed is a blocky, stepped-back structure that redeems itself by opening up a good view of the splendid Matson and Pacific Gas & Electric (PG&E) buildings in the next block west. In front of the building there is a ponderous loggia with roof plantings. The **Matson Building** (7) at 245 Market, now owned by PG&E, is also the work of Bliss & Faville. From 1922 to 1947 it served as headquarters for the shipping company established by Captain William Matson that plied the waters between Hawaii and the West Coast. This building is a good example

of the office building structured as a classical column with a four-story "base" with columns and an entry arcade, nine stories of "shaft," and a richly ornamented "capital" consisting of arched windows under a cornice.

Designed by John Bakewell Jr. and Arthur Brown Jr., the **PG&E Building** (8) next door was completed in 1925 as the company's corporate headquarters. Construction occurred during a period of consolidation that made PG&E the largest power company in northern California. Bakewell and Brown were the city's most prominent neoclassical architects. Educated at the École des Beaux-Arts, they designed City Hall and the War Memorial Opera House and Veterans Building. The PG&E Building was obviously designed to complement the Matson Building. The divisions between base, columns, and capital are aligned, and the terra-cotta surface harmonizes with the Matson Building. Terra-cotta, favored by contractors, was used to clad both buildings because of its light weight and its proven ability to withstand fire. Gladding, McBean, the Bay Area's leading terra-cotta manufacturer, developed a tile called Granitex, which could be colored to look like stone—in this instance Sierra white granite—for the PG&E building. The building is distinguished by magnificent lamps on either side of the door and sculptural work evoking California themes by Edgar Walter—the heads of bighorn sheep on the keystones of the base arcade, grizzly bears and their paws over the entrance.

The SP, Matson, and PG&E buildings present a striking contrast to the row of modernist office towers on the north side of Market, which were built during the height of Manhattanization in the 1980s. John Portman Jr.'s **Hyatt Regency** (9) stands at the foot of California Street right next to the cable car stop. Terraced with a revolving, circular restaurant on the roof, the build-

The Matson Building, bracketed by two towers of the Embarcadero Center. *Peter Booth Wiley.*

ing has a huge interior atrium with hanging vines, fountains, and glass elevator shafts, perhaps best known as the setting of Mel Brooks's hilarious portrayal of a psychiatrist with vertigo in *High Anxiety*. **Number One California** (10) is a good example of a dull, generic office tower complete with characterless modern banking temple. One block west is **101 California** (11), a striking glass silo designed by Johnson/Burgee. Philip Johnson, who was still practicing architecture in New York in his nineties in the year 2000, played a major role in introducing European modernism to the United States via the 1931 New York Museum of Modern Art show on International Style.

Cross to the south side of Market and turn left into Beale Street. In an attractive though heavily shaded pocket park on the right, there is a railroad car museum. The car, named **WaaTeeKaa** (12) by the wife of Bechtel Corporation founder Warren Bechtel, was home to Steve and Laura Bechtel and their children in the 1920s when Steve was travel-

ing the West, supervising construction projects. The car is now a museum. Bechtel, a global powerhouse and one of the last of the great San Francisco family-owned businesses, has its headquarters next door at **50 Beale Street** (12), a Miesian knockoff designed by Skidmore Owings Merrill (SOM) in 1968.

Return to Market Street and turn left. The SOM-designed building (1987) at **388 Market** (13) is the modern equivalent of a flatiron building, well adapted to the triangular lot typical of the intersections north of Market Street. The green framing around the windows harmonizes well with the building's reddish granite skin. The apartments on the top six floors of the building are fitted with balconies that create a grill-like surface, which contrasts nicely with the polished surface below. West of Front Street in the next block is the **Sanwa Bank Building** (14) (1982) at 444 Market, also by SOM. The rolling vertical curves are shaped in aluminum, and the top of the building features a series of setbacks with trees on terraces that predate the

388 Market Street.
Peter Booth Wiley.

Planning Department's regulation calling for setbacks in 1985. The end of Bush Street farther west on Market has been closed to extend the plaza surrounding the **Mechanic's Monument** (15) (1901). The granite base was designed by Willis Polk, and the sculpture, a monument to Peter Donahue, one of the founders of industrial San Francisco, is by Douglas Tilden, the city's foremost sculptor, who was a deaf mute.

The Mechanic's Monument Plaza provides an excellent point from which to view the **Crown Zellerbach Building** (16) (see illustration on page 139). This 1959 building by SOM and Hertzka and

Knowles was one of San Francisco's first flirtations with the International Style — a modern glass, steel, and aluminum high rise with no surface ornamentation. The architects also broke with the prevailing way of arranging office buildings shoulder to shoulder by creating a tower in a plaza setting à la Le Corbusier. The building is considered structurally innovative because its steel girders, which reach across the entire width of the building, eliminated the need for interior columns, thus creating office space that could be adapted to shifting organizational forms. Although it is a high rise, the building seems modest in proportions when contrasted with the surrounding megaliths. The building was constructed at a time when Market Street was in decline, thus SOM placed the entrance on Bush Street and faced the service tower, which is clad in greenish mosaic tile, toward Market Street. The small circular building, **Web Street Securities,** was originally a banking temple, the most innovative of the various modernist attempts along Market Street. The roof is made of precast folded concrete plates sheathed in copper.

The Crown Zellerbach Building is the center of Downtown's most fascinating and concentrated cityscape. Just across Bush Street from the Crown Zellerbach Building, George Kelham's **Shell Building** (17), in the Moderne style of the 1920s, is an excellent example of the previous generation of skyscrapers. Kelham, one of several graduates of the École des Beaux-Arts who made major contributions to local architecture, came to San Francisco in 1906 to supervise construction of the Palace Hotel. He settled in the city, and his work on five major downtown buildings marked the transition from the Chicago style to Moderne structures. Kelham is also credited with changing the role of architects in the construction of commercial buildings by hiring a general contractor. Before general contractors were utilized, the architect assumed responsibility for hiring workers and acquiring materials. Like that of Timothy Pflueger, Kelham's work was influenced both by New York architects who were tapering their buildings in response to zoning laws passed in 1916 and by Eliel Saarinen's entry in the 1922 Chicago Tribune Tower competition. In fact, the top of the Shell Building closely resembles Saarinen's much-imitated design. Kelham emphasized verticality at a time when major buildings rose 10 to 15 floors above their Chicago style neighbors. Indeed, Kelham's buildings defined the upper limits of the downtown skyline in the 1920s. The building's ornamentation

combines abstracted shell designs with Egyptian motifs, notably the lotus flowers in the tower.

Wedged into a 20-foot lot next to the Shell Building is one of Downtown's true gems. Designed by George Applegarth, another Beaux-Arts graduate, the **Heineman Building** (18) at 130 Bush was built as a belt, tie, and suspender factory in 1910 and is reminiscent of the pre-1906 downtown when light manufacturing shared space with office workers. The gracefully rounded windows are separated by hammered

The narrow façade of the Heineman Building. *Peter Booth Wiley.*

copper paneling and topped with a Gothic parapet. Prismatic glass was used to direct light into the workspace. To the left of 130 Bush is the **Adam Grant Building** (19) by Howard and Galloway, which started out as a six-story building with a dry goods whole-saler and manufacturer as its main ten-ant. In 1926 the owners added eight more stories, and the building was con-verted to office use.

Both sides of the 200 block of Bush Street are lined with **Standard Oil buildings** (20). The first, built in 1916 at 115 Sansome at the northwest corner of Bush and Sansome, was designed by Benjamin MacDougall. Designed in the Chicago style, the exterior features a granite base with two floors of gray limestone topped by dark brown pressed brick and terra-cotta colon-nades under the cornice. The building, when it opened in 1916, was noted for having the most sumptuous interior downtown. "It expresses to a nicety the princely character of one of the world's wealthiest corporations and it impresses the visitor most profoundly with the

importance, the perfection, and the power of this most efficient and most successful of all America's business organizations," explained *Architect and Engineer.* For the mighty Standard Oil Company, one building was not enough. In the early 1920s George Kelham designed a larger building across the street at 225 Bush, modeled after New York's Federal Reserve Bank. Standard Oil continued to expand across Market Street, opting for space and ugliness in two towers at **555 and 575 Market Street** (21), by Hertzka and Knowles, built in 1964 and 1975. In what is per-haps a hope to redeem these buildings that rank with the worst of the down-town high rises, the towers are separat-ed by a **park** by Theodore Osmundson and John Staley that looks appealing but is usually too cold to sit in.

One Sansome Street at Market and Sansome (22) is a neoclassical building (1910) designed by Albert Pissis for the **London-Paris National Bank,** added onto by Kelham, and gutted to become the entrance portico to the undistin-guished **Citicorp Center** (1984) by

One Sansome, a banking temple gutted to become the portico for a modern office building. *Peter Booth Wiley.*

Pereira and Associates at its rear. This is one of several examples of the creative or reductive—depending on your point of view—integration of banking temples into modern structures. A 30-ton remnant from the **façade of the Holbrooke Building,** which stood on the site of the Citicorp Center, has been incorporated into the **Citicourt Café** on the ground floor. Note the wall display about the history of the site on the left as you enter the café. Inside the portico on the right is a statue, the *Star Figure,* which is a reproduction of a parapet ornament sculpted by A. Sterling Calder for the Panama Pacific International Exposition. Pissis was the first of the late-nineteenth-century architects to bring the results of a Beaux-Arts education to San Francisco. Born into a French family in Mexico, he started by designing conventional Victorian homes until he won the competition to design a new Hibernia Bank at Jones and Market. Pissis's work quickly drew the attention of the new generation of architects who were enamored with classicism. Where Sutter strikes Market, creating a small triangular lot, is the **Flatiron Building** (23) by Havens and Toepke (1913). Viewed from the right angle, the characterless high rises on the south side of Market provide a fitting backdrop for this finely detailed building.

The 500 block on Market Street contains two works by Willis Polk, **564 Market** (24) and the renowned **Hobart Building** (25) at 582 Market, thought to be his favorite commercial structure. Polk was the most active architect during the reconstruction of the city after the earthquake, designing 106 buildings between 1906 and 1914. He also proposed numerous imaginative additions to Market Street. Two of them, a new civic center at Market and Van Ness, as envisioned in the Burnham Plan, and a triumphal arch and peristyle that would frame the Ferry Building and provide a grand entrance to Market Street, were

very ambitious but never realized. Polk was a careful student of context, which is demonstrated in his few remaining drawings and by his work with large-scale photographs of street sites on which he sketched building designs. When Burnham thought that his plan might be implemented after the fire and earthquake of 1906, he rushed to open a San Francisco office under the direction of Polk, who had been trained in his Chicago office. But Polk was a poor manager, a contentious critic of his colleagues, and a lover of public stunts. Burnham closed his office in 1910, and Polk continued to practice on his own. Polk set out to build the Hobart Building, conceived during this difficult period, in record time (11 months), which led to charges of recklessness. The body of the building rises to a flattened oval tower with fine terra-cotta ornamentation in the Renaissance/ Baroque manner.

Across the street at 581 Market, **Stacey's Bookstore** (26) has a fine collection of architecture books, and **Rand McNally's** (27) at 595 Market offers maps. On the south side of Market Street between Second and New Montgomery is a good example of the "funny hats" that resulted from the Planning Department's 1985 guidelines for the tops of buildings — in this case bulbous pseudo-cornices, an oversized clock, and pointy pole. The building, **33 New Montgomery** (28), straddles the old **Hoffman Grill.** The developer gave the Planning Commission the impression that the historic restaurant would be saved. In fact, nothing remains besides the façade, the tiled floor, and mezzanine.

The **Palace Hotel** (29), the building that brought George Kelham to San Francisco to supervise its construction, stands on the southwest corner of Market and New Montgomery. It was designed by the New York firm of Trowbridge and Livingston and opened in 1909. This Palace Hotel, a modest but handsome and well-proportioned neo-classical structure, replaced William Ralston's famed hotel, which he had touted as the biggest and best of everything in the West, after it was destroyed in 1906. The interior follows the style of the original hotel with the exception of the **Garden Court,** which replaced an interior courtyard that served as a carriage entrance. There are vaulted ceilings, plenty of gilding, and Austrian leaded crystal chandeliers. The Garden Court features imported marble columns and a lovely art glass ceiling. **Maxfield's,** a redwood-paneled bar, was built to showcase Maxfield Parrish's *Pied Piper of Hamlin.*

Another bar and restaurant, the **House of Shields** (30), occupies part of the ground floor of the Chicago style **Sharon Building** (1912) across the street, also designed by Kelham. The building was once favored by architects for their offices. Along part of its frontage the structure is only 20 feet deep and is actually a façade for the parking garage behind it. The House of Shields's ornate bar was meant for the Palace but was moved across the street when Parrish's large painting did not leave enough room for the bar.

Return to Market and turn left. **Lotta's Fountain** (31) (see illustration on page 35) at the intersection of Market, Kearny, and Geary, is another public monument that survived the 1906 disaster. Lotta Crabtree was a vaudevillian who got her start as an eight-year-old performing in San Francisco dance halls. So popular with miners that they showered her with gold nuggets, she reciprocated by donating this elaborate public drinking fountain to the city in 1875. It became a favorite gathering place. Annually, the few survivors of the 1906 earthquake congregate here at 5:18 A.M. every April 18. Eight feet were added to the column during the 1916 beautification of Market Street to make it conform more closely to the new streetlight standards. The fountain was restored and cut down to its original size in 1999.

With the construction of the **Chronicle Building** (32) (1890) at 690 Market, Burnham's first building in San Francisco and the first high rise in the city, the corner of Third and Market, sometimes referred to as "Newspaper Angle," became one of the most prestigious addresses downtown. Old timers also called the corner "Cape Horn" because of the wind that whipped around the buildings. According to *San Francisco, The Bay and Its Cities,* a 1940 guidebook put together by writers hired by the Works Progress Administration (WPA), this corner also drew another type of crowd: "Here lounged young wastrels whose delight it was to observe the skirts of passing damsels wafted knee-high by sudden gusts."[58] In an effort to one-up the de Youngs, Claus Spreckels had the Reid Brothers design a taller tower for the *Call* (see illustration on page 42) on the southwest corner of Third and Market and Kearny in 1898. Both buildings were gutted by fire and restored after 1906. They are still here, but you would never know it inasmuch as they have been thoroughly transmogrified. The original Romanesque Chronicle Building was enlarged twice, following designs by Willis Polk, before it was stripped of its exterior features and clad with enameled metal porcelain in 1962. The domed **Call Building** (33) was likewise a striking edifice. (Architect George Applegarth had his office in the dome.) It was so well engineered that its foundation and frame could accommodate six more floors, which were added in 1938 when the dome was removed, making it into an architectural nonentity.

Fortunately, a successful imitation of the Call Building, the **Humboldt Bank Building** (34) (1906) by Meyer and O'Brien at 783-85 Market, still exists. The **Hearst Building** (35) (1909) on the

Chicago architect Daniel Burnham designed the city's first modern office building for Michael de Young's *San Francisco Chronicle* in 1889. The façade has been stripped away, but the outline of the building remains. *San Francisco Public Library.*

southeast corner of Third and Market, with its delightful terra-cotta detailing, was designed for the *Examiner* by New York architects Kirby, Petit and Green. The bank building at **700 Market** (36) (corner of Geary) by William Curlett is another pre-earthquake structure (1902); it was restored after the fire and later (1964) paired up (see illustration on page 142) with an interesting example of postmodern adaptation by Charles Moore and Clark and Beuttler.

Return east to Montgomery Street and walk north along Wall Street West.

The entrance to Montgomery Street is marked by another deconstructed bank building with a complicated history. The original **Crocker Bank Building** (37) (1908) (see illustration on page 133) at 1 Montgomery, now Wells Fargo, was the work of Willis Polk. When another architect copied his design for an extension of the banking hall along Montgomery, Polk sued him for plagiarism. By 1960 the sandstone façade was crumbling. So Milton Pflueger, whose brother Timothy was the city's most influential architect in the 1930s and 1940s, redesigned the façade for the upper floors. When Crocker proposed a new world head-

quarters tower and galleria further west on Post Street, the city provided air space in exchange for the demolition of the upper floors of the building at 1 Montgomery. The banking temple with its lavish original interior is now topped by a roof garden, and the **Crocker Galleria and Office Tower** (1983) by SOM are stacked up to the west of it on Post Street. The Galleria is particularly attractive.

Across the street at 57 Post is the **Mechanics Institute Library** (1909) (38) by Albert Pissis. The Mechanics Institute was founded in 1854 to provide education for workingmen. Some of its board members formed the nucleus of

Willis Polk's glass-fronted Hallidie Building. *Peter Booth Wiley.*

the group that founded the city's public library system.

The **Fidelity Investments Building** and **banking temple** (39) at 44 Montgomery Street were designed to be the new world headquarters building for Wells Fargo by John Graham, architect for the Space Needle in Seattle. When it was completed in 1969, it was the tallest office building in the West. Note the vertical aluminum fins, a flourish derived from the work of Mies van der Rohe.

Two of Downtown's most spectacular buildings are located in the 100 block of Sutter just west of Montgomery. The **Hunter-Dulin Building** (40) on the left at 111 Sutter was built on property whose ownership and inflated value tells much about the rise of the city's great fortunes. Originally owned by James Lick, the eccentric millionaire philanthropist, it passed into the hands of "Silver King" James Fair and then on to a company controlled by Rudolph Spreckels and James Duvall Phelan. The Los Angeles investment firm of Hunter, Dulin & Company bought the property in 1925 for a price estimated to have been well in excess of $1 million. Hunter, Dulin hired the New York firm of Schultze and Weaver to design an office building. (Leonard Schultze was chief of design for New York's Grand Central Terminal, and with his partner, Spencer Fullerton Weaver, designed a number of the most extravagant hotels built during the 1920s, including the Pierre, the Sherry Netherlands, and the Waldorf Astoria in New York and the Breakers in Palm Beach.) The Hunter-Dulin Building is a tripartite French Renaissance Revival structure clad with sand-colored Granitex on its primary façades and brick on the others. The shaft rises to an elaborate gabled mansard roof of terra-cotta tile with copper-coated cresting. The ornamentation is particularly elaborate, with flower and bird designs, medallions representing the four seasons, and the heads of men facing each other in some of the window alcoves.

The building's most famous tenant was fictitious: Dashiell Hammett's detective, Sam Spade.

The **Hallidie Building** (41), Polk's 1917 radical masterpiece, is across the street at 130 Sutter. A careful examination of the neighborhood (for example, the 1908 **Bemiss Building** (42) by George Applegarth at 266 Sutter) reveals that other architects were moving in the direction of the glass curtain wall building. Polk hung a glass wall in front of the structural frame of the building, finishing the façade with exquisitely patterned railings, fire escapes, and a Gothic cornice. The ornamentation suggests influences from William Morris and Art Nouveau. The building looks backward — toward elaborate ornamentation characteristic of the late Victorians, of which Polk was a vociferous critic — and forward to the unadorned glass wall, which Walter Gropius had already successfully developed in Germany. The local chapter of the American Institute of Architects is located here. With his sense of context, Polk designed the Hallidie Building to fit with the **French Banking Building** (43) at 110 Sutter. *Splendid Survivors* describes the buildings on this block of Sutter and the next block west "as a capsule history of downtown San Francisco architecture, which has come together in an aesthetically highly successful group." [54]

Continue north on Montgomery. From the corner of Montgomery and Bush, a half-block foray west brings you to **Sam's Grill** (44), one of a handful of traditional businessmen's luncheon places that are still open. Sam's was founded in 1867 as an oyster bar and saloon in an open-air market on California Street on the southern edge of the Produce Market. The oysters came from beds in the Bay, which have not survived. Sam's moved to its present location in 1946.

When it was built in 1891, the **Mills Building** (45) at 220 Montgomery Street was the epitome of modernity because of its entirely steel frame (the first in San Francisco), its high-speed elevators, its innovative use of terra-cotta, and its organization of 420 offices around a light well. Designed by Burnham and Root, it was built for Darius Ogden Mills, head of the Bank of California. This structure is considered the finest pre-earthquake example of a Chicago style building in the city. The base, with its Romanesque arch (similar to that of Burnham's Chronicle Building), is Inyo white marble with brick and terra-cotta ornamentation above. Despite the claim that it was fireproof, the building suffered extensive interior damage in 1906; it was rebuilt in 1908 and enlarged twice in 1914 and 1918, according to drawings by Polk. His restored lobby still features the lavish use of marble. The Mills Tower at the back of the building was designed by Lewis Hobart and added in 1931.

George Kelham's **Russ Building** (46) (1927) at 235 Montgomery is nicely paired with the Mills Building as an example of the second, post-Chicago style, generation of high rises. As one can see from the detailing around the doorway, the gargoyles, and the emphasis on verticality, Kelham was again following the Gothic style of contemporary skyscrapers. The Russ Building was one of the first to include a basement garage, a portent of the downtown traffic jam. Like the Hunter-Dulin Building, the upper stories of the Russ Building are best viewed from behind.

Even as the Russ Building was going up, commercial buildings were moving toward Deco-influenced modern designs, such as James Miller and Timothy Pflueger's **Pacific Coast Stock Exchange** (47), which is one block east of Montgomery on the corner of Pine and Sansome. The Stock Exchange started out as a U.S. Treasury Building, designed by Milton Dyer in 1915. Ironically, it was the collapse of the stock market that led to the building's remodeling as a stock exchange in 1930 after the Treasury Department moved out. For the Stock Exchange, Miller and Pflueger, emerging as the city's leading architects, streamlined a rather conventional neoclassical building, giving it more modern lines by adding massive corners to interrupt the Doric colonnade. The granite figures in front are by Ralph Stackpole. The skylight over the trading floor features innovative metal louvers to filter the natural light.

Pflueger persuaded the Stock Exchange owners to spend lavishly on interior work for **155 Sansome Street** (48), just around the corner to the right. The building lobby is done in a variety of marbles with a paper-folded gold leaf ceiling. The **City Club** (formerly the **Stock Exchange Club**) on the tenth and eleventh floors represents the most successful integration of architecture and the arts in San Francisco. The interior was designed by Michael Goodman, who introduced Pflueger to the collaborating artists. The project was driven by Pflueger's desire that the artists' contributions, as Goodman put it, "had to be something nobody else was doing." (The overall motif has been described as Deco, but Goodman insisted, "We never mentioned Deco. The truth is, there is no style here.")[55] There are, however, ample signs that the artists were drawing on Asian and Hispanic themes in a significant shift away from traditional Eurocentrism. Among the incredible array of design features are elevator doors designed by Goodman and executed in monel (an alloy of nickel and copper), brass, and bronze and a lounge with walls of goat parchment. The originals were eaten by rats as soon as they were installed, and new ones had to be backed up with galvanized sheet metal. There are also bas relief work by Adaline Kent and Ralph Stackpole; four murals representing the gathering and consumption of food in four different cultures by Robert Boardman Howard (Kent's husband and the son of architect John Galen Howard); glass panels in the bar painted to look like stained glass by Otis Oldfield; corner pieces and panels by Kent, Ruth Cravath, and Clifford Wright; and sculpture by Arthur Putnam. Several rooms are fitted with custom furniture, some designed by Goodman, featuring the lavish use of ash, ebony, pear, mahogany, marble, and brass.

The centerpiece of this abundance is the **first mural** executed by **Diego Rivera** in the United States. Rivera, a friend of Stackpole's, was hired at the urging of Pflueger, the influential art patron Albert Bender, and William Gerstle. Gerstle, a member of the Gerstle-Sloss clan, divided his life between his shipping interests and painting at his studio in the Montgomery Block. Rivera arrived in the city after being denounced for his "communistic" views by the *Chronicle* and *Examiner* and a number of the city's leading artists. While the city in a *volta face* embraced Rivera and his wife Frida Kahlo—they were even taken to a Stanford football game—he worked in Stackpole's studio at 716 Montgomery Street preparing the sketches for his *Allegory of California,* using tennis star Helen Wills Moody and Stackpole's son Peter as his two central models. Tours available.

Return to Montgomery Street and turn right to California, the third axis of the Downtown Financial district. In the two blocks west of Montgomery on California, there is a cluster of modern buildings, the most dominant of which is the **Bank of America** (B of A) **Building** (49) (1969) at 555 California by Wurster, Benardi and Emmons and

The Bank of America Building with the International Building in the foreground. *Peter Booth Wiley.*

SOM with Pietro Belluschi as consultant. In topping the city skyline along with the Transamerica Pyramid, the B of A Building indicates the direction in which Downtown was headed before the numerous campaigns against high rises. Clad in carnelian granite, the 52-story tower is faceted to provide views from every window. There is a large banking hall on the southwest corner of California and Montgomery, and the tower shades a large plaza, served by tapered steps, with a massive black sculpture by Masayuki Nagare, which local wags call the **"Banker's Heart."** Since the B of A was gobbled up by NationsBank of North Carolina, the building has been a reminder that fewer and fewer locally headquartered corporations can claim to be global giants.

Across the street, **580 California** (50) (1987) was designed by Johnson/Burgee. Its rounded bays complement the faceted bays on the B of A Building. The cornice below the mansard roof features three strange figures that look like variations on the Grim Reaper. The **International Building** (51) at 601 California by Anshen and Allen is an early high rise (1962), considered innovative in its time. The top 18 floors were cantilevered to create corner pockets with vertical air-conditioning ducts that carry away heat generated by the plate glass windows.

Turning east on California, you come to two blocks east of Montgomery that feature significant Chicago style buildings from the pre- and post-1906 building booms. First, there is another block dominated by the work of Willis Polk. The **Kohl Building** (52) on the northeast corner of Montgomery and California was designed by Polk in 1904 and then restored after the fire. Polk also designed the **Merchant's Exchange Building** (53) (1904) at 465 California and its later companion, the

Insurance Exchange (54) (1913) at 433 California. When San Francisco was still a port city, the Merchant's Exchange was a beehive of activity. Arriving ships radioed the tower on the roof, and messages were relayed to the businessmen waiting below, who hurried off to meet their ships. According to *Splendid Survivors*, Polk's building became the template for many later buildings, with its massive base with columned entryway, shaft with rustication emphasizing horizontal lines, a detailed capital with columns, cornice, and roof belvedere. The interior features a marble lobby and merchants hall by Julia Morgan. The restored murals in the bank at the back of the lobby are by Walter Coulter and Nils Hagerup. Morgan's office was on the 13th floor. An associate told of visiting her, only to find her coming in a top-floor window dressed in a neat gray suit covered with plaster dust. She had climbed down from a small scaffold from which she had been examining damage to the terra-cotta on the cornice of the building.

Further east, at 400 California, is what is regarded as the city's finest banking temple, the **Bank of California** (55) (1907) by Bliss and Faville. It sits on the site of William Ralston's original Bank of California building (see illustration on page 33). On the south side of the 300 block of California are the **J. Harold Dollar Building** (56) by George Kelham (1920) and the more elaborate **Robert Dollar Building** (57) by Charles McColl (1919) with maritime ornamentation befitting the headquarters of what was one of the city's largest shipping companies. Between the two Dollar buildings is the entrance to the **California Center** (58) by SOM (1986). By building in the middle of the block during the contentious 1980s, SOM preserved a number of historic buildings. The twin towers have been renamed "the Roach Clip."

As an example of early modernism in San Francisco (1959), the **Industrial Indemnity** (originally **John Hancock) Building** (59) at 255 California by SOM stirred up as much excitement as the Crown Zellerbach Building. The building sits on piers whose curving arches pick up the shape of the windows on the top floor of the Dollar Building across the street. The façade is unadorned except for the slightly raised panels between the windows. At 14 floors, this modern building, as compared with 345 California, fits well with its older companions. Lawrence Halprin's lovely **Japanese garden,** accessible from the second floor, seemed neglected in 2000.

Tadich's Grill (60) across the street is another venerable eating establishment. Also a nineteenth-century Produce Market restaurant, Tadich's migrated around the financial district until the Redevelopment Agency forced the owner to relocate in 1967 to the site of a 1920s restaurant on California Street. The beautiful and colorful façade by Crim and Scott fronts a simple room with a long horseshoe bar and private eating nooks along one wall.

Around the corner to the north on Front Street is **Schroeder's German Restaurant** (61), a reminder that the city once was home to a sizeable Teutonic population. Schroeder's started as a men's restaurant and beer hall, finally abandoning the male tradition in 1970. The interior has tall wooden wainscoting, a mahogany and rosewood bar, polished oak tables, and murals by Herman Richter (1932).

Just to the right of Schroeder's, at **222 Front Street** (62), is an attractive contextual essay by Tai Associates, which was designed according to Landmarks Board guidelines. The building was constructed for two brothers from Hong Kong who wanted to honor their father, a well-known Southeast Asian businessman. Their father did not think the four narrow columns in front of the building

were necessary. Tai made them removable so that they can be taken down when the father visits.

Return to Montgomery and California and turn right. The **Wells Fargo History Museum** (63) is located at 420 Montgomery. Next door, **Montgomery Plaza** is an unimpressive high rise built over two banking temples so as to preserve their street level façades. Turn left on Sacramento to **Jack's Restaurant** (64) (1907) at 615 Sacramento. Opened in 1864 on this site, it is perhaps the oldest restaurant in the city. The owners claim that Alfred Hitchcock and Louis Lurie, a local real estate baron, invented the mimosa here.

Return to Montgomery and turn left. Note how the **Bank of Canton** (65) at 565 Montgomery was built astride the old Subtreasury Building, which is described in on pages 148–149. The Italianate building on the southeast corner of Clay and Montgomery, now the **Bank of San Francisco** (66), served as headquarters of A. P. Giannini's Bank of Italy from 1908 to 1920. (The Bank of Italy was renamed the Bank of America in 1921.) It was here that Giannini, perhaps the most innovative banker of the twentieth century, invented branch banking. F. T. Shea designed the building, which is faced in granite and sandstone, but Giannini personally supervised every detail of its construction. Giannini's office was in an open space on the ground floor where his customers could see and talk with him on a regular basis.

Continuing north, you will come to the **Transamerica Pyramid** (67) at the corner of Montgomery and Clay. San Franciscans have come to accept, if not embrace, this tower as one of its signature buildings. The pyramid was designed by William Pereira & Associates and can be said to have inspired the city's spirited campaign against high rises. The building's distinctive shape is supported on an exposed cat's cradle of structural members. The Redwood

Garden to the east was designed by Tom Galli.

At the pyramid, turn right on Clay Street, then left on Battery, and walk to Washington to find the former **U.S. Custom House** (68), another relic from the days when San Francisco was a bustling port. The building was planned by Eames and Young, St. Louis architects for other federal buildings. Construction started right after the 1906 earthquake but, because of labor shortages, was not completed until 1911. The building's foundation sits on the timbers of a gold rush period steamship that was tied up to a wharf at the same location. The squat granite structure is typically Renaissance style in its detailing, with an elaborate lobby and stairways in black and white marble.

Directly across the street are the **Golden Gateway Apartments** (69), the city's first redevelopment project. The general plan for the development, drawn up by SOM, emphasized towers and town houses in a park and plaza setting—a modernist design concept influenced by the work of Le Corbusier and the Bauhaus architects. Unlike the buildings in the rest of the downtown, which stand side by side with very little open space, these buildings are distributed over eight blocks. The design called for open space one level above the street so that the entire complex, which includes One Maritime Plaza and the Embarcadero Center to the south, is connected by walkways and pedestrian bridges. The city's premier architectural firms, Wurster, Bernardi & Emmons, Anshen and Allen, and DeMars and Reay, worked on the project, which was completed in 1963. Wurster et al. teamed with DeMars and Reay to design the towers, garages, and a set of town houses, and Anshen and Allen did a second set of town houses.

To explore the complex, turn right at Jackson and walk one block to **Sidney Walton Park** (70). Walton was a long-

time member of the board of the San Francisco Redevelopment Agency. In a later phase completed in 1982, Fisher Friedman Associates designed a **low-rise mixed-use complex** (71) around the east and north sides of the park. Situated beside the park with additional green space provided by the closure of Pacific Avenue, this project has a more natural feel than the sterile plazas in the Golden Gateway Towers. Note the ivy-covered **portals of the Colombo Market** (1876) on the west side of the park, the first structure in what would become the Produce Market.

Enter the Golden Gateway complex via the stairs and pedestrian bridge leading up from the park. Wander south through the complex and cross another pedestrian bridge to **One Maritime Plaza** (72), designed by SOM in 1964 as part of the first phase of the Golden Gateway Project. Even with the demolition of the intrusive Embarcadero Freeway ramps, which flanked the Plaza on the north and south, the street-level pedestrian is still presented with the unrelenting ugliness of blank concrete walls and garage and service entrances on three sides of the building. This is unfortunate, because once you find your way onto the Plaza, you are in for a treat. The Plaza, a collection of mini-parks with sculpture and fountains, is an ideal viewing platform—free of hustle and bustle—from which to study downtown architecture. On both sides of the office tower, with its distinctive exposed sway bracing, there are sleek one-story buildings of glass and brick, which are modernist gems.

From Maritime Plaza, cross one of the footbridges to the south to the **Embarcadero Center** (73), four towers designed by John Portman Jr. in another phase of the Golden Gateway Project completed in the 1980s. Portman emphasized verticality by massing attached towers with narrow vertical windows. The buildings are most appealing at night during the Christmas season when they are outlined with white lights. The first two floors are devoted to shops, restaurants, and a movie theater complex. West of Embarcadero Center One across Battery Street is **Embarcadero West** (the former **Federal Reserve Bank**) (74) by George Kelham (1924). The federal government was committed to Grand Buildings. So we get a double stack of banking halls, which is a bit overwhelming as compared, say, with the grace of Bliss and Faville's Bank of California on California Street. Kelham, as seen in some of his other buildings, started with strictly classical references in the Doric colonnade at the front of the building on Sansome Street and progressed toward more modern ornamentation in the upper stack. Inside

there is a large banking hall with murals at the west end of the lobby depicting the origins of banking in Venice by Jules Guerin. The bank, which was converted to offices in 1991, sits on top of the wreck of the Apollo, another gold rush ship that served as a storeship, saloon, and lodging house before disappearing under bay fill.

Exit onto Sansome, turn left, and left again on Sacramento, walking east across Drumm Street to **Justin Herman Plaza** (75) on the east side of the Hyatt Regency. The Plaza is a monument to the man who reshaped the area through which you have just walked. Part of Market Street beautification, it used to stand in the shadow of the Embarcadero. The fountain, by Armand Vaillancourt, is one of the ugliest structures in the city.

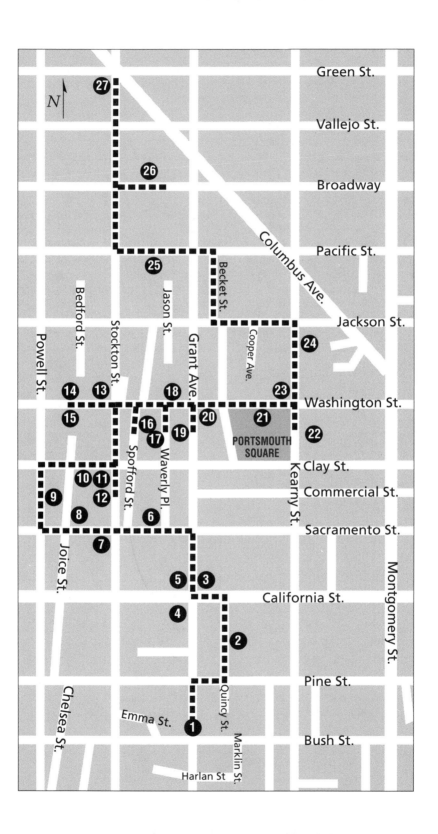

N

Green St.

Vallejo St.

Broadway

Pacific St.

Columbus Ave.

Jackson St.

Bedford St.

Jason St.

Becket St.

Cooper Ave.

Powell St.

Stockton St.

Grant Ave.

Washington St.

PORTSMOUTH
SQUARE

Clay St.

Commercial St.

Sacramento St.

Spofford St.

Waverly Pl.

Kearny St.

Joice St.

Montgomery St.

California St.

Pine St.

Chelsea St.

Emma St.

Quincy St.

Marklin St.

Bush St.

Harlan St

11

Chinatown

A two-hour walk with one steep climb. The tour begins at Bush and Grant and ends near North Beach.

San Francisco's Chinatown was the country's first, and it remains the city's most ethnically distinct neighborhood, a fitting symbol of the strength of Chinese culture and traditions in the face of the very seductive ways of the dominant society. The distinction can be measured with one's senses: the click of mah-jongg tiles heard in any alley, the use of certain bright colors (red for happiness and vitality, green for life and abundance, yellow or gold for wealth), the smell of incense and a thousand different dishes cooking in dozens of restaurants, and the sight of numerous apothecary shop windows filled with strange (at least to Western eyes) herbs.

The best way to get a sense of Chinatown before 1906 is to view the photographs of Arnold Genthe in his memoir *As I Remember* or *Genthe's Photographs of San Francisco's Old Chinatown* (selection and text by John Juo Wei Tchen). About the new Chinatown Genthe wrote, "On brilliantly illuminated streets, smoothly asphalted, filled with crowds in American clothes, stand imposing bazaars of an architecture that never was, blazing in myriads of electric lights." It is this "architecture that never was" that you will see in today's Chinatown. For most of the "Chinese" buildings are little more than ersatz Oriental façades and pagoda features applied to conventional brick, concrete, and woodern structures.

San Francisco's first Chinese settlers were merchants and traders from a prosperous area known as the Three Districts near Canton in southern China. They arrived starting in 1838 via clipper ships, which linked the West Coast with the Chinese ports forced open four years later by the British during the Opium Wars.

GOLD MOUNTAIN

By the early days of the gold rush, China was suffering through the slaughter and deprivation that accompanied the Taiping Rebellion. When news of the "Gold Mountain" reached China, the number of Chinese emigrants grew rapidly, most of them heading for the diggings where they were barely tolerated. Driven away from the richest deposits, the Chinese resorted to working claims that had already been picked over or became workers for the mining companies, which were replacing the early pick-and-shovel miners. Thus, early on the Chinese became a source of cheap labor, which was very much in demand as most whites preferred the diggings to other forms of manual labor.

By 1852, according to one estimate, 20,000 Chinese had entered the city, many of them directed there by Chinese merchants engaged in the coolie trade with the West Indies and Latin America. The first arrivals opened shops on Sacramento Street (called the Street of Chinese People by the Chinese) between Kearny and Grant. From this modest beginning, San Francisco's only ghetto gradually took shape. Chinese fishermen cobbled together a fishing village at Rincon Point and, later, several more along the bay shore north and south of the city. Their primary catch was bay shrimp, most of which was dried and exported to Japan, Hawaii, and China.

Until the 1870s the bulk of the Chinese population lived and worked outside the city. The Chinese were skillful farmers, mostly working as sharecroppers and the state's first migrant farm laborers. They built roads, levees, and bridges, dug out caves for wine cellars in the Napa Valley, and quickly replaced the Irish working on the western portion of the transcontinental railroad. Blasting their way through Sierra granite was dangerous work, and the Chinese paid a fearful price. Twenty thousand pounds of bones, the remains of 1,200 railroad workers, were shipped back to China in 1870. In the city, whites took advantage of Chinese workers' willingness to work for lower wages, and a number of Chinese businessmen started their own factories. By 1870 fully half of the city's manufacturing workers were Chinese. Chinatown continued to grow with the arrival of railroad workers looking for new jobs.

A Chinese fishing village on the shores of Rincon Point in 1859. Oil painting by Frederic A. Butman. *California Historical Society.*

San Francisco's reception of the Chinese at first was far from a hostile one. In 1850, Mayor John Geary spoke at a gathering for the Chinese in Portsmouth Square, where he presented the attendees with books and religious pamphlets printed in Chinese and invited them to participate in the funeral procession for President Zachary Taylor. The *Alta California* predicted that the Chinese would attend the same schools as Americans, vote in the same elections, and share the same religion. Governor John McDougal proposed offering land grants to the Chinese, and another prominent citizen put forward a resolution welcoming them to the city. This friendly attitude, however, was short-lived. As early as 1854, Governor John Bigler was urging Chinese exclusion.

With the economic collapse following the completion of the transcontinental railroad in 1869, white farmers, miners, and workers turned their anger on the Chinese, blaming them for the growth of unemployment among whites. Agitators formed "anticoolie clubs" and then the Workingmen's Party, one of whose slogans was "The Chinese Must Go." Mobs drove the Chinese out of many rural communities; other groups, inspired by the leaders of the Workingmen's Party, harassed and attacked the Chinese in San Francisco. Chinese students were barred from public schools, the Chinese school itself was closed, and numerous laws were passed—some later found unconstitutional—proscribing the activities of the Chinese population. In 1882 anti-Chinese sentiment was enshrined by Congress in the Chinese Exclusion Act, which barred Chinese workers from entering the country. Chinese merchants, teachers, students, tourists, and government officials, however, were permitted entry. Not surprisingly, the number of Chinese in the United States peaked just before 1882 and fell to half its highest level by 1920 as many returned to their native country.

San Francisco's dwindling Chinese community was restricted to Chinatown, not by law, but by the ever-present threat of attacks by street thugs on any Chinese person who left the confines of the neighborhood — unless, of course, he was a servant living in his master's home. And the residents of Chinatown were preponderantly male. Men had migrated from China to work so that they could send their wages back to their families and return themselves some day. A small number of merchants brought their wives with them or arranged for the importation of women for purposes of marriage, concubinage, or prostitution, but the community itself remained overwhelmingly male well into the twentieth century.

CLANS AND TONGS

Chinatown became a community apart, with its own culture, economy, and political structure. The community was run by a cluster of benevolent associations organized by clan members who had migrated from specific districts near Canton. The first, the Kong Chow Association, was formed in 1849. By 1854 there were six such organizations, and leaders in the community decided to form a new supra-organization to settle disputes between the existing associations. Out of this *kung saw* (public hall), the Chinese Consolidated Benevolent Association, or Six Companies, was formed in 1882. Until the turn of the century scholars were recruited in China to run the clan associations. Since then, they have been run by local businessmen. The Six Companies and the benevolent associations served as a kind of parallel government, helping to provide for educational, recreational, and health needs, burying the dead or shipping their remains back to China, caring for tombs, settling disputes between members (the Chinese were barred by law from testifying in the courts), and involving themselves in lawsuits. Before the establishment of diplomatic relations between the United States and China, the Six Companies acted as the official liaison between the Chinese imperial government and the United States.

In marked contrast to the clan associations were the tongs, purely criminal organizations that were the offspring of secret societies in China. The tongs controlled gambling, drugs, prostitution, and the traffic in Chinese women, the last vestige of slavery in the United States and the ugliest feature of Chinatown's "bachelor society." The first tongs were formed in the 1850s, but their time of ascendancy did not come until the 1880s and 1890s when the Six Companies were weakened by their unsuccessful attempts to challenge the Exclusion Act. This was the era of the so-called tong wars, when "hatchet men," or hired killers, terrorized the community during a prolonged struggle over control of criminal activities. Until he was assassinated in 1897, Fung Jing Toy, or Little Pete, ran the most powerful tong in Chinatown. Interestingly, Little Pete spoke English, using an interpreter to deal with his gang members. Guarded by three white bodyguards, he wore a steel plate under his hat and a chain mail coat when he left his home on the corner of Washington Street and Waverly Place.

White San Francisco maintained a laissez faire attitude toward Chinatown. What happened there was a Chinese problem. The police force, understaffed during the first few decades of the city's history, vacillated between indifference and predatory forays to secure their cut of the funds generated by criminal activity. Part of the problem was that the bulk of the heroin entering the country—an estimated half million pounds between 1884 and 1892—came through San Francisco. According to an 1885 report, there were 26 opium dens in Chinatown. In addition, the Chinese were inordinately fond of gambling, an addictive vice in the white community as well. The most sinister crime in the community was the slave trade in women. In a predominantly male community—which means all of San Francisco regardless of race until the 1890s—the prospects of marriage were often remote, and prostitutes fetched a premium. The problem was exacerbated by the generally negative attitude toward female offspring in traditional Chinese society and the debasing poverty of the Chinese peasantry. Working at times with corrupt customs officials and shipping companies, the tongs smuggled girls and young women into the city. The children became house servants until they were old enough to become concubines or prostitutes. The older girls were sent directly either to the fancier parlor houses on Grant Avenue, Ross Alley, and Waverly Place or to the grim little hovels with barred windows in the doors, known as cribs, that lined Jackson, Washington, and numerous alleys.

Stopping the female slave trade became a major objective of a number of San Francisco women beginning in 1873. They worked through white missionary organizations operating in Chinatown, particularly the Presbyterian Mission, which built a home for girls and young women at 920 Sacramento Street. The women who ran this settlement house launched an aggressive attack on the slave trade. When they could, they confronted young women on the streets. But because most slaves were closely confined, the missionary women enlisted the assistance of sympathetic police officers to conduct raids. These often turned into assaults on the buildings where servants and prostitutes were confined.

Donaldina Mackenzie Cameron was the most beloved and effective of the crusaders against female slavery. Born in Scotland, she went to work at the Presbyterian Mission in 1895, leading many a foray along the streets and alleys of Chinatown. Naturally enough, she was hated by the tongs, who threatened her regularly and even planted dynamite on the doorstep at 920 Sacramento. Cameron and her associates rescued hundreds of girls and young women from slavery over the years. In time Cameron, who was supported by the Chinese-language press, was joined by Chinese reformers, such as Sieh King King, an 18-year-old woman student from Shanghai who denounced the slave trade before an audience at a Chinese theater in 1902. This was the beginning of the prolonged upheavals in China that led to the seizure of power by Chinese Communists in 1949. Reform organizations were gathering support both in China and San Francisco—witness the ransacking of a number of Jackson Street brothels by young Chinese in 1904.

Over time the campaign against the slave trade gained momentum, and the number of prostitutes declined. In 1910 a new immigration law was passed providing for the arrest and deportation of foreign women brought into the country for illicit purposes and the arrest and punishment of those engaged in such traffic. Heartened, Cameron urged a general attack on racist legislation directed against the Chinese. She was told in no uncertain terms by her male supporters to let lawyers take care of the law. The slave trade continued into the 1930s, finally disappearing during World War II.

EARLY TOURISM

Whites treated Chinatown as a fascinating bit of exotica; it was one of the city's first tourist attractions. A visit to a real live opium den was a *must* on any tour of Chinatown. Eager to oblige the tourists, guides put together fake opium dens, complete with sinister "hatchet men" or "highbinders," as the tong enforcers were called, lurking near the entrances. There were some, such as the renowned photographer Arnold Genthe, who developed a more subtle and less racist appreciation of Chinese culture. At first he tried to draw its buildings and inhabitants, then taught himself how to work a camera. His photographs capture the sense of crowding and claustrophobia, the deplorable conditions of women, the predominance of males, the occasional family, the dilapidated buildings, and the filthy streets. Genthe was particularly fond of Chinese opera. Chinese performers came to San Francisco as early as 1852, and the first theater was built in Chinatown in the same year. Chinatown's most popular theater, on Jackson Street, was owned by Little Pete.

PRESERVING CHINATOWN

Even within the confines of Chinatown, the Chinese population was not entirely secure. Their proximity to Downtown was a source of constant annoyance and temptation to the city's real estate developers. The bulk of the property in nineteenth-century Chinatown was owned by non-Chinese, but developers still wanted to see this valuable real estate cleared of Chinese. One proposal put forward in 1905 called for the relocation of Chinatown to a site south of the city border where it would be recreated for tourists. With the total destruction caused by the fire and earthquake of 1906, the idea of moving Chinatown surfaced again, this time to Hunter's Point. Chinese landowners had to go to court to get permission to rebuild after the earthquake. Once secure, they went to work quickly, using Oriental motifs in their façades, an idea supported by the San Francisco Real Estate Board.

The earthquake proved to be a boon to the Chinese community in an unexpected way. With the destruction of most public records, many Chinese were able to establish citizenship, arguing that their papers had burned in the fire. Newly arriving Chinese continued to be subjected to harsh treatment at the hands of immigration officials. In 1905 a boycott of American goods was organized in a number of Chinese cities to protest the treatment of immigrants in the United States. Some of the more obnoxious regulations were done away with, but the federal government continued to screen new arrivals aggressively, strictly limiting the number of those permitted to stay. In response to complaints from the Chinese community and Chinese officials, a new immigration station was opened on Angel Island in 1910. Here the arrivals were segregated by sex and confined to spartan dormitories surrounded by fences with guards posted nearby. Privacy was limited, the food was poor, and the sanitary arrangements were deplorable. In 1922 the immigration commissioner declared the facilities unfit for human habitation, but the facility remained open until 1940, when a fire destroyed the administration building. The Exclusion Act was repealed in 1944 as an embarrassment to the United States' wartime alliance with the Chiang Kai-shek regime in China.

THE NEW CHINATOWN

The post-1906 Chinatown was a vast improvement over the earlier ghetto. New buildings with *faux* Oriental façades went up along Grant Avenue and other main arteries. Grant, Washington, Jackson, Sacramento, Clay, and Stockton were lined with restaurants, bazaars, clothing stores, meat, fish, and poultry shops, and two new theaters. In these years Chinatown played an important role, along with other overseas Chinese communities, in financing and supporting revolutionary activity in China. Sun Yat-sen, on his way to overthrowing the Manchu dynasty in 1911, visited Chinatown three times. Inspired by events in China, a handful of Chinese men formed the Chinese-American Citizen's Alliance to campaign for the rights of Chinese residents, and a group of women from San Francisco's and Oakland's Chinatowns, excluded from the Alliance, formed the Chinese Women's Self-Reliance Association. Numerous other community organizations, including a YMCA and a YWCA, were formed.

Many of the residents, particularly with the growth of the second generation beginning in the 1920s, were becoming more Westernized, at least in
appearance. There were numerous residents who were more comfortable
speaking English than one of the numerous southern Chinese dialects. Men
adopted Western dress, cutting off their queues to celebrate the establishment
of the first Chinese republic under Sun in 1912. Chinese children were admitted to public schools in the 1920s.

Nevertheless, the community remained a ghetto. Racism was expressed
less in terms of thuggish violence but continued to exist, as every nonwhite
San Franciscan knew. Although the number of families increased, men still
outnumbered women by three to one. The men continued to work in low-
income jobs as laborers, servants, and factory workers in cigar and garment
shops while women took jobs in the canneries and garment shops. The pros-
perous-looking shops along the main streets hid the poverty and overcrowding epitomized by the numerous back alley apartments, many of them little
more than bachelor dormitories. More than other second-generation immigrants, Chinese-Americans, because of their isolation, felt themselves torn
between two worlds, neither of which they really belonged to. "I have learned
to acknowledge that the better jobs are not available to me and that the
advancement of my career is consequently limited in this fair land," wrote
Kaye Hong in a 1936 essay. "As I express my desire to return to China to create
a career, however, I am constantly being reminded that I am American as
American can be, that the chaos of China's government offers me no promise
of economic security." [56]

Ironically, the Depression helped break down some barriers between
Chinatown and the rest of San Francisco. Chinese San Franciscans were not
discriminated against in the distribution of relief. After Chinese workers
joined the picket lines in the 1934 General Strike and organized a successful
strike against a garment factory owned by National Dollar Stores, they were
admitted to the city's progressive unions. Moreover, the Chinese found it easier to rent and then buy property on Nob Hill west of Stockton Street.

More barriers came down during World War II. Many Chinese-Americans
served in the armed forces, and others worked for the first time in better-
paying jobs outside Chinatown. In the postwar years, as middle-class Chinese
were able to purchase homes in other parts of the city and the suburbs,
Chinatown became a gateway neighborhood through which immigrant families, admitted in increasing numbers under the 1965 Immigration and
Naturalization Act, made their way into the larger Bay Area community.

Chinatown has a long tradition of political activism dating back to the
passage of the Exclusion Laws, but it was an activism that focused most often
on the plight of the motherland. At home, less than half of the registered voters went to the polls. When Phillip Burton took on the Democratic machine
in his run for the state assembly in 1956, he turned to Lim P. Lee, a law school

buddy. Lee worked for Albert Chow, the unofficial mayor of Chinatown. A friend of Harry Truman, Chow was aligned with the Democratic machine, which did little to further the interests of Chinese-Americans. Burton was presented with an opportunity to build support in Chinatown when the Justice Department subpoenaed the membership lists of every major organization in Chinatown, including the Six Companies, in an effort to ferret out illegal immigrants. Burton was the only major political figure to attack the subpoenas, which were eventually quashed.

It would take years of political organizing and a healthy increase in the Chinese population before Chinese-Americans emerged in the 1980s as a significant force in San Francisco politics. By then the Chinese population had grown to the point where the original Chinatown had spilled over Broadway into North Beach, and a second Chinatown had grown up along Clement Street in the Richmond District. At the end of the 1990s there were signs of polarization in the Chinese community between Chinatown Democrats, who were closely aligned with Mayor Willie Brown, and the more conservative and wealthier Chinese from the western half of the city.

IN THE SHADOW OF DOWNTOWN

To a remarkable degree Chinatown escaped the ever-present danger of an expanding downtown. In the absence of research on the subject, one would suspect that Chinatown was protected, to a degree, by its residents' ability to gain control of property in the neighborhood. However, Chinatown did suffer one of the great architectural atrocities of the Manhattanization period with the construction in 1969 of a Holiday Inn on Kearny Street across from Portsmouth Square. The Holiday Inn is remarkable for its ugliness (a male space fantasy?), but the crime was city permission to build a bridge into Portsmouth Square. The bridge ate up part of Portsmouth Square, which is probably the most heavily used public space in the city and the city's original civic center. In 2000 the square was being redesigned to provide more space.

The other significant encroachment occurred in Manilatown, once a subdistrict of Chinatown. Beginning in the twentieth century, Chinatown also became home to small Japanese and Filipino communities. Starting in the 1920s, Filipinos, many of them originally seasonal farm workers who had stopped over in Hawaii on their way to the mainland, formed a bachelors' community near the intersection of Jackson and Kearny Streets. By the 1960s, the International Hotel at the corner of Jackson and Kearny had become a residential facility for Chinese and Filipinos and the headquarters for a number of community organizations. In 1968, Walter Shorenstein, who had bought the hotel, proposed tearing it down to "get rid of a slum." Nineteen sixty-eight was a significant year in the development of Bay Area activism, for it marked the emergence of nonwhite students as a political force. Saving the International Hotel became a rallying point for numerous Asian activists and organizations, such as the Chinese Progressive Association, as well as the United Farmworkers Association. Shorenstein backed off extending the tenants' leases for three years and then sold the building to a Hong Kong investor. Finally, in 1977, the tenants were evicted and the hotel was torn down, leaving an empty hole in the ground. The fight over the International Hotel was an important moment in the struggle to protect low-income housing in San Francisco, and the new investors were hesitant to raise the issue once again. In 1994, the Catholic Church made plans to relocate St. Mary's Chinese Catholic Center, which had been damaged in the 1989 earthquake, to the site. In 2000 construction will begin on a new school, a community center, and the International Hotel Senior Housing Center. "Finally justice is being served," Emil de Guzman, the former head of the International Hotel tenants' union, told a local reporter.

Despite its colorful façade and the prosperity of the city's burgeoning Chinese-American community, Chinatown is still plagued by poor housing and overcrowding. Six days a week, thousands of Chinese women, most of whom are recent immigrants with limited knowledge of English, still take the bus out of Chinatown, headed for minimum-wage jobs in the city's

numerous nonunion sweatshops. The significant difference is that today San Francisco is increasingly an Asian-Latino city, and Chinese-Americans, once a hated minority, are moving closer to becoming coequals in the city's potpourri.

A street lamp on Grant Avenue in Chinatown, a blend of Asian and Art Nouveau styles. *Peter Booth Wiley.*

The Sing Chong Building at the corner of California and Grant. *Peter Booth Wiley.*

Begin the Chinatown tour at the entrance to Chinatown, at the corner of Bush Street and Grant Avenue, and walk north. **Grant Avenue** is Chinatown's main street. It was also the city's first street, *Calle de la Fundacion*. This is why it narrows north of Bush in conformity with the city's first survey in 1839. The **Chinatown Gate** (1), designed in 1970 by Clayton Lee, faces south in accordance with the principals of *feng shui*, a form of traditional geomancy by which a structure is aligned to enhance its relationship with positive forces thought to exist in the atmosphere while minimizing the impact of negative forces. On a wooden plaque the words "All under heaven is for the good of the people," a quote from Sun Yat-sen, are inscribed. The dogs on either side are there to ward of evil spirits, and the dragons on the tile roof are symbols of power and fertility. The **streetlights** were installed in 1915 for the Panama Pacific International Exposition.

Continue north on Grant and turn right on Pine for a short detour to **St. Mary's Square** (2), a quiet, shaded refuge on the left designed by Eckbo, Royston & Williams in 1960. The **statue of Sun Yat-sen** is by Beniamino Bufano. Walk through the park and turn left up California a few steps, to the intersection with Grant. On the northeast corner of Grant and California is **Old St. Mary's Church** (3). Designed by Englishman William Crain and Irishman Thomas England in the tradition of the towered Gothic church, it was built between 1852 and 1854 by Chinese workers on a foundation of granite imported from China. The church served as the city's Catholic cathedral until 1891. It has been gutted by fire twice, in 1906 and in 1969, and is being restored for the third time.

The **Sing Fat Building** (4) on the southwest corner of Grant and California and the **Sing Chong Building** (5) (both 1908) on the northwest corner mark the entrance to the pre-1906 Chinatown. Their architect, T. Patterson Ross, initiated the post-1906 trend toward Chinese-style architecture in Chinatown. Tong Bong, owner of the Sing Fat Building, was one of the first antiques and arts dealers in Chinatown. Look Tin Eli, owner of the Sing Chong Building, was the founder of the Bank of Canton in California.

Continue north on Grant, turning left on Sacramento. A target of numerous missionary efforts, Chinatown has the highest concentration of Christian churches in San Francisco. Missionary work, along with nationalist and Marxist politics, was an important part of the reform ethic that led to fundamental changes in Chinese society both at home and in the diaspora. As part of that effort, the **Baptist Church** rebuilt the **Mission Home** (6) at the corner of Waverly and Sacramento in 1908, using brick scavenged after the 1906 fire, according to a design by G. E. Burlingame.

Continuing west on Sacramento; on the southwest corner of Stockton and Sacramento are the **Mei Lun Yuen housing complex** and **Chinatown and Geen Mun Neighborhood Centers** (7), designed by Architects Associated in 1982. Boxy and unadorned, this complex combines private and public units as part of the effort to meet Chinatown's need for low-cost housing. Farther west at 920 Sacramento, the **Donaldina Cameron House** (8) is the first of four Chinatown buildings designed by Julia Morgan. This structure, which was home to the hundreds of young women and girls that Cameron and her associates rescued from the slave trade, was completed in 1908 with the use of the firebrick saved from the ruins of the original

building after 1906. Morgan worked with the mission's board of directors, which permitted Cameron no input about the design of the interior. Cameron disliked the size and layout of the upstairs living quarters because they did not contribute to the family atmosphere she was trying to create. Fortunately for both Cameron and Morgan, they were able to collaborate on a remodeling job in the 1940s.

Continue west on Sacramento and turn right on Powell. In her capacity as the YWCA's district architect, Morgan also designed the **Chinatown Women's Residence Hall** (9) at 940-950 Powell Street in the style of a Tuscan villa. Continue north on Powell and turn right on Clay. The YWCA's **Clay Street Center** (10) (1931) at 965 Clay is another Morgan design, this time in a more accommodating Oriental style. The Chinese Historical Society of America acquired the building and plans to transform it into a museum.

Continue east on Clay to Stockton and turn right at Stockton. Don't be fooled by the modern brick and glass structure on the southwest corner of Clay and Stockton. Its top floors are the home of the **Kong Chow District Association** (11), the oldest benevolent association in Chinatown. The Chinese community is still organized according to district and family associations, of which there are presently 52 in Chinatown. The **Kong Chow Temple,** the oldest Chinese temple in North America, was reinstalled on the fourth floor at 855 Stockton and is open to the public. Many of the ornamental pieces date back to the nineteenth century. The headquarters of the Chinese **Consolidated Benevolent Association (the Six Companies)** (12) is located at 843 Stockton Street. The Six Companies served as the virtual government of Chinatown in its earliest years and is still the most powerful organization in Chinatown. Note the flag of the

Republic of China, symbolic of the Six Companies' long association with the Chiang Kai-shek's Kuomintang, for many years the ruling power in Taiwan.

Turn around and walk north on Stockton to Washington. **The Methodist Church** (13) (1911) on the northwest corner of the Stockton and Washington replaced one designed by Morgan that burned in 1906. It is the work of Clarence Ward. The **Gum Moon Residence** (also the **Asian Women's Resource Center)** (14), farther up the hill at 940 Washington, was designed by Morgan in 1912 for the Methodist Church. Note the simple but attractive terra-cotta work in the arch leading to the front door and under the cornice. Across the street is the **Commodore Stockton School Annex** (15) designed by Angus McSweeney in 1924. When Chinese children were finally admitted to public schools in the 1920s, most of them attended Commodore Stockton elementary school, where they experienced de facto segregation and substandard education for years.

Walk east on Washington. There are four alleys off Washington between Stockton and Grant. **Spofford Alley,** the first on the right, was originally called New Spanish Alley because it was the location of a number of brothels patronized by Hispanics. Historian Thomas Chinn recalls his family barricading themselves in their storefront home at 24 Spofford at night in the 1920s to protect themselves from petty criminals and the tong wars. The **Chinese Free Masons Building** (16) at 36 Spofford, designed by Charles Rousseau in 1907, was home to the *Chinese Free Press*, which espoused the views of Sun Yat-sen. The alley was modernized in 1995 as part of an effort by community organizations to put together a Chinatown plan that would provide for preservation, affordable housing, and opportunities for new immigrants.

Waverly Place and **Ross Alley,** parallel to Spofford and a few steps farther east on Washington, were the site of the fancy bordellos known as parlor houses. Today these alleys are home to a number of benevolent and family associations. The **Tin How Temple** (17) on the top floor of 125 Waverly is another of the city's oldest temples. It is dedicated to the Queen of Heaven, who favors offerings of red paper, and is open to the public. The **Golden Dragon Restaurant** (18) at 816-822 Washington is perhaps the most notorious site in modern Chinatown. In 1977 gunmen affiliated with a gang called the Joe Boys opened fire on customers in an attempt to assassinate members of the rival Wah Ching. Five people were killed and eleven wounded. The incident highlighted problems with gangs, protection rackets, and illegal gambling in Chinatown, which continue today.

The Tin How Temple at 125 Waverly Place. *Peter Booth Wiley.*

Walking east on Washington, make a quick detour south on Grant. The **Grant Avenue Arts and Gifts Center** (19) at 801-807 Grant is a particularly fine example of the Sinicization of Chinatown's architecture. Return to Washington and turn right. The **Bank of Canton** (20) (1909) at 743 Washington was once Chinatown's telephone exchange. Furnished with teakwood chairs inlayed with mother of pearl and tables lacquered black, and fitted with windowpanes made of imitation oyster shell, it was one of the most sumptuous buildings in Chinatown. Calls were placed through operators who knew the name of every Chinatown resident with a phone and the numerous dialects used in the community.

Continue east on Washington to **Portsmouth Square** (21), which you will recognize as the center of gold rush San Francisco. In the northwest

corner of the square you will find a **monument to Robert Louis Stevenson,** who lived nearby on Bush Street in 1879, struggling to make ends meet as a writer while waiting for his lover Fanny Osbourne to divorce her husband. Stevenson would return in 1888, a successful author preparing to explore the South Seas in a 100-foot yacht he bought in the city. The monument was the result of an effort by Willis Polk and his friends in the Guild of Arts and Crafts to bring works of art to the streets and squares of San Francisco, the first such undertaking in the city. The idea was Bruce Porter's, the sculpture is by George Piper, and Polk designed the base.

When the Redevelopment Agency targeted Chinatown in the 1960s, the result was the very ugly **Holiday Inn** (22) (1971) by Clement Chen and John Carl Warnecke and Associates to the east of

The International Hotel and St. Mary's Catholic Center at the corner of Jackson and Kearny. *Gordon Chong & Partners.*

Former prostitute's crib in Beckett Alley. *Jerry Schimmel.*

Portsmouth Square. The **Chinese Culture Center** was installed in the hotel to offset the damage done to Portsmouth Square. Its galleries are open to the public. **Buddha's Universal Church** (23), by Wesley Wong, on the northwest corner of Washington and Kearny is a former nightclub. After its purchase in 1951, it took volunteers 11 years to convert it to a temple; hence its name, "the Church of a Thousand Hands."

Continue north on Kearny. On the southeast corner of Kearny and Jackson, the new **International Hotel and St. Mary's Catholic Center** (24) by Gordon H. Chong & Partners with Herman Stoller Coliver Architects, Tai Associates, and Greg Roja and Associates will soon be under construction, filling a lot that has been vacant for years since the destruction of the original International Hotel. The complex includes senior housing, a new K–8 school, and community recreation facilities.

Turn left on Jackson and walk west to **Beckett Street,** an alley on the right. In 1913 there were 24 brothels lining both sides of this alley. The door-ways at 8, 10, and 12 Beckett look very much as they did then.

Continue north to Pacific, turn left, and cross Grant. One of the first buildings in the **Ping Yuen Housing Complex** (25) occupies most of the block on the left. Construction of the first phase of the Ping Yuen complex in 1952 was the result of a housing survey conducted by Works Progress Administration employees during the New Deal. With a few design flourishes—the long balconies and red concrete pillars—an ordinary concrete box was transformed into an attractive building.

OTHER ATTRACTIONS

The Chinese Historical Society (26) is located temporarily at 644 Broadway, Suite 402, between Grant and Stockton. It has a permanent exhibit about the history of Chinatown. **Eastwind Books and Arts** (27) at 1435 Stockton near Columbus has an excellent collection of books about Chinese subjects in Chinese and English.

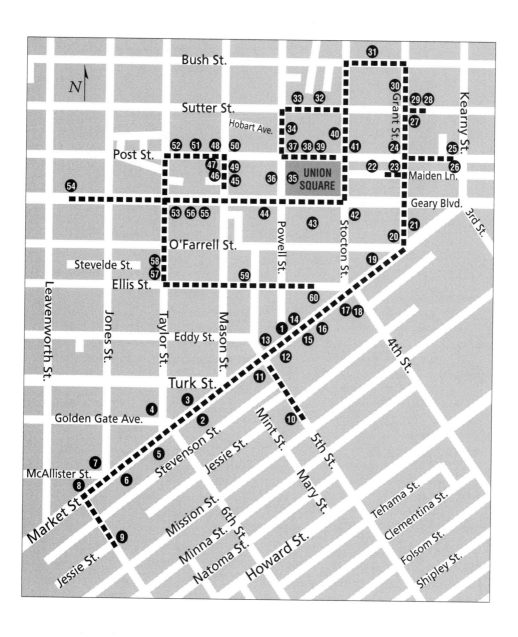

Bush St.

N

Sutter St.

Hobart Ave.

Post St.

54

O'Farrell St.

Stevelde St.

Ellis St.

Turk St.

Golden Gate Ave.

McAllister St.

Market St.

Jessie St.

Leavenworth St.

Jones St.

Taylor St.

Eddy St.

Mason St.

Stevenson St.

Jessie St.

Mint St.

Mission St.

Minna St.

6th St.

Natoma St.

Mary St.

5th St.

Howard St.

Tehama St.

Clementina St.

Folsom St.

Shipley St.

4th St.

3rd St.

Powell St.

Stocton St.

Grant St.

Kearny St.

Maiden Ln.

Geary Blvd.

UNION SQUARE

31
30
33 32
29 28
27
34
40
25
37 38 39
41
24
26
52 51 48 50
22 23
21
47 49
46 45 36
35
20
53 56 55
44
43
42
19
58
57
59
60
14
17 18
1
16
13
15
12
11
10
3
4
2
5
7
6
9

12

The Union
Square Area

*A two-hour walk with some gradual climbs. The tour starts and ends at the
cable car turnaround at Powell and Market.*

Union Square is the heart of the city's upscale shopping, hotel, and
theater district. More than Downtown, this area, with its generally
lower skyline, has maintained much of the ambience of the Chicago
style city that grew up before and after the earthquake and fire of
1906. One of the most architecturally elegant shopping districts to be found
anywhere, the area was protected for a time by a tacit agreement that office
building development would take place Downtown and the Union Square
area would retain its retail character. There was no agreement, however,
about the sanctity of historic buildings in the area. They were saved only by
the Downtown Plan of 1983.

The area's architecture provides a running commentary on the history of
merchandising and the fate of the city's prominent merchant families. Many
of the significant buildings, such as the City of Paris, the White House, the
Emporium, I. Magnin's, and Hale Brothers, were built for local merchant-

princes. The arrival of Nieman Marcus in the 1970s marked a transition in the fortunes of these venerable institutions. They were being bought up by trendy national chains, such as Macy's, Nordstrom, and Sak's, much in the way that a number of great San Francisco corporations would later become the victims of merger mania. As the third largest generator of retail dollars in the country, the Union Square area remains under relentless pressure from chains, such as Bloomingdale's, to provide space for new outlets.

Start at the **cable car turnaround** (1) at Powell and Market. You are now on a part of **Market Street** with a different history and character as compared with the sober business blocks east of Kearny Street. The blocks between Kearny and Van Ness were the main artery of a part of town that just before and after the 1906 earthquake offered all the amenities of the Barbary Coast for a more respectable, if that is the word, clientele. Here saloons, dance halls, billiard parlors, theaters, and, later, movie houses were interspersed with office buildings, such as the Phelan and Flood buildings, and major department stores, such as Hale Brothers' and the Emporium. The blocks east of Powell and north of Market were known as the Upper Tenderloin. They were packed with watering holes, gambling dens, cabarets, swank restaurants, and bagnios. Here were located some of the best known of the French restaurants with rooms for private entertainment upstairs. During cocktail hour Market Street became the "Pathway to Propinquity" as the city's working women paraded up and down dressed in their finest. The neighborhood's most popular madam was Tessie Wall, who had migrated north after leaving a large Irish family South of the Slot. Known as the Queen of the Tenderloin, she presided from a three-story building of brick and terra-cotta at 337 O'Farrell (where the Hilton Hotel stands) designed for her by a friend, architect Milton

Latham, and packed with expensive antiques. Wall was a particular favorite of the police department, which she supported by buying large numbers of tickets so that she and her ladies could attend the annual Policeman's Ball. When she died in 1932, she left a portion of her sizeable estate to her friend and advisor, the captain of the Stanyan Street police station.

Though never as lively as in the years before Prohibition, Market Street remained a popular entertainment spot through World War II, declining only with the flight to the suburbs, the rise of urban paranoia, and the massive disruption caused by the construction of the Bay Area Rapid Transit System (BART). In the years since BART was completed, the area around the cable car turnaround has revived, becoming a favorite shopping district where hordes of tourists brush shoulders with chess players, street artists, musicians, soap box preachers, and homeless people.

Walk west on Market from Fifth, where the next two blocks with their "discount" clothing and camera stores, porno and pawn shops have continued to resist prettification. There are a number of handsome buildings in these blocks, however, including the **Wilson Building** (2) at 973 Market, perhaps by Willis Polk. Across the street at 982-98 Market, the **Warfield** (3) (1921) is a popular rock venue, and the **Golden Gate Theatre** (4) (1922) with its Moorish and Spanish Revival motifs at

The Eastern Outfitting Building, 1017-21 Market. *Peter Booth Wiley.*

the corner of Taylor, Golden Gate, and Market offers Broadway reruns. Both buildings were designed by G. Albert Lansburgh. West of Sixth are the **Eastern Outfitting Building** (5) (1909) by George Applegarth at 1017-21 Market, with its enormous Corinthian columns, and the **Lippert Building** (6) (1924) by an unknown architect at 1067-73 Market. The Eastern Outfitting Building is another of Applegarth's experiments with glass facades.

The Hibernia
Bank, Jones and
Market. *Bancroft
Library.*

The United
States Court of
Appeals, Seventh
and Mission. *U.S.
Court of Appeals.*

On this stretch of Market, one of the saddest sights is Albert Pissis and William Moore's beautifully proportioned deserted masterpiece, the **Hibernia Bank** (7) at the corner of Market, McAllister, and Jones. Pissis and Moore used only the most expensive materials in the building, which has granite exterior walls with an interior of marble, wrought iron, bronze, and mahogany. The building was gutted in 1906, then rebuilt, and became the headquarters of the police chief for a time. The **Renoir Hotel** (8) across

McAllister Street on Market is by H. A. Minton. It was built in 1926 on top of the two-story remains of a pre-earthquake building by Pissis.

Cross Market and turn left on Seventh Street. The **U.S. Court of Appeals** (9) (1905) is on the left at the corner of Mission. One of the finest buildings in the city, it was designed as a post office and courthouse in the style of an Italian Renaissance palazzo by James Knox Taylor, supervising architect of the U.S. Treasury Department. The lot was bought for $1 million, and another $3,555,000, enormous sums in those days, was spent on construction and one of the most lavish interiors of any building in San Francisco. The interior of this brick structure faced with granite has been compared to the Library of Congress. It is the work of Italian wood-carvers, stonemasons, and marble workers, who were brought to the city for the job. The corridors, which feature terrazzo tile, are finished with mosaics, and marbles from the United States, Italy, and North Africa. Wood finishes and carvings throughout the building were done with Mexican and white mahogany, East Indian woods, redwood, and oak. The marble-walled courtrooms abound in elaborate marble carving, mosaics, and frescoes. The lamps on either side of the entrances are modeled after those at the Palazzo Strozzi in Florence.

When fire swept down on the building in 1906, postal employees closed all the windows, moved flammable records to the vault, and plugged the fuel oil line. The fire burst through one window on the third floor but was contained by ten employees who covered the doors with wet sacks. The only other damage occurred when parts of the granite façade peeled away from the building. In the 1989 quake the building was damaged again when the granite façade pulled away from the brick. During a $91 million retrofit and

restoration, the building's structural columns were cut off and set down on 256 friction pendulum base isolators, slightly concave stainless steel disks. The base isolators will permit the building to rise slightly and move as much as 24 inches in a major earthquake. Tours available.

Return to Market, turn right, and walk back to Fifth Street. One block south of Market on Fifth Street is a delightful but sad sight, the **Old U.S. Mint** (10) (see illustration on page 127), which was designed by Treasury Department architect Alfred Mullett and opened in 1874. This Mint was built to accommodate the huge flow of silver and gold that poured from the Comstock lode. Before the construction of Fort Knox, a third of the nation's gold and silver was stored here. Because work on the building was begun soon after the earthquake of 1868, the granite foundation is massive. That precaution and the valiant effort to keep the 1906 fire, which scorched its walls, at bay meant that it would be one of the very few buildings within the fire zone to survive intact. A fine example of Classical Revival architecture, its lines are modest and graceful. The exterior sandstone has, unfortunately, suffered from exposure to air pollution. By comparing the Mint with the U.S. Court of Appeals, one can see the evolution from the simple, almost severe lines of a Classical Revival building to the incredibly ornate design and finishings of the neoclassical court building. Once a museum, the Old Mint is now closed as a result of cuts in federal spending.

Return to Market Street. The building on the southwest corner of Fifth and Market was once the **Hale Brothers Department Store** (11) (1912), and then J.C. Penney's until it was left empty for a time. In 1985 it was gutted and converted to mixed use. The building's designers, James and Merritt Reid, were

The San Francisco Centre with the Powell Street BART station in the foreground. Fifth and Market. *Peter Booth Wiley.*

important local architects with numerous significant buildings to their credit. James was one of the founders of the local chapter of the American Institute of Architects.

Across Fifth Street the **San Francisco Centre** (12) (1989) provides a running commentary on its neighbors, the Hale Brothers building on one side and the former Emporium (soon to be Bloomingdale's) on the other. Architects Whisler-Patri aligned the Shopping Center's cornice with Hale Brothers and stepped back the upper floors to meet the roofline of the Emporium. The grated windows are borrowed from the neoclassical, and the concave verticals framing the windows serve as indented pilasters, a reversal of the neoclassical. On the north side of Market facing the entrance to BART is the **Bank of America** (13) (1920) by Bliss and Faville. This building became the bank's headquarters in 1920. Bliss and Faville,

who modeled the building after the University Club in New York, were the subject of an essay in *Architect and Engineer* about "the line between inspiration and plagiarism." The author pronounced the building of "unusual distinction" without commenting on its originality. To the east of the cable car turnaround is the **Flood Building** (14) by Albert Pissis. Constructed in 1904 for James Flood, son of the Comstock Silver King, its exterior survived the 1906 disaster.

Across Market from the Flood Building, the façade of the **Emporium** (15) (1898), by Albert Pissis and William Moore, was braced and preserved after 1906 while a new building was constructed behind it. It is a particularly fine example of early neoclassical work. Bloomingdale's acquired the building and initially planned to tear down the façade to make way for a store, shopping arcade, and hotel. The façade was at variance with the firm's image as "an up-to-date, modern retailer," according to a company spokesperson. In its latest proposal Bloomingdale's has agreed to restore the façade, but has increased the height of its hotel tower from 10 to 20 stories. Under Mayor Willie Brown, an enthusiastic supporter of the project, jurisdiction over its design was transferred from the Planning Department to the Redevelopment Agency. The Redevelopment Agency is permitted by state law to bypass zoning and planning guidelines, such as height limits, which Bloomingdale's is planning to exceed with its plans for a hotel. "There are probably going to be enough battles over the Bloomingdale's project to make the developers wish they were carried off by a swarm of flying monkeys," commented *Chronicle* columnist Ken Garcia.

Walk east on Market to discover the **James Bong Building** (16) (1908) at 825-833, designed by Lewis Hobart. It features bronze cherubs flying over an elaborate Art Nouveau entranceway and lobby, which also incorporates beautiful marble work. Next door, C. F. Whittlesey borrowed generously from his mentor Louis Sullivan's Carson Pirie Scott building in Chicago for ideas, particularly the corner tower, for the **Old Navy Building** (17) (1907) on the southwest corner of Market and Fourth Streets. Whittlesey objected to the dull colors of the begrimed granite and terra-cotta façades in many downtown buildings. Comparing the building's exterior to a lady attired in a stylish outfit with a satin cravat, he clad the lower floors in red tile and the shaft in green, using cream-colored terra-cotta for trim. Whittlesey defended his use of color saying, "This town is so shady in color as well as morals that a little spot of white…attracts attention like a diamond dropped in the mud."[57] Gensler Associates converted the building into an Old Navy department store and the **Palomar Hotel** (18) in 1999, but could

not persuade the owner to restore the cornice, which is presently covered with concrete. Farther east at 760 Market is the **Phelan Building** (19) (1908) by William Curlett, where James Duvall Phelan's offices were located (for information on the Humboldt Savings Bank Building across the street, see page 164).

Turn left on Grant Avenue, on either side of which are two neoclassical banking temples evoking an era when most of the entrances to the blocks north of Market were marked by bank buildings. The **Emporio Armani** (20) (1919) at 1 Grant Avenue was designed by Bliss and Faville in the spirit of the Roman Pantheon. The **Wells Fargo Bank** (21) (1910) across Grant is by Clinton Day. The interior of white marble with pyrite highlights and green marble tiles on the floor is suitably elaborate.

Continue north on Grant and turn left into Maiden Lane, named for the women who once worked there and were decidedly not maidens. The only San Francisco building designed by Frank Lloyd Wright, the **Folk Art International Gallery** (22) (1949), is at 140 Maiden Lane. Aaron Green, Wright's former associate, restored the building in 1998. Instead of employing the usual glass front found on retail stores, Wright clad the two-story building in honey-colored brick and created a deep, arched entryway. Inside are signs of Wright's wrestling with the ideas that were incorporated in New York's Guggenheim Museum. The central motif is circular, with a ramp sweeping up to the second floor. During restoration, furnishings designed by Wright—curved walnut cabinetry, display tables, bottom-lit display stands, and an acrylic planter suspended from the ceiling—were retrieved from the basement, and other fixtures, including the bubbled acrylic lighting screen on the ceiling, had to be remanufactured using original drawings and photographs.

Frank Lloyd Wright's only San Francisco building, 140 Maiden Lane. *Peter Booth Wiley.*

Return to Grant Avenue and walk north to the corner of Grant and Post. **Brooks Brothers** (23) (1909) on the southwest corner and **Shreve & Company** (24) (1905) on the northwest corner, both by William Curlett, are typical of the grand Chicago style buildings in the area. Turn right on Post. **Talbot's** (25) (1909) at 128 Post, with its gracefully curved corner that turns into an alley is another fine example of the work of Albert Pissis. Across the street is **Gump's** (26) (1910), moved in recent years to this building at 135 Post Street. Designed by Reid Brothers, it features some lovely ornamental work in terracotta around the entrance to the **Rizzoli Bookstore.**

Return to Grant and turn right. The 1908 **White House** (now the **Banana Republic**) (27) is located on the southeast corner of Grant and Sutter. Here is another wonderful example by Pissis of the grand department store, with a curved façade similar to Talbot's. The attic floor was added later. Rafael Weill, founder of the White House, was one of the city's earliest merchant princes. A

bon vivant, he served on the Vigilante Committee of 1856 and was a prominent member of the Jewish community. The entire block of Sutter east of Grant, with the exception of one new building, has been preserved. The **Goldberg Bowen Building** (28) (1909) by Meyers and Ward at 250 Sutter, named after a delicatessen that used to occupy the ground floor, has particularly elegant floral detailing in the ribs of the vertical shafts and clusters of flowers on the cornice. The **Sather Building** (29) (1911) at 266 Sutter, by an unknown architect, demonstrates that architects were experimenting with glass façades before Willis Polk designed the Hallidie Building.

Return to Grant and turn right. The authors of *Splendid Survivors* single out the **Pacific Bell Building** (30) (1908) at 333 Grant, by Coxhead and Coxhead, as unique among the downtown commercial buildings because of its "assertively, intelligently 'incorrect' use of [oversized] detail" in the façade. Continue to Bush and turn left. **Notre Dame des Victoires Church** (31) at

566 Bush was designed by Louis Brouchoud in the Romanesque style with baroque features in 1915. The church was founded in 1855 in an area known as Frenchmen's Hill, so-called because it was here that French argonauts pitched their tents. Named to commemorate the victory of the western European powers in the Crimean War, the church houses a very fine organ, built in the city and still in working order.

Continue west on Bush to Stockton Street and descend the stairs to the left. Turn right on Sutter. The **Medico-Dental Building** (32) (1929) at 450 Sutter is Miller and Pflueger's influential masterpiece. The rhythmic pattern of the walls and the columnar thrust of the building are formed by small bay windows with spandrels featuring Mayan designs in relief. The narrow lobby incorporates purple marble shot through with white, elaborate relief work on the elevator doors and ceilings, and a beautifully fashioned fan over the entrance. Once again Pflueger turned away from Europe to more proximate influences for his design work. Built in the year of the stock market crash, this was the last major office building constructed in the city until after World War II. The **Crown Plaza Hotel** (33) next door is an interesting case of attempted contextual design. Its larger bays pick up the rhythm of the Medico-Dental Building, but the thought seems to dissipate at the top of the front wall.

Turn left on Powell; the **Sir Francis Drake** (34) (1928) in the 400 block is among the city's best known old-line hotels. The design by Weeks and Day is consistent with Gothic themes popular at the time. The hotel originally featured a penthouse apartment that was occupied by its one-time owner, real estate baron Louis Lurie. The unity of the façade was interrupted when the **Star Lite Room** replaced the penthouse apartment and a horizontal plate glass window was slashed into the building.

The ornate entranceway, lobby, and grand staircase are fashioned with caenstone, imported marble, and walnut. The murals depicting scenes from the life of Sir Francis Drake are by W. F. Bergman.

Farther south on Powell you enter **Union Square** (35). The Square appeared as open space in Jasper O'Farrell's 1847 plan, was laid out in 1850, and was later named for the prounion rallies held here during the Civil War. Unfortunately, the imperatives of the automobile and modern retailing—the construction of a garage under the square and the arrival of Sak's and Nieman Marcus—have not been friendly to the architectural ambience of one of the city's two traditional focal points, the other being the Civic Center Plaza. The **monument** by Newton Tharp in the center of the square commemorates Admiral George Dewey's victory in Manila Bay during the Spanish-American War. The bronze figure of a woman is by Robert Aitken. His model was Alma de Bretteville, a voluptuous young beauty who would become the lover, and later the wife, of Adolph Spreckels, the man who headed the committee that selected the design for the monument. The Square was reshaped when a **garage** designed by Timothy Pflueger was completed in 1942. Pflueger's design was hailed as a great innovation—a parking garage under a city park—but the park, with its sloping surface, never seemed to be particularly inviting to the public. In 1998 after a design competition whose entrants included a miniature Golden Gate Bridge, a fog fountain, and a museum in the shape of a heart at the bottom of a pit, landscape architects April Phillips and Michael Fotheringham were chosen to redo the square. Their design is meant to evoke an open Italian piazza surrounded by the existing palm trees, with alternating stripes of colored paving stone continued into the surrounding streets.

The **St. Francis Hotel** (36), another old-line hotel, occupies the entire west end of the Square and is a good example of the mismatches that occur when the modern meets the traditional. The hotel was the brainchild of Mark Gerstle of the Sloss-Gerstle clan. Designed by Bliss and Faville, its construction was funded by the estate of Southern Pacific railroad baron Charles Crocker. The hotel opened in 1904; after 1906 it was gutted and rebuilt and then added onto in 1913. Ben Swig made his grand entrance into San Francisco by purchasing the St. Francis in 1944. The original C-shaped design in the Renaissance Revival style was meant to provide every room with an outside window, an ambition frustrated by the addition to the north side of the C along Post Street. There are marble columns at the entrances to the light wells, and the somber color comes from the use of granite in the base and gray Colusa sandstone in the façade. The lobby is a remodel. *Splendid Survivors* notes its "ersatz magnificence" and that a cocktail

lounge designed by Pflueger with black patent leather walls and a Lucite ceiling was destroyed during remodeling. The unfortunate tower, with its ugly, blank verticals and top section, is the work of William Pereira Associates in 1972.

On the north side of the Square, **Sak's** (37) (1981) leveled the Fitzhugh Building and Helmuth, Obata & Kassabaum created a juxtaposition of concrete columns and panels, which add up to very little, in its place. Next door at **350 Post** (38) Skidmore Owings Merrill (SOM) designed an unadorned building with a lovely polished marble façade in 1972, which looks great when compared with Sak's. The building at **340 Post** (39) (1923) by Reid Brothers evokes in its scale an earlier era. Turn left on Stockton. The delightful **Ruth Asawa Fountain** (40) (1972) on the Stockton Street steps of the Hyatt Union Square was a community project involving schoolchildren, family, and friends, who made the original model with bread dough. The only significant building on the east side of the Square is

A fountain by Ruth Asawa in front of the Grand Hyatt Union Square, 345 Stockton. *Peter Booth Wiley.*

Art glass from the original atrium of the City of Paris, which was incorporated into the new Neiman Marcus Building at Stockton and Geary. *San Francisco History Center, San Francisco Public Library.*

278-99 Post Street (41) (1910), on the northeast corner of Stockton and Polk, by Willis Polk.

It is still hard to forgive **Nieman Marcus's** (42) destruction of the City of Paris, which stood at the southeast corner of Union Square (see page 98). Johnson/Burgee's replacement (1982), with its varicolored diamonds, stands out without shouting. Do not miss the old atrium and its art glass ceiling by Harry Wile Hopps, which was incorporated into the new building. Pflueger stripped and reclad a 1905 steel frame for I. Magnin's on the southwest corner of Stockton and Geary when Magnin's moved to Union Square in 1946. Pflueger's design was celebrated as the city's first essay in high modernism. (It does significantly predate the Crown Zellerbach and John Hancock Buildings described in the Downtown Walking Tour in Chapter 10.) Pflueger maintained that the flat façade of white Vermont marble was meant to pigeon-proof the building. After turning an ugly face to the south side of the Square, **Macy's** (43), which has expanded into both of the former Magnin company's buildings, finally upgraded with a fine new glass façade by Patri-Merker in 1998.

Walking west on Geary past Powell, sports fans will find a traditional watering hole and steam table, of which there are very few remaining, at **Lefty O'Doul's** (44) at 333 Geary. O'Doul was a local baseball hero who came up through the Pacific Coast League and went to the majors as a pitcher for the Red Sox and the Yankees. After his arm gave out, he played outfield for the Giants and the Phillies, where he batted .398 in 1929 and won the batting crown. O'Douls greatest claim to fame was that he sent Joe DiMaggio from the San Francisco Seals to the Yankees in 1936. Turn right at Mason. The **Native Sons Building** (45) (1911), by Righetti and Headman with E. H. Hildebrand, is an eye-grabber, particularly its columned loggia under a dramatic cornice. The terra-cotta work, some of it blocked from view by the theater marquee, shows scenes from California history. The bas relief portraits of California pioneers are by Jo Moro.

Willis Polk's **Spring Valley Water Company Building** (46) (1922), now the San Francisco Water Department, at 425 Mason evokes an era when the city's water supply was in the hands of a monopolist, Polk's friend William Bowers Bourn II. Polk apparently inspired some fumbling contextualism in the **Donatello Hotel** (47) (1969) next door, with its circular imagery, and the **Pan Pacific Hotel** (48) (1990) by Portman Associates across the street, with its tubular spouts over arched windows outlined with odd metal bars topped by two black balls.

The **First Congregational Church** (49) (1913) on the southwest corner of Post and Mason seems strangely out of place. But this was a primarily residential area at one time, and the church has been located here since 1879. The church was founded by Timothy Dwight Hunt, the city's first and only official chaplain, who arrived in 1848. When Hunt recruited a woman to sing at his services, the locals emptied the gambling halls and streamed to the church, where they packed the room to overflowing to hear the first devout woman's voice that they had heard in a long time. This church, designed by Reid Brothers, was meant to evoke the predominantly neoclassical look of downtown buildings as well as the New England background of its founders.

The **Medico-Dental Building** (50) (1925) on the northeast corner of Post and Mason, by George Kelham and William Merchant, is an interesting contrast with Pflueger's building of a similar type that was designed four years later when the Chicago style was dying out and Pflueger was experimenting with modernity. Turning west on Post, you come to two of the city's most exclusive clubs. The **Olympic Club** (51) (1912) by Paff & Baur at 524 Post, said to be the oldest private athletic club in the nation, is a harmonious assemblage of sandstone, brick, and terra-cotta. The **Bohemian Club** (52) (1934) on the northeast corner of Post and Taylor, by Lewis Hobart, was formed in 1872 by a group of journalists who soon recruited members of the arts world and an occasional enlightened businessman. Many of the great names of late-nineteenth and early-twentieth century Bohemia, such as Ambrose Bierce, Gelett Burgess, Porter Garnett, Jack London, John Muir, Frank Norris, William Keith, and George Sterling, were members of the club. The all-male organization was devoted to having a good time with readings, an array of theatricals, and lots of carousing. Eventually the club was taken over by the city's elite. Most of today's artists wouldn't make it past the front door. The club's annual retreat at the Bohemian Grove in Sonoma County became a gathering place for the global elite, symbolic of the worldwide reach of corporate San Francisco.

Turn left on Taylor. The **Clift Hotel** (53) (1913) on the southeast corner of Taylor and Geary, by MacDonald and Applegarth, is another grand old hotel.

The flat look of the façade is the result of removing the cornice, an earthquake precaution. The hotel's finest feature is the **Redwood Room** designed by G. Albert Lansburgh and Anthony Heinsbergen in the Moderne style in 1935. You may want to take a quick walk west on Geary to see the **Alcazar Theatre** (54) (1917) at 650 Geary Street, an outlandish Islamic fantasy by T. Patterson Ross.

Return east on Geary. Next to the Clift are two of San Francisco's major theaters, the Curran and the Geary. The **Geary** (55), by Bliss and Faville, and the older of the two (1909), is the home of the American Conservatory Theatre, the city's principal dramatic company with a national reputation for developing young talent. Before 1906, San Francisco was a theater town. Eight downtown theaters were destroyed in 1906, but were replaced soon after. By the 1950s, San Francisco's theater belt, centered on Geary Street, could be "more accurately described as a 'garter'," according to newspaper columnist Herb Caen. The Geary's ornate interior with its sunburst chandelier was devastated in the 1989 quake and then restored. Its elaborate terra-cotta exterior is best viewed under the lights at night. The **Curran** (56) (1922), by Alfred Henry Jacobs, is a rerun house. Although more subdued in its exterior design, it fits well with the Geary.

Return to Taylor and turn left. On the northwest corner of Taylor and Ellis is the **Glide Memorial Church** (57), where the Reverend Cecil Williams presided until 1999. Williams is a political force in San Francisco, and the church is known for both its community services and its hard-rocking gospel choir, which performs every Sunday. The new **Cecil Williams Glide Community Home** (58) (1999) next door at 333 Taylor was designed by Michael Willis and Associates and T. C. Moore to accommodate the church's outreach programs and provide housing for homeless people. Note the soaring wing-shaped roof canopy.

Turn left on Ellis. On the northwest corner of Ellis and Cyril Magnin, the building housing the **Hana Zen Restaurant** (59) (1994) by Sadich Mohindroo and Silvan and Siskind is a fine contemporary comment on neo-classical architecture. The long, curving façade starts off with a very narrow front on Eddy Street and then sweeps gracefully up Cyril Magnin. Farther east, **John's Grill** (60) at 63 Ellis is a National Literary Landmark. This classic men's restaurant, now, of course, open to all, is where Sam Spade ate dinner in the *Maltese Falcon*. Author Dashiell Hammett worked in the Flood Building nearby before drinking interfered with his day job. He is alleged to have written part of the *Maltese Falcon* at a table in the restaurant.

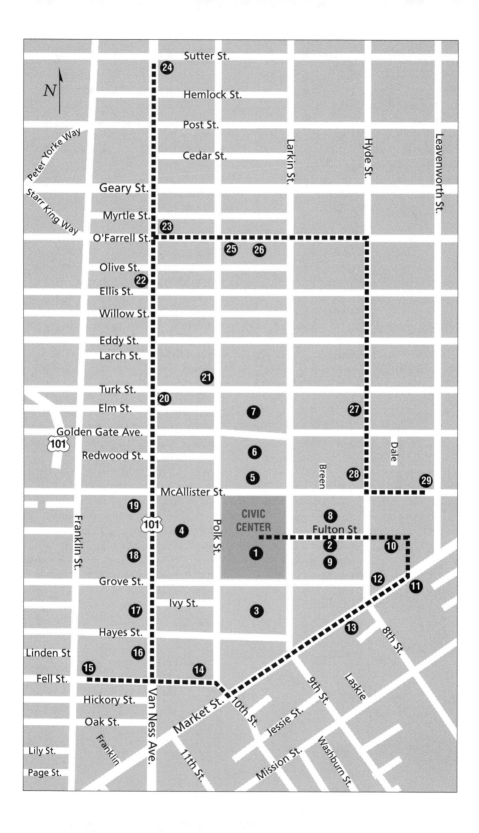

13

The Civic Center

A 1½-hour walk on level ground, except for a gradual climb as you walk north on Van Ness. Docent tours will take additional time. The tour begins at the Civic Center Plaza and ends nearby.

Portsmouth Square was the city's first civic center. But then a group of real estate speculators came up with the idea of moving City Hall to the western edge of the city—now the site of the New Main Library and the Asian Art Museum—to enhance the value of the surrounding property. In 1870, the Board of Supervisors chose the city cemetery, once located here, as the new site for the new City Hall (see illustration on page 51). "It [the cemetery] lies in a hollow among miserable looking sand-hills, which are scantily covered with stunted trees, worthless ground, and is still among the most dreary and melancholy spots that surround the city," wrote the authors of *The Annals of San Francisco.*[58] The dunes were leveled and the bodies were disinterred, causing the first of many scandals connected with the construction project. For it was the practice of the grave diggers, who were paid by the body, to try to make at least two bodies out of each bundle of bones.

This was an era when good government was equated with budgetary frugality. The less money in the public treasury the less there was for politicians to steal, was the prevailing sentiment. So City Hall was to be built for a modest price of $1.5 million, using funds that were to be parceled out over time. A special commission hired Augustus Laver to design the building. Laver had established a reputation as a distinguished architect with the design of the parliament buildings in Ottawa and the New York state capitol in Albany. He submitted a plan that called for a Second Empire structure with a tall clock tower and a mansard roof. Construction commenced in 1872. Critics pointed out that Laver's ambitious design would cost more than the allotted sum. And they were right: The foundation alone cost $600,000. Laver was replaced by John Clifford, an associate of Denis Kearny, a sandlot agitator who often mounted his attacks on corrupt politicians, Nob Hill millionaires, and the Chinese from a crude stage thrown together in the shadow of the construction site. When Clifford turned out to be a fraud—he had secured his appointment with a forged letter purportedly signed by a respected English architect—he was replaced by a committee from the local chapter of the American Institute of Architects. The final result, which cost $6 million dollars and took 24 years to build, looked as though it had been designed by a committee whose members barely spoke the same language. The building accurately reflected its method of construction: It was a patched-together collection of semirelated structures topped by an oddly disproportionate dome.

The City Beautiful movement, an outgrowth of the Chicago Columbian Exposition of 1893, inspired plans for a new civic center for San Francisco. After serving as mayor, James Duvall Phelan headed a committee that hired Chicago architect and city planner Daniel Burnham, chief of construction at the Columbian Exposition and the man most closely associated with the City Beautiful movement, to draft a plan for San Francisco. Burnham's plan called for a civic center at the intersection of Market and Van Ness. Public buildings, including a new City Hall, would be built around a semicircular plaza with a monument at the intersection. Burnham's plan, illustrated by Willis Polk, gained new supporters after City Hall suffered major damage in the 1906 earthquake and was gutted by fire. The plan, however, was defeated at the ballot box in 1909.

In 1908 the city had renewed its efforts to persuade Congress to make it the site for an exposition to celebrate the opening of the Panama Canal. San Francisco's civic leaders wanted to use the exposition to send the message that this Pacific Rim capital was once again open for business. Plans for a new civic center could not be allowed to die. Three years later James "Sunny Jim" Rolph ran successfully for mayor on a platform that called for another civic center bond measure. The measure passed overwhelmingly, and Rolph appointed an advisory committee made up of University of California architecture professor John Galen Howard and architects Frederick Meyer and

John Reid Jr. The advisory committee reviewed the Burnham-Polk plan and another submitted by British-born architect B. J. S. Cahill, which called for a civic center defined by Van Ness, McAllister, Hyde, and Grove streets, with a new City Hall on Van Ness between Grove and McAllister, a civic auditorium, a public library, a state office building, an opera house, a civic center power plant, and the fire, police, and health departments. The Civic Center was conceived in the spirit of the Burnham Plan, Howard acknowledged, but it was Cahill's plan that came closest to the final results.

Writing about the plan, Howard reviewed the history of civic centers dating back to ancient Greece, but said nothing about architectural style. It appears to have been an unspoken, but obviously very large, assumption that the style would be neoclassical inasmuch as that was the dominant if waning architectural fashion and many of the city's leading architects were graduates of the École des Beaux-Arts.

To begin this two-decade-long construction project—the first phase of Civic Center construction—Howard, Meyer, and Reid designed the first building, the Civic Auditorium, now known as the Bill Graham Civic Auditorium. With an eye to the tourist and convention business that would be inspired by the Panama Pacific International Exposition, the business community contributed $1 million for its construction. The Civic Auditorium was finished in 1915, with City Hall completed according to a design by John Bakewell Jr. and Arthur Brown Jr. in the same year. The Civic Center Plaza, later named for Mayor Rolph, was completed soon after.

Construction on the Main Library (now the Asian Art Museum) was delayed by the San Francisco Labor Council's hatred of Andrew Carnegie, who had offered the city $750,000 toward a new main library and several new branches in 1901. Carnegie was regarded as an enemy of organized labor because of his close association with Henry Clay Frick. Frick had crushed a strike at Carnegie's Homestead steel mill in 1892, during which Pinkerton detectives had fired into a crowd, killing nine workers. The San Francisco Labor Council maintained that Carnegie's money had been earned "by notoriously questionable means," which reflected his "cruel, heartless and degrading policy toward his employees." However, when the question of whether to accept Carnegie's money was put on the ballot in 1913, San Franciscans voted two to one to take it. With funds in hand, the library's trustees organized a design competition whose jury awarded the contract to George Kelham, the architect who had made a name for himself after coming to town to supervise the construction of the second Palace Hotel. The library was completed in 1917, but not until one contestant sued, arguing that Kelham had copied the design of juror Cass Gilbert for the Detroit Public Library. Three more buildings were added in the 1920s: a state office building, a power plant, and the city health department. The first phase of construction of the Civic Center was complete, with the exception of the opera house.

THE HIGH ARTS

Civic Center planners set Marshall Square aside for a new opera house. San Franciscans since the days of the gold rush were mad for opera, but the city lacked both a company and a truly grand venue for performances. The locals were instead dependent on touring companies and visiting performers. In conjunction with the construction of the Civic Center, opera supporters raised funds for a permanent home based on drawings by Willis Polk. However, the arrangement between the city and the private builders of the opera house was found to be in violation of the city charter. In a fit of populism Mayor Rolph denounced the opera as undemocratic and calculated to encourage aristocratic pretensions. Later, Rolph calmed down, promising that a new opera house would be built in Marshall Square. In 1918 opera supporters raised $2 million for a new house, and Major Charles Kendrick proposed building the opera house as a memorial to World War I veterans. In 1923, Gaetano Merola formed the San Francisco Opera Company, and four years later a bond measure was passed providing funding for the War Memorial complex—two buildings, one an opera house, the other an auditorium with additional space for a museum and veterans groups. The complex, moved to the west side of Van Ness between McAllister and Grove, was designed by Bakewell and Brown.

The opening of the War Memorial Opera House in 1932 marked the beginning of a significant cultural transition for San Francisco. The Opera House became home to the San Francisco Symphony, which had been founded in 1911, and then the Opera Ballet, later the San Francisco Ballet Company, the oldest professional ballet company in the country. San Francisco's wealthiest families, who in the era of the Comstock lode epitomized conspicuous consumption and freewheeling philistinism, were now committing their considerable wealth to high culture. Once again San Francisco, despite its size, aspired to world-class status, and the Civic Center would become the center of the high arts.

The federal government joined the Civic Center complex in 1936 with the construction of a building in the block east of the library, also designed by Bakewell and Brown. In the years after the war, the Civic Center, renowned as the most complete example of a civic complex in the Beaux-Arts style in the United States, fell on hard times. There were more public employees at all three levels of government, hence the need for more buildings, but the public seemed to shun the Civic Center. The library suffered from particular neglect. The city's first families were able to find the money to build the ballet, opera, and symphony into institutions with national and international reputations, but neither the city's philanthropists nor its politicians could come up with funds to run a decent public library system in a city with a long history of literary accomplishments.

THE SECOND PHASE OF CONSTRUCTION

To meet the need for more space for government offices in the 1950s, the Department of City Planning turned to modernist design ideas for new public buildings. The neoclassical design of the Civic Center's buildings, according to *An Introductory Plan for the Civic Center* (1953), evoked an era when "the search for a native architectural style had hardly begun...when the greatest achievement in civic reconstruction, the opening of the boulevards of Paris by Haussmann, was still fresh and accepted uncritically as a model for all civic building endeavors." The Department suggested construction of "new buildings of simple and straightforward design."[59] In 1958 two well-known modernist firms, Skidmore Owings Merrill (SOM) and Wurster, Bernardi & Emmons, drew up a plan for the Civic Center calling for a second ring of buildings around the Civic Plaza. The drawings in the report, although meant only to be suggestive, show buildings of glass and steel in a sleek, horizontal style. On its way to orthodoxy, the International Style, which never was "a native architectural style," was having an impact in American cities, and this was one year before the first two modernist office buildings, both designed by SOM, would be built downtown. Modernism reached the Civic Center in 1959, the same year that SOM's Crown Zellerbach Building went up. The result was the Phillip Burton Federal Building, a tall, characterless slab with gestures of verticality that overshadowed the Civic Center. With the federal government breaking through the Civic Center skyline, a number of tall, poorly designed buildings followed, including Fox Plaza on Market between Ninth and Tenth, which was built after the demolition of the Fox Theatre, one of the city's grand old movie houses. For a time it looked as though the Civic Center would be surrounded and darkened by towering tombstones.

THE POLITICS OF CULTURE

The first civic building constructed in the spirit of the 1958 plan was the Davies Symphony Hall. It was conceived amid controversy: Mayor Joseph Alioto backed the symphony's effort to locate its new hall in Marshall Square, which had been promised for a new main library. By the late 1950s the public library was being branded a national disgrace. To remedy the situation, a handful of library supporters led by three very strong-minded women formed a new Friends organization and in the early 1960s secured a vague commitment from the city to build a new main library in Marshall Square. However, no one in city hall would back a bond measure for the ballot.

In 1974, Alioto called the president of the Library Commission to his office and introduced him to three of the symphony's most powerful backers:

Samuel Stewart, retired vice chairman of the board of the Bank of America, Gwinn Follis, retired chairman of Standard Oil of California, and Harold Zellerbach, retired chairman of Crown Zellerbach. Alioto explained that these gentlemen proposed to build a new symphony hall in Marshall Square. Taken aback, the commission president stood his ground, suggesting that Symphony Hall be built at the corner of Grove and Van Ness, which is where it ultimately was built—but not until the Friends of the Library mounted a grass roots campaign to save Marshall Square for a new main library.

In designing Davies Symphony Hall, named for Louise Davies, the symphony's most generous benefactor—SOM followed its own suggestions in the 1958 plan. Although modernist and thus devoid of ornamentation in contrast to the highly ornamented Beaux-Arts buildings of the inner Civic Center, it neither overwhelmed nor clashed with these earlier structures. The same can be said of the new state office building on the corner of McAllister and Van Ness, which was also designed by SOM and completed in 1984. And, finally, in its finest contribution to the Civic Center, SOM designed another state office building that stands between the Burton Federal Building and the 1926 State Office Building on the north side of the Plaza.

After the construction of Symphony Hall, library supporters pressed doggedly ahead with their plans for a new main building. The library system improved for a time, but the passage of Proposition 13, the statewide tax cut initiative, in 1978 threatened the system, particularly its branches, as never before. When a consultant recommended the closing of some of the branches in 1982, the neighborhoods responded with a torrent of disapproval, enough to convince Mayor Dianne Feinstein to increase the library's budget and keep all branches open. Feinstein quickly learned what the Friends already knew: There was widespread support in the community for protecting and improving the library system. The Friends convinced the mayor to see the construction of a new library in Marshall Square as part of the completion of the Civic Center. Plans at first called for the Museum of Modern Art (MOMA) to move into the old library, but when MOMA abandoned the Civic Center for the Yerba Buena complex, the Asian Art Museum was invited to move into the library. In a final state of the city speech in 1987, Mayor Feinstein called for the completion of the Civic Center with a new main library in Marshall Square.

Funds to build the library were raised by a public bond measure, but the library had to be furnished with private donations. With no history of significant philanthropic support, the public library, its fund-raising consultants found out, would be competing with the city's elite cultural institutions. The ballet, opera, and symphony "are perceived as the causes of choice," the consultants concluded. "They are more often patronized by such donors, most of whom, while voicing a belief in the importance of libraries, never enter the San Francisco library or its branches." [65]

Undaunted, the leaders of the New Main Campaign turned conventional approaches to fund-raising ideas on their head after encountering resistance from a number of the city's wealthiest philanthropists. Rather than secure donations from large donors first, the New Main Campaign encouraged library supporters to organize a series of grass roots campaigns mirroring the way in which the city is organized politically. In the spirit of friendly competition, various affinity groups—African-American, Hispanic-Latino, gay and lesbian, and others—raised millions from small donors, ultimately convincing the city's big philanthropists that they should support the New Main effort too. The New Main Library, a striking though controversial addition to the Civic Center, opened in April 1996. In 1998, with the opening of a new Civil Courts Building at the corner of Polk and McAllister, the Civic Center was completed.

TO PRESERVE OR NOT TO PRESERVE

Recent changes to the Civic Center, a national landmark, have stirred repeated controversies over the responsibilities of preservationists. The Pioneer Monument, the last artifact from the pre-1906 city hall complex, until recently stood at its original site at the corner of Hyde, Grove, and Market just east of the Grove Street entrance to the library (see illustration on page 5). When the New Main Library was being designed in the early 1990s, architect James Ingo Freed hoped to propitiate preservationists by building the new structure around the monument. And there was yet another perspective. Native Americans have long been offended by one of the four groups of statues that surround the monument. This group shows a supine Indian being urged by a Franciscan with an uplighted finger to do something in a heavenly direction while a white settler looks on. At the hearings on the monument, one Native leader suggested tossing it into the ocean. Freed found that he would have to reduce the size of the library substantially to incorporate the monument. It was decided, over the objection of a number of preservationists, to move the monument to the middle of Fulton Street between the New Main Library and the Asian Art Museum.

The next controversy was stirred up by plans to retrofit and restore City Hall after the 1989 quake. The quake torqued City Hall's majestic dome, buckling steel girders in the drum, cracking masonry piers and hollow tile walls, and showering the inside of the building with plaster and stone fragments. No one was injured, but a stronger shock or a few more seconds of shaking, according to structural engineers, might have brought the whole structure down on hundreds of city employees. To restore City Hall, architects and engineers embarked on one of the most ambitious retrofit and restoration projects ever undertaken. First, the 171-million-pound structure had to be jacked up and braced while its 530 steel supporting columns were sawed off at the base and then set down on base isolators, shock-absorbing devices that look like giant motor mounts, made of steel and rubber. New foundations were poured, thousands of pounds of new steel and concrete were added, and the building was restored at the cost of $293 million. Mayor Willie Brown insisted on restoring the building to its original splendor, which meant removing a rabbit warren of offices from two grand skylit assembly rooms on the main floor. Brown, known for his love of elegant parties, was accused of providing new entertainment space for his wealthy backers at public expense.

Across the Civic Center Plaza at the new Asian Art Museum, preservationists lost a major battle to protect the integrity of the old Main Library after the museum announced plans by Italian architect Gae Aulenti to make major changes to the interior and exterior of the building to accommodate what is arguably the greatest collection of Asian art in the Western world. Both the interior and exterior were supposedly protected by the building's national landmark status. Aulenti, known for her conversion of the Gare d'Dorsay from a railroad station into the Musée d'Orsay, proposed gutting the interior of the building, retaining only the main staircase and one of three grand rooms on the second floor. Her plans also called for the removal of historic murals by Gotardo Piazzoni and Frank du Mond—all in a structure supposedly protected by National Landmark status. These plans were vehemently opposed by the Landmarks Preservation Board, the National Trust for Historic Preservations, San Francisco Heritage, and dozens of preservation professionals around the world as being in clear violation of the city's planning code. The code requires that alterations of landmark buildings adhere to standards spelled out by the Secretary of the Interior. With Mayor Brown showing little interest in preservation issues beyond the restoration of City Hall, the Planning Commission upheld the museum's proposal and Heritage's legal challenge was denied in the courts. Facing a powerful, well-connected museum board, wealthy and influential donors such as Senator Dianne Feinstein and her husband Richard Blum, and no prospect of support from the mayor, the preservation community abandoned its opposition to the museum's plans.

With the resolution of the dispute over the future of the Asian Art Museum, there is one more job left in the Civic Center: the restoration of the Plaza itself to its original glory, a financial burden that San Francisco voters have so far refused to shoulder.

For a true appreciation of the **Civic Center,** start in the **Plaza** (1), which is bounded by Grove, Polk, McAllister, and Larkin, and look around. The pre-1906 City Hall and a separate, circular structure called the Hall of Records occupied the two blocks on the east side of the Plaza where the Asian Art Museum and the New Main Library now stand. In the middle of Fulton Street between the New Main and the Asian Art Museum is the **Pioneer Monument** (2) (1894) on the site to which it was moved during the construction of the library. The monument is the work of sculptor Frank Happersberger. Despite the recent addition of a plaque on the east side of the monument that disclaimer on a plaque on the east side of the monument, from time to time mysterious individuals express their dislike of the racial symbolism of the reclining Native American figure in the easternmost group of statuary by coating it with red paint.

On the south side of the Plaza is the **Bill Graham Civic Auditorium** (3) (1915) designed by John Galen Howard, Fred Meyers, and John Reid Jr. Clad in California granite, as are all the buildings in the Civic Center, it is a fairly conventional example of French High Baroque Revival. It is also evocative of a time when a relatively small building such as this could be used for conventions. Among the memorable events staged here were the 1920 Democratic Party convention, at which elegantly dressed hostesses kept the delegates supplied from 60 barrels of excellent bourbon, which, according to journalist H. L. Mencken, were charged to the tab of the local smallpox hospital. For many years the auditorium was the site of the infamous Grateful Dead New Year's Eve Concerts.

City Hall (4) (1915) is the true masterpiece of the Civic Center (see illustration on page 131). The design was actually rendered by Arthur Brown Jr., John

Bakewell serving as the managing partner in the firm. Brown, who was a student of Bernard Maybeck and a graduate of the École des Beaux-Arts, took his ideas from the Church of Les Invalides in Paris, which was built in the seventeenth century and then became Napoleon's tomb. The 308-foot-high dome was designed so that it would be taller by about a dozen feet than the capitol dome in Washington. The sculpture is by Henri Crenier, and much of the interior design was done by Jean Louis Bourgeois. Skilled craftsmen were imported from France and Italy to work on City Hall as well as a number of buildings being constructed for the Panama Pacific International Exposition. The central staircase surmounted by the dome is truly inspiring. Brown designed the structure around two light courts that open onto skylights over ceremonial chambers. The southern chamber houses a small city museum. The spectacular legislative chamber of the Board of Supervisors at the top of the stairs is paneled in Manchurian oak and is open to the public at meeting times. The mayor's office and connected meeting rooms on the Polk Street side of the building on the second floor are also paneled in Manchurian oak, but are less accessible to the public. Tours are available.

Bliss and Faville's **State Office Building** (5) (1926) on the north side of the Plaza was never meant to be as impressive as City Hall, but the **New State Office Building** (6) (1999) designed by Skidmore Owings Merrill (SOM) is the most pleasing modern addition to the Civic Center. Using the same granite in its façade and plenty of glass, this gracefully curved structure provides a striking but not overpowering transition from the neoclassicism of the 1926 building to the ugly modernism of the **Phillip Burton Federal Building** (7) (1959) designed by Albert

The New State Office Building provides a backdrop for the Old State Office Building and a screen to hide the Federal Building in the rear. *Peter Booth Wiley.*

The new loggia inside the Asian Art Museum. In a move opposed by preservationists, historic murals were removed and most of the old Main Library was gutted to create a modern museum space. *Asian Art Museum.*

Roller, Stone Marraccini & Patterson, and John Carl Warnecke, while successfully screening it from viewers in the Civic Center Plaza.

On the east size of the Plaza is the **Asian Art Museum** (8), which was originally designed by George Kelham to house the Main Library. The old main library has an interesting architectural patrimony stretching back to the Bibliothèque Ste. Geneviève in Paris, one of the first Beaux-Arts structures, by way of the Boston and Detroit main libraries. Kelham designed the interior to resemble an Italian Renaissance palazzo, with two readings rooms with beamed ceilings. To accommodate the Asian Art Museum, scheduled to open in the fall of 2002, the building was redesigned by Italian architect Gae Aulenti in association with Hellmuth, Obata & Kassabaum, LDA Architects, and Robert Wong. Aulenti retained the façade while giving the building a new heart. This will be accomplished by transforming the entrance hall and grand staircase, which is topped by a loggia, into a central light court. Aulenti

also inserted an additional floor into the structure by putting a mezzanine around the former library's two main reading rooms.

To the right of the Asian Art Museum is the **New Main Library** (9) (1996) by Pei Cobb Freed & Partners and Simon Martin-Vegue Winkelstein Moris. Confronted with the problem of fitting his design into the context of the Beaux-Arts Civic Center, James Ingo Freed, who designed the Holocaust Museum in Washington, D.C., decided to offer a second design motif for those parts of the building facing Market Street. The façades along Grove and Hyde evoke the modernist boxes along Market Street, and the curtain wall façade on Larkin and Fulton is Freed's commentary on the neoclassical Asian Art Museum. To retain this sense of bipolarity, Freed cantilevered the periodical reading room out into the atrium, aligning it with the streets south of Market. The stainless steel columns topped with I-beams in the Larkin and Fulton Street façades are Freed's comment on structural elements in the building. Freed

The "neoclassical" curtain wall on the New Main Library. *Peter Booth Wiley.*

was encouraged to design a grand building, and indeed the building features a large central atrium and several multistory reading rooms wonderfully illuminated with natural light. However, Freed did not include enough space for the library's collection nor proper workspace for back office employees. The building is undergoing a redesign of the interior. The **San Francisco History Room** is on the sixth floor. On the same floor, there is a special kiosk where you can view "Shaping San Francisco," a multimedia presentation of the city's history.

Walk east between the New Main Library and the Asian Art Museum into **United Nations Plaza** (10). The **Federal Building** (1936) on the left is a testament to the staying power of the Beaux-Arts tradition, employed here again by Bakewell and Brown two decades after designing City Hall. The Plaza and fountain by Lawrence Halprin (1980) memorialize the signing of the United Nations Charter in the Herbst Theatre at the War Memorial Performing Arts Complex in June 1945.

Turn right on Market Street; directly across from the fountain is **One Trinity Center** (11), a successful postmodern work by Backen, Arrigoni & Ross from 1989. The European style **Caffé Trinity** on the first floor features **murals by Carlo Marchiori** (1992). Farther west on Market on the right side of the street is the **Orpheum Theatre** (12) (1926), which was designed by B. Marcus Priteca as a vaudeville theater for Alexander Pantages. Priteca took his ideas for the Moorish façade from the twelfth-century cathedral in Leon, Spain, and the lobby was inspired by a palace in the Alhambra. Succumbing to changing times, Pantages went out of business and the Orpheum became a movie house in 1929. The interior, which was restored in 1998 for Broadway shows, is filled with elaborate carving

and relief work. For some reason, the city and the Shorenstein family, owners of the Orpheum, the Curran, and the Golden Gate theaters, have never been able to settle on what to do with the ugly blank wall at the back of the building that frowns on the United Nations Plaza.

Continue west on Market, noting the modernist backside of the New Main Library. The **Ramada Plaza Hotel** (13) at 1231 Market was once the Whitcomb Hotel, which was built quickly after the 1906 earthquake and served as city hall for a time. Turn right at an oblique angle onto Fell Street where Polk meets Market. The **New College of California School of Law** (14) (1932) at 50 Fell is a Spanish Revival work by Willis Polk. Continue west on Fell, crossing Van Ness. The original **High School of Commerce** (15) (c. 1912), the boarded-up building on the northeast corner of Fell and Franklin, was built after the 1906 earthquake at Grove and Larkin across from what is now the New Main Library. It was moved almost immediately to this site. Return to Van Ness and turn left. This 1927 addition to the former High School of Commerce at 135 Van Ness, which now houses offices of the **San Francisco Unified School District** (16), was designed by John Reid Jr. as part of the larger Civic Center complex. The Moorish structure will be retrofitted and redesigned to accommodate the School of the Arts, the city's public high school for the arts. The school district is threatening to tear down the original School of Commerce in the process, a move opposed by preservationists. Further north on Van Ness on the left is **Davies Symphony Hall** (17), designed by SOM in 1981. SOM designed the building to showcase City Hall. The three floors of glass-fronted lobbies serve as viewing platforms from which a concert-goer's gaze is directed toward the dome. The building

The Louise M. Davies Symphony Hall. *Peter Booth Wiley.*

interior is sleek and understated in cream and salmon colors. The hall itself, however, has proved less than successful acoustically. It has been the subject of a series of auditory retoolings, which have included moving its walls inward, placing seats behind the stage, and hanging plastic shields and devices that look like rumpled window shades from the ceiling. The hall also features the largest pipe organ in any concert hall in North America. The horizontal jug handles on the exterior are unfortunate.

The **Opera House** (18) (1932) was designed by Arthur Brown Jr., its interior the work of G. Albert Lansburgh. Brown drew inspiration from Garnier's Opera House in Paris, but he specifically rejected some of the characteristics of other grand opera houses. The auditorium, Brown argued, was for viewing the performance, not for the audience to view itself. Thus, he faced the boxes forward in a wonderfully

curved balcony rather than placing them in a horseshoe facing each other and eliminated the grand staircase where members of the local aristocracy were wont to strut and preen. The lobby, with its arched ceiling, rosettes, and sandstone columns, is particularly noteworthy. The abundance of gold in the interior is actually due to the widespread application of Dutch metal, an alloy made up of 90 percent copper and 10 percent zinc. Gold leaf was reserved for the large masks on either side of the proscenium arch, the decorative detail in the arch itself, and the wood and plaster molding in the boxes. The silver sunburst chandelier set in an oval opening in the auditorium ceiling was Lansburgh's one concession to modernism.

A companion structure to the north of the Opera House is the **Veterans Building** (19) (1932), also the work of Bakewell and Brown. The building was

The War Memorial Opera House. *Peter Booth Wiley.*

designed to provide space for veterans organizations, an arts museum, and the Herbst Theatre. The **Performing Arts Library and Museum** is located on the fourth floor. The **Herbst Theatre** was designed as a small recital hall around the murals of Frank Brangwin, which were removed from the Panama Pacific International Exposition before its buildings were torn down. The Herbst Theatre was the location of the signing of the United Nations Charter in 1945. A tour of the Symphony Hall, Opera House, and Veterans Building is available.

Walk north on Van Ness, noting the bright yellow **Tenderloin Elementary School and Community Center** (20) with marvelous decorative tilework by schoolchildren on the east side of Van Ness between Golden Gate and Turk. This was the final work of noted architect Joseph Esherick before his death in 1998. The school marks the transformation of the Tenderloin into a family neighborhood populated by Southeast Asians. The school's vibrant color scheme inspired MacDonald's to brighten up its building too. One block to the east on Turk at the corner of Polk is the former German Association Building (1913), now **California Hall** (21), by Frederick Meyer. This Teutonic hulk includes a rathskeller in the basement where students at the California Culinary Academy operate a restaurant.

Return to Van Ness and continue north to **Automobile Row.** American infatuation with new technologies found architectural expression in the elaborate movie houses of the 1920s and the automobile showroom. On the left at 901 Van Ness is the former **Earl C. Anthony Packard Showroom** (22) (1927), now a Jaguar dealer, by Bernard Maybeck. The white columns are actually red marble that has been painted over. In walking west, you can see the former Cadillac showroom (1923), now the **AMC Theatres** (23) at 1000 Van Ness, the work of Weeks and Day. Note the bears on the columns and the elaborate interior tile work. This stretch of Van Ness was the site of civil rights

Bernard Maybeck's drawing for the Earle C. Anthony automobile showroom, 901 Van Ness. *Documents Collection, College of Environmental Design, University of California–Berkeley.*

demonstrations in 1964 that challenged the all-white hiring practices of the automobile dealers. Three blocks further at Van Ness and Sutter is the **Galaxy Theatre** (24) (1986). This wonderful collection of glass boxes is the work of Kaplan, McLauglin, Diaz.

Walk east on O'Farrell. Since the 1970s, the **Mitchell Brothers Theatre** (25) on the southeast corner of Polk and O'Farrell has offered the city's most notorious sex shows. A number of well-known x-rated films were shot here. After years of drugs and dissolution one brother murdered the other. The **Great American Musical Hall** (26) at 859 O'Farrell opened as a French restaurant and bordello in 1907. Since 1972 it has been one of the city's premier music venues graced by the likes of Duke Ellington, Jerry Garcia, Van Morrison, Etta James, Joe Pass, Maynard Ferguson, and Stephane Grapelli. Turn right on Hyde. You are in the heart of one of San

Francisco's newest neighborhoods, where recent immigrants, many from Cambodia and Vietnam, rub shoulders with low-income retirees, ex-cons, and street people. There are numerous restaurants to explore. In the 1930s, Hyde Street was the center of the city's small film industry. The Deco buildings at **245, 251, 255, and 259 Hyde** (27) by the O'Brien brothers and **125 Hyde** (28) by Wilbur Peugh, all built in 1930s, were early film studios. Bay Area musical legends such as Creedence Clearwater, the Grateful Dead, the Jefferson Airplane, and Carlos Santana recorded albums at **Wally Heider's Studios** at 245 Hyde. Continue south on Hyde and make a left turn on McAllister. The former **William Taylor Hotel** (29) by Miller and Pflueger (1929) at 100 McAllister was built by the Methodist Church to provide its members with a "dry" hotel and a chapel in an otherwise sinful city.

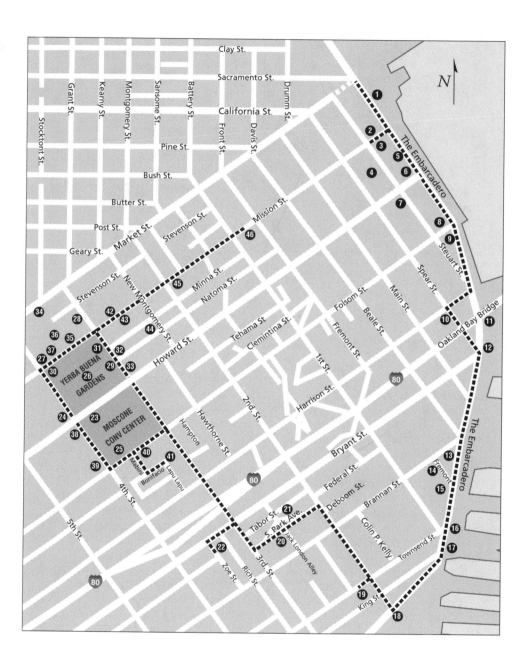

14

South of Market

This is a long walk over level ground, except for the gradual climb up and over Rincon Hill along Second Street. Three to four hours. The tour begins in front of the Ferry Building and ends at First and Mission.

Start in front of the Ferry Building at the foot of Market Street. Walk south along the Embarcadero past the Agricultural Building at 101 Embarcadero. From here south, the **Herb Caen Promenade** (1)—named after the city's most famous newspaper columnist, who died in 1998—runs along the seawall. Since the disappearance of shipping activity along the northern waterfront, the city is converting selected parcels on the east side of the Embarcadero into waterfront park.

Cross the Embarcadero at Mission and walk west to the intersection of Steuart and Missions Streets. On the northeast corner of Mission and Steuart is the **International Longshore and Warehouse Union's monument** (2) to

strikers killed in the 1934 General Strike. From this intersection a police officer fired into a crowd of men in front of strike headquarters in the **Audiffred Building** (3) on the southeast corner, killing two and injuring one. The monument, a series of acrylic paintings on steel plates, was done by a group of Mission District artists to memorialize Howard Sperry and Nick Bordoies, the two men killed, on the 50th anniversary of the 1934 strike. Now home to the **Boulevard Restaurant,** the Audiffred Building, once abandoned and fire-scarred, is one of the few reminders of the pre-1906 waterfront. Designed by William Cullen, it was built in 1889 by Hippolite Audiffred, evoking similar buildings in his native France. It has

The Audiffred Building, Mission and the Embarcadero. *Peter Booth Wiley.*

been a sailors' saloon, the first head-quarters of the Sailors' Union of the Pacific, and served as the strike committee's headquarters during the General Strike of 1934.

Across Steuart is the **Rincon Center and Towers** (4). The old Rincon Center post office, designed by Gilbert Stanley Underwood, was built in the Moderne style by the Public Works Administration in 1939–1940. It is the site of significant **murals by Anton Refregier** (1948) depicting the history of the state and the city. Refregier, a Russian-born leftist, set out to create a series of paintings based on the Works Progress Administration guide to San Francisco. Forced to make dozens of changes— deleting references to a successful strike and improving the physical appearance of Native Americans (judged to be too thin) and a priest (judged to be too fat), for example—Refregier needed seven years to complete his work. Fain and Johnson of Pereira Associates designed

Rincon Towers (1988) to include the post office as a forecourt. Behind the post office there is a large central atrium where a fountain, surrounded by various eating establishments, rains from the ceiling.

Return along Mission Street to the Embarcadero and turn right. The **YMCA** (5) at 166 Embarcadero was designed by Carl Werner in 1924. To the south, Tower Architects created a nautical bookend for the larger YMCA with **Bayside Plaza** (6) at 188 Embarcadero. Turn right at Howard. The **Folger Coffee Company Building** (7) (1905) at 101 Howard (southwest corner) was designed by Henry Schulze. Its construction marked a transition in structural design and the use of materials in warehouses, which resulted in only minimal damage in the earthquakes of 1906 and 1989. The first warehouses were prefabricated metal structures imported at the time of the gold rush. After the fires of the early 1850s, the next warehouses featured thick brick walls sitting on granite foundations with iron shutters to protect their contents from fire. Reinforced concrete was used as early as the 1880s, but was widely used only after World War I. The Folger Building is brick around a steel frame sitting on concrete and granite foundations. Built on fill, 40-foot wooden pilings were driven into mud so that they remained below water level to keep them from deteriorating. They were topped with concrete pile caps and then surrounded by 12 to 18 inches of concrete. Brick and concrete were used as piers for steel channel columns. The building was a combination office, coffee manufacturing, and warehouse space.

The Folger Company was the oldest family-owned coffee importing business in San Francisco. San Francisco was once one of the largest coffee importing and processing centers in the world. Folger introduced San Franciscans to Central American coffee beans at the Panama Pacific International Exposition in 1915. By the late 1930s Folger had offices in El Salvador and Mexico, establishing one of the early links that brought Central Americans to San Francisco.

Walk south on Steuart and turn left on Folsom. The new **Gap Building** (8) designed by Robert Stern going up on the left is to be completed in early 2001. This building is a monument to the emergence of Donald Fisher, founder and chairman of The Gap clothing chain, as one of the city's most influential movers and shakers. Robert Stern was one of the first architects to use the term postmodern and is one of the foremost exponents of contextualism. For context, Stern studied the

From the left, Hills Plaza and the Gap Building. This illustration and one of Pacific Bell Stadium on page 266 show the impact of height limits on skyline, which declines in altitude as one moves south. *The Gap.*

neighborhood's brick warehouses, the Ferry Building tower, and the Hills Brothers building to the south. The Gap was able to acquire this premium piece of property at a substantial discount from the San Francisco Redevelopment Agency. In exchange, The Gap is paying for a 2-acre park on the east side of the Embarcadero, which is being designed by Lauri Olin and will feature a sculpture of Cupid's bow and arrow by Claes Oldenburg. The San Francisco Redevelopment Agency (SFRA) is developing plans to turn Folsom Street into **Folsom Boulevard,** widening the street from the waterfront to the Moscone Convention Center.

On the south side of Folsom fronting on the Embarcadero is **Hills Plaza** (9). The north end of the blockwide complex is a modern tower and office building designed by Whisler-Patri in 1992. The original Hills Brothers Coffee Factory (1933), another major importer of coffee, lies to the south. It was designed by George Kelham in a Romanesque Revival style. Turn right off the Embarcadero on Harrison. The **Hathaway Warehouse** (10), one of the oldest warehouses on the waterfront, is at the southwest corner of Harrison and Spear. It was originally a one-story building dating from the 1850s; a second floor was added in 1891.

SOUTH BEACH

Continue south on Spear, passing under the Bay Bridge. The cable anchorage for the west end of the Bay Bridge sits atop what is left of Rincon Hill, once San Francisco's most fashionable neighborhood. South of the Bay Bridge, you come to the first of a number of new residential complexes that face the Bay and will eventually extend to the new developments in the Mission Bay Project. Many of these units are part of an SFRA plan to provide affordable residences. This area, known as **South**

The Delancey Street Center, the Embarcadero and Brannan Street. *Beau Wiley.*

The new Oriental Warehouse after Fisher Friedman Associates nested live-work spaces inside the burned out walls of the old warehouse. *Charles Callister.*

Beach, was home to a number of shipyards in the early days of the city and later was one of the most active parts of the waterfront. Note the two remaining **Mission Revival bulkhead buildings** (11) at Piers 26 and 28 under the bridge. The **Boondocks Restaurant** and **Red's Java House** (12) just to the south are typical of the dozens of bars and greasy spoons that once served sailors and longshoremen along the waterfront. These may not last as there are plans to build an elaborate cruise ship terminal here. Also note the square **black and white pillars** along the east side of the Embarcadero. These display historical information and photographs about South Beach.

Continuing south along the Embarcadero, you come to the **Delancey Street Center** (13) (1992) just south of Brannan, designed by Bracken Arrigoni & Ross in the Mediterranean Revival style. Known for its work with drug addicts and ex-convicts, the Delancey Street Foundation is one of the most successful social rehabilitation organizations in the country. Eighty percent of the work on the complex, which includes residences, the Foundation's offices, a restaurant, a meeting hall, and a movie theater, was done by residents; numerous program graduates who went into the construction business contributed time and materials to bring the buildings in at half their estimated cost. Just south of the Delancey Street complex, turn right. Behind Delancey Street is the **Oriental Warehouse** (14) (1868). In 1996 Fisher Friedman Associates nested 66 live-work lofts within the walls of the old warehouse. The Pacific Mail Steamship Company built the warehouse to store items, such as tea, silk, and coffee, arriving from Asia. The land south of here was once **Steamboat Point,** the site of the Pacific Mail's piers, warehouses, machine shops, and coal yards. The Pacific Mail operated 25 steamships and brought most of the Chinese workers who arrived in the nineteenth century

Pacific Bell Park, the new home of the San Francisco Giants. *San Francisco Giants.*

through this area into the city. The warehouse was heavily damaged in the 1989 earthquake and two later fires before being redeemed by Fisher Friedman. Fisher Friedman also designed **Bayside Village** (15) (1991) and **South Beach Marina** south and west of the Oriental Warehouse.

Cross the Embarcadero at Townsend and walk toward the sailing ship sitting atop the piers, passing the **Java House** (16) another old greasy spoon. The **Sailing Ship Restaurant** (17) was built in France in 1862 and later chartered by Jules Verne when he was doing research for *Twenty Thousand Leagues Under the Sea.* The Embarcadero ends at the new **Pacific Bell Park** (18) (2000), home of the San Francisco Giants. The stadium is the fourth major league facility designed by HOK Sports to resemble baseball parks of the past. A four-story prefabricated brick curtain wall, with plenty of glass between the columns, surrounds steel bleachers surmounted by light towers. The stadium designers were presented with an odd-shaped lot running along the waterfront and the usual wind problems. The result is a stadium positioned to block the wind with a short right field fence (307 feet at the foul pole), a deep alley in right center (420 feet), and a longer left field line

(335 feet). There is a waterfront walkway south of the stadium, with an open fence through which strollers can watch games. The Giants' decision to move to an urban setting triggered a real estate boom in the area, which still includes numerous brick warehouses, and promises to add to the congestion in a rapidly growing neighborhood. There is plenty of public transit nearby, but will the fans use it?

WAREHOUSES AND LOFTS

Across from the ballpark, walk north on Second Street to the intersection with Townsend. You are entering one of the city's most intact warehouse districts. To the right, the **Townsend Building** (19) (1904) at 123 Townsend is typical of the brick warehouses in the area. With walls 16 inches thick, it was built for the Southern Pacific by the Haslett Warehouse Company, the largest warehouse company in the city. To its immediate right is another **Haslett warehouse** (1911), this one designed by MacDonald and Applegarth and built of reinforced concrete.

Continue north on Second and turn left into **South Park** (20). Nothing remains of the city's first upscale housing development laid out by George

Gordon in 1856, except the park itself (see illustration on page 29). South Park, with its smart cafes and restaurants, is the heart of Multimedia Gulch. Scattered along the alleys from here west are examples of the newest live-work architecture, some of which evoke the early years of modernism with their clean, streamlined look. Levy Design Partners conceived **86-88 South Park** (21) to be built entirely of sustainable materials—lightweight steel, recycled newspaper for insulation, and wood flooring from sustained yield forests. Note **Jack London Alley** bisecting the Park from north to south. London was born near here in 1876. Walk west out of the park to Third Street, turn right on Third, then left on Bryant. The second alley on the left is Zoe Street. Tanner Leddy Maytum Stacy crammed a 4,000-square-foot aluminum and steel building into a small lot (20 by 75 feet) at **25 Zoe** (22) (1992). There is an office and a garage on the first floor, an apartment on the second, and a well-lit photography study on the third.

YERBA BUENA GARDENS

Return to Third Street and walk north three blocks to Howard Street. Turn left and you are standing in front of the Moscone Convention Center. From here to Market Street and in the surrounding blocks you will experience modern San Francisco, about as extensive a remake of the city as you will find anywhere. Like the rest of South of Market (SOMA), this area is the center of a modernist revival in the tradition of the great European architects such as Walter Gropius and Mies van der Rohe. Although not contextual in Stern's sense, many of the exteriors, fashioned from brick and corrugated metals, evoke the industrial history of the neighborhood, reminding us that Gropius was fascinated by American grain silos and factories.

The blocks bound by Folsom, Fourth, Mission, and Third are known as **Yerba Buena Gardens.** This cultural-convention-entertainment complex was built from the ground up over the last two

Moscone Convention Center West, to open in 2003 at Fourth and Howard. *G. Ratto.*

decades. Originally conceived as a commercial development centered on a convention center and sports arena, a combination of economics (the bankruptcy of the developer Olympia &York) and politics (local opposition to the destruction of a neighborhood offering low-income housing) led to the transformation of the complex into something very different. The Gardens were built in pieces that do not quite fit together.

The most exciting thing about the **Moscone Convention Center** (23) (1981), which was designed by Hellmuth Obata and Kassabaum, is hidden away underground: the 880- by 300-foot exhibit hall, at the time the largest ever built below ground. University of California engineer T. Y. Lin spanned the room with eight pairs of 5-foot-wide bowed arches stiffened by huge roof girders. In a bold display of functionalism, the structural system is exposed along Third Street as part of the exterior design, and a series of gigantic trusses are used to cover the entranceway. Otherwise, the building is an unappealing stack of flat slabs. Notice the bird-beak **streetlights.** During the day they stand up vertically, dropping to the horizontal at night.

The Convention Center has been added to over the years, starting with the meeting rooms on the east side of Moscone South and a second underground hall, Moscone North, across Howard Street. Gensler Associates have drawn up plans for a third addition, **Moscone West** (24), which will be built on the southeast corner of Howard and Fourth and open in 2003. A sleek glass front will curve around the corner, breaking into a series of cantilevered bay windows on Howard Street and leaving the massive lobby exposed to passersby.

The **Rooftop at Yerba Buena Gardens** (25), designed by Adele Naudé Santos, opened in 1998. The Rooftop is on top of the Convention Center and can be entered by a stairway to the west of the Convention Center entrance. You immediately come upon a carousel, which has sentimental meaning for longtime San Franciscans. The carousel with its hand-carved animals was built in 1906 for Playland, a funky amusement park at Ocean Beach, which was torn down in 1972. Next to the carousel is a tapered cylinder, which is part of the **Zeum,** a high-tech production facility where young people can explore and produce visual, performing, and media arts. For the rest of the building's exterior, the architect favored corrugated siding and bright pastel colors, giving the design a machine shed look. The **Children's Garden,** up the stairs to the left, is the work of M. Paul Friedberg & Partners. In the back of the garden is a spectacular public **skating rink,** which can best be appreciated from inside. Plain columns hold the canopy ceiling aloft, and tall windows offer a panoramic view of the downtown skyline. There is also a bowling alley and a child development center offering care for 90 infants.

Return to the carousel and cross the pedestrian bridge to the north to the **Esplanade Gardens** (26) (1993), which were designed by Romaldo Giurgola/MGA Partners. To the right on a balcony overlooking the lawn below are a restaurant and the ever-present caffeine dispensary. To the left is a long, curved ribbon of water running over granite with a bench above it. This platform is an ideal spot for contemplating the dissonant strains of the downtown skyline. Unfortunately the two most prominent buildings in the foreground, the **Marriott Hotel** (27) (1989) by Daniel, Mann, Johnson & Mendenhall to the left, called the Wurlitzer because it looks like a jukebox when lit up at night, and the **Argent Hotel** (28) to the

Yerba Buena Center for the Arts Theater. *Richard Barnes.*

The Esplanade and the Metreon at Yerba Buena Garden. *Peter Booth Wiley.*

right, are among the least successful South of Market.

For another interesting contrast, note the Museum of Modern Art to the right with the Pacific Bell Building as a background (see illustration on page 134). Below the platform is a lovely rolling lawn with the **Martin Luther King Jr. Memorial Fountain** by architect Joseph De Pace and sculptor Houston Conwill as its south wall. This green space is a delightful oasis in an area that is completely lacking in public parks. Unfortunately, the entrance to the Esplanade on Mission Street to the north and the view from the ground level are obscured by cement block "dog houses," which contain exit stairs for the Convention Center below.

To the east is the **Yerba Buena Center for the Arts** (29) (1993), a cultural center that showcases artists who reflect San Francisco's remarkable diversity. The theater to the right as you face east and the gallery and sculpture garden must be circumnavigated to be appreciated. The theater, the work of James Stuart Polshek & Partners, is an attractive, straightforward collection of geometric shapes variously covered with ceramic tile, glass, polished aluminum, and black and white brick. The gallery and sculpture garden designed by Fumihiko Maki Associates combine a streamlined nautical look with more neo-machine-shed siding. Although there is an entrance on Mission Street, most of the façade facing the street is composed of service entrances and blank walls, a most unappealing look. The sleek, beautifully lit interior and sculpture garden are a welcome contrast to the industrial exterior.

On the west side of the Garden is Sony's **Metreon** (30) (1999), designed by Simon Martin-Vegue Winklestein Moris and Gary E. Handel & Associates. This multimedia entertainment complex is a commercial venture that generates substantial income to support Yerba

Buena Garden's public amenities. The Metreon includes a Microsoft store, a 15-screen movie theater, a 3-D IMAX theater, interactive family attractions based on the works of French graphic novelist Jean Giraud (Moebius)'s *The Airtight Garage,* Maurice Sendak's *Where the Wild Things Are* and *In the Night Kitchen,* and David Macaulay's *The Way Things Work.* The Metreon's gray western wall and green-tinted glass blend nicely into the Esplanade Gardens, which are gradually being screened from the building by young trees.

Walking east from the Esplanade Gardens, pass between buildings of the Center for the Visual Arts and through Omi Lang's **East Garden** (31) to reach Swiss architect Mario Botta's **Museum of Modern Art** (32) (1995), one of the most commanding structures to be built in San Francisco in recent years. Botta has written of public buildings that can "awaken the memory of forms and images that may be dormant." [60] Botta, like his teacher Le Corbusier, is preoccupied with elemental forms—the rectangle, square, and cylinder. MOMA is a stacking of brick-clad cubes with a cylinder in the center. Whereas the downtown skyline is vertical, the Museum of Modern Art (MOMA) is horizontal, setting the tone for the Yerba Buena structures that came later. The prefabricated brick exterior panels with their intricate design patterns evoke the traditional brickwork of the Jessie Street Substation and St. Patrick's Church on Mission Street. Light pours through the top of the central cylinder combining with natural light from skylights to illuminate the interior, where there is also an excellent bookstore. Ultimately, Yerba Buena Gardens manifests both the reassertion of modernism and a successful citizens' campaign to address the need for public space in the downtown area.

The Yerba Buena area is being walled off to the east and north by the latest generation of high rises. The Museum of Modern Art will be bracketed by the 30-story **W San Francisco Hotel** (33) by Hornberger & Worstell to the right of its entrance, which opened in 1999, and a not-yet-built 40-story luxury hotel and condominium high rise designed by Skidmore Owings Merrill to wrap around the historic Williams Building to the left. Across the street is a new 28-story office tower. On Market Street there will be a new entrance to the Yerba Buena Gardens between the Marriott and the new 37-story **Four Seasons Hotel** (34) and residential complex designed by Gary E. Handel and Associates. With these buildings architects, for the most part, have gone beyond the "funny hat" designs of the period immediately following the passage of the Downtown Plan to fashion more elegantly sculpted shapes.

Exiting the Museum of Modern Art, turn right on Third and then left on Mission. The right side of the open space on the north side of Mission across from Yerba Buena Gardens is the site for Ricardo Legoretta's **Mexican Museum** (35), which is still some years off. The area between the Mexican Museum and St. Patrick's will become Jessie Square, a terraced plaza designed by Kay Kajiwara with a 100-foot-long reflecting water sculpture by James Carpenter. On the north side of the square is the **Jessie Street Substation** (36), which will be converted into the **Jewish Museum** by Daniel Libeskind, scheduled to open in 2003 (see illustration on page 144). One of the fortuitous results of the demolition that preceded construction of Yerba Buena Gardens was the emergence of this old Pacific Gas and Electric power plant from behind the surrounding buildings. The original building went up in 1881 and was remodeled twice between 1905 and 1909 by Willis Polk after it was damaged in the earthquake and two fires. Polk added or replaced the central archway

and door, added a new door with cherubs in terra-cotta above it to the left, and extended the building to the east, adding four more windows.

St. Patrick's Church (37) between the Substation and the Marriott was built in 1872 to replace the original St. Patrick's on Market Street. It was gutted in 1906 and then rebuilt by Shea and Lofquist minus the original spire. The church, which once had 30,000 parishioners, is a lonely reminder that SOMA was a heavily Irish working class neighborhood. Its stained glass windows describe episodes from Irish religious history and the life of St. Patrick. Today the parishioners are mostly Filipino.

HOUSING

Walk west on Mission and turn left on Fourth Street to see the extensive low-income housing developments that were built as a result of a neighborhood movement to resist the SFRA's plans for the area. The fight was led by Tenants and Owners in Resistance to Redevelopment (TOOR), which then formed the Tenants and Owners Development Corporation (TODCO). Over the past 20 years TODCO has built or rehabilitated more than a thousand units of housing in the blocks that extend from Fourth to Seventh Streets. Other low-income developments have been built or restored by the Salvation Army and Mercy Charities.

TODCO hired Robert Herman Associates to design **Woolf House** (38) on the southwest corner of Fourth and Howard. Named after TOOR founder George Woolf, it opened in 1979. The apartment building features a solarium and a 3,500-foot roof garden with 28 separate growing plots. A second attached unit was added on Howard Street in 1982. Herman Associates also designed the 93-unit **Ceatrice Polite Apartments** (39) south of Woolf House on Clementina. Herman Associates' finest design, **Mendelsohn House** (40) (1990), is to the left on Folsom just past Mabini. On Folsom, turn right into Mabini and then left on Bonifacio. Note the windows, bays, and balconies and the trellised garden facing Bonifacio. Behind Mendelsohn House, TODCO leases 18,000 square feet for the **Alice Street Gardens** (41) replacing earlier gardens started by Chinese residents on empty lots in the area.

Return to Folsom, turn right, then left on Third and right on Mission. The **California Historical Society** (42) at 678 Mission moved from a crumbling mansion in Pacific Heights to this old

hardware store in 1995. It was redesigned as a gallery and archive with an excellent bookstore by Adolph Rosekrans, a descendant of the fabled Spreckels family. The **Ansel Adams Center for Photography** (43) moved into another former commercial space across the street at 655 Mission in 2000.

Continue east on Mission Street, turning right on New Montgomery. The **Pacific Bell Building** (44) (1925) at 140 New Montgomery was designed by Miller and Pflueger and is one of the city's finest. Its Gothic towers are topped with Moderne sculpted eagles and lotus flowers. The lobby, with its black-veined

The courtyard at Mendelsohn House, a TODCO project, at 737 Folsom. *Herman and Colliver.*

marble, has a ceiling decorated with mythic Chinese figures.

Return to Mission Street and turn right. On the right at the corner of Mission and Second, **101 Second Street** (45) is an elegant new office tower designed by Skidmore Owings Merrill, the first to be built after eight years (1991–1999) when no new office towers went up downtown. The thin window casings and tinted curved glass give the building a delightful sense of lightness and transparency. Continue

east on Mission to First. Timothy Pflueger and Arthur Brown Jr. collaborated on a functional Moderne design for the **Transbay Terminal** (46) (1939) on the right. The terminal was built as a turnaround for the Key System railroad, which brought commuters across the Bay Bridge from the eastern suburbs. Today it is a bus terminal. From here east on the north side of Mission Street are the last office towers built during the Manhattanization of Downtown.

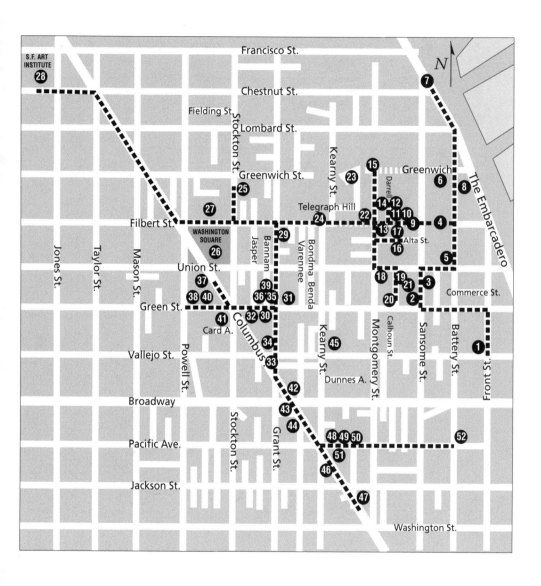

15

Telegraph Hill, the Barbary Coast, and North Beach

A three-hour walk with a steep climb over Telegraph Hill. The tour starts at Vallejo and Front and ends at Battery and Pacific.

The city's hills are its most prominent geographical feature. Even before accessibility was enhanced by the advent of the cable car, they proved, with their sweeping views of the Bay and the Golden Gate, to be appealing home sites for some, too isolated for others. The beach at Yerba Buena in the days of the Spanish was hemmed in to the north and west by Telegraph Hill (Loma Alta), Nob Hill, and Russian Hill, and they soon became distinctive communities.

TELEGRAPH HILL

The western flank of Telegraph Hill was the site of a dairy farm owned by Juana Briones, the widow of a soldier at the Presidio during Mexican rule. Her kitchen garden was located where Washington Square Park is today. When the U.S. Navy seized Yerba Buena in 1846, sailors built an adobe fort with a signal flag on the hill to warn of approaching vessels. Four years later a marine telegraph station with a hand-operated semaphore replaced the signal flag. In 1853 it was replaced by an electric telegraph. Hence the name Telegraph Hill.

Before the gold rush there was nothing but a narrow beach covered at high tide along the eastern foot of Telegraph Hill. In 1846, William Squire Clark built an adobe house and the city's first pier at the foot of Broadway near today's Front Street. At the time the southern flank of Telegraph Hill crossed Broadway. When Broadway was first graded, it ran through a 25-foot-deep cut. Clark extended his pier 150 feet into the Bay. Soon there were a number of piers at the foot of Telegraph Hill, which were favored by large clipper ships.

With the arrival of the argonauts, a number of tents and crude shelters were thrown up on Telegraph Hill, as well as more permanent wooden structures. The area became the favored location for Australians and Hispanics and, later, for Germans and the Irish. Some of the Australians, known as the Sydney Ducks, clustered in Sydney Town, the collection of saloons, brothels, and gambling halls that sprang up near the Broadway Wharf.

The Fremont Hotel, tents, and shacks on the east side of Telegraph Hill at the beginning of the gold rush. Today Battery Street runs along the edge of the cliff. *Library of Congress.*

While new buildings, including a hotel, went up on the steep slopes of Telegraph Hill, crews blasted away at the east side of the hill to provide level ground for what would become Sansome and Battery Streets. More rock was taken from the hill to backfill behind the new seawall, installed in two stages in the 1860s and 1870s. Even with the completion of the seawall, Telegraph Hill was the site of a number of quarries. Constant blasting and an occasional house tumbling down the hillside kept the neighbors in court, fighting the quarry companies until they ceased operations in 1914.

In 1876 four businessmen bought the top of the hill and gave it to the city to maintain as Pioneer Park. In 1882, Frederick Layman, a local entrepreneur, built an elaborate "German castle" complete with observatory and concert hall next to the park. To provide access to his resort, Layman ran a cable car line up Greenwich Street, but it failed within a few years for lack of passengers. Even the staging of broadsword fights on horseback could not attract enough people to keep the resort open. It was destroyed by arsonists in 1903.

THE BARBARY COAST

After 1849 the city's most notorious neighborhood flourished along the southern flank of Telegraph Hill. According to a popular ditty:

> The miners came in forty-nine,
> The whores in fifty-one;
> And when they got together
> They produced the native son.

With the arrival of the first prostitutes, the city's fanciest bagnios opened near the gambling halls around Portsmouth Square. Sydney Town, which stretched along Broadway and Pacific between Grant and the waterfront, became the center of the city's tawdriest entertainment district. With time the area expanded into the surrounding streets and alleyways and came to be known as the Barbary Coast, named after the dangerous ports of call on the southern shores of the Mediterranean. During the day sailors, who lived in shabby boarding houses, lounged about or shopped at cheap clothing stores and auction houses. Nightlife abounded with saloons, gambling dives, brothels, and dance halls, one establishment featuring a live bear chained in front. The press inspired periodic campaigns to close down the Barbary Coast, and women were even barred from working there in 1869—to little avail. Terrific Street, as Pacific Street was called, became a regular stop for guides bringing tourists from Chinatown after a tour of an opium den. Here they rubbed shoulders with local "slummers," members of the city's fast crowd who flocked to the area for the latest music and dances. By the 1890s, San Francisco had gained the dubious reputation of being "the wickedest city in the world."

In the aftermath of the Abe Ruef–Eugene Schmitz political scandals after the 1906 earthquake, the Barbary Coast came under attack. Ruef and Schmitz epitomized the way in which politicians squeezed the purveyors of vice for protection money, and the Barbary Coast proved to be the most visible target for reformers. When a Red Light Abatement Law was passed in 1914, the police department descended on the Barbary Coast. By the early 1920s it had become almost impossible for its denizens to operate in the old ways. In the 1930s the area was renamed the International Settlement. A number of popular nightspots lingered, and a city investigator listed about two dozen houses of prostitution in the area by address in 1937. But the days of open and outrageous debauchery were over.

NORTH BEACH: AN ITALIAN COMMUNITY

The piers along the eastern side of Telegraph Hill were a favorite disembarkation point for immigrants from Italy, who sought out inexpensive housing in the neighborhood. The first Italians returned from the mines to settle near the intersection of Broadway and Columbus in the 1850s with Mexicans, various Hispanics, Basques, and the French in what became known as the Latin Quarter. Grant Avenue north of Broadway was soon described as Little Italy, and as the Italian population grew it pushed through the saddle between Russian and Telegraph Hills, spilling over into North Beach. Today North Beach is used to describe the area from Chinatown to Fisherman's Wharf.

The number of Italians in the Latin Quarter grew slowly until the 1880s. Then the collapse of Italy's farm economy, brought about in large measure by the import of American wheat, forced many young Italian males to seek their fortune in the United States. In 1880 there were 2,500 Italians in San Francisco. By 1920, when the number reached 46,000, Italians were the largest foreign-born group in the city. Almost all of those who came to San Francisco emigrated from the provinces of Genoa, Lucca, Cosenza, and Palermo, with 70 percent coming from the northern provinces of Genoa and Lucca.

Among the first immigrants, the Genoese established themselves in the 1850s as farmers, working land both within the city and in nearby towns. The Genoese were followed by Luccans, but the Genoese farmers were well organized and able to keep the Luccans from becoming the middlemen between Italian farmers and their markets. In 1876, a Genoese farmers' organization opened the Colombo Market on Sansome Street near California. The Market became the center of the Produce Market, which was torn down in the 1950s to make way for the Golden Gateway redevelopment project. Retaining as much control of the market as possible, the Genoese made room for the Luccans in the business, but only as employees or as peddlers selling produce on the streets of San Francisco. In time the Luccans opened fruit and vegetable stands throughout the city, moving eventually into grocery stores, delicatessens, and the restaurant trade. Men from Lorsica near Genoa became scavengers and garbage men, those from Verbicaro in Cosenza monopolized the shoe shining trade, and the Genovese went into fishing until forced out by the Sicilians. Some Italians moved to other parts of the city, such as Potrero Hill and the Mission, but North Beach remained the heart of the Italian community. "Only in North Beach do Italians feel completely at home," reported the Italian consul in 1903. "On Sunday afternoon the Italians who live in other areas of town get together there: it is a way of recreating the security of the Italian village they have left behind." [61]

The principal appeal of North Beach and Telegraph Hill was cheap housing. The 1906 fire burned most of the buildings in the area except for a few blocks around the summit of Telegraph Hill. These were saved by starting backfires and the judicious application of wine-soaked rugs and bags to several structures. After the fire, ramshackle structures were thrown up to accommodate those burned out. Then Italian developers put up "Romeo flats," buildings divided into nine or more units on lots that were legally meant to accommodate four. Soon Telegraph Hill was judged one of the poorest neighborhoods in the city.

As the latest immigrant group to arrive, Italians entered the lowest-paying jobs, in part because the city's union leaders refused to admit Italians as members. Popularly identified with farming, the Produce Market, retail grocery stores, and fishing, Italians in fact moved into a wide range of employment, including jobs at the canneries near Fisherman's Wharf, the largest employer of Italians in the city, and worked as wood-carvers, stonemasons, and marble workers on major public buildings, such as the U.S. Court of Appeals and City Hall.

The last wave of Italians, who arrived between 1910 and 1926, when the federal government put an end to immigration until the postwar period, tended to be better off and more highly educated. By this time, a number of Italians, like the French, Jews, Germans, and Irish before them, had moved into the business class, in a few cases founding some of the great corporations, specifically in agribusiness and banking, that were emblematic of San Francisco's economic ascendancy after 1906. For example, in 1916, Marco Fontana, the son of a Genoese marble cutter, played a leading role in organizing the Del Monte Corporation, at one time the largest seller of canned goods in the United States. By 1910, the DiGiorgio Corporation, started by Giuseppe DiGiorgio, a Sicilian and thus one of the few southerners to become a powerful figure in the business community, was the largest fruit grower in the United States. And Amadeo Peter Giannini from Genoa organized the Bank of America and built it into the largest commercial bank in the world.

Italian-Americans also became a force in city politics. Giannini, a supporter of the reformism of James Duvall Phelan, played a major role in breaking Christopher Buckley's hold on North Beach–Telegraph Hill voters. When Buckley threatened to use violence against the reform forces, Giannini, according to a biographer, "immediately hired seventy-five wagons with his own money and recruited a small force of men armed with rifles. He personally escorted the wagons carrying voters to the polls."[62] In 1932, Angelo Rossi became the city's first Italian-American mayor, followed by Joseph Alioto in the 1960s and George Moscone in the 1970s.

By the 1920s, North Beach had changed from a poor immigrant community to a neighborhood with a solid middle class. By 1930, Italian-American home ownership ranked just below Irish-American. As the community began to take pride in its accomplishment, a new sense of national identity, no doubt negatively enforced by anti-Italian sentiment, swept the community, and many Italian-Americans came to identify with Benito Mussolino and his fascist movement. "I am deeply convinced," wrote the editor of *L'Italia,* North Beach's conservative evening newspaper, "that of all social and political reforms since the time of the French Revolution, Fascism has been the most beneficial for every social class."[63] North Beach became one of the most significant centers of fascist support in the United States. When the war began, a number of prominent Italians and Italian-Americans were interned, and even naturalized citizens were barred from jobs near defense or debarkation areas.

THE SAN FRANCISCO RENAISSANCE: ARTISTS AND WRITERS

Next to the Chinese, the Italians created the most ethnically distinctive community in the city. Italians were attracted to California because of its Mediterranean climate, and North Beach, nestled between two hills in the shadow of Saints Peter and Paul in Washington Square, had all the ambience of a neighborhood in an Italian hilltown. It was this European atmosphere and the nearby San Francisco Art Institute that attracted artists in large numbers to North Beach and Telegraph Hill after 1906. What came to be known as the San Francisco Renaissance had many originators, but among the most important were three groups of writers, one that formed around Jack Kerouac, Allen Ginsberg, and William Burroughs in New York, a second group consisting of conscientious objectors, including the poet William Everson (Father Antoninus), who were interned in Oregon during World War II, and a third overlapping circle of writers who gravitated to Berkeley after the war. The Berkeley group included Everson, Kenneth Rexroth, Henry Miller, Anaïs

Nin, Robert Duncan, and Kenneth Patchen. This group, according to Lawrence Ferlinghetti, looked to "European avant-garde poets and painters, especially to French Surrealists in exile in New York during the war and former American expatriots.... [They] expressed anti-war, anarchist or anti-authoritarian, civil libertarian attitudes, coupled with a new experimentation in the arts."[64]

It was San Francisco's rebellious past—and present, a little more than a decade after the General Strike—its bohemian tradition, and the general lack of a Puritan ethic that drew many artists to North Beach. "In the spiritual and political loneliness of America of the fifties you'd hitch a thousand miles to meet a friend," poet Gary Snyder once said. "Whatever lives needs a habitat, a proper culture of warmth and moisture to grow. West coast of those days, San Francisco was the only city; and of San Francisco, North Beach." Bars and coffeehouses, such as the Black Cat, the Place, the Cellar, the Co-Existence Bagel Shop, Vesuvio, and Caffé Trieste, provided this fecund habitat. In 1953, Ferlinghetti and Peter Martin started City Lights Books, the first all-paperback bookstore in the country.

In *The Dharma Bums,* Kerouac described a reading at the Six Gallery on Fillmore Street, in October 1955, as the "the night of the birth of the San Francisco Poetry Renaissance." Rexroth acted as emcee, introducing Ginsberg, Snyder, Michael McClure, Philip Whalen, and Philip Lamantia. Ginsberg read "Howl," Snyder a poem derived from a Native American coyote tale and translations from a Chinese poet from the T'ang Dynasty, and on and on into an evening turned increasingly ecstatic as Kerouac collected change to pay for the big jugs of red wine passed from hand to hand.

The Beats were claiming turf, a place to live unfettered lives according to their utopian notions of how the world should work, a California tradition reaching back to the gold rush. Not surprisingly, as the lively scene in North Beach drew wannabes, hangers-on, and finally tour buses, it also attracted the authorities. In March 1957, City Lights' second printing of "Howl," coming across the piers from England, was seized by U.S. Customs officials as obscene material because of its references to homosexuality. When City Lights continued to sell the poem, the San Francisco police department arrested Ferlinghetti and the bookstore's manager for selling obscene materials. The trial, which ended in acquittal, proved to be an important landmark in the fight against censorship.

Besides unsettling the postwar literary world, North Beach also made a significant contribution to the emergence of an openly gay community in San Francisco. There were numerous gay artists, and bisexuality was common. The Dash, at 574 Pacific Street in the heart of the Barbary Coast, may have been the city's first gay bar. It featured female impersonators and was shut down by the police in 1908. Finocchio's on Broadway, which opened as a speakeasy with female impersonators in 1929, was another important gathering place for gays and lesbians, as were Mona's, a lesbian club on Broadway, and the Black Cat, one of North Beach's renowned watering holes. The gay and lesbian scene was by no means confined to the old Barbary Coast and North Beach. But it was the Beat denizens of North Beach who openly challenged the straight world to come to terms with their sexuality.

In time the Beat scene fragmented. Some artists returned to New York, others wandered off in search of new experiences, while hardcore San Franciscans like Ferlinghetti remained, but in a very different world. As with Bret Harte and Mark Twain, San Francisco proved to be a city for cultural sojourners rather than a permanent home. North Beach in the 1960s became notorious for its topless, and then bottomless, joints, and jazz clubs flourished and then declined. The neighborhood retains its European ambience, and it is still home to some Italian-Americans. But many Italians, like immigrants before them, blended into less distinctive neighborhoods, such as the Marina, and then left the city altogether for the homogeneity of the suburbs. Meanwhile, Chinatown has been growing apace, crossing Broadway into the streets and alleys that were once the heart of the Latin Quarter.

Start at the **Daniel Gibb & Company Warehouses** (1) on the southwest and northwest corners of Vallejo and Front. Before the gold rush there was nothing along the eastern foot of Telegraph Hill but a narrow beach covered at high tide until William Squire Clark built the city's first pier at the foot of Broadway. This warehouse and a second one across the street were built on the Broadway pier in 1852 and 1855. Gibb and his brother were Scots commission merchants, whose first office was in the *Niantic,* a ship turned warehouse. They imported a wide variety of goods—liquor, blasting powder, coal, iron and iron products including corrugated siding, oatmeal, and bicarbonate of soda. Most of the buildings along the waterfront up to a line one to two blocks north of the Gibb warehouses were burned in 1906. The Gibb warehouses were gutted, partially destroyed, and rebuilt.

These warehouses mark the beginning of the city's second concentration of restored and repurposed warehouses and a significant shift in the city's archi-

tectural destiny. In the 1960s Telegraph Hill residents initiated the campaign against downtown high rises and were adamantly opposed to the construction of similar buildings blocking their views. Their opposition created an incentive to reuse the old warehouses in the area. Walk north on Front Street and turn left on Green. The modest warehouse on the northwest corner of Green and Sansome is where **Philo Farnsworth** (2) invented the television tube in 1927. Turn right on Sansome. In 1970, Wurster, Bernardi & Emmons restored **Icehouses One and Two** (3) on the right on the corner of Union, which were originally built in 1914.

Turn right on Union and left on Battery. The campus style **Levi Strauss Plaza** (4) (1982) was designed by Helmuth, Obata & Kassabaum after Chairman Walter Haas found the company's headquarters in one of the Embarcadero Center towers to be an uninviting work environment. As part of the complex, the architects restored the **Cargo West Warehouse** (5) on the

Daniel Gibb & Company Warehouse, Front and Vallejo. In 1865 the warehouse was located on the piers. *Beau Wiley.*

Lawrence Halprin's fountain and landscaping, with Levi Plaza and the Italian Swiss Colony Warehouse in the background. *Peter Booth Wiley.*

northwest corner of Battery and Union and the **Italian Swiss Colony Warehouse** (6) (Hemenway and Miller) on the northern side of the complex. The Cargo West Warehouse was built in 1907 to provide offices for a lumberyard with lodgings upstairs. The Italian Swiss Colony Warehouse was built in 1903 to increase the wine maker's storage capacity, a mark of the success of Andrea Sbarboro's 1,500-acre wine-making operation at Asti in

Sonoma County. Lawrence Halprin did the landscape design and fountains. This complex, with its verdant park space and human scale, marked a significant rejection of the corporate community's infatuation with the office tower.

Continue north on Battery to the Embarcadero and turn left. At the corner of the Embarcadero and Sansome is the **Beltline Roundhouse** (7). This wedge-shaped structure was used to repair and service the engines that pulled cars along the waterfront. The Beltline Railroad was begun in 1890. When it was completed in 1912, it was considered to be the most complete waterfront railway in the country. Built in 1914, the roundhouse provided space for five engines and included a drop-pit machine shop, blacksmith shop, storeroom, and engine house. Return to Battery. On the left is the **Fog City Diner** (8) (1987), a modern rendition of an old favorite designed by restaurateur Pat Kuleto. This fashionable eating establishment is parodied as the Fog City Dumpster in Phil Frank's daily cartoon, "Farley," in the *Chronicle*.

Walk west through Levi Plaza to Filbert and Sansome, and climb the **Filbert Street Steps** (9) toward the top of Telegraph Hill. You are climbing into a fascinating neighborhood of narrow streets, back alleys, and cul de sacs. There are numerous small cottages evoking the past when this was an ethnically mixed neighborhood with many residents of modest means. Note the results of quarrying on the hillside as you climb, and, yes, those are the famous Telegraph Hill parrots squawking in the trees. "It requires physical exertion to mount a Telegraph Hill stairway," a resident wrote in 1888, "but that is nothing in comparison with the mental effort necessary in finding one's way after reaching the top. We jump a ditch that serves as an open channel for sewage, make a detour around a pile of

Ace Architects' condominium at 34-36 Darrell Place, a tribute to the architects of the Second Bay Style. *Christopher Irion*.

tomato cans, bring up in a blind alley that purports to be a street leading directly to the house we seek, try a path that ends abruptly on the edge of the cliff, and narrowly escape a landslide that goes careening down the bluff." [65] With houses interspersed with vacant lots, Telegraph Hill retained a semirural atmosphere until the 1920s. Goats grazed here until 1928, when a city ordinance barred them. Besides sailors, immigrant families, and the usual comers and goers attracted to San Francisco, the hill, because of its proximity to the San Francisco Art Institute on Russian Hill, became a favorite living place for various artists, most of them known only to their friends.

At the first house on the right, **218-20 Filbert** (10), the owner gardened from a boatswain's chair. Englishman Phillip Brown built **228 Filbert** (11), a

Built in 1853, 31 Alta and its neighbors are still there. *Library of Congress.*

good example of carpenter's Gothic, for his family in 1882. There are numerous other houses from the same period along Napier Lane and Darrell Place. Note the condominiums at **34-36 Darrell Place** (12). They are the work of Ace Architects (Lucia Howard and David Weingarten) and were designed, according to the architects, as a homage to Bernard Maybeck, William Wurster, Joseph Esherick, and Charles Moore.

The Deco gem at the top of the stairs on the left at **1360 Lombard** (13) (1936) was designed by S. W. Goldstein. Turn right on Montgomery. Gardner Dailey designed **1420 Montgomery** (14) in 1960 for Mrs. Henry Potter Russell, a patron of the arts and member of the Crocker family. Dailey was a local architect associated with the Second Bay Tradition. The southwest corner of Montgomery and Greenwich

was the site of one of two known artists' communes in the area, which date from the post–World War I period. This one was made up of five modest structures surrounded by a fence. They were built very much like the butcher block structures designed by hippies in the 1960s. Artist and newspaperman Harry Laffler scavenged lumber for the buildings on the hill, taking some of it from the large "Welcome" sign erected in honor of the arrival of the Great White Fleet in 1908. At the end of Montgomery is **Julius' Castle** (15) (1922), designed by Louis Mastropasqua for Italian immigrant restaurateur Julius Roz.

Return south on the left side of Montgomery Street. Turn left on Alta Street, another site of some of the earliest houses built on the hill. A sea captain built **31 Alta Street** (16) in 1853. During Prohibition the wife of a sailor turned it into a successful speakeasy and restaurant. The **Duck House** (17) at 60-62 Alta is covered with murals by Helen Forbes and Dorothy Pucinelli, who also did the murals in the Mothers' House at the Zoo (see page 385). Return to Montgomery and turn left. The Italianate structure at **1254-62 Montgomery** (18) on the southeast corner of Montgomery and Union was built as a rooming house in 1865 on the site of a coffee mill driven by wind power. This is one of the buildings saved in 1906 when its walls were draped with burlap sacks dipped in wine. Continue south on Montgomery and turn left on Union and right on **Calhoun Terrace** (19). This street was partially destroyed by quarrying and then restored by the Works Progress Administration (WPA) in the 1930s. The

Coit Tower. *Peter Booth Wiley.*

house at **9 Calhoun Terrace** (20) dates from 1854. Famed International Style architect Richard Neutra, known for his work in southern California, designed the Kahn House at **66 Calhoun Terrace** (21). Return to Montgomery Street, turn right, and continue up the Filbert Steps. Painter and sculptor Ralph Stackpole, a ringleader of the group of artists who worked on the Stock Exchange (City) Club and Coit Tower, built the house at **312 Filbert** (22) in 1932. Stackpole was a central figure in both radical and artistic circles in the 1920s and 30s.

Coit Tower (23), at the top of Telegraph Hill, is the legacy of one of San Francisco's most colorful characters, Lillie Hitchcock Coit. According to popular myth, Coit, who came to San Francisco with her family in 1851, was saved from a fire by a member of the Knickerbocker Fire Company No. 5. The Knickerbocker Company adopted her as a kind of mascot, eventually making her an honorary member, and she reciprocated by wearing the company's helmet, red shirt, wide belt with a company medallion, and underwear with the number 5 embroidered on them. In 1868 she married Howard Coit, the caller at the San Francisco Stock Exchange. Their marriage, however, was not a happy one. For one thing, Coit, who by now had become a society belle, was a very independent woman: She found a shot of bourbon, a good cigar, and a game of poker as entertaining as a grand ball.

When Coit died in 1929, she left money for each surviving member of the Knickerbocker Engine Company, for a monument to volunteer firemen, and for a fund to add to the beauty of the city she loved. In accordance with Coit's bequest, Haig Patigian, one of the city's foremost sculptors, was hired to fashion a monument, which stands today in Washington Square. Coit had spoken of buying the top of Telegraph

Hill and building an observatory there. The city honored her wishes by hiring Henry Howard, an architect in the office of Arthur Brown Jr., who had designed City Hall and the War Memorial Opera House, to design a tower on the top of the hill. Howard was the son of John Galen Howard, the Berkeley architecture professor whose Civic Center advisory committee had chosen Brown to work on City Hall and the Opera House.

Howard's plan for a 180-foot-tall tower, a simple fluted column, inspired one of the earliest rows over height limits for buildings. A group of artists argued before the newly formed Art Commission that the tower was too tall for the 228-foot hill. Once the tower was completed in 1933, the Board of Supervisors voted to rezone Telegraph Hill "so that the skyscrapers of the future would not interfere with the view or detract from the beauty of Coit Memorial."

Howard designed the tower's interior to provide public space for artwork and historical exhibits. The completion of the tower coincided with the beginning of a federal pilot program in the arts. Inspired by the three great Mexican muralists, Diego Rivera, David Alfaro Siqueiros, and José Clemente Orozco, associates of Franklin Roosevelt convinced him to fund a program that would pay artists to paint murals in public buildings. San Francisco responded by forming a committee of prominent citizens from the arts, architecture, and museum world, which championed the idea of murals in Coit Tower. Simultaneously, painter Bernard Zakheim was working with painter and poet Kenneth Rexroth to urge the federal government to find employment for local artists. Twenty-six artists and their helpers, including Victor Arnautoff, John Langley Howard (Henry's brother), Clifford Wight, Ralph Stackpole, and Suzanne Scheur, went to work in the tower. Wight was a former assistant

of Rivera; Stackpole lent Rivera his studio when he came to the city to work on his mural in the stairwell of the Stock Exchange Club.

The Coit Tower muralists were at work in the midst of the charged atmosphere surrounding the 1934 longshoremen's strike. With the local press searching out "Reds" to blame for the strike, some reporters turned their attention to these artists. Careful examination of the murals found telltale traces of the dreaded Bolshevism—*The New Masses* and the *Daily Worker* on a rack with other publications in a newsstand (depicted by Victor Arnautoff), a miner reading the *Western Worker* (John Langley Howard), a reader reaching for *Das Kapital* in a library (Bernard Zakheim), and the slogan "United Workers of the World" with a hammer and sickle above a window (Clifford Wight). When the Art Commission's inspection of the murals confirmed "opposition to the generally accepted tradition of native Americanism," the tower was padlocked. It was later reopened after the offending hammer and sickle and slogan were excised.

Walk down Telegraph Hill Boulevard and continue west down the Filbert Steps. Esherick, Homsey, Dodge & Davis redesigned the **Garfield Elementary School** (24) at 420 Filbert Street in 1981. Continue west on Filbert Street, turning right on Stockton. Bernard Maybeck designed the **Maybeck Building** (25) (1907) at 1736 Stockton to be the Telegraph Hill Neighborhood House (1907). Two women formed the Telegraph Hill Neighborhood Association in 1888 to provide assistance to immigrant families. Returning on Stockton, you enter **Washington Square** (26), the site of Juana Briones' rancho in the 1830s and 1840s. See the monument near the corner of Stockton and Filbert. The square was laid out as one of the city's three original parks by William Eddy in 1849. In 1855 it was described as "the receptacle for all the vile compounds, dead dogs, cats, and rubbish generally, which can be found in the city." [66] The city used chain gangs from the city prison to begin work on the park in 1860. In the late 1950s the city floated plans to dig up the park for an undercover garage. When they were opposed, Lawrence Halprin designed a new park, which was landscaped by Douglas Baylis, a resident of North Beach. Near Columbus Avenue is **Haig Partigian's statue** in honor of the city's firemen, which was funded by the estate of Lillie Hitchcock Coit. Overlooking the park on the north is the church of **Sts. Peter and Paul** (27), still an important gathering place for Italian-Americans. Joe DiMaggio's funeral was held here in 1999 before a respectful crowd with very little fanfare. The original church was founded, at the direction of the Vatican, in 1884 to serve the Italian community. The present structure dates from 1922 and was designed by Charles Fantoni, combining elements of Gothic and Romanesque design. On the first Sunday of October, a statue of the Virgin is carried from here to the Fisherman's Wharf for the annual blessing of the fishing fleet. The altar and sanctuary are finished in various Italian marbles inlaid with onyx from Brazil and Morocco.

Walk west on Filbert to Columbus and turn right, then left on Chestnut. Walk west on Chestnut to Jones. The **San Francisco Art Institute** (28) is on the right. In 1926, City Hall architects Bakewell and Brown were moving beyond the neoclassical to a more stripped-down concrete building in the Mediterranean style. The 1970 addition by Paffard Keatinge Clay on the north side of the block was influenced by Le Corbusier. Diego Rivera painted his second mural in the city in an interior gallery here in 1931. In *Making a Fresco, Showing the Building of the City,* Rivera not only memorialized architecture and construction, but also

the process of mural painting itself. That's his backside perched on the scaffolding. The mural includes portraits of architects Arthur Brown Jr., Michael Goodman, and Timothy Pflueger and artists Will Gerstle, Matthew Barnes, Ralph Stackpole, and Clifford Wight.

Return to Grant and Filbert and turn right. **Grant Avenue,** the site of a number of popular bars, coffee houses, and jazz joints during the Beat era, was described at the time as a three-block-long open-air mental hospital. **The Place** (29), a bar that offered an open mike to poets on Blabbermouth Night, was located at 1546 Grant. The **Co-Existence Bagel Shop** (30), another hangout where the cops were fond of parking a police van out front, was located on the southwest corner of Grant and Green. Just east of Grant the **Old Spaghetti Factory** (31), now the Maykadeh Restaurant, was at 468-70 Green Street. Originally the Italian-American Paste Company, it was a restaurant and bar frequented by the Beats. West of Grant at 576 Green **The Cellar** (32) offered jazz and poetry. Continuing south on Grant, the **Caffé Trieste** (33) on the southwest corner of Grant and Vallejo has been a North Beach gathering place since 1956 and is still owned by the Giotta family. To the west on Vallejo is the church of **St. Francis of Assisi** (34). When the first argonauts arrived, Mission Dolores did not offer mass regularly and was too remote for the inhabitants of this area. So Father John Brouillet, vicar general of the diocese of Walla Walla, Washington, built the first Catholic church in the city under American rule on this site in 1851. This Norman Gothic structure dates from 1860. It was gutted by fire in 1906 and then rebuilt. In 1994 the church was closed along with six others because of the declining number of Catholics in San Francisco. In 1999, the National Conference of Bishops named St. Francis the National Shrine of

Club Fugazi, 678 Green.
Peter Booth Wiley.

St. Francis. Within there are stained glass windows and murals depicting his life.

Return on Grant to Green and turn left. This block has retained much of the flavor of old North Beach. **Soldini's Trattoria** (35) at 510 Green is one of a handful of traditional Italian-American restaurants, as is **Dante Benedetti's New Pisa** (36) at 550 Green. There are also the **Golden Spike** (37) at 527 Columbus and **Capp's Corner** (38) farther west, at the corner of Green and Powell. **Gino and Carlo's** (39) at 548 Green, where the Beats rubbed shoulders with the locals, is still a popular neighborhood hangout.

Continue west on Green across Columbus to the **Club Fugazi** (40) at 678 Green Street, the historic meeting place of the city's contending visions of itself. The hall, designed by Italo Zanolino, was given by wealthy travel agent John F. Fugazi to the Italian-American community in 1912 to foster a sense of national identity in a community fragmented by regionalism. Fugazi's bust is above the cornice. Besides housing numerous Italian-American neighborhood organizations, in the 1930s the hall became the home to a number of recreational youth groups of fascist inspiration. In the 1950s the Beats organized the first public poetry readings in North Beach here. Since 1975 it has hosted a major tourist attraction, the wacky and continuously revised musical revue *Beach Blanket Babylon.*

Return to Columbus. Just to the right, at 1435 Stockton, the **North Beach Museum** (41) is housed in the BayView Bank. Go right on Columbus. The **Condor Sports Bar** (42) on the northwest corner of Columbus and Broadway is where Carol Doda began the topless dancing craze in 1964. Across the intersection at 261 Columbus is **City Lights Booksellers and Publishing** (43) founded by Peter Martin and Lawrence Ferlinghetti in 1953 to sell paperback books. The bookstore, with its excellent collections of little magazines and poetry, is the most famous of San Francisco's fine assortment of independent bookstores. City Lights Publishers, which began with the works of authors such as Gregory Corso, Diane di Prima, Allen Ginsberg, Gary Snyder, Bob Kauffman, Jack Kerouac, and Ferlinghetti, continues to be a significant literary press. Across Jack Kerouac Street is **Vesuvio** (44). The building, designed by Italo

Zanolini in 1913, features extensive use of pressed tin. It was once an Italian language bookstore, but then became a favorite Beat watering hole and is still a lively place.

Walk east on Broadway to Kearny. Go left and climb up to the first alley on the right. Pasquale Gogna, a baker who owned several hotels in the neighborhood built the odd **tower** (45) at the end of the alley in 1930 for his residence. Walk south on Kearny and notice the **Columbus Tower** (46) (1905) by Field and Kohlberg at the corner of Kearny and Columbus. In recent years filmmaker Francis Ford Coppola bought the building, hence the **Niebaum Coppola Café** on the ground floor. The lovely white terra-cotta building on the left at the corner of Columbus, Montgomery, and Washington was originally the **Fugazi Bank** (47) (1911) by Field and Kohlberg. Fugazi, because he owned a large safe at his travel agency,

Terrific Street (Pacific Avenue), the heart of the Barbary Coast sometime between 1900 and 1910. Spider Kelly's, the Hippodrome, and Purcell's So Different Club. *San Francisco History Center, San Francisco Public Library.*

became North Beach's first banker. A. P. Giannini started his banking career as a member of the board of directors of Fugazi's bank, knocked heads with him, and set up the rival Bank of Italy, which was housed here for a time and later became the Bank of America. The building also once served as headquarters of the Transamerica Corporation, the holding company set up by Giannini to control his banking operations.

Return north on Columbus and turn right on Pacific Avenue. It is hard to imagine that this sedate block was once called **Terrific Street,** the center of several square blocks of dives, whorehouses, opium dens, dance halls, and cheap hotels, which made up the **Barbary Coast.** After the 1906 earthquake Terrific Street became home to a thriving jazz and dance scene. Jelly Roll Morton, King Oliver, and Kid Ory played here, and music historian Tom Stoddard argues that the word *jazz* entered the vocabulary as a way to describe the new music and dances introduced here.[67] **Spider Kelly's** (48) was located in the three-story brick building at 570-74 Pacific. Next door to the right, at 560 Pacific, was the original **Hippodrome** (49). This new brick façade replaced an ornate white entryway marked by two classical columns. **Purcell's,** or the **So**

Different Club (50), where the popular dance the "Texas Tommy" originated in 1911, was located at 550 Pacific. "All the new dances came from Purcell's, which hired the best colored entertainers from coast to coast," a musician told Stoddard.[68] Purcell's was owned by two African-Americans who had quit their jobs as sleeping car porters to open a saloon near the Presidio to serve black soldiers, known as Buffalo Soldiers, stationed there. At some point the Hippodrome moved across the street, replacing the Moulin Rouge, or Red Mill. The original façade of the second Hippodrome at **555 Pacific** (51) is still intact. Note the columns that become bare-breasted women, the only remnant of a naughty past.

Continue east on Pacific to Battery. The **Old Ship Saloon** (52) (1861) on the northeast corner is one of the last of the old waterfront bars. The original Old Ship Saloon was the ship *Arkansas,* which was overtaken by the waterfront after its arrival in 1849. In 1859, the *Arkansas* was cut up and replaced by this brick building, which was both a saloon and a boarding house. Sailors stayed here at their peril, as crimps operated from the saloon, providing men by one means or another for ships' captains.

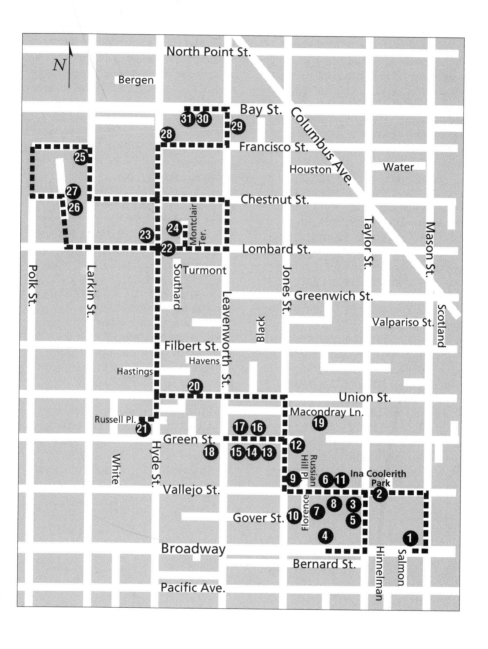

North Point St.

Bergen

Bay St.

31 30

28

29

Francisco St.

Houston

Water

25

Chestnut St.

27
26

Montclair Ter.

24

Lombard St.

23

22

Turmont

Southard

Greenwich St.

Jones St.

Taylor St.

Mason St.

Valpariso St.

Scotland

Black

Leavenworth St.

Polk St.

Larkin St.

Filbert St.

Havens

Hastings

20

Union St.

Macondray Ln.

Russell Pl.

21

19

Green St.

17 **16**

18

15 **14** **13**

12

White

Hyde St.

Russian Hill Pl.

Ina Coolerith Park

9

6 **11**

2

Vallejo St.

Gover St.

10

7 **8** **3**

5

1

4

Broadway

Bernard St.

Hinnelman

Salmon

Florence

Pacific Ave.

N

Columbus Ave.

16

Russian Hill, Nob Hill, and Pacific Heights

RUSSIAN HILL

Two hours, with steep climbs around the top of the hill. This tour starts at Broadway and Mason and ends near Fisherman's Wharf. There are good restaurants near the intersection of Union and Hyde.

Russian Hill provides ample opportunity to examine the evolution of the Bay Area Tradition. The top of Russian Hill is the famous incubator of the First Bay Tradition. As you explore the northern slopes of the hill, you will find various examples of modernism and the Second and Third Bay Traditions, styles that became popular with the city's gentry starting in the 1930s.

When the forty-niners explored the heights of the hill to the west of Telegraph Hill, they found the graves of seven Russian sailors, hence the name Russian Hill. Because of the hill's craggy summit, it was years before streets were built to the top. Instead, footpaths and wooden stairways criss-crossed the heights. Even today Broadway and Vallejo end in steps on the eastern side of Russian Hill, there are numerous cul de sacs, and Lombard

Street eases its way down from Hyde Street in a series of curves that are a famous tourist attraction. As a result Russian Hill, although close to downtown, remained very much a world apart. While Nob Hill became the home of the moneyed elite, Russian Hill attracted a mixed community of businessmen, skilled workers, artists, and newspaper people.

Thanks to the work of architectural historian William Kostura, we have a remarkably detailed account of the history of the top of hill where two groups of friends, a generation apart, made significant contributions to the architecture of San Francisco.[69] The first development began in 1849 when William Squire Clark, the builder of the Broadway Wharf, bought the block on the southern side of the summit bounded by Broadway, Vallejo, Taylor, and Jones—six lots for $37.50 a lot. In 1853, Charles Homer, a building contractor, bought the property from Clark for $5,000 and then sold all but one lot to associates in the construction business. Also in 1853, Homer supervised construction of the United States Marine Hospital at Rincon Point, the largest structure to be built in San Francisco in the 1850s.

At about the same time he formed a partnership with Joseph Atkinson, a bricklayer from Pennsylvania, and William Ranlett, a New York architect. A close look at the structures shows that Ranlett was the likely designer of the homes for the families of all three men: a large Gothic Revival home at the corner of Taylor and Broadway for Homer, which no longer stands, and homes in the Italianate style for his own and Atkinson's family on adjacent lots. Ranlett was a well-known architect in eastern circles and publisher of an influential periodical called *The Architect*. His journal promoted the ideas of architect Alexander Jackson Davis and landscape designer Andrew Jackson Downing. Through their work and two books written by Downing, *Victorian Cottage Residences* and *The Architecture of Country Homes*, they played a major role in promoting the Gothic Revival, Italianate, and Romanesque styles, which were just becoming popular for country and suburban homes. Ranlett's and Atkinson's homes were probably the first Italianate buildings in San Francisco; the Atkinson house is the oldest surviving home of this type in the city. Thus, Ranlett is a very obvious connection between fashionable East Coast architecture and the emerging architecture of the booming metropolis on the Pacific.

The second development began in the late 1880s. As the flow of construction pressed ever westward block after block toward the end of the nineteenth century, the top of Russian Hill remained isolated and what today we would call "funky," with an occasional goat browsing in empty, garbage-strewn lots. Gradually, homes were built in clusters or one at a time. In 1888 the wife of the owner of property at the top of the hill asked Joseph Worcester, pastor at the Swedenborgian Church, to design three houses to be built on part of the parcel. Worcester's design, like Ranlett's three decades earlier, was to have a major impact on Bay Area architecture. Worcester, who was influenced in his thinking by Ralph Waldo Emerson, John Ruskin, and William Wordsworth, "viewed the natural world as a manifestation of God and felt that buildings should relate well to the environment rather than disrupt it," according to Kostura.[70] Worcester had built a home in the Oakland Hills, a simple rustic affair with a low hipped roof, overhanging eaves, unpainted shingles on the outside, and redwood on the inside. Although he lacked formal training in architecture, Worcester was experimenting with a vernacular shingled design just *before* Henry Hobson Richardson, the architect most closely associated with the Shingle Style, began designing shingled homes in New England.

The three homes at the top of Russian Hill designed by Worcester were a radical departure from the elaborate Victorians that filled the blocks of the ever-expanding city. Gone were the stickwork, turrets, bay windows, brackets, and other elaborate ornamentation. In their place Worcester created simple shingled houses. Worcester's designs marked the beginning of the revolt against Victorianism and the origins of the First Bay Tradition.

Worcester built a cottage for himself to the east of the three new shingled houses. To his home he attracted a group of artists and intellectuals who shared his reverence for nature and a love of simple living. William Keith, the landscape painter who contributed canvasses to the Church of the New Jerusalem over whose construction Worcester would preside, was a close friend, as were John Muir and Charles Keeler. Keeler was an advocate of the Arts and Crafts movement, an ardent supporter of the work of Bernard Maybeck, and the author of *The Simple Home*, which he dedicated to Maybeck. In about 1890, Willis Polk moved into a dilapidated house across the street from the Worcester houses and became a friend of their designer. Polk immediately went to work remodeling the ground floor of the house he was renting, paneling the walls with redwood much in the manner of the interior of Worcester's modest home.

Although only 23 when he moved to Russian Hill, Polk had already made a name for himself by publishing the short-lived *Architectural News,* which featured classical buildings in Europe, articles on the California missions, and newer designs from the East. Polk's home soon became a gathering place for young artists, writers, and architects, including John Galen Howard and Ernest Coxhead, and Polk and his friends visited with Worcester, who served as a kind of mentor and father figure. Worcester and Polk shared an antipathy to the excesses of Victorian architecture, which Polk would attack in *The Wave* in 1897. Worcester never designed another building, but he was the guiding force behind the construction of the Church of the New Jerusalem, the first example in San Francisco of the integration of architecture, painting, and domestic crafts (see page 278.) Over the next two decades Polk would make a number of contributions to the design of hilltop houses, including a home that he, his brother, and his father built for their family.

The Battle for Russian Hill

After World War I, Russian Hill began to change, eventually becoming the pre-serve of wealthier San Franciscans. When sculptor Haig Patigian built his home at the corner of Hyde and Francisco Streets in 1914, he spent $30,000, a handsome sum in those days, on a lovely half-timbered structure. Starting in 1941, Russian Hill residents began to mobilize to save their views and pre-serve the neighborhood as a place for small apartment buildings and single-family dwellings. In 1952 residents argued unsuccessfully for a 40-foot height limit on the top of the hill. When a developer proposed a 14-story apartment house for the corner of Chestnut and Hyde in 1954, the neighborhood rose up in arms. "One of the most vocal of the property owners," reported the *Chronicle*, "is Mrs. Oscar Sutro, wife of a Standard Oil Co. executive...who enjoys a breathtaking view of the bay." Once again hilltop dwellers, and well-to-do residents at that, were in the forefront of the battle over height limits. The apartment building went up, but the brawls continued as even taller buildings were constructed. In 1959 residents represented by Caspar Weinberger, later Ronald Reagan's secretary of defense, persuaded a local judge to bar the construction of a 23-story apartment building at Bay and Leavenworth. The judge was overruled by the state supreme court.

Residents were successful in their effort to get the Planning Commission to impose height restrictions along the waterfront after construction of the Fontana Apartments near Aquatic Park in 1961, but the top of the hill contin-ued to be zoned for high-rise apartments. In 1962 a developer bought Joseph Worcester's cottage and one of the houses that he had designed and tore them down without notifying the neighbors. The next year Joseph Eichler began construction on a disproportionately tall apartment tower at Jones and Green (see illustration on page 124). The skirmishes continued, but slowly the tide was turning. Neighborhood resistance to willful destruction of historic buildings and uncontrolled development was gaining ground—at least in wealthier parts of the city. In 1970 the city imposed a 40-foot height limit on Russian Hill, thereby guaranteeing that much of the neighborhood would remain intact.

Start at **Nuestra Senora de Guadalupe** (1) by Shea and Lofquist, on Broadway just west of the intersection with Mason. Although the name evokes the Hispanic miners who camped near here during the gold rush, the church dates from 1906 (rebuilt in 1912) and is thought to be the first reinforced concrete church built in the city. Walk north on Mason and turn left on Vallejo. Vallejo ends in a set of steps that take you through **Ina Coolbrith Park** (2), named for the early San Francisco poet. Houghton Sawyer designed the large house at **1001 Vallejo** (3) on the southwest cor-ner of Taylor in 1906 for Robert Hanford. Hanford was a mining promot-er and one of the men who bought up the city's streetcar companies in 1901 and 1902 and sold them to an eastern syndicate in what was regarded at the time as the largest acquisition in U.S. history.

Beginning with the Atkinson House on Broadway near Taylor, the summit of Russian Hill has some of the most historically significant homes in the city. Turn right on Taylor and walk down to Broadway. The second house on the right from the corner of Taylor and Broadway, best seen from across the street, is the **Atkinson House** (4) (1853). Probably designed by William Ranlett, it is the oldest Italianate house in the city. Willis Polk redesigned the interior of the first floor in 1893, installing sumptuous redwood paneling, columns, cabinets, and a mantel over a terra-cotta fireplace. Returning north on Taylor, you pass the house at 1637 Taylor, which Ranlett designed for his family in 1853. It was known as the **House of Many Corners** (5) because of its stepped-back façade. The house is difficult to see; it was significantly altered in the 1890s when it was cut in half, perhaps as a result of a divorce settlement.

Continue north on Vallejo and climb the stairs to your left. Once you are in the 1000 block of Vallejo, look at the buildings in chronological order, because understanding the relationships between them will tell you a lot about the origins of the First Bay Tradition. Joseph Worcester, the Swedenborgian minister and amateur architect, designed the two shingled houses at **1034 and 1036 Vallejo** (6) (1889) (see page 124). Worcester broke with the Victorian style, cladding these houses with shingles while eschewing the elaborate ornamentation and complex façades that were popular at the time. In the same year, Worcester built his own house where the Hermitage stands at 1020 Vallejo. He finished the interior with plain redwood paneling, giving it a rustic look.

In 1890, Willis Polk rented the **Livermore House** (7) (1865) at 1045 Vallejo, which is secluded behind trees just south of the corner of Florence and Vallejo. Having become a friend of Worcester's, Polk remodeled the entryway and living room of the Livermore

The Atkinson House, one of the oldest in the city. Interior by Willis Polk. *Courtesy of Alan Nichols/ William Kostura.*

House in late 1890 and early 1891 in a manner similar to Worcester's. (Robert Stern remodeled and added to the Livermore House in 1990.) The next year Polk worked with his father and brother to design and build the **Polk-Williams House** (8) at 1013-1017 Vallejo. He skillfully blended elements of Gothic, late Medieval, and the contemporary Shingle Style in his design. By 1914, Polk was working on improvements in the neighborhood, such as the access ramp at the west end of the 1000 block Vallejo and to **Russian Hill Place,** which marked the passing of the hilltop's isolated bohemian years. Polk also designed the attached houses at **1, 3, 5, and 7 Russian Hill Place** (9).

As part of the gentrification of the top of the hill, Charles Whittlesey designed the Pueblo style houses at **35, 37, and 39 Florence Street** (10) at about 1920. Return to the east end of the block to look at Esherick, Homsey, Dodge & Davis's **Hermitage** (11) (1984) on the left. This is a truly San Francisco design,

given that the architects were working within both the historical context of this famous block and the regulations laid down by the Planning Commission after numerous fights over high rises and preservation. So, naturally, we have a shingled structure à la Worcester and Polk sitting on the site of Worcester's own cottage and shaped to provide for height limits, view lines, setbacks, easements, and air rights.

Go west on Vallejo to Jones and turn right to the corner of Green. The disproportionately large (35 stories) glass and concrete tower on your right at **999 Green Street** (12) gives you a good sense of why the neighborhood rebelled against high-rise apartments. This building was designed for Joseph Eichler by Neil Smith and Associates and Claude Oakland and was completed in 1965.

Walk west on Green Street. The Newsom Brothers designed **1039-43 Green** (13) in the Italianate style in the 1880s. It was moved here after 1906. Julia Morgan remodeled **1055 Green**

The Polk-Williams House, 1013-17 Vallejo. *California State Library.*

The Feusier Octagon House, 1067 Green. *Peter Booth Wiley.*

(14) in 1915, transforming an Italianate home into a stucco villa. **Feusier Octagon House** (15) (1859) at 1067 Green was designed by an unknown follower of nineteenth-century New York phrenologist Orson Fowler, who wrote in *A Home for All* that octagon houses provided a salubrious residential environment and a cheap domicile for the "new age." Perfect for California! A second story, the mansard roof, and a cupola were added sometime after the house was built. Lewis Hobart designed the Classical Revival apartment building at **1050 Green** (16) (1913). Newton Tharp designed **Engine House No. 31** (17) (1908), one of the last firehouses built to house horse-drawn equipment, at 1088 Green in a combination of Tudor Revival and Craftsman styles to fit in with local residences. Philanthropist Louise Davies, after whom Symphony Hall is named, bought the firehouse, restored it, opened the ground floor to neighborhood organizations, and gave the building to the National Trust for Historic Preservation. Herman Baumann, the noted Art Deco architect, designed **1101 Green** (18) (1928) on the southwest corner of Green and

Engine House Number 31, 1088 Green. *Peter Booth Wiley.*

Leavenworth. This was one of Baumann's first Deco designs. He went on to design 500 buildings in San Francisco.

Return east on Green Street and turn left at Jones, heading down the hill to **Macondray Lane** (19), the Barbary Lane of Armistead Maupin's newspaper serial, *Tales of the City,* which was reprinted as a wildly successful book and then made into a television film about San Francisco life in the 1970s. Continue north on Jones to Union, turn left, and, noting the fine Deco apartment building by Albert Larsen at **1150 Union** (20) (1936), walk up to Hyde. Turn left at Hyde and make a quick right into Russell Place. Jack Kerouac lived with Neal Cassady and Carol Cassady at **29 Russell Place** (21) in 1952 while writing *On the Road, Visions of Cody,* and *Doctor Sax.*

Return to Hyde, turn left, and walk north to **Lombard.** You are now at the top of **"the crookedest street in the world"** (22). Willis Polk designed **1100 Lombard** (23) (1900) on the northwest corner for Fannie Osborne Stevenson, the widow of Robert Louis Stevenson. The original design has been obscured by subsequent additions. This block of Lombard Street is a San Francisco landmark. A continuing traffic jam during the tourist season, it was designed in 1922 to provide automobile access to houses built on a 27 percent grade. Walk down the hill to Montclair Terrace on the left. Gardner Dailey designed **65 Montclair Terrace** (24) (1938), an essay in the International Style.

Turn left on Leavenworth and left on Chestnut, noting the three large houses with ample yards on the left. Turn right on Larkin. Wurster, Bernardi & Emmons designed the Second Bay Tradition beauty at **2745 Larkin** (25) in 1951. Follow Larkin around to Francisco, turn left onto Polk, and then left into the Chestnut Street cul de sac. Joseph Esherick designed **20-24 Culebra Terrace** (26) for himself with additional rental units at **26-30 Culebra** (27) (1963). Climb the stairs at the end of Culebra and turn left on Chestnut, then left again on Hyde. Sculptor **Haig Patigian's home** (28) (1914) on the northeast corner at 898 Francisco was designed by Ward & Blohme. Continue east on Francisco and turn left on Leavenworth. Clark & Beuttler and Charles Moore designed the studio over the entranceway at **2508 Leavenworth** (29) (1961). Moore is regarded as one of the elders of the Third Bay Tradition. Continue down Leavenworth to Bay and turn left. William Wurster designed the apartment complex at **737 Bay Street** (30) (1937) and then remodeled the terraced homes at **757-63 Bay** (31), which were built in the 1850s, the same year.

NOB HILL

A 1½-hour walk, with some steep climbs. This tour starts at Washington and Mason Streets and ends on Polk Street on the west side of Nob Hill. You can return downtown via the California Street cable car.

In the gold rush era, Nob Hill, which was then known as Clay Street or California Street Hill, was an undistinguished neighborhood of frame houses with a handful of interesting exceptions, such as the Roman style villa set in a garden, built by William Coleman, the head of the second Vigilante Committee. The vast fortunes made from the Comstock lode and the construction of the Central Pacific railroad, the invention of the cable car, and the demise of Rincon Hill as a fashionable neighborhood changed all that. In 1873, Andrew Hallidie ran the first cable car line up Clay Street. Three years later Leland Stanford and a group of associates began work on the California Street Cable Railroad.

Quickly the city's new millionaires—those who did not build along Van Ness Avenue—George Hearst, his partner James Ben Ali Haggin, Richard Tobin (founder of the Hibernia Bank), the Big Four (Mark Hopkins, Leland Stanford, Charles Crocker, and Collis Huntington), Silver Kings James Fair and James Flood, and their fellow parvenus, covered the top of the hill with their mansions. Haggin, who admired good horse flesh, built a 60-room house on the block bounded by Washington, Taylor, Jackson, and Mason with stables for 40 horses and 18 carriages. Stanford's 50-room home, completed in 1876 at a cost of $2 million, was touted as "the most elegant private residence in the country." It featured a three-story entrance hall with a skylight of amber-colored glass shining down on the signs of the zodiac done in black mosaic on a white marble floor, ceilings covered with frescoes by Italian artists, doors and woodwork in French walnut, birch, toa, mahogany, and rosewood with inlays of ebony and precious stones, a room filled with the Chinese furniture exhibited at the Centennial Exposition in Philadelphia in 1876, and an art collection worth an estimated $2 million. The Hopkins monstrosity, a curious mismatch of architectural styles, sat next door (see illustration on page 130). Hopkins, however, died in 1878 before it was completed. A taciturn, even mysterious figure, Hopkins preferred his cabin in the Sierras and a nearby cottage to this building, which he liked to call the "Hotel de Hopkins." His mansion was the pet project of his wife, a much younger woman, whose own son claimed was Hopkins's housekeeper, not his wife.

After fire swept the neighborhood in 1906, almost nothing remained of the great mansions that had squatted on the shoulders of Nob Hill. The Flood Mansion and the Fairmount Hotel, which was under construction, were gutted and rebuilt. And there is the granite wall that railroad barons Leland Stanford and Mark Hopkins built around the block (Mason, Pine, Powell, and California) where their huge houses stood. After the earthquake and fire, the city's moneyed elite preferred to rebuild in Pacific Heights or the suburbs south on the Peninsula. Nob Hill became known for its hotels and luxurious apartment houses. The Fairmount hotel had been within weeks of opening when it was gutted by the fire. Rebuilt under the supervision of Julia Morgan, it was soon joined by the Stanford Court, the Mark Hopkins, and the Huntington. Nob Hill became a marketing myth to be sold to well-heeled tourists and those who could afford to live there. "The idea is to give 72 rich Americans and their families the opulent, gracious way of life maintained a century ago in the Nob Hill mansions of the Mark Hopkinses, the Floods, the Crockers, and the Huntingtons," wrote a *Chronicle* reporter, describing a 22-story apartment tower being built near the top of the hill in 1961.

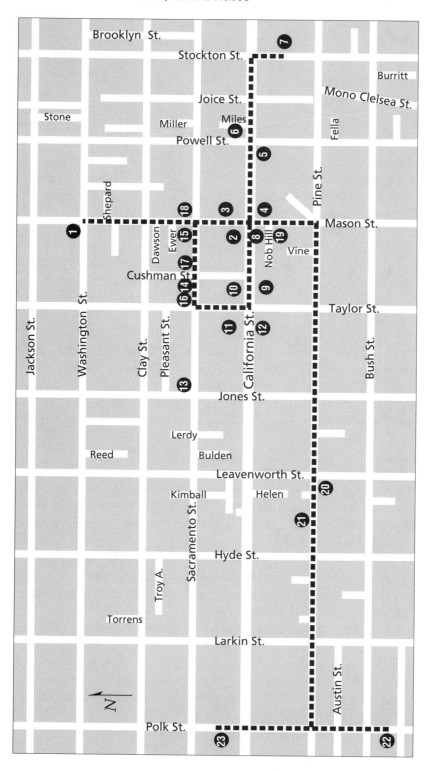

Brooklyn St.

Stockton St.

Stone

Miller

Joice St.

Miles

Powell St.

Burritt

Mono Clelsea St.

Fella

Pine St.

Shepard

Dawson

Ewer

Nob Hill

Vine

Mason St.

Cushman St.

Jackson St.

Washington St.

Clay St.

Pleasant St.

California St.

Taylor St.

Bush St.

Jones St.

Lerdy

Reed

Bulden

Leavenworth St.

Kimball

Helen

Sacramento St.

Troy A.

Hyde St.

Torrens

Larkin St.

Austin St.

N

Polk St.

The top of Nob Hill. From the right, the Flood Mansion (now the Pacific Union Club), the Colton Mansion, and the Crocker Mansion before the 1906 earthquake. *Library of Congress.*

The **Cable Car Barn and Museum** (1) (1909) at 1200 Mason Street at Washington is the logical place to start, inasmuch as cable cars turned Nob Hill into an accessible and fashionable place to live. The key to the development of the cable car was the invention of wire cable with a tensile strength of 160,000 pounds per square inch by the father of Andrew Hallidie, a Scottish immigrant. Hallidie was not the first to think of cable cars, but he solved two fundamental problems: what to pull them with (his wire cable, which runs beneath the street powered originally by steam, now by electric engine) and how to attach the car to the cable. He developed the grip to attach ore buckets to the cable at the mines. The operations of the cable system are explained by placards in the barn.

Originally, there were eight cable car lines covering 112 miles. Over time cable cars were replaced, first by electric trolleys and later by gasoline buses, and the system became a tourist attraction rather than a means of mass transit. Today there are four lines covering 4.4 miles. This building was retrofitted and restored by Chin and Hensholt Engineers, working with Ernest Born as consulting architect, when the entire system was rebuilt between 1982 and 1984. The historic photographs in the museum give you a sense of the scale and complexity of the mechanical equipment manufactured for the mining and transportation industries in San Francisco in the nineteenth century.

Walk south on Mason Street to the top of Nob Hill at the corner of Mason and California, where the cable car line built by Leland Stanford still runs. Before 1906 you would have been standing in the midst of a line of extravagant mansions—owned by Leland Stanford, Mark Hopkins, James Flood, Collis Huntington, Charles Crocker, and lesser beings—that stretched up and down California Street. Their designs ranged from the subdued neoclassicism of David Colton's mansion, which Willis

Polk described as the most artistic building in the city, to the Gothic flamboyance of the Hopkins house.

August Laver, the original architect for the first City Hall built in the Civic Center, designed the Italianate Flood Mansion (1886), which later became the **Pacific Union Club** (2) on the northeast corner of Mason and California. James Flood and William O'Brien were the owners of the Auction Lunch Saloon. With James Fair and John MacKay, they wrested control of the Comstock silver lode from the grasp of William Ralston and went on to strike the Big Bonanza. Impressed by mansions in the East, Flood insisted on brownstone, which was brought precut from a quarry in Connecticut. The use of brownstone in this 42-room, $15 million structure saved it from total destruction in 1906 when it was gutted, while the rest of the Nob Hill mansions, ersatz stone fashioned from wood, were reduced to ashes along with most of their precious furnishings, libraries, and artwork. Flood's daughter sold the gutted structure to the Pacific Union Club, which held an architectural competition for its restoration. Albert Pissis won with a proposal for an Acropolis-like structure on the site. The club turned him down, awarding the job to Willis Polk, another club member. Acquiring brownstone from the same quarry in Connecticut, Polk designed a lavish interior, complete with swimming pool surrounded by Minoan columns and an illuminated stained glass ceiling, and added the semicircular wings on the eastern and western sides of the building and a third floor. The original bronze fence surrounds three sides of the mansion. Forget about getting into this very exclusive club.

James Fair's daughter, Theresa Alice Oelrichs, hired the Reid brothers in 1903 to design the **Fairmount Hotel** (3) on the site of a mansion on Mason between Sacramento and California that her father had begun but never finished.

When the project proved too costly and time-consuming, she traded the unfinished building in 1906 for another on New Montgomery Street. The new owners finished construction and were just preparing for a grand opening when the earthquake struck. For a time the ballroom became the city government's command post—until fire swept over the top of the hill. Julia Morgan, in practice for only two years, drew up the plans to restore the fire-blackened hulk. Ben Swig bought the Fairmount and the St. Francis as the centerpieces of his ready-made real estate empire in 1945. Swig added the tower by Mario Gaidano on the back of the building in 1962, the top of which is an excellent place from which to view the city. The Fairmount, the most ornate hotel in the city, has recently been restored to its original condition. Particularly noteworthy are the triple-domed Laurel Court, the Venetian Room, one of the city's swankest supper clubs, and the Deco Cirque Room, which was designed by Timothy Pflueger.

Weeks and Day designed the **Mark Hopkins Hotel** (4) (1925) as a residential hotel for a wealthy mining engineer. The Gothic massing of its towers evokes the Hopkins mansion, which sat on this site. The only remaining vestige of the Hopkins mansion is the stone retaining wall that surrounded both Hopkins's home and Leland Stanford's to the east and the turret that marked the stables in the rear on Pine Street. The famous **Top of the Mark** has been redecorated several times, obliterating most of the Deco design, also by Pflueger. It still has an excellent view. The **Stanford Court** (5), another of the hilltop's exclusive hotels located down California Street to the east, was designed by Creighton Withers and built in 1911 on the site of Stanford's mansion. On the northeast corner of California and Powell is the somewhat tattered **University Club** (6) (1912) by Bliss & Faville. Farther east down California Street on the right at

Grace Episcopal Cathedral. *Peter Booth Wiley.*

the corner of Stockton is the **Ritz Carlton Hotel** (7) (1909), arguably the city's most luxurious. The center of the building on Stockton Street was designed by Napoleon Le Brun & Sons of New York as the western headquarters of the Metropolitan Life Insurance Company. Added onto five times, it became Cogswell college in 1973 and then the Ritz Carlton in 1991. Kajima Associates and Whisler-Patri gutted the building and rebuilt the interior to accommodate guests and added a coach entrance. The hotel's 18,000-square-foot garden, which overlooks Downtown, was designed by Thomas Church and has been partially restored. The interior is filled with eighteenth- and nineteenth-century antiques and artwork. The **tableau** (1920) in the pediment over the entrance depicting the American family protected by insurance is by Haig Patigan.

Return up California Street; across from the Mark Hopkins on the left are the **Morsehead Apartments** (8)

(1914), a very attractive French style structure by Houghton Sawyer.

Continue west on California to the **Huntington Hotel** (9) (1924) at the southeast corner of Taylor and California, another creation of Weeks & Day. The hotel's **Big Four Restaurant** with its clubby atmosphere has an excellent collection of photographs of the old Nob Hill. **Huntington Park** (10) across the street was the site of David Colton's mansion. Colton was vice president of the Southern Pacific. Huntington bought Colton's mansion, which burned in 1906. In 1915, Huntington's widow gave the site to the city for a park to honor her husband, the most shameless of the four buccaneers. It is thought that this beautiful little park was designed by John McLaren, longtime head of the city's park system, who oversaw the completion of Golden Gate Park.

Turn west to face the front of **Grace Cathedral** (11), the seat of the Episcopal bishop of California. Lewis

The Chambord Apartments, Jones and Sacramento. *Peter Booth Wiley.*

Hobart designed this French Gothic structure, reminiscent of Notre Dame, after earlier plans were abandoned. It was built over more than a half century, beginning in 1910, on land, once the site of Charles Crocker's mansion, that was donated by his family. The exterior was fashioned from reinforced concrete, brush hammered to appear like stone. Construction was completed in 1964 with the installation of copies of Ghiberti's bronze doors, from the baptistry at the Duomo in Florence, at the main entrance. The cathedral features an exceptionally fine collection of stained glass windows. Tours are available. Across California Street the **Masonic Temple and Auditorium** (12) (1958) by Albert Roller presents a striking contrast with its sleek Vermont marble surfaces.

Continue west on California and turn right on Jones to Sacramento. The **Chambord Apartments** (13) (1921), on the northeast corner of Jones and Sacramento, were originally designed by James Francis Dunn, with references to Antonio Gaudi and Beaux-Arts styles. The ornamentation on this sculpted building was stripped off the balconies in the 1950s and then carefully restored by Marquis & Stoller in 1985. Interestingly, the original plans showed details that did not correspond with the one photograph of the building located by the architects.

Turn right on Sacramento and walk east. The next block offers a sense of the evolution of apartment building architecture in an upscale neighborhood. To view these buildings in chronological order, begin with the diminutive **1182 Sacramento** (14) (1908). The association of French style with gracious living may have been established right after the earthquake with this building by an unknown architect. Next look at the Park Lane Apartments at **1100 Sacramento** (15) (1924), Edward Young's design in the Moderne style. Angus McSweeney designed **1190 Sacramento** (16) in the International Style in 1954, five years before that style began to influence downtown office building design. Rony Rolnizky designed **1150 Sacramento** (17) (1987) to conform with the hilltop's 65-foot height limit.

Across Mason Street on the northeast corner of Sacramento, M. V. B. MacAdam poured her fortune into the **Brocklebank** (18) (1926), hoping to build an apartment house that would be, she said, "a credit to San Francisco and myself." She hired Weeks & Day, who were also working on the Mark Hopkins Hotel, which explains the complementarity of the two buildings'

designs. MacAdam's effort broke her, but she left one of the city's most exclusive addresses as her legacy.

Walk south on Mason and down the hill past a row of town houses at **831-43 Mason** (19) (1917) by Willis Polk. Turn right on Pine and walk to the 1200 block, where there are two striking apartment buildings designed by James Francis Dunn. Little is known of Dunn, who died before the Chambord Apartments were completed in 1921, beyond his ability to come up with original combinations of French Beaux-Arts motifs. Two of his most elegant are the **apartments at 1201 Pine** (20) (1909) and **1250 Pine** (21) (1919).

Continue west on Pine to Polk Street. There are two traditional seafood restaurants on Polk, **Maye's Original Oyster House** (22) to the left at 1233 Polk, and the **Swan Oyster Depot** (23) to the right at 1517 Polk. You can return downtown via the California Street cable car, which departs from Polk and California.

PACIFIC HEIGHTS

This is a long walk (allow four hours) with a number of steep climbs. It begins at Lafayette Park and ends at Arguello and Lake. You can return downtown on a California Street bus. If you want to stop for lunch, Fillmore Street between Pine and Washington offers a number of good restaurants. Or you may want to divide the tour in half, stopping after seeing the Bourn Mansion at 2250 Webster.

During the first decade or so of the city's history, Pacific Heights was an empty ridge top, dotted by an occasional home overlooking the farms and dairies of Cow Hollow to the north. Construction, beyond the building of an occasional isolated home, did not begin until the early 1870s when J. W. Tucker, described as "an old-time builder," erected a collection of one-story bay-window cottages known as Tucker Town around a square defined by Jackson, Webster, Washington, and Buchanan. The cottages were very modest in size, and only one survives today. Further development quickly followed the arrival of the cable car and trolley lines beginning in 1873. Soon contractors, such as The Real Estates Associates (TREA) and the Hinkel family, began building row houses for "middle-class" families in the same area.

The construction of row houses was first noted in the city at about 1860, but little is known of these early developments because most of them were destroyed in the 1906 fire. An early means of development was the formation of homestead associations. "About 170 of these corporations were formed in the 1860s," stated architectural historian Anne Bloomfield, "in order to turn a profit by breaking up large landholdings and encouraging house-lot ownership among workingmen." Aspiring home owners became members for a small fee and made monthly payments until they owned a lot. The homestead associations then offered plans and contractors. These developments led to the construction of many of the Victorians so closely associated with the image of San Francisco.

The Real Estate Associates, said Bloomfield, "claimed to have built more detached houses than any other person or company in the United States in a similar time span [more than 1,000 in the 1870s]. Its work includes familiar rows of detached, nearly identical, Italianate houses." TREA, in this early example of mass production of housing, built for people of varying income levels: "A few larger and several medium-priced houses on the more important streets, slightly less expensive houses on the side streets, and inexpensive houses on interior streets [alleys] that the company cut through blocks."[71] The more expensive houses cost $6,000 and more, and those for the families of skilled working men and lower-level professionals sold for $2,500 to $4,000. Terms were one fifth to one half down, the balance to be paid over 1 to 12 years at 8 to 10 percent a year. TREA crews, totaling 300 to 400 men, worked on numerous sites simultaneously.

TREA began by speculating in land but soon moved into construction. Its board of directors included owners of a planing mill and a firm of stair builders, scroll sawyers, and wood turners, reflecting at least an attempt at vertical integration in the home-building business. Eventually they hired two architects, John Remer, a theater designer who signed his name to designs that did not appear significantly different from those in popular pattern books, and David Farquharson, who designed the Bank of California for William Ralston and commercial buildings for TREA. TREA operated out of an ornate five-story building complete with a mansard roof at 230 Montgomery Street.

TREA, according to its manager, was eager "to serve the great middle class" and "transform the sandy wastes outside the business part of the city into...neighborhoods, composed of frugal and industrious people." Excellent sentiments, but according to Bloomfield, TREA practices were both ruthless and shady. "The process of getting possession [of land] came to resemble a grade-B western, with destruction by night, forcible takeover by day in overwhelming numbers, and unceasing armed watch, all punctuated by gunshots that may or may not have been random." [72] TREA ultimately fell prey to the stock market collapse following William Ralston's unsuccessful attempt to gain control of the Comstock lode. TREA had gone deeply into debt, purchasing land worth more than its assets. In 1881 a group of its creditors drove the company into bankruptcy.

The middle-class neighborhood on the southern slope of Pacific Heights was overshadowed by the rows of Victorian mansions built along the ridge top, starting at Van Ness in the 1880s. Members of the vast, intermarried clan of German Jews that began when Louis Sloss and Lewis Gerstle married the Grunebaum sisters were among the first to build in this area. The Sloss family lived on Van Ness near California and was soon joined by the Gerstle family, which moved in aross the street. Both homes burned in 1906. When Sloss's daughter Bella married Ernest Reuben Lilienthal, Sloss built a house for them a little more than a block away near California and Franklin. Their son Samuel married into the Haas family, eventually inheriting the nearby mansion known as the Haas-Lilienthal House, today the headquarters of San Francisco Heritage (see page 130). This classic Queen Anne was built by Samuel's father-in-law, William Haas, for his wife, who was Bella Sloss Lilienthal's first cousin. There are three other nineteenth-century houses built by the Haas family in the immediate neighborhood. Many of these "Gothic" behemoths were demolished to make way for modern apartment buildings, some of which contained apartments with as many as 20 rooms.

In the 1890s, as moneyed families moved west along Pacific Heights, they began to hire the young architects, such as Ernest Coxhead, A. Page Brown, Willis Polk, and Bernard Maybeck, who prided themselves on their break with Victorian styles. Some of the homes designed by Coxhead, Maybeck, and Polk are the earliest examples of the First Bay Tradition. In the same area a generation later modern architects such as William Wurster, Gardner Dailey, and Joseph Esherick designed houses, which proved to be an even more radical break with the past and are representative of the Second Bay Tradition.

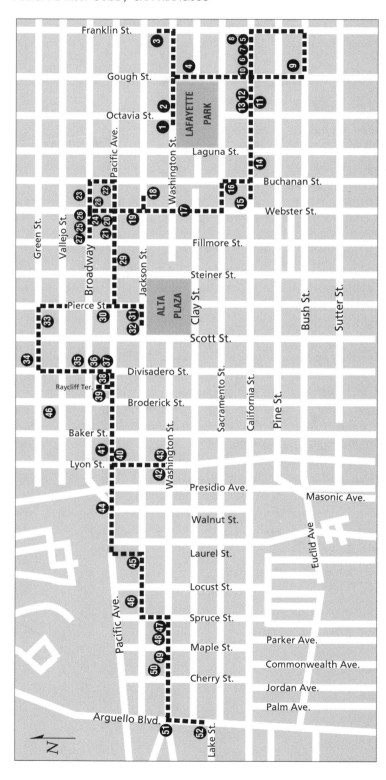

Begin at the **Mary Phelan Mansion** (1) (1915) at 2120 Washington Street on the north side of Lafayette Park, one of the city's most fashionable addresses starting in the late nineteenth century. James Duvall Phelan, former mayor, U.S. senator, and exponent of the City Beautiful movement, built this house for his sister and maintained a suite here. Neither of them married, although Phelan kept a mistress, Mrs. Florence Ellon, for whom he maintained a separate flat. The house was designed by Charles Peter Weeks.

Walk east on Washington to **2080 Washington** (2) (1913), which was designed for Alma Spreckels by MacDonald and Applegarth (see pages 377–379 for a discussion of her role in the city's cultural affairs). The design illustrates the dramatic shift from late Victorian to neoclassical styles. Big Alma, who convinced her husband to fund the California Palace of the Legion of Honor, was in love with all things French. George Applegarth, who also designed the Palace, was a graduate of the École des Beaux-Arts. Spreckels kept her very fine collection of Rodin statuary here before moving it to the Palace. The interior reflected the expensive and garish tastes of the city's millionaires. There was a long entry hall with a Tiffany glass ceiling and gold mosaics set in Italian stone, a Pompeian court with a fountain and a ceiling covered with cherubs and cupids, a ballroom along the entire west wall of the building, and an Italian room with a floor-to-ceiling fireplace bracketed by two Nubian slave figures decked out in purple loincloths and orange collars studded with rhinestones.

Continue east to Franklin and turn left to the **Haas-Lilienthal House** (3) at 2007 Franklin (see illustration on page 130). None of the grand houses lining Van Ness Avenue survived 1906, but some of the smaller (!) houses built nearby before the earthquake, such as

The Spreckels Mansion, 2080 Washington. *San Francisco History Center, San Francisco Public Library.*

Alma de Bretteville Spreckels in 1904.
San Francisco History Center, San Francisco Public Library

this one, remain. Headquarters of the Foundation for San Francisco's Architectural Heritage, the house is a monument to efforts to preserve the city's architectural treasures. William Haas, a German Jewish immigrant and head of Haas Brothers, a merchant house trading for food staples around the Pacific Basin, built this home for his bride in 1886. Designed by Peter Schmidt, it is a classic example of late Victorian Queen Anne with some suggestions of the coming Shingle and Colonial Revival styles. The house, which was turned over to Heritage in 1973, is beautifully preserved and open to the public. Heritage also offers walking tours of Pacific Heights.

Return on Washington to Gough and turn left to Clay. The **C. A. Belden House** (4) at 2004 Gough is another superb Queen Anne, designed by Walter Mathews in 1889. Walk south on Gough and turn left on California. *Here Today* describes the houses clustered around the intersection of California and Gough and farther west on California as

part of "one of San Francisco's most valuable and architecturally distinguished districts." Edward Coleman, owner of a Grass Valley gold mine and timberlands, built the elaborate Queen Anne at **1701 Franklin** (5) in 1895 after a design by W. H. Lillie. Coleman wanted to locate near his brother John, who bought **1834 California** (6) and remodeled it according to plans by Percy & Hamilton in 1895. Isaac Wormser, a grocery merchant who was the "W" in S&W Foods, built the original house in 1876. Louis Sloss, one of the founding patriarchs of the intricately intermarried Sloss-Gerstle-Haas-Lilienthal-Bransten-Fleisshacker-Stern-Koshland clans, built **1818 California** (7) as a wedding present for his daughter Bella and her husband, Ernest Reuben Lilienthal. Sloss's mansion was nearby on Van Ness Avenue, and the neighborhood became home to some of his extended family.

Ernest and Bella's daughter, Florine, married Edward Bransten (originally Brandenstein), the owner of MJB Coffee. The **Bransten Mansion** (8) (1904), a brick veneer over wood Colonial Revival designed by Herman Barth, is located at 1735 Franklin. The Branstens bought 1701 Franklin and 1818 California, providing them with a lovely family compound with gardens. Samuel Lilienthal, another of Ernest and Bella's children, married William Haas's daughter Alice. (Bella Lilienthal and Alice's mother were first cousins.) Samuel and Alice moved into the Haas-Lilienthal House after William's death.

Continue south on Franklin to Bush and turn right. **Trinity Church** (9), a massive Gothic affair of Colusa sandstone at the corner of Gough and Bush, is thought to have been designed by A. C. Schweinfurth in 1896 when he was working as a draftsman for A. Page Brown. Turn right on Gough and return to California. The apartment building at **1800 Gough** (10) (1923) is typical of

Trinity Church, Bush and Franklin. *Peter Booth Wiley.*

Dominga de Goni Atherton House, 1990 California. *Peter Booth Wiley.*

the large structures built to replace the late-Victorian mansions in the area.

Walk west on California. Willis Polk designed the Tudor home at **1969 California** (11) (1915) for Constance de Young (Mrs. Joseph O. Tobin), Michael de Young's daughter. De Young's mansion, now demolished, stood next door. Another daughter, Helen (Mrs. George Cameron), never carried out her plans to build a similar house adjacent to her sister's. They were to be connected by the unfinished arch to the right. The lavish Queen Anne at **1976**

California (12) (1883) was designed by Schmidt & Havens. Its bizarre neighbor to the west at **1990 California** (13) was designed by Moore Brothers for Dominga de Goni, the widow of Faxon Dean Atherton, a Massachusetts native who came to Yerba Buena in the 1830s to trade hides and tallow with merchants in Valparaiso, Chile, and later made substantial investments in city real estate. De Goni was the daughter of a wealthy Valparaiso merchant. (Author Gertrude Atherton was Faxon's daughter-in-law.)

Continue west on California, where there are numerous late Victorians to admire. The Newsom brothers, Samuel and Joseph Cather, designed **2129** and **2145 California** (14) in 1882. Their work, among the most significant in the city, epitomizes the bourgeois fascination with the decorative hyperbole of late-Victorian style. These young Canadians, who came to San Francisco in the 1860s, began their practice in a third brother's office and went on not only to design numerous buildings throughout California but also to promote their work through pattern books and a periodical, *Up-to-Date Architecture*.

Temple Sherith Israel (15) (1904) at 2266 California was founded by Polish Jews in 1854 after an irreconcilable split with their German brethren over who would control kosher slaughtering. Designed by Albert Pissis in the Romanesque style, the building survived the 1906 earthquake and, as one of the few remaining public buildings, housed the superior court for a number of years. It was here that Boss Abe Ruef was tried for extortion (see page 61). The ark within dates from the construction of the congregation's first temple in 1854, and the building houses a particularly fine library.

Return east on California, turning left on Buchanan. In 1904, Willis Polk remodeled the house at **2139-41 Buchanan** (16), originally built in 1880, for his father-in-law, Fernando Barreda, ambassador from Spain and Peru to the Court of St. James and the United States. Continue north on Buchanan,

Temple Sherith Israel, 2266 California. *Peter Booth Wiley.*

Victorian row houses in Pacific Heights, 2200 block of Webster. *Peter Booth Wiley.*

turn left on Sacramento, and right on Webster. TREA built the classic Italianate row houses at **2244, 2250, 2311, and 2315-21 Webster** (1878–1879). Henry Hinkel designed the row houses at **2209-53 Webster** (17) (1878–1879). Various members of the Hinkel family, conveniently made up of an architect, two carpenters, and a sawyer, built numerous houses in Pacific Heights, the Western Addition, and the Mission. Continue north on Webster and turn right on Jackson. The cottage at **2209 Jackson** (18) is the only structure remaining from the original Pacific Heights development known as Tucker Town. Return to Webster and turn right. James Francis Dunn, architect for a number of fine apartment buildings on Nob Hill, designed the Francophile apartment house at **2411 Webster** (19) (c. 1915).

Turn left on Pacific to see **2340 Pacific** (20) (1929), a Deco apartment building by Herman Baumann, and **2360 Pacific** (21) (1929), which combines a Churrigueresque entryway with

Deco detailing on the upper floors. Return east on Pacific; there is another Deco apartment building at **2230-50 Pacific** (22) with Mayan detailing.

Turn left on Buchanan and left on Broadway. Broadway to the west is dotted with large mansions for the next nine blocks. James Flood, son of the famed Silver King who lived on Nob Hill, built the first of two mansions at **2120 Broadway** (23) (1900–1901), now the Hamlin School, from a design by Julius Kraft. G. Albert Lansburgh designed the mansion at **2201 Broadway** (24) (1914). The second Flood mansion, by Bliss & Faville, is across the street at **2222 Broadway** (25) (1915). With a panoramic view of the Golden Gate, this Italian palazzo features a 140-foot-long reception hall, hand-carved hardwood interiors, and elaborate marble fireplaces. Flood's widow gave the building to the Catholic Church, which turned it into the Convent of the Sacred Heart, an exclusive girls' school. The school also owns the **Grant Mansion** (26) at 2200

Convent of the Sacred Heart School, formerly the Flood Mansion, 2222 Broadway. *Peter Booth Wiley.*

The Bourn Mansion, 2250 Webster. *Peter Booth Wiley.*

Broadway (1910), designed by Hiss & Weekes. Andrew Hammond built the mansion at **2252 Broadway** (27) (1905), now the Stuart Hall School. Hammond was a lumber baron while Joseph Grant was a founder of the Save the Redwoods League and has a grove

of trees in Del Norte State Park named after him.

Return to Webster and turn right. Willis Polk designed the **Bourn Mansion** (28) at 2550 Webster in the style of an English town house for his friend William Bourn II in 1896. Polk successfully crammed this clinker brick structure with 28 rooms and 14 fire-places into a small lot. Bourn inherited a rich Grass Valley gold mine from his father and became president of the Spring Valley Water Company, which controlled the city's water supply. Polk did some of his finest work for Bourn, including the water company's office building on Mason Street, an elaborate stone "cottage" and office building at the Empire Mine, and Filoli, his estate near Woodside.

Turn right on Pacific. The **Leale House** (29) at 2475 Pacific, the house for a 25-acre dairy farm, is one of the few remaining early farmhouses. Built circa 1853, it was remodeled two decades later. Continuing west, you will come to one of the early modern hous-es in Pacific Heights, William Wurster's design at **2600 Pacific** (30) (1937). Turn left at Pierce and right on Jackson. Irving Murray Scott, owner of the Union

Iron Works, hired Ernest Coxhead, one of the architects associated with the First Bay Tradition, to do the drawings for a house for his daughter and her husband at **2600 Jackson** (31) (1897) for his daughter and her husband. It was the first electrified house in San Francisco. Appropriately, Coxhead's colleague Willis Polk designed what was intended to be a country home at **2622 Jackson** (32) (1894) when the area still had a rural atmosphere. This was probably Polk's first independent commission.

Walk back to the corner of Jackson and Pierce and turn left down the hill. Continue on to Green and turn left. Ernest Coxhead designed both **2421 and 2423 Green** (33) (1893 and 1895), the former for himself. Continue west to **2508 Green** (34) (1901), a half-timbered Craftsman house designed by Edgar Matthews.

Turn left up the hill on Divisadero. You are beginning to see more modern homes designed by architects associat-ed with modernism and the Second Bay Tradition. John Elkin Dinwiddie combined modernist elements—a flat roof, ribbon windows, minimal trim—with local materials, redwood siding with a partial board and batten finish, in a classic Second Bay Tradition home at **2660 Divisadero** (35) (1938). William Wurster designed **2560 Divisadero** (36) (1939). Esherick Homsey Dodge & Davis were still working in the same style in 1990 when the firm designed **2550 Divisadero** (37). Paul Williams, the country's first prominent African-American architect, is responsible for **2555 Divisadero** (38) (c. 1930).

Continue south on Divisadero, turn right onto Pacific and right again into Raycliffe Terrace, a modernist enclave. Gardner Dailey designed **1 Raycliffe Terrace** (39) (1951). Wurster, Bernardi & Emmons did **25 Raycliffe** (39) (1959), and Joseph Esherick **75 Raycliffe** (39) (1951). Most of these

The Second Bay Tradition, 2660 Divisadero. *Jan Cigliano.*

Interior of the Church of New Jerusalem, with unpeeled madrone logs supporting the ceiling, chairs by Bernard Maybeck, and landscapes by William Keith. Lyon and Washington Streets. *Courtesy of the Swedenborgian Church.*

houses seem quite commonplace if not banal today, but they were startling when they were first built in the 1930s. Return to Pacific and turn right. There is another Wurster, Bernardi & Emmons house at **3095 Pacific** (40) (1959), with an Esherick house across the street at **3070 Pacific** (41) (1953).

Continue on Pacific to Lyon and turn left, walking to the corner of Washington. The **Church of the New Jerusalem** (42) (1894) is the collective work of A. Page Brown, A. C. Schweinfurth, Bernard Maybeck, William Keith, and Bruce Porter, all working under the supervision of Joseph Worcester, the Swedenborgian pastor (see pages 254–255). Porter supplied a drawing of a chapel in the Po Valley of Italy. Schweinfurth mined the vernacular, ranging from European chapels to California missions, for its design. Worcester went to the Santa Cruz

Mountains to select unpeeled madrone logs to support the roof. Maybeck is thought to have designed the rush chairs, which Gustav Stickley acknowledged as the inspiration for his Mission furniture; Porter fashioned the stained glass windows, and Keith painted four murals. Note the Craftsman apartment building across the street at **2106-10 Lyon** (43) by Edgar Mathews (c. 1905).

Return to Pacific and turn left. Continuing west on Pacific, you will find a **large cluster of shingled houses designed by the practitioners of the First Bay Tradition** (44) located ideally on the edge of the Presidio forest, which nicely complements their wooden exteriors. Ernest Coxhead's houses are **3151 Pacific** (1912), **3255 Pacific** (c. 1910), remodeled by Polk), **3234 Pacific** (1902), Bruce Porter's home, and **3232 Pacific** (1902, remodeled in 1959), one of his best known. Polk also remodeled **3203 Pacific,** and Maybeck designed **3233 Pacific** (1909). Samuel Newsom designed **3198 Pacific** (1898). Julia Morgan showed her affinity for the new Shingle Style with **3377 Pacific** (1908), and Esherick added a modern commentary on the tradition with **3323 Pacific** (1963). Albert Farr was the architect for **3333 and 3343 Pacific.**

Turn left on Laurel. On the northwest corner of Laurel and Jackson is Maybeck's striking masterpiece, the **Roos House** (45) (1909). The house was given to Elizabeth Roos by her father, the owner of the Opheum Theatre Company. Roos also owned the Roos Brothers clothing store. The house appears modest in size but is actually 9,000 square feet. Designed in the Tudor style, it features fantastically carved ornamental woodwork on the exterior, a forest of redwood paneling inside, and numerous light fixtures, lanterns, and fireplaces designed by Maybeck. Even the foundation—a lattice of heavy wooden beams attached to wooden piles to secure the house in an earthquake—is an original. Michael Goodman, who oversaw interior design at the Stock Exchange (City) Club, offers another modern essay at **3550 Jackson** (46) (1940).

Walk west on Jackson and turn left on Spruce. As you approach Washington, note the **Goldman House** (47) (1951) on your right, which sits on the corner of Washington and Spruce. You are entering another enclave of the extended Haas family, which owns Levi Strauss. Rhoda Goldman is a Haas. The delicacy of the framing and the expanses of glass give Esherick's design an airy, see-through look. At the end of the block at **3778 Washington** (48) (1952) is the home of Madeline Haas Russell, the only Bay Area residence designed by the well-known European modernist Eric Mendelsohn. Mrs. Russell was the granddaughter of William and Bertha Haas, the first occupants of the Haas-Lilienthal House.

The First Bay Tradition, 3232 Pacific Street. *Jan Cigliano.*

Le Petit Trianon (49) (1902), the grand mansion in the next block west on Washington, was designed by Frank Van Trees for Marcus and Corinne Koshland. The Koshlands were Boston wool merchants, who bought their wool from ranchers throughout the Intermountain West. Mrs. Koshland asked Van Trees to copy Marie Antionette's favorite palace. The Koshland's son Daniel partnered with his brother-in-law Walter Haas, to take control of Levi Strauss in the 1920s. Just around the corner to the right at **116 Cherry** (50) (1892) is another early Willis Polk house.

Continue on Washington to where it ends at Arguello Boulevard. Across Arguello is the entrance to **Presidio Terrace** (51), the city's most exclusive enclave, through portals designed by Albert Pissis. Laid out in 1898 on land being used as a vegetable garden, it was the city's first planned neighborhood since George Gordon modeled South

The Roos House, a Bernard Maybeck masterpiece, at Laurel and Jackson Streets. *Peter Booth Wiley.*

Park after a fashionable London crescent in 1855. Antoine Borel, a Swiss banker and real estate developer, bought the land and partnered with the realtors Baldwin & Howell to create a private enclave for wealthy families. For a model, they looked to garden city developments, such as Bedford Park in London and Tuxedo Park in the New York suburbs. The lots here are wider (50 to 75 feet) than others in the city, and the entrance gate provides a sense of exclusivity (and a place to hang a Private Property sign.) Original deeds spelled out a number of restrictions, including no saloons, billboards, ugly buildings, spite fences, overhead wiring, nor people of color.

The enclave is a compendium of fashionable architectural styles from the post-1906 period. Realtor Archibald Stewart Baldwin's in-laws built the first home at **2 Presidio Terrace,** designed by Frank Trees in the Italianate style, and lived there with Baldwin and his wife. Kenneth MacDonald Jr., of the firm of MacDonald and Applegarth,

designed **3, 4, and 5 Presidio Terrace** (1908, 1908, and 1911), purchasing the Mediterranean Revival home at 4 Presidio Terrace for himself and his wife. **Five Presidio Terrace** is MacDonald's essay in the Shingle Style. It was built for Dr. Hartland Law, who with his brother bought the fire-ravaged Fairmount Hotel from Theresa Fair and hired Julia Morgan to reconstruct it.

Charles Whittlesey, the architect for **10 Presidio Terrace** (1909), began his practice in Chicago under the influence of Louis Sullivan and Frank Lloyd Wright and brought some of Wright's Prairie Style to this design. Whittlesey designed six other homes in the development, including **19 Presidio Terrace** in the Pueblo style (1909). T. Patterson Ross, architect for the Moorish Alcazar Theatre and collaborator on the Sing Chong and Sing Fat Buildings in Chinatown, was fond of exotica. He designed **22 Presidio Terrace** (1910) in the Mission Revival Style. Whittlesey introduced a rare and unique reference to Japanese architecture in his design for **24 Presidio Terrace** (1909). Note the stacked and exposed beams under the eaves.

The Reid Brothers designed **26 Presidio Terrace** (1909) in the Colonial Revival style for merchant prince Marshall Hale, the owner of the Hale Brothers department store at Fifth and Market, which they also designed. MacDonald and Applegarth did the drawings for **30 Presidio Terrace** (1909) for Fernando Nelson, the San Francisco contractor who built some 4,000 homes in the city. This massive Elizabethan "cottage" is the home of Senator Dianne Feinstein and her husband Richard Blum. The senator grew up across the street at **1 Presidio Terrace.** The Beaux-Arts mansion at **34 Presidio Terrace** (1909) by MacDonald and Applegarth was a forerunner of Alma Spreckels's grander

mansion on Washington Street. It was the home of Mayor Joseph Alioto. Julia Morgan designed **36 Presidio Terrace** (1911) in the Beaux-Arts style.

Return to Arguello and turn right to **Temple Emanu-El** (52), the house of worship built in 1926 by the city's prominent German Jewish families. Emanu-El was established after Polish and German Jews split in 1854. According to a member of one of the pioneering German Jewish families, after 1861 "the *Hinterberliner* [those from east of Berlin] could not hope to pass" through the doorways of Emanu-El, which is no longer true.[73] This massive Byzantine structure was designed by Bakewell and Brown with assistance from Sylvan Schaittacher and advice from Bernard Maybeck, G. Albert Lansburgh, and Edgar Walter. Bruce Porter did the interior decoration.

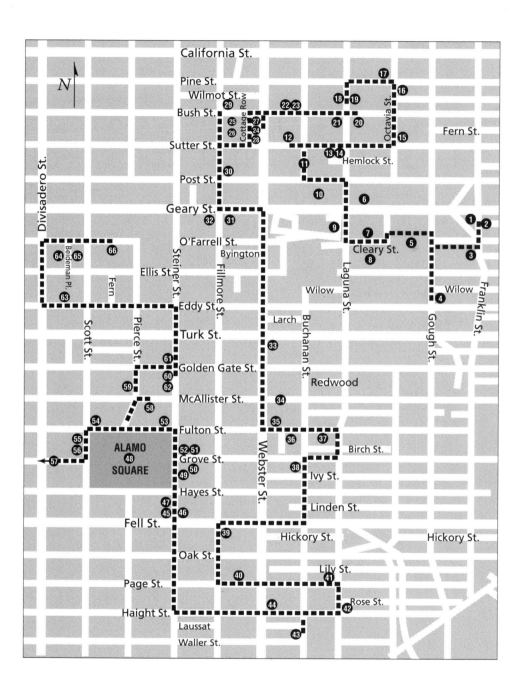

17

The Western Addition, the Mission, and the Haight-Ashbury

I n the 1850s the development of San Francisco beyond the waterfront was confounded by the city's lack of a clear title to the Outside Lands, a broad arc of sand dunes, swales, and rocky outcrops to the south and west of downtown. Larkin and Eighth Streets—representing a line that runs roughly north and south from today's Civic Center—were regarded as the western border of the city. As the population grew rapidly, the city sought to extend its claim to lands beyond the boundaries of the pueblo of Yerba Buena, which were established in 1834, but the federal government argued that the city had no title to any land. There was a small village including a number of farms adjacent to Mission Dolores, shacks and houses built by squatters, who numbered in the thousands, and an occasional country estate scattered here and there in the dunes and along the hillsides. The question of title did not deter squatters, who were willing to defend their homes with firearms and often did.

Mayor James Van Ness brought a semblance of order to the problem of land titles through an 1858 ordinance. Some squatters' titles were confirmed; others were not, which resulted in further violence. Thereafter, development in the new "suburbs," as they were called beginning in the 1880s, followed a familiar pattern. Real estate speculators bought up blocks of land. Those who were not already on the public payroll prevailed upon city officials, through the judicious distribution of boodle, to grant horse car franchises. Once the horse car lines were running, construction of new housing began. The dispersal of development created a series of little villages—on Fillmore, Haight, and Mission Streets—where the new residents bought their food and housewares. Big-ticket shopping was reserved for a trip downtown, which could take some time in those days. These little villages were the first of San Francisco's highly self-conscious neighborhoods.

THE WESTERN ADDITION

This tour covers a lot of ground with moderate climbs. Allow three hours. It starts on Gough between O'Farrell and Geary and ends near O'Farrell and Scott. You can return downtown on the Geary Street bus.

"The Van Ness Ordinance," according to Mel Scott in The San Francisco Bay Area, "is important from the standpoint of city planning...because it determined the pattern of streets and public squares in the area known as the Western Addition."[74] Away from the crowding and congestion of the waterfront, the city was more generous with the establishment of public parks. Three were created in the Western Addition, including Alamo Square, one of the centerpieces of Victoriana.

Systematic development came to the Western Addition in 1859 when real estate speculator Thomas Hayes, after a six-year term as county clerk, built a railroad through the sand dunes along Market Street to the 160-acre plot he had acquired in what is today known as Hayes Valley (along either side of Hayes Street from Franklin to Fillmore.) With the construction of streetcar lines connecting the Western Addition to the downtown, it became one of the first districts where substantial construction of "middle-class" homes in the spirit of the Real Estate Associates took place (see pages 268–269). Larger homes were built around Alamo Square. The first apartment buildings went up in the 1880s, but the city remained overwhelmingly a community of single-family dwellings until the 1906 disaster.

The Western Addition epitomized the popularity of Victorian architecture in all its permutations. It also became the target of the critics led by Willis Polk. Polk described the Western Addition as "that architectural nightmare conceived in a reign of terror and produced by artistic anarchists who are continually seeking to do something great, without any previous experience or preparation for their work." "The real estate speculators, speculative contractors, and disappointed carpenters who have passed themselves off on an indulgent public as architects all over the country," he went on, "seem to have found their last refuge in San Francisco."[75]

When the entire city east of Van Ness was destroyed by the fire of 1906, Fillmore Street, already the principal shopping district in the Western Addition, became for a time the city's most important commercial strip. After 1906, the Western Addition remained very much like other middle-class neighborhoods, a mixed community of workers, professionals, and successful businessmen with occasional businesses, such as a lumberyard, a brewery, a sausage factory, and a bakery, interspersed with homes. The first signs of change came when Jewish and Japanese families began to move into the neighborhood. In the nineteenth century, the Jewish community, primarily German immigrants, remained small. Jewish immigration in significant numbers began with the pogroms that followed the assassination of Czar Alexander II in 1881. The first new arrivals, small in number as compared with those who went to New York City, settled south of Market, moving after the earthquake to the Western Addition. Many of the city's established Jewish families contributed funds to assist both their brethren still in Russia and those who had immigrated. But there were a few in the community who agreed with Rabbi Jacob Voorsanger of Temple Emanu-El when he wrote that the new immigrants were "uncouth" and an embarrassment and that further immigration should be barred by the U.S. government.

The first Japanese immigrants lived either in Chinatown or on Rincon Hill after its decline as a fashionable neighborhood. After 1906, the Japanese settled in Japan Town on Post and Sutter Streets east of Fillmore. In addition, there was a small number of African-American families living on Ellis and Scott Streets and a smattering of French, Irish, Italians, and Russians.

World War II brought changes to the Western Addition that would ultimately lead to its decimation at the hands of the Redevelopment Agency. By 1943 crowding, caused by the rapid influx of African-American war workers, was so serious in the Western Addition that a congressional committee reported that people were living in "stores, rear porches, in fact practically any space available." Some of the pressure on housing in the Western Addition was relieved by the confinement of most of the Japanese-American population in internment camps in 1942. After the war some of the internees returned to their former neighborhood while the black population found that the prospects offered by wartime employment were now circumscribed by job and housing discrimination.

Despite its problems, the Western Addition was a vital community with numerous churches, locally owned businesses, and a substantial middle class. By the 1950s jazz musicians, such as Duke Ellington, Miles Davis, Charlie Parker, John Coltrane, and Billie Holiday, were appearing at after-hours clubs in the Western Addition—Jimbo's Bop City, the New Orleans

Swing House, and Elsie's Breakfast Club. The Western Addition was the most important jazz center west of Chicago.

None of this mattered to the city's white establishment. In 1947, the Planning Department explained that the Western Addition was too close to the financial district for the city not to take advantage of the opportunity to build on "slopes on which apartments with fine views could be erected." Unfortunately, Planning acknowledged, only a small number of the "colored and foreign-born families" could expect to return there after redevelopment. Because of these families' low incomes, the Department concluded, "only a relatively small proportion of them may be expected to be in a position to occupy quarters in the new development." Planning did not address where displaced blacks might live in a community where segregated housing drew national attention in 1958 after the New York Giants moved to San Francisco. Not even Willie Mays could buy a house in a white neighborhood. A private housing association offering its own plan for the Western Addition was a little more color-conscious in its characterization of the district. The neighborhood was "not white" like the "clean and bright" Marina District, popular with upwardly mobile Italian-Americans. "It was gray, brown, and an indeterminate shade of dirty black."[76]

The destruction of Western Addition Victorians in the 1960s. *San Francisco History Center, San Francisco Public Library.*

Redevelopment's A-1 Project

The Western Addition became the San Francisco Redevelopment Agency's (SFRA) first target. Known as the A-1 project, the area ran along both sides of Geary Boulevard between Post and Eddy Streets from Franklin to Broderick and was later expanded to include 60 more blocks from Post north to California between Presidio and Van Ness. SFRA plans, which were developed in the early 1950s with the help of architects Albert Roller and Vernon DeMars, called for the transformation of Geary into a six-lane boulevard with an underpass at Fillmore, apartment houses on the heights near Franklin and Geary, and a tourist-oriented development in Japan Town. The SFRA planned to demolish thousands of homes, leaving only 35 of the original structures and rehabilitating others in the blocks north of Post.

The SFRA claimed to have plans to relocate the area's 13,500 residents, 90 percent of whom were renters, most of them paying very low rates. A number of families would be moved to new housing just south of A-1. Redevelopment, however, had no plans for replacing demolished homes with public housing.

The SFRA plan appeared to have widespread support initially, but as early as 1954, problems began to develop. Shady real estate dealers descended on the neighborhood, offering to buy and sell options on houses in what an SFRA employee called "a campaign of fear." In this climate of uncertainty, some residents moved even before demolition began in 1957, often because landlords stopped maintaining their buildings, knowing that the SFRA would be buying them.

When demolition got under way, it soon became apparent that the SFRA would not fulfill its legal obligation to provide dislocated people with housing. The city was not going to build replacement housing, and the supply of low-rental properties was limited, particularly given many landlords' refusal to rent to blacks. The SFRA disavowed responsibility for those who had moved before their property was acquired by the Agency, and its earlier claim that home owners would be permitted to rehabilitate their property turned out to be false. Instead, the pace of condemnation was stepped up.

In April 1959, M. Justin Herman came to the SFRA. In his first annual report, Herman acknowledged that "private housing resources for families of low or modest incomes...are very limited" and that new housing in the area was going to be for people in "the upper to luxury brackets." Herman quickly made efforts to moderate the strategy of the SFRA in hope of propitiating the feds and members of the community, who were increasingly alarmed by the destruction around them. But his efforts were largely cosmetic. The agency sold property to Jones Memorial Methodist Church for senior citizens housing developments and worked with the International Longshore and Warehouse Union (ILWU) to build a moderate-income housing co-op and with the Lutheran and Presbyterian churches to provide housing for seniors.

Working with the Jones Memorial Methodist Church and the ILWU was an astute move on Herman's part. Jones Memorial was the place where the National Association for the Advancement of Colored People (NAACP) organized some of the first protests against racism in housing and employment. Ever since the 1930s, the ILWU had been organizing black workers even while many of the city's unions admitted whites only. The ILWU project, St. Francis Square designed by Marquis & Stoller and completed in 1964, became a showcase for integrated, moderate-income housing. In SFRA literature, which was increasingly defensive about the dislocation of low-income families, St. Francis Square loomed larger than life. However, only one displaced family moved into the co-op. For most people even this and the other co-op's modest rents were too high. According to the *Chronicle,* in the end only three of the thousands of displaced residents returned to the A-1 area.

The most significant part of the development became known as Cathedral Hill. It was centered on the new St. Mary's Cathedral and the Lutheran church's St. Martin's Square and was decidedly upscale, which was, after all, the SFRA's original intent. Geary Boulevard, once the site of a proposed subway line to serve the western part of the city, instead became an urban superhighway contributing to the traffic congestion downtown. With its spacious settings for apartment towers, garden apartments, the Japanese Cultural and Trade Center, and the Miyako Hotel built around the ultramodern Cathedral as a kind of centerpiece, the final results were a second (after the Golden Gateway Towers), more impressive, undertaking in the International Style.

The A-2 Project

With construction in A-1 well on its way, Herman announced plans in 1964 to expand the reach of the SFRA to another, larger section of the Western Addition. The A-2 district wrapped around A-1, picking up the earlier extension north of Post Street, then running east to Van Ness, south to Grove, and west to Broderick. The area, already overcrowded with those displaced by the SFRA's demolition of the adjoining blocks, was home to an estimated 13,500 people, more than half of them black. The core of the SFRA plan called for a new commercial district on Fillmore Street, the leveling of most of the blocks between Fillmore and Franklin followed by the construction of garden-style apartments, and the rehabilitation of the Victorians west of Fillmore. In contrast to its plan for A-1, the SFRA promised to save 25 percent of the buildings in the area.

With A-2, Herman was operating in a very different political environment. The civil rights struggle had been under way in San Francisco for four years. The NAACP and the city's automobile dealers were just about to sign an agreement ending job discrimination on Automobile Row, and demonstrators were turning their attention to the same issue at the Palace Hotel. There was no chance that young activists would sit around and watch their neighborhood be leveled. Even before the SFRA announced its grand plans, the United Freedom Movement and ILWU members living in the area called for the formation of an organization to encourage people not to move until adequate replacement housing was built. "We will see not only picketing," wrote Allen Temko, the *Chronicle's* architecture critic, "but Negroes and their white sympathizers—whom Mr. Herman to his discredit denounces as 'liberal intellectual do-gooders'—placing their bodies before bulldozers."

Redevelopment meetings began to draw large hostile crowds. Major John Shelley suggested that perhaps demolition should be carried out in piecemeal fashion so that new housing would be available simultaneously, but representatives of the city's AFL-CIO unions voted unanimously against the plan. After many delays, the Board of Supervisors, promising to oversee relocation, voted to support the A-2 project.

Despite the scale of the original A-1 presentation, Herman's actual plans for A-2 were decidedly less grand than those for A-1. A-2 real estate was in a less desirable area than A-1. In addition, the federal government, buffeted by criticisms of urban renewal, was offering backing for low-interest mortgages and rental subsidies that would help at least some low-income people to live in redevelopment housing. As for public housing, the city planned to scatter 200 units around the area.

Herman was particularly eager to work with Western Addition church leaders and businessmen. Terry François, the city's first black supervisor, was an avid supporter of redevelopment and representative of the fact that there were members of the black community who, either for personal gain or out of genuine concern for the condition of the neighborhood, wanted to see it rebuilt. Gradually, a pro-redevelopment bloc of black leaders emerged in the Western Addition. During the Shelley and Alioto administrations African-Americans were appointed to the SFRA board and the Housing Authority. This new elite, sometimes reluctantly, sometimes enthusiastically, came to reconcile itself to the evisceration of the city's first black neighborhood.

Demolition began soon after the Board of Supervisors approved the project, and the protests continued. In 1967, with numerous blocks looking as though they had been carpet-bombed, a group of young church leaders and home owners formed the Western Addition Community Organization (WACO) to escalate the protest against redevelopment. WACO temporarily stopped some of the demolition, but its most potent weapon turned out to be the use of the legal system. Working with lawyers from the Neighborhood Legal Assistance Foundation, WACO asked the Department of Housing and Urban Development (HUD) to stop financing for the A-2 project because the SFRA was not providing adequate replacement housing.

On the eve of the mayoral election in October 1967, the Board of Supervisors voted to stop the A-2 project. A year earlier rioting had broken out in Hunter's Point, another African-American community, which had become a dumping ground for people forced out of the Western Addition. Mayor Shelley, whose career was on the line in the election largely because of his handling of redevelopment, vetoed the supervisors' vote. Shelley did not run, and WACO sued the SFRA in federal court. Early in 1968 a dozen WACO members stood in front of dump trucks and graders as they began work on A-2's first housing development in Martin Luther King Square. The protests continued for months until the SFRA negotiated a construction contract with a black construction firm from New York, which was 49 percent owned by Boise Cascade. The WACO protest and lawsuit, however, did not halt demolition in the neighborhood. In June 1968, the SFRA embarked on what the *Chronicle* described as the "most massive demolition of buildings in San Francisco since the destruction following the 1906 fire." At the end of the year a federal judge issued an injunction halting the flow of funds to the A-2 project and stopping the removal of residents until HUD, the SFRA, and WACO could agree on a relocation plan. This was the first instance in the country in which local residents had stopped an urban renewal project.

Soon after the injunction was issued, a new, pro-redevelopment organization, the Western Addition Project Area Committee (WAPAC), was formed by neighborhood ministers and businessmen who had invested in SFRA-sponsored housing developments. Initially, WAPAC tried working with WACO. But once the SFRA received approval for a new relocation plan, the Agency worked exclusively with WAPAC, isolating WACO and portraying it, with help from the established press, as an angry fringe group. Eventually, the SFRA put WAPAC on the dole, paying its annual budget.

By the early 1970s the fate of the Western Addition was sealed. The fight continued over relocation housing, with the same federal judge holding up funding a second time. But the opposition had fragmented, thousands of people had moved from the area, and enough of the established community leadership now had a stake in the construction of new housing, security contracts, and other goodies dispensed by the SFRA that no one would effectively oppose the Agency again. The ILWU built a second housing development for low-income people. It also bought a choice lot in the A-2 district on Franklin Street for its new headquarters.

The SFRA's legacy in the A-2 district, although it was still incomplete at the end of the twentieth century, is not a particularly glorious one. The Agency demolished one of the city's most historically significant pre-1906 neighborhoods, evicting its residents and grinding hundreds of Victorian homes and apartments—constructed with the finest virgin redwood—to pulp, which was used for landfill. Herman inveighed against liberal do-gooders and black militants, promising to replace what he considered a slum with a nice new neighborhood. Instead, SFRA-sponsored architects and contractors built a drab collection of garden apartments stretching block after block through the heart of the Western Addition. Some of the construction was shabby. Some was of a higher quality. But there is hardly an example of note-worthy architecture in the area, particularly considering what the new build-ings replaced and in contrast to the more appealing modernism of Cathedral Hill. The SFRA tore up the fabric of the community, leaving only a few church-es where there were once corner stores, shops, pharmacies, restaurants, juke joints, gambling halls, and jazz clubs. Here and there are vacant lots sur-rounded by chain link fences, and there is still airy talk about reviving Fillmore Street—where the SFRA once proposed construction of "an interna-tional city," then "a community shopping center"—as a jazz district, a sort of Dixieland returns as Disneyland for jazz fans.

The Birthplace of Preservation

In retrospect, the people of the Western Addition—and the city—would have benefited enormously from the rehabilitation of the Western Addition's housing stock. Thousands of lives would not have been disrupted, nor would the number of historic buildings have been reduced so dramatically. To insist on rehabilitation would have required a powerful citywide movement—with the protection of the rights of low-income people as a central goal—willing to challenge the basic concepts of urban renewal. No such movement was formed to support the residents of the Western Addition. Instead, each neigh-borhood—South of Market, the Mission, and the Western Addition—was left to fight the redevelopment juggernaut with limited assistance and varying results.

The SFRA did not even begin to seriously consider rehabilitation as an alternative until 1961 when it noted a new objective: the retention in the area of buildings of architectural or historical merit. A San Francisco Conservation Committee was formed under the leadership of a local attorney to survey the A-2 and purportedly received advice from the California Historical Society, the American Institute of Architects, and the Society of Architectural Historians, among others. It is not clear what advice, if any, these organiza-tions gave the SFRA. The committee reported in 1962 that there were 30 struc-tures with sufficient visual merit to warrant preservation and one [sic] struc-ture of historic merit. The historic building was St. Patrick's, which had been built among sand dunes at the corner of Market and New Montgomery in the early 1850s and moved to the Western Addition. The SFRA described St. Patrick's as "one of the city's few [sic] historic monuments." When the Junior League published *Here Today: San Francisco's Architectural Heritage*, the semi-nal work that helped mobilize the preservation community, Roger Holmsted noted in the introduction that "the wholesale destruction of a large part of the Western Addition in the name of 'Redevelopment'," represented the bankrupt-cy of traditional approaches to preservation.[77]

Some rehabilitation was carried out under the auspices of the SFRA. The Agency, for example, pointed proudly to the restoration of row houses along the south side of Bush Street between Fillmore and Webster Streets. In general there was less destruction north of Geary and on the western edges of the area, particularly around Alamo Square, where by the early 1970s gentrification was under way.

In 1971, Charles Hall Page and Harry Miller began discussing the destruction in the Western Addition in the context of the need for a preservation organization. Page wanted an organization that would go beyond what the Landmarks Preservation Advisory Board could do—that is, tell people what they could *not* do with landmark buildings—to provide an incentive for preservation. "When we were thinking about this," Hall said, "the Redevelopment Agency was busy knocking down everything in sight…They had already decimated A-1, and they were knocking down A-2. We were trying to decide what we were going to do to encourage a little more retention and a little less demolition."[78] Hall and Miller started the Foundation for the Preservation of San Francisco's Architectural Heritage with backing from some of the city's most prominent families. Heritage approached the SFRA to see whether the Agency was receptive to selling houses in the Western Addition that could be restored. The Agency agreed on the condition that the houses be moved to a new location. Over the next five years Heritage found buyers for 12 houses and lots to move them to.

There were some difficult moments associated with the move. Because of its relationship with the SFRA, WAPAC was asked by the Agency to approve the sale and removal. WAPAC's director told a reporter that there was particular resentment among WAPAC members because all of the new home owners were white, leaving him to explain to the people who grew up in the houses how white people had come to own them. For this reason, Heritage and the SFRA were asked to stay away from the meeting at which the removal was approved.

For a time Heritage experimented with an approach to restoration that would benefit low-income home owners. With funds from the city, it set up a historic preservation loan program in 1977, and a small number of homes were restored before funding was cut off. A more extensive restoration program targeting low-income home owners was carried out under the Federally Assisted Code Enforcement (FACE) program. Home owners around Alamo Square successfully pushed for inclusion in the FACE program as a way to keep redevelopment, which was inching westward toward this increasingly gentrified neighborhood, out. When President Richard Nixon trimmed funding for FACE in 1974, the city started the Rehabilitation Assistance Program, which made some further small contributions to the preservation of housing for low-income residents. One of the great tragedies of urban renewal was the lack of commitment to rehabilitation.

Cathedral Hill. St. Mary's Catholic Cathedral *(center)* with the Carillon Tower to the far right. *Peter Booth Wiley.*

To understand the transformation of the Western Addition under the Redevelopment Agency, start on Franklin between Geary and O'Farrell. You are standing between the **First Unitarian Church** (1) and the **headquarters of the International Longshore and Warehouse Union** (2). Thomas Starr King, the Boston Preacher who became wildly popular during the Civil War and then died suddenly at the age of 39, was the church's first minister. This church, which combines elements of Gothic with Romanesque, was built in 1889 according to a design by George Percy and added to in the 1960s and 1970s. King's tomb is in the churchyard. The ILWU headquarters (1969) is the work of Anshen & Allen.

Walk South one block on Franklin. On the right is **St. Mark's Square** (3) (1965), which includes the Lutheran Church's **Urban Life Center** on the right; the **Martin Luther Tower,** the first church-sponsored housing project backed by the Redevelopment Agency on the left, both designed by Architecture (Donald Power Smith and Bert Lowell Smith); **St. Mark's Church,** through the courtyard and garden behind 1301 Franklin, was designed by Henry Geilfuss and built in 1895. It is the oldest Lutheran church in the west. The **Carillon Tower,** the circular apartment building farther west, which was a moderate-income cooperative organized by St. Mark's pastor and a group of St. Mark's parishioners. To make way for the development, dozens of Victorians were leveled during what the pastor called a tragic time. In their place emerged a modern urban development, which could trace its lineage to Le Corbusier's tower in the park.

Continue west to Gough and turn left. The **Family Service Agency** (4) (1928) at the corner of Gough and Eddy is the work of Bernard Maybeck. Note the wonderful spiral fire escape in the indentation on the south side of the building. Turn around and walk north on Gough to **St. Mary's Cathedral** (5) (1971), one of the city's landmark buildings. The Redevelopment Agency's plans originally called for a supermarket to be built on this site. Then St. Mary's, located on Van Ness, burned in 1962, and the

Catholic Church acquired the land for a building designed by Pietro Belluschi in association with Pier Lungi Nervi and McSweeney, Ryan & Lee. The building, with its flat roof and tower made up of hyperbolic paraboloids, is a dramatic essay in abstractions and an example of the early use of computers in structural design. Nervi, an expert in thin shell concrete work, consulted on the engineering. The Cathedral commands the heights from a plaza of brick and travertine marble. The spectacular interior was designed in the spirit of the Second Vatican Council, which emphasized the meeting of the clergy and the congregation at the altar. From the plaza, note the surrounding high rises, including the **Sequoias** (6) (1969), the Presbyterian Church's elegant apartment building for senior citizens designed by Stone, Marraccini & Patterson. North of the Cathedral, it is the apartment tower to the left.

Walk around to the west side of the Cathedral and continue west on Cleary court. Jones and Emmons designed the 15-story high rise at **66 Cleary Court** (7) (1963) for Joseph Eichler, one of Northern California's largest developers, as the first apartment tower in the A-1 complex. Eichler also built the **Laguna Heights Apartments** (8) across the street, from plans by Claude Oakland. In this secluded enclave with landscaping by Sasaki Walker, Eichler wanted to provide urban apartment dwellers with all the amenities of a single-family home in the suburbs. Continuing west, enter **St. Francis Square** (9) (1964), the cooperative housing complex financed by the International Longshore and Warehouse Union. The SFRA frequently pointed to this development as a model of what it wanted to achieve in the Western Addition. However, its benefit to dislocated families was minimal. Marquis & Stoller's design evokes the Second Bay Region style.

Walk north on Laguna, crossing **Geary Boulevard.** In the initial phase of the A-1 project, several blocks of buildings north and south of Geary were demolished. The street was widened and dropped below street level at Fillmore, according to a master plan by Vernon DeMars, in order to speed the flow of automobiles from the western suburbs to the downtown. You are entering the heart of what was a vital Japanese community before the residents were relocated to internment camps in 1942. A few returned to try to put their lives together after the war, but were soon confronted with the redevelopment bulldozer.

The **Miyako Hotel** and the **Japanese Cultural and Trade Center** (10) (1968), the work of Minoru Yamasaki and Van Bourg Nakamura, were meant to be the commercial centerpieces of a redeveloped Japan Town. Today a number of community buildings and religious institutions, which serve the small Japanese community, are located in this area. Meanwhile, the Buddhist temples in the area have attracted more ethnically diverse followers. The Trade Center includes numerous shops, restaurants, a multiplex movie theater, an excellent Japanese bookstore **(Kinokuniya),** and a bathhouse. Cross Post on the north side of the Trade Center. The more modest **Nihonmachi Mall** (11) (1976), with a well-designed public space by Okamoto & Murata and Van Bourg Nakamura and a fountain and street furniture by Ruth Asawa, connects Post and Sutter north of the Trade Center.

Walk through the mall to Sutter and turn left. The **Japanese-American History Archives** are located in the **Japanese Cultural and Community** (12) (1987), by Wayne Osaki, at 1840 Sutter Street. Return east on Sutter. This fascinating mini-neighborhood marks the interpenetration of the old Western Addition, although residents prefer to call it Lower Pacific Heights, and the Western Addition as influenced by the arrival of the Japanese after the 1906 earthquake. The **Nichibei Kai Cultural Center** (13) (1972) at 1759 Sutter, with its traditional Japanese look, is the work of Mitsuru Tada & Associates. On the southwest corner of Sutter and Laguna is the **Soto Zen Sokoji** (14) (1984), a modern Buddhist temple by VBN Corporation with elements of traditional Japanese architecture such as the projecting roof timbers.

Continue east on Sutter. The **Queen Anne Hotel** (15) (1890) at 1590 Sutter, the northeast corner of Sutter and Octavia, was designed for Silver King James Fair by Henry Schulze to be Miss Lake's School for Young Ladies and is now an elegant bed and breakfast. Walk north on Octavia to Pine. The **Buddhist Church of San Francisco** (16) (1937) on the southeast corner of Pine and Octavia, designed by Gentoko Shimamato, is an unassuming building except for the stupa in the center, which contains relics of the Buddha given to the temple by the King of Siam in 1935. The worship hall is a spectacular affair modeled after the mother church in Kyoto. Across the street at 1801 Octavia is the **St. Francis Xavier Roman**

Catholic Mission for the Japanese (17), designed by Henry Minton in 1935 and named for the Jesuit who reached the shores of Japan in 1549.

Continue west on Pine and turn left on Laguna. The row of Eastlake structures at **1801-63 Laguna** (18) (1889) were designed by William Hinkel. Across the street at **1800-32 Laguna** (19) (1877) are a row of Italianate Real Estate Associates homes. The very dilapidated and empty **Ohabai Shalome Synagogue** (20) (1895) at 1881 Bush was designed by Moses Lyon, using redwood to create a Moorish-Venetian effect. The synagogue was founded in 1863 by a group of defectors from Temple Emanu-El. When they gave up the location, two different Buddhist sects and a Christian congregation occupied the building. A group of non-Asian followers of Shunryu Suzuki Roshi founded the highly successful San Francisco Zen Center here in the 1960s before moving it to 300 Page Street in 1969. The **Konko Church** (21) (1973) at 1909 Bush is the home of a Shinto sect founded by a Japanese farmer in 1859. Designed by Van Bourg,

The Konko Church of a Shinto sect, Bush. *Peter Booth Wiley.*

Nakamura, Katsura, and Karney in the Japanese post and lintel style, the roofline is modeled after the famous Shinto shrine at Ise, Japan.

Continue west on Bush. You are entering that part of the Western Addition saved from the bulldozer after years of protests against the SFRA's willful destruction of hundreds of historic buildings in the neighborhood. The **Stanyan House** (22) at 2006 Bush was built for Charles Stanyan in 1852. As a member of the Board of Supervisors, Stanyan chaired the Outside Lands Committee, which set aside land for Golden Gate Park. This house, one of the oldest in the city, was prefabricated in New England and shipped around Cape Horn. Its unadorned exterior contrasts sharply with the elaborate Eastlake Victorians at **2000 and 2001 Bush** (23), which the Stanyan family built in 1885 as income property.

Turn left at the corner of Bush and Webster. The **Vollmer House** (24) (1885) at 1735-37 Webster was one of the houses saved and moved by the SFRA in 1975. Considered one of the finest façades designed by Samuel and Joseph Cather Newsom, it was originally located on Turk Street near Franklin. Return to Bush and turn left into the **Bush Street–Cottage Row Historical District,** which includes 20 residences in the Italianate style on Bush, Sutter, and along the Cottage Row Mews on your left, which joins the two streets. These houses were built by two developers, the Real Estate Associates (TREA) and Charles Taylor, a Maine native who at various times owned a lumber business, manufactured sash and blinds, sold insurance, and was in the shipping and commission business. TREA bought the block west of Cottage Row in 1874 and divided it into 23 lots, which sold at prices ranging from $4,200 to $6,623, and then built houses on them for the new owners. TREA houses are at **2115-2125 Bush** (25)

and **1942-48 Sutter Street** (26). TREA followed its typical pattern, building more expensive homes on the side streets (Bush and Sutter) and less expensive homes on Fillmore, which was a commercial street. The new owners were small businessmen and professionals. Taylor's homes, built between 1874 and 1882, are at **2101-2107 and 2109-11 Bush** (27) and numbers **1 to 6 on Cottage Row** (28). They were designed by Taylor & Copeland — architect Frederick Taylor may have been a relative — and built by Thomas Nash, who lived at 2 Cottage Row.

Continue west on Sutter or Bush, turning right on Fillmore. The commercial building at the corner of Fillmore and Bush, **1940-46 Fillmore** (29) (1882), is a typical Italianate building of the period with commercial space on the ground floor and apartments above. The building was designed by Wildrich Winterhalter for Jonas Schoenfeld, an importer and dealer in tobacco and cigars. This block of Fillmore and the next two north, lined with groceries, bakeries, shoe stores, restaurants, dry goods stores, dressmakers, and a dentist, have been the commercial strip for this middle-to-upper-class neighborhood for more than one hundred years. Return south on Fillmore. **Marcus Books** (30), the African-American bookstore at 1712 Fillmore, was once **Jimbo's Bop City,** one of the most popular jazz joints in the Western Addition. The building was moved here in the 1970s from Post and Webster.

Continue south on Fillmore across Geary. The apartment towers by Daniel, Mann, Johnson & Mendenhall on the southeast corner of Fillmore and Geary are part of the **Fillmore Center** (31) (1988), an 8.95-acre mixed commercial and residential development that replaced the old Victorian neighborhood after years of delay. Across the street on the southwest corner of Geary and Fillmore is the **Fillmore**

Auditorium (32), a music venue associated both with the history of black music in the Western Addition and with the beginnings of the San Francisco sound in rock and roll. Opened as the Majestic Hall and Academy of Dancing in 1912, it was turned into a venue for black musicians by a promoter, who booked numerous musicians, including Duke Ellington, Ray Charles, Little Richard, Ike and Tina Turner, and Bobby Blue Bland. In 1966 rock impresario Bill Graham rented the hall for the first time, presenting numerous Sixties legends, such as the Jefferson Airplane, Jimi Hendrix, Eric Clapton, Janis Joplin, the Grateful Dead, Santana, and Credence Clearwater Revival, mixed generously with famed black musicians such as Count Basie, Muddy Waters, Jimmy Reed, and Howlin' Wolf. The Fillmore displays a large collection of rock posters and photographs. Graham also produced performances at **Winterland,** the ice skating rink turned funky rock palace, which was located at Post and Steiner north of Geary before it was torn down.

Walk east on Geary and turn right on Webster. The **Rosa Parks Senior Apartments** (33) at the corner of Webster and Turk were originally a notorious housing project known as the Pink Palace, one of San Francisco's two unsuccessful experiments with modern, vertical slab public housing. This one was built in the early 1960s to accommodate local residents displaced by redevelopment and was redesigned as senior housing by Marquis Associates with Young & Associates in 1985. Continue south on Webster to the corner of McAllister. **McAllister Street** (34) between Fillmore and Laguna was the commercial strip for the Western Addition's Jewish community when it grew in size after 1906. The local synagogue was near the corner of Webster and Golden Gate.

Continue to Fulton and turn left. The

African-American Historical and Cultural Library and Archives is located in the **Center for African-American Art and Culture** (35) at 762 Fulton Street. This community facility was the headquarters of the Redevelopment Agency during the turbulent 1960s. The **Bannecker Homes** (36) across the street, built partially on the foundations of an old brewery, is typical of the shabby construction sponsored by the SFRA as part of it's A-2 project. The **Bryant Mortuary** (37) at 635 Fulton retains a sense of the old Western Addition.

Continue to Laguna, turn right on Laguna and right on Grove. The brick building on the southwest corner of Grove and Buchanan was originally built for the Hebrew Free Loan Association and the **Jewish Educational Society** (38) (1925). Today it is headquarters for the **Korean Residents Association.** Turn south on Buchanan and right on Fell. **Sacred Heart Church** (39) on the southeast corner of Fell and Fillmore was designed by Thomas Welsh and John Carey and built between 1896 and 1908. A Renaissance Revival building, it has three lovely Carrara marble altars. Father Eugene Boyle, a progressive priest presided over this parish in the 1960s, and the Black Panther Party ran a breakfast for children program in the parish house.

Turn left on Fillmore and left on Page. The spectacular Queen Anne at **584 Page Street** (40) (c. 1895) built by contractor-builder Daniel Einstein is one of the most intact, internally and externally, of this style in the city. Einstein built at least 90 houses between 1891 and 1906. Continue east on Page to the **San Francisco Zen Center** (41) (1922) at 300 Page. This building was designed by Julia Morgan as the Emanu-El Sisterhood Residence, a home for single Jewish women. As home to one of the most successful Buddhist sects in the

The San Francisco Zen Center by Julia Morgan, 300 Page. *Peter Booth Wiley.*

The Nightingale Cottage, 201 Buchanan Street. *Peter Booth Wiley.*

Western hemisphere, the Zen Center epitomizes Californians' love affair with Eastern culture, which dates back to the beginning of the twentieth century. The Zen Center owns Green Gulch Farm in Marin County, the Greens Restaurant at Fort Mason, and the Tassajara Zen Mountain Center in the Big Sur.

Turn right on Laguna. On the northeast corner of Haight and Laguna is the **Parsonage** (42) (1883), another late Italianate beauty complete with carriage house, now a be and breakfast (see illustration on page 129). The original structure designed by Australian-born Thomas Welsh included 22 rooms with six fireplaces, two water closets, and a single bathtub. Cost: $12,000.

Turn right on Haight and left on Buchanan. The **Nightingale Cottage** (43) at 201 Buchanan (1882) built for a forty-niner is an eye-popper. Return to Haight and turn left. The new structures on Haight between Buchanan and Webster are a second-generation **public housing project** (44). The original project was built in the 1960s and torn down in the late 1990s to be replaced by attached single-family homes. Walk west on Haight. This trendy commercial strip, the land of tattoos and piercings, is known as the Lower Haight.

At Steiner turn right and walk north. The enormous Queen Anne at 601

Steiner (45) (corner of Fell) was designed by Charles Hansen for a Scottish immigrant. The house features a third-floor ballroom accessible by elevator. It is now the **Henry Oloff House,** a recovery center named for the Episcopalian minister who ran the Canon Kip Community House south of Market from 1915 to 1942. The apartment building across the street at **898 Fell** (46) (1901) on the northeast corner of Steiner and Fell was designed by T. Patterson Ross for an owner-occupant who rented out the upstairs flat. The house was stripped of its ornamentation and covered with asbestos siding, then restored in the 1990s. The twin Queen Annes towering over you at **637 and 639 Steiner** (47) (1894) were designed by Moses Lyon for two French immigrant brothers named Marx, who were furriers on Market Street. Lyon was the architect for the exotic Ohabai Shalom Synagogue on Bush Street.

Continue south to **Alamo Square** (48), which begins at Hayes. This property was claimed by a squatter, who had been run out of town by the Vigilante Committee of 1856 for shooting a theater manager and stuffing ballot boxes, returned to the city four years later and tried unsuccessfully for 17 years to reestablish his title. The park was graded and developed starting in 1892. Before that, according to a resident, it was "a primeval forest of rocks...the whilom paradise of a thousand boys...[who] played at being trappers, or scouts, or wild Indians of the boundless prairie." The houses facing the park at **710 to 720 Steiner** (49) (1894–95) are known as **Photo Row** because they are probably the most photographed in the city. (See the cover of this book.) They were designed by Matthew Kavanaugh, who built **722 Steiner** for his family.

Turn right on Grove. Samuel and Joseph Cather Newsom designed **975 Grove** (50) (1886) with some unique variations on their usually elaborate exteriors. Note the plaster and shingle work and the sunburst and grizzly bear ornamentation. The Classical Revival **mansion** (51) (1897) at 926 Grove was built for John Koster, who sold vinegar, pickles, and barrels and owned a vineyard and a steamship line that ran between San Francisco and Eureka. In 1922 it became the Jewish Community Center. Moshe Menuhin, father of the famed violinist Yehudi Menuhin, taught Hebrew here. During the war the government took the building over to provide housing for military personnel and stripped its interior. Albert Pissis and William Moore designed **940 Grove (The Burt Children's Center)** (52) on the northeast corner of Steiner for "a studious and bookish English rector who through his knowledge of chemistry accumulated a fortune in the Nevada mines."

Walk west through the park, favoring the north side. The French château style **mansion** (53) by Frank Shea on the northwest corner of Fulton and Steiner was built in 1904, providing luxurious quarters for the politically influential Archbishop Patrick Riordan. Archbishop Riordan decided to build a new home after he was criticized for living on California Street near the original St. Mary's Cathedral, "a stone's throw away from the Barbary coast reeking of infamous filth." It is now a bed and breakfast. The 28-room **Westerfeld House** (54) (1889) designed by Henry Geilfuss at 1198 Fulton (see illustration on page 129) is one of the finest Stick Style homes in the city. Originally built for a successful baker and confectioner, it was owned for a time by the contractor who built the St. Francis and Palace Hotels. In the 1920s it was bought by a Russian community organization, which operated a restaurant and ballroom.

Diagonally across the intersection with Scott at 1201 Fulton is the **Lucy House** (55) (1896), Edgar Matthews's version of a Tudor cottage. The Arts and Crafts interior features redwood paneling with butterfly joints, cabinetry, bookcases, and window nooks. Next door at 719 Scott Street is the **Baum House** (56) (1895). Designed by German-born architects Kenitzer and Barth for Charles Baum, the home reflects the transition from Queen Anne to Classic Revival. Baum was a German national who was raised in Russia before coming to San Francisco, where he made his fortune in the fur and ice trades. The two buildings are operated as the **Alamo Square Inn.** Continue south on Scott and turn right on Grove. The **John Peters Livery Stable** (57) (1894) at 1336 Grove, designed by William Smith and Eugene Freeman, is a rare surviving example of a ubiquitous institution before the arrival of the automobile. It was at such stables that many a city dweller either kept a horse and carriage or rented the same for an occasional drive.

Return to Scott and Fulton. Turn right on Fulton and left on Pierce. Continue north on Pierce and turn right on McAllister. James Francis Dunn designed another of his Parisian Belle Époque apartment buildings at **1347 McAllister** (58) (c. 1900). Return to Pierce and turn right. The apartments at **915 Pierce** (59) (1934) by Irvine and Ebbetts are a rare example of Deco in this neighborhood. Note the beautiful lobby.

Continue north on Pierce and turn right on Golden Gate. The spectacular

Seattle Block and the **Château Tivoli** (60) (1892) on the right at the corner of Steiner were built at the same time. Ernestine Kreling, the owner of the Tivoli Opera House, bought the corner house in 1898. In 1917 the building became the Emanu-El Sisterhood Residence until it was moved to Julia Morgan's new building on Page Street in 1923, when it was converted to the Jewish Folk School House, whose activities were supported by a kosher restaurant. In the 1950s the Workmen's Circle, a socialist fraternal order, met here. Decorated in 22 colors with gold leaf on the turrets and towers, the Château Tivoli is now a bed and breakfast. Sharon Row, across the street at **1400-12 Golden Gate** (61) (1884), was designed by John Gaynor as income property for Senator William Sharon, William Ralston's close associate. Sharon ended up with most of Ralston's assets after his death, including the original Palace Hotel, which was designed by Gaynor. The Queen Anne at **1043 Steiner** (62), south of the intersection of Golden Gate and Steiner, is where Yehudi Menuhin's family lived in the 1920s.

Continue north on Steiner and turn left on Eddy. The abandoned **Holy Cross Parish Hall** (63) at 1822 Eddy is old St. Patrick's (1854), the Catholic church that sat amid the dunes at the

Deco entranceway at 915 Pierce. *Peter Booth Wiley.*

The Seattle Block and the Château Tivoli, Steiner and Golden Gate. *Peter Booth Wiley.*

Sharon Row,
1400-12 Golden
Gate. *Peter Booth
Wiley.*

corner of Market and New Montgomery before it was moved twice. Walk west on Eddy, turn right on Divisadero, right on Ellis, and left on **Beideman Place.** This enclave was created when the newly formed Foundation for San Francisco's Architectural Heritage worked with the SFRA to find buyers for and then move two Italianate Victorians to this location in 1974. The houses at **33-35 Beideman Place** (64) were built circa 1876; those at **45-57 Beideman** sometime in the 1870s or 1880s. The townhouses and cottages across the street at **20-40 Beideman** (65) (1989) are by Daniel Solomon. Solomon copied a typical nineteenth-century arrangement, a town house on the street and a cottage

behind, in this contemporary commentary on the Victorians across the street.
Solomon, a University of
California–Berkeley architecture professor, explores what he calls "the tension
between context and the logic and
rationality of the modernist building." [79]

Continue north on Beideman and
turn right on O'Farrell. **Amancio
Ergina Village** (66) (1985) on the
right, past Scott, another contextual
essay by Daniel Solomon, is the second
cooperative development funded by
the ILWU.

THE MISSION

*This tour, which begins on level ground and then climbs upward in the Noe
and Castro Valleys, starts at Sixteenth and Dolores and ends at Castro and
Eighteenth. You can return downtown from Castro and Market on a historic
streetcar. Allow three hours.*

Unlike the Western Addition, the Mission (or Inner Mission), which is bor-
dered by 101 North, Potrero Avenue, Cesar Chavez (Army) Street, and
Dolores started as a separate village of farms and adobes centered on the
Mission Dolores. Before the gold rush, the Mission was the site of ranchos
owned by the Bernal, Noe, Valencia, and Guerrero families. The 4,443-acre
Noe rancho was the largest. Don Miguel Noe's adobe stood at the corner of
Eighteenth and Dolores Streets. In a continuing state of decline after secularization in 1833, the Mission Dolores became the site of a regular market and
numerous fiestas with horse racing, dancing, and bull and bear fights.

In 1851, the Mission Plank Road, a toll road that ran along present-day
Mission Street ending at Sixteenth, and a second plank road along Folsom
Street brought pleasure seekers to the Mission Dolores and its environs,
which became known for their resorts, some of them notoriously rowdy. Part
of the Mission Dolores became a roadhouse and bar. The Willows, a resort
near Mission and Eighteenth, included a small zoo, outdoor cafe, bar, hotel,
and open-air pavilion for moonlight dancing. The more elaborate
Woodward's Garden offered an amusement park and museum near Mission
and DuBoce. There were two racetracks, one owned by Senator David
Broderick, who was killed by Judge David Terry in a duel in 1859. The
Mission was also the site of the city's first baseball game and three different
stadiums, including Seals Stadium where the Giants played before they
moved to Candlestick in 1961.

The ever-active city clerk Thomas Hayes of Western Addition fame built
the first horse car line from Market and California to the Mission Dolores in
1857. The first streetcars arrived in 1866 as the Mission became a collection
of developments separated by vacant lots. During the years when the railroad entered the city through the gap between Bernal Heights and Diamond

Heights, which is now San Jose Avenue, one could board the train at Twenty-fifth and Valencia to travel downtown. The Outer Mission (or Excelsior), which was still being farmed in the 1890s, was even more remote. An Italian farmer recalled to a *Chronicle* reporter how it took three and half hours by wagon to get from there to North Beach.

During the first three decades after the gold rush, the Mission, a semirural "sunbelt" where the fog burned off earliest in the morning and returned latest in the evening, was one of the favored locations for city's wealthier families. François Pioche, the French-born banker, merchant, real estate speculator, and mining investor for whom the boomtown of Pioche, Nevada, was named, built a country mansion called the Hermitage next to Mission Dolores. Pioche was a major conduit for French capital pouring into the city. He is said to have contributed to the city's love for fine cuisine by importing 40 French chefs and a boatload of French wines. John Spreckels, son of the sugar baron and developer of San Diego, built a spectacular home at Twenty-first and South Van Ness. Mayor (later U.S. Senator) James Duvall Phelan lived on Valencia between Sixteenth and Seventeenth, and Mayor James "Sunny Jim" Rolph's home was at the corner of Twenty-fifth and San Jose. There were other elegant homes along South Van Ness and on the hillsides along Guerrero and Dolores.

As the Mission and Potrero Point to the east became industrial centers, working class families, predominantly Irish but with a mixture of Italians, Germans, and other European immigrants, occupied most of the small houses and apartments on the flatlands. As in the Western Addition and Pacific Heights, the Real Estate Associates and other home-building companies played a role in their development. There were factories, breweries, a woolen mill, and a tannery in the north Mission, with other tanneries along the creek that became Cesar Chavez. There was even a wharf on Mission Creek adjoining the tannery at Nineteenth and Folsom before Mission Creek was filled in. Where more than half of the city's union were founded, the Mission typified nineteenth-century blue-collar San Francisco and became even more representative after many families moved there from South of Market after 1906. Mission dwellers felt a sense of isolation from the rest of the city, even developing a distinct accent, a sort of West Coast Brooklynese. In the postwar years Hispanics moved into the northern parts of the district, and by the 1960s many white working-class families had moved out. Mission and Twenty-fourth Streets between Valencia and Potrero would become the principal axes of the Hispanic community.

In 1962 the *Chronicle*, in a series of articles, described the Mission as "almost cut off from the rest of San Francisco, a city within a city," still steeped in the culture of the city's working class, now with 15,000 Hispanic residents. Supervisor Joseph Tinney recalled the annual rock fight between the kids from Paddytown along Cesar Chavez and the enemy, who lived on the south side of Bernal Heights. Another resident remembered shooting ducks in the marshy creek where Alemany Boulevard is today. "The Mission isn't run down enough to get the attention of redevelopment officials," lamented the reporter.

Not for long. Four years later the city began construction on the Bay Area Rapid Transit System (BART), which would run under Mission Street, and Mayor Shelley called for the Mission to become a redevelopment district. Mission Street, planning consultants told the city, was going to sprout high rises and "smart shops." Mission residents, despite their reputed insularity, were not blind; they knew what the SFRA was doing to the Western Addition. So when the SFRA started talking about 60 percent of the structures in the neighborhood being substandard and the need to replace 5,000 buildings, they could hear the bulldozers. The first opposition came from small businessmen and home owners who opposed the Agency's "confiscation of private property" and soon broadened as antipoverty workers and church activists fanned the flames of discontent. "This is one of the last low-cost housing areas in the city, and it is now being destroyed," a member of the Catholic Council for the Spanish Speaking told a public meeting, at which redevelopment director Justin Herman was roundly booed.

Shelley's problem was getting sufficient support to push his proposal through the Board of Supervisors. The SFRA was totally devoid of credibility, particularly when it came to relocation. In December 1966, the supervisors voted 6 to 5 against redevelopment, and despite Shelley's best efforts the proposal failed a second time.

Model Cities

Soon after his inauguration, the leaders of the resistance to redevelopment asked Mayor Alioto to look into securing Model Cities funding for the Mission. The Model Cities program, part of Lyndon Johnson's War on Poverty, promised citizen participation in its decision-making process. In 1971, the Mission received $2.92 million as its share of Model Cities funding for the Bay Area. The funds were divided between job training, housing, child care centers, education, and citizens' participation. A small amount of funds went into working on a neighborhood plan, which was developed by the nonprofit Mission Housing Development Corporation (MHDC), an affiliate of the community-based Mission coalition (MCO).

A Plan for the Inner Mission District, published in 1974, envisioned a Mission that retained many of its existing characteristics, but with more amenities such as parks, day-care centers, and schools. With regard to housing, the plan, recognizing that "it is unclear if or when housing subsidies will be available," called for greater emphasis on preservation, rehabilitation, and "creative approaches to satisfying housing needs." These creative approaches were undertaken by the MHDC in much the same way that the Tenants and

Owners Development Corporation (TODCO) did in the South of Market Area (see pages 110–111). Since its formation in 1971, MHDC has built 676 units of affordable housing, with another 356 units either in construction or about to be completed. It has also rehabilitated more than a 1,000 privately owned units in the neighborhood.

The Mission Plan's call for greater emphasis on rehabilitation and preservation grew out of the emergence of a neighborhood group called the Victorian Alliance. The Alliance was started by a group of home owners who were seeking information about how to restore their aging homes. Members also hoped to educate the public about "misguided improvements," such as removing decorative trim and ornamentation and replacing redwood siding with aluminum or asbestos shingles. Following its promotion of restoration, the Alliance went on to encourage home ownership. Of course, this was in the tradition of many of the original Victorians, inasmuch as they were built to broaden the social base of home ownership. Alliance members, painfully aware of the destruction in the Western Addition, were eager to provide an alternative to the SFRA's approach to housing issues.

"We felt that old housing [should be preserved] because it was better made, and it had more character and because in some cases it was better suited for larger families," recalled Toby Levine, one of the founders of the Alliance. "We called the old buildings oldies, but goodies. We had to sell them to people. People viewed them as pests. They cost money to keep up. They were big, and they had these high ceilings and were hard to heat."[80] The Alliance's effort ran up against the fact that the Mission was redlined, meaning that lending institutions were restricting funding in this predominantly working-class neighborhood. So the Alliance fought redlining while producing a guide to historic homes in the Mission. Levine became head of the Mission Planning Council, an affiliate of the Mission Coalition (MCO), which worked with the MHDC. Through this connection, the Alliance's perspective on restoration and home ownership was incorporated into the Mission Plan.

The Mission Today

The legacy left by the complex network of organizations that came together to save the Mission has been by and large a positive one, particularly as compared with the destruction of the Western Addition. The Mission has retained much of its original character. There was no wholesale demolition of its housing stock. Mission Street did not become a commercial high rise corridor. The Mission is still a vital working-class community with numerous small businesses, social service organizations, and cultural facilities. As modest as it was, Model Cities funding spawned a number of these organizations, and the MHDC added to the stock of low-income housing. Today Mission residents are still working on the implementation of many of the Inner Mission Plan's recommendations. One can only speculate about what might have been done in the Mission if the Model Cities program provided the tens of millions of dollars that the federal government made available to the SFRA.

The Mission, like all low-income neighborhoods in the city, still faces serious challenges and may ultimately become a very different place. In the area of home ownership and low-cost housing, efforts such as those of the Victorian Alliance and the MHDC were only marginally successful. Home ownership remains low, and the need for low-cost housing far outstrips the supply. At the beginning of the twenty-first century, the Mission is experiencing a housing boom, particularly in the formerly industrial North Mission. New apartment houses are going up and old factories are being converted into lofts, live-work spaces, and office space for dotcoms. With the exception of a small number of low-cost developments, this new housing will be priced to a market that has skyrocketed during the boom years. In the surrounding neighborhoods, and now in the heart of the Mission, gentrification is entering its second generation, and the Mission is headed for a future very much like South of Market. As rents and home prices soar, the need for affordable housing grows daily. But as long as there is no political commitment to providing housing for low-income residents, the vast majority of units will be built for white-collar professionals rather than low-income Latinos.

Today Mission Street looks threadbare. The arrival of warehouse outlets in the city has driven many shopkeepers out of business. There are continuing problems with street crime, particularly gang activity, and the neighborhood's schools, like all inner-city schools in California, have never recovered from the negative consequences of the drastic tax cuts mandated by Proposition 13. One block away along Valencia Street, the old Mission mixes uneasily with the new. Bookstores, coffeehouses, and upscale restaurants intermingle with tacquerias and distinctly ethnic shops. The trend on a street that a generation ago had an abandoned look is toward a future that caters to the young professional. How these two streets ultimately interact will be a guide to the future of San Francisco.

Only certain blocks in the north Mission were destroyed by fire in 1906, leaving hundreds of delightful Victorians in what was once a very fashionable part of town. Begin at the **Mission Dolores** (1) at Sixteenth and Dolores Streets. This mission, the oldest building in San Francisco, was either the fourth or the fifth to be built in the immediate area, the earlier structures having been torn down or, in one case, damaged by a severe winter storm.

Inspired by Spanish and Mexican ecclesiastical architecture, Father Francisco Palou designed the building and organized Indian converts to build it between 1785 and 1791.

The mission's 4-foot adobe brick walls sit on stone foundations. The redwood ceiling beams and trusses were originally fastened together with rawhide and manzanita pegs, as were the door and window frames, and the roof was covered with clay tile. An

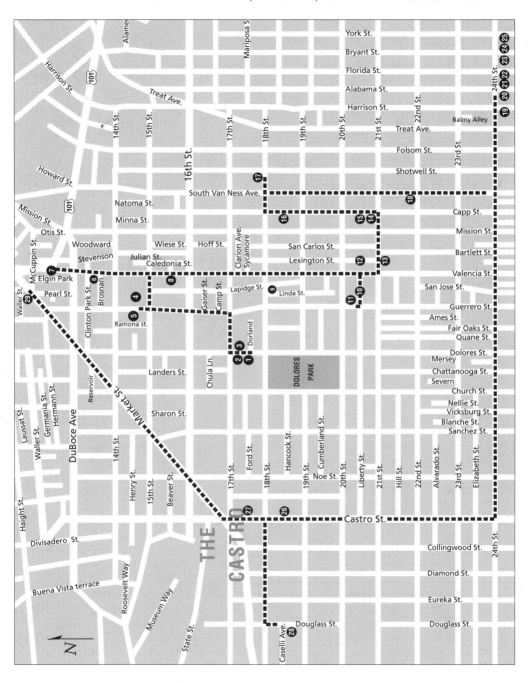

Mission Dolores, the oldest building in the city. *Peter Booth Wiley.*

example of the beam construction can be seen in the small museum in a room behind the altar, where a window in the wall reveals the original adobe work. In the façade four squat columns support a wooden balcony and six half columns with three niches for bells in between. The bells, which are original, were brought from Mexico. Each of them honors a saint: The righthand bell, for example, is inscribed, "Ruelas made me, 1797. I am called Joseph, Holy Mary most pure."

Inside the chapel to the left are the original confessional doors. The ceiling is a repainted version of the original, which was done by Indians using vegetable dyes in a characteristic native design. The elaborate baroque gilded altar was brought in pieces from Mexico, as were the two side altars. The mission has been the subject of three restoration efforts. Willis Polk led one such endeavor in 1916, hiding reinforcing steel in the roof to support the beams and trusses.

Beneath the floor lie the remains of José Joaquin Moraga, leader of the 1776 expedition that brought the first group of settlers to San Francisco; members of the Noe family, a prominent California family whose rancho adjoined the mission to the south and William Leidesdorff, a pioneer black businessman from the West Indies.

Part of the original cemetery is accessible by going through the chapel. It contains the remains of a curious collection of individuals from the city's early history: Captain Luis Antonio Arguello, the first governor of California under Mexican rule; Francisco de Haro, the first alcalde (mayor) of Yerba Buena; James Casey, who was hanged by the first Vigilance Committee after he shot newspaper editor James King of Williams for revealing that Casey had served time in prison before coming to San Francisco; Italian-born theater owner Charles Cora, who also died at the hands of vigilantes; the prize fighter James Yankee Sullivan, who died under mysterious circumstances after being jailed by the vigilantes for stuffing ballot boxes. Throughout this garden of native plants are scattered the graves of other Catholics—French, German, Irish, and Italian—who represent the influx of immigrants once San Francisco had become a booming city. Finally, there is a monument to the more than 5,000 converted Indians who were buried in unmarked graves somewhere outside the walls of the existing cemetery. Many of their names are listed in a directory in the museum.

To the right of the Mission is the Churrigueresque Revival **Basilica of San Francisco** (2) (1913, towers added in 1926), which was built on this site after the original church was damaged in 1906 and then torn down. Across the street is the former **Notre Dame High School** (3) (1907), the first girls' school in the city, designed by Theodore Lentzen. The original building was dynamited in 1906 to protect the Mission.

Walk east on Sixteenth Street, the oldest street in San Francisco, and turn left on Guerrero. **Valencia Gardens** (4) (1943), on the right just beyond the intersection with Fifteenth, was designed by William Wurster following guidelines written in Washington, D.C.,

and influenced by the work of his wife, Catherine Bauer. Wurster drew on three traditions for his design: Scandinavian cooperative housing, Mexican court-yards, and the work of Ernest May, an architect and planner close to the Bauhaus. The two-story Valencia Gardens was built on a human scale that emphasized each individual family unit, a marked contrast to the huge ugly blocks of housing projects that would go up in major cities after World War II. The courtyard, which opens onto Fifteenth Street, features sculpture by Beniamino Bufano, a project funded by the Federal Arts Project. Note the **Sheet Workers Hall** (5) (1906) at 226 Guerrero, a reminder that the Mission was home to many union workers.

Walk east on Fifteenth and turn left on Valencia. The **Levi Strauss Factory and Design Center** (6) (1906) at 250 Valencia is now a museum. Tours by appointment. Continue north to the **Baha'i Center** (7) (1932) at 170 Valencia, a Deco union hall designed by Harold Stoner and built for the Woodmen of the World.

Valencia Gardens with statuary by Beniamino Bufano, Guerrero and Fifteenth Streets. *Peter Booth Wiley.*

Levi Strauss Factory and Design Center, 250 Valencia Street. *Peter Booth Wiley.*

Mission Housing Development Corporation's Plaza del Sol, 440 Valencia Street. *Mission Housing Development Corporation.*

Turn around and walk south on Valencia, a wonderful interface between the Latino and young and hip communities, particularly lively at night. **Plaza del Sol** (8) (1994) at 440 Valencia Street, with 38 units for very-low-income families and 20 for low-income households, was designed by Hood Miller Associates with Alan Martinez and was built by the Mission Housing Development Corporation. Built around a secure courtyard, the complex, which offers tutoring for students by two graduate students from the

Women's Building at Eighteenth and Lapidge. *Peter Booth Wiley.*

University of San Francisco, is a modern effort in the spirit of William Wurster. Continue south on Valencia, turn right at Eighteenth, and walk to the corner of Lapidge on the left, where the **Women's Building,** or **Edificio de Mujeres** (9), stands. This building was originally a Norwegian-American meeting hall. The bar on the left was the Dovre Club, where Paddy Nolan, the city's leading Irish nationalist, presided until his death in the 1990s. The mural here (1995) is by Juana Alicia and Associates. (The Mission is filled with murals.)[81]

Return to Valencia, turn right, and then right on Liberty Street. The **Liberty Street Historic District** (10) is both an enclave of fine Victorians and a living guide to the evolution of Victorian styles. The land was originally part of the Noe Rancho. The first two houses, at 7 and 17 Liberty Street, were built in 1867 and 1869 in the Italianate style with half-octagonal bays rising to a cornice and classical ornamentation, such as Corinthian columns. Seventeen more Italianate houses (2, 3, 6, 8, 12, 17, 22, 24, 27, 30-32, 35, 37, 39, 42, 44, and 49) were built in the 1870s on double

The Liberty Street Historic District, 35-37 Liberty Street. *Peter Booth Wiley.*

and even triple 25-foot lots. Those built in the 1880s (37, 38, 50, and 51) are in the Stick-Eastlake Style, with rectangular bays and ornamentation with fruit and floral motifs. Six Queen Annes were built in the 1880s (4, 5, 9, 18, 19, and 20) with a variety of bays, rounded arches, towers, and various types of ornamentation. The last group of Classical Revival buildings (11, 15, 33, 46, and 47), are actually pairs of flats built between 1902 and 1911.

Walk west on Liberty to Guerrero and turn right. The **John McMullen House** (11) at 827 Guerrero was originally a Stick Style home completed by an unknown architect in 1881. McMullen made his fortune in the construction business, specializing in dredging, harbor improvements, bridges, and waterworks, including the dredging of the Oakland Harbor, building a section of San Francisco's seawall, and building the first dry-dock at Hunter's Point. McMullen hired Samuel Newsom in 1890 for the first of several additions to the house, which were carried out over the next 14 years. The house was a hospice in recent years; it was subsequently damaged in a fire and then restored.

Return to Valencia. The block bounded by Valencia, Twentieth, Mission, and Twenty-first is the most complete **development by the Real Estate Associates** (12), which claimed to be the largest home construction company in the United States in the 1870s. As with Cottage Row in the Western Addition, TREA built larger houses on the main streets, favoring corner lots for the most expensive houses, and more modest homes in the Lexington and San Carlos street alleys. See, for example, the larger houses at 929 to 945 Valencia; then turn left on Twenty-first and left again on Lexington to see the more modest homes at 330 to 340 Lexington. For a striking contrast, note **La Casa de la Raza** (13) (1987), a state-financed low-income housing development by Conrad Associates, on the southwest corner of Twenty-first and Bartlett, built, unfortunately, on top of a toxin-generating garage.

Continue east on Twenty-first and make a left on Capp. Dan Fontes painted the mural ***Salud!*** (14) (1997) on the south wall of the Bethany Center, a low-income seniors residence, at the corner of Twenty-first and Capp. Fontes included

The Community Music Center at 544 Capp Street.
Peter Booth Wiley.

St. Peter's Parish Hall, with murals, Twenty-fourth and Florida. *Peter Booth Wiley.*

portraits of the residents. The Italianate building at 544 Capp (c. 1885) was once a home and is now the **Community Music Center** (15), which provides instruction and performances for people of all ages, backgrounds, and income levels. Founded in 1921, its most famous graduates are Johnny Mathis and Lucine Amara, soprano, who sang with the New York Metropolitan Opera for years. Note the attractive recital hall (1925) and gardens. Continuing north, you come to the **Mission Neighborhood Center** (16) at 362 Capp Street, a good example of the shingled First Bay Tradition by Ward & Blohme. The center was originally the San Francisco Girls Club, founded in 1896 by Rachel Wolfsohn to assist young women south of Market. Wolfsohn moved the Club to this building after the 1906 fire wiped out the original structure. In the 1930s, the Club decided to reach out to the entire neighborhood as a community center. These two centers are the products of the long tradition of civic activism that has helped to stabilize this working-class community.

Turn right on Eighteenth Street and cross South Van Ness. **St. Charles School** (17) at Eighteenth and Shotwell is a grand Italianate from about 1880. Return to South Van Ness and turn left. You are walking along what was once a street lined with large Victorians, a handful of which have survived. The white church to the west of South Van Ness at Twenty-second Street is **St. John's Lutheran Church** (18) (1900), once a German parish.

Turn left at Twenty-fourth Street, along with Mission, the principal axis of the Latino Community. The **Balmy Alley murals** (19) on the right east of Folsom were painted by thirty artists in 1985 to protest U.S. involvement in El Salvador. The **Precita Eyes Murals Art Center** (20) at 2981 Twenty-fourth was founded by some of the original Mission muralists. **China Books and Periodicals** (21) at 2929 Twenty-Fourth Street was the only business licensed to trade with the People's Republic of China when it opened here in 1964. The mural (1978) by Precita Eyes is one of the earliest in the Mission. Founded in 1867, **St. Peter's Catholic Church** (22) at the corner of Twenty-Fourth and Florida was originally the home parish of the Mission Irish. There were predominantly German and Italian parishes nearby. St. Peter's most famous priest was Father Peter Yorke, who challenged the anti-Catholic American Protective Association in the 1890s, championed the city's labor unions, and was an ardent supporter of Irish republicanism. In the 1950s, Hispanic families began worshiping at St. Peter's, and the parish went through another period of activism in the 1960s and 1970s when parish priests supported the United Farmworkers Union and opposed the war in Vietnam. St. Peter's became a member of the Mission Coalition, the organization formed to stop redevelopment, and one of its parishioners, James Bourne, headed the Mission Planning Council and was the first director of the Mission Housing Development Corporation. In the **murals** (1993) on the rectory on the southwest corner of Twenty-fourth and Florida, Isais Mata memorialized a number of historical figures, including Mexican revolutionary Father Miguel Hidalgo and Martin Luther King Jr., but did not include Father Yorke. There are many Latino restaurants along Mission and Twenty-fourth Streets. The Galeria de la Raza (23) (1970) was founded by artists active in the Chicano civil rights movement. For a true sense of the past, don't miss **Roosevelt's Tamale Parlor** (24) at 2817 Twenty-fourth Street, a typical Mexican restaurant named for FDR, and the **St. Francis Fountain and Candy Shop** (25) at 2801 Twenty-fourth Street, which looks just as it did when it opened in 1918.

To avoid a long walk to the **Castro District,** take the bus west on Twenty-fourth, change to the 24 going north at Castro, and get off at Eighteenth and Castro. If you walk, enjoy exploring the numerous streets and alleys north and south of Twenty-fourth. The Castro played a historic role in the emergence of gay and lesbian culture around the world, and Harvey Milk, who owned a camera store at **575 Castro** (26), was its most significant leader. Reviled in many communities, homosexuals sought refuge in San Francisco and were inspired by the election of Milk, the nation's first avowedly gay politician, to the Board of Supervisors in 1977. Milk was assassinated the next year, along with mayor George Moscone, by Dan White, a former supervisor. The gay community responded to White's conviction for the lesser crime of manslaughter with a march that originated in the Castro and ended up in the White Night Riot at City Hall. The **Castro Theatre** (27) (1923) just north of Eighteenth Street is a delightful piece of exotica. It was the first of seven movie theaters designed by Timothy Pflueger, this one in the Spanish Baroque style. The interior, with an organ that rises up in front of the stage on an elevator, is lavishly furnished to look like an enormous tent.

The heights to the east and west of Castro Street are filled with quiet, tree-lined streets and fine homes, the most grandiose of which is **Nobby Clarke's Folly** (28) (1892) at 250 Douglass Street at the corner of Caselli, three blocks west of Castro and a block to the left. That a mere clerk to the police chief could build this pile on 17 acres tells a lot about San Francisco politics in the nineteenth century.

You can return downtown via the historic streetcars on Market Street. On the left, at Market and Octavia, is the site of the new **Lesbian-Gay-Bisexual-Transgender Community Center** (29), which will open in May 2001. Architects, the Cee/Pfau Collaborative, decided to incorporate and restore the historic Fallon Building (1894) on the corner into their plans after preservationists opposed a proposal to tear it down.

THE HAIGHT-ASHBURY

Two hours with two steep climbs. The tour starts at Oak and Divisadero and ends at Frederick and Arguello, adjacent to the Golden Gate Park.

The Haight–Ashbury, which became world famous during the Hippie era, remained remote and only partially developed as late as 1900. South and west of the Western Addition, it was part of the Outside Lands, which were in dispute until the U.S. Supreme Court settled title on the city in 1865. Protected by Twin Peaks from the strong southwesterly winds that accompany winter storms, and by Lone Mountain from the prevailing northerlies, the Haight before the arrival of the Spanish was known for its springs, trees, and thick stands of berry bushes harvested by the local Indians. The Spanish were less impressed by the terrain, referring to it as *la tierra de las pulgas,* or "land of the fleas." After the gold rush, a number of farms were located in the area.

When work began on Golden Gate Park in 1871, the Panhandle—the narrow extension of the park between Baker and Stanyan—became a favorite place for San Franciscans to venture forth on horseback or in carriages for a leisurely ride. In the 1880s cable car lines were extended along Haight, Oak, and McAllister Streets, and numerous elegant homes were built near the Panhandle or scattered along the sides of Asbury Heights.

At this time the Haight was still as much a recreational as a residential area. In 1885 a stadium for California League baseball games was built across from Golden Gate Park at Stanyan and Waller, and a decade later the Chutes, an amusement park featuring a 60-foot-high water slide, roller coasters, a vaudeville theater, carnival booths, and a zoo, opened on Haight between Clay and Cole. A photograph of the Chutes shows cable cars running along Haight Street to the east past blocks of empty lots, with houses built along Page and Oak.

The Haight attracted its share of elegant homes and grand apartments in the style of the late nineteenth century—spacious living room and dining room, perhaps a parlor, numerous bedrooms, and at least one room for a servant in the back with as much floor space as a generous-sized house. Because development came later to the Haight than to the Western Addition and the Mission, many of its most distinctive buildings were in the Queen Anne style, which had become fashionable toward the end of the Victorian era. The 1906 fire and earthquake triggered a building boom in the area, and by the 1920s the neighborhood, for the most part, was built up.

According to neighborhood historian Donna Gouse, the Haight began a gradual decline in the 1930s that stretched on until the 1970s, when gentrification began. During the 1930s home ownership fell, buildings began to deteriorate, and large flats and houses were subdivided into smaller units, a trend accelerated by the pressures on housing during World War II.

Neighborhood demographics also changed as the area became more working class and more African-American, particularly as blacks were pushed out
of the Western Addition starting in the late 1950s. The Haight did offer spacious quarters in once monumental homes at very low rents.

From Beatniks to Hippies

Offering low rents and proximity to Golden Gate Park, the Haight and the
Western Addition attracted counterculture types well before the "Summer of
Love" in 1967. The cultural scene in the Haight and its environs was very
much a continuation of what had started in North Beach, but in a locale with
fewer tourists and a lot less police attention. Kenneth Rexroth, father figure to
the Beats, lived in the Western Addition off and on starting in 1927. For seven
years, beginning in 1959, Jay Defeo worked on her monumental painting *The
Rose,* a 2,300-pound mandala made up of layer after layer of paint, in an
apartment building on Fillmore Street near Haight, which was inhabited by a
number of Beat figures, including poet Michael McClure.

"We were just interested in being beatniks then," Janis Joplin told the
Village Voice, describing her arrival in North Beach in 1963 before she moved
on to the Haight to form a band with Big Brother and the Holding Company.
Big Brother, the Grateful Dead, the Jefferson Airplane, and a handful of other
groups, were soon associated with the San Francisco Sound, a distinctive part
of the new rock music. Indeed, the Beats referred to their younger counterparts as "Hippies," meaning young hipsters. Neal Cassady, Jack Kerouac's
sometime soulmate and the model for Dean Moriarty in *On the Road,* acted
as a kind of mascot and chauffeur to Ken Kesey's Merry Pranksters. This
group of Stanford students and hangers-on formed a commune on the peninsula south of San Francisco and then took their show on the road in the
school bus named "Furthur," funded by Kesey's royalties from *One Flew Over
the Cuckoo's Nest.* Jerry Garcia, the son of a San Francisco bar owner and
lead guitarist for the Dead, hung around the fringes of the Pranksters scene
after he got out of the army until his band, the Warlocks, became the house
band at the Pranksters' Acid Tests. It was also significant that Beat poets Allen
Ginsberg and Gary Snyder occupied center stage at the human be-in at the
Polo Field in Golden Gate Park in January 1967.

Music making and a kind of free-form dancing were core rituals in
Hippie life, particularly music played before large crowds in auditoriums with
walls colored and laced by light shows, such as the Longshoremen's Hall at
Fisherman's Wharf, the Fillmore Auditorium, the Avalon Ballroom, and the
Straight Theatre on Haight, or in open spaces, such as the Panhandle or
Speedway Meadows. Drugs reshaped and heightened the experience. And
the Haight, with its abundant supply of cheap rentals in houses and apart-
ments with elaborate Victorian interiors, seemed the perfect setting for young

people who were drawn to vibrant colors and ornate patterns in their clothing and artwork. The standard black outfit of the Beat was being shed in favor of homemade tie-dyes.

The Haight was the site of elaborate efforts to build an alternative to what young people considered a repressive and greed-based society. The Diggers, a loose collection of individuals who took their name from an anarchist group formed during the civil wars in seventeenth-century England, were the main movers in this effort. Started by performers, some from the San Francisco Mime Troupe, the Diggers spoke of "life acting," taking theater into the streets while handing out free food and maintaining free stores in the Haight.

What Was That?

The free public spectacle, whether a street fair, an open-air rock concert in the Panhandle, or a Digger event such as the Death of Money, was endemic to the whole undertaking. The Hippies went beyond the Beats, proclaiming, "the streets belong to the people." This redefinition of public space was accompanied by the organization of the Artist Liberation Front by some Diggers and Mime Troupers. Beyond bringing culture to the people free of charge, they wanted to shift attention away from the established arts to new artistic voices speaking out in the neighborhoods and communities of color. Over the next three decades, this generation of artists would bring new energy to the city's arts world. They would force the city to distribute moneys from the hotel tax fund to neighborhood groups, as well as to the ballet, opera, and symphony, playing a part in the relocation of the Davies Symphony Hall and helping to shape the final plans for the Yerba Buena Center.

The Diggers celebrate the Death of Money on Haight Street in 1966. *Gene Anthony.*

Young people by the tens of thousands flocked to the Haight during the Summer of Love. Many stayed on, some left, and others came later. Tourist buses and the police also showed up. The Hell's Angels, friendly with Kesey and the Diggers, had already made their presence known. The flower children, once deemed innocents, were indulging in heroin and speed as well as marijuana and LSD. "Rape," one handout announced, "is as common as bullshit on Haight Street." Two drug dealers were murdered. For the new arrivals the Diggers set up free crash pads, counseling services, and a runaway location center, and the Haight-Ashbury Free Clinic was organized by a young medical student and staffed by 30 doctors. The Grateful Dead house was busted, and the Diggers and their allies decided to celebrate the "Death of Hippie" with a sunrise service and taps played on the top of the hill in Buena Vista Park.

"What was that?" asked *Rolling Stone* reporter Charles Perry. "Basically the biggest LSD party in history," he concluded.[82] Really, it was many things, Perry and others have acknowledged: a new theater form, a paean to spontaneity, a naïve attempt at building community, a power trip in the guise of a leaderless revolution led by a group of very imaginative, young, white, male intellectuals, the most flamboyant episode in a long history of American utopianism, a waste of positive energy. Whatever it was, it peaked in the Haight in 1967, although the Haight remained a Hippie stronghold for many years to come. By 1968 new arrivals in the city were warned, "Stay away from the Haight." Many of the original Hippies had fled to rural communes starting in 1967. And what remains is a bedraggled gathering of homeless outcasts.

The Haight Becomes Gentrified

The arrival of Flower Power caused enormous problems for the Haight's long-time residents. The Haight had played a leading role in the Freeway Revolt. So there was a tradition of neighborhood-based activism to draw on. However, the issues changed as the Hippies turned into street people, and the neighborhood gradually gentrified. In 1970, Mayor Alioto called for the restoration of the Haight, which was enough to make everyone nervous, given the mayor's long entanglement with the SFRA. The community responded by working with other neighborhoods to impose a height limit on new construction. In 1974, the Haight became part of the city Rehabilitation and Assistance Program, an updated version of the Federally Assisted Code Enforcement (FACE) program. "The program...resulted in large scale displacement of both low income tenants whose rents were increased and homeowners who could not afford to rehabilitate their buildings," reported Donna Gouse, neighborhood historian. It was redevelopment on a small scale with a velvet glove. The African-American population declined; the gay and white professional population increased. The neighborhood organized against attempts by chain stores to move into the community. A McDonald's was built at end of Haight Street across from

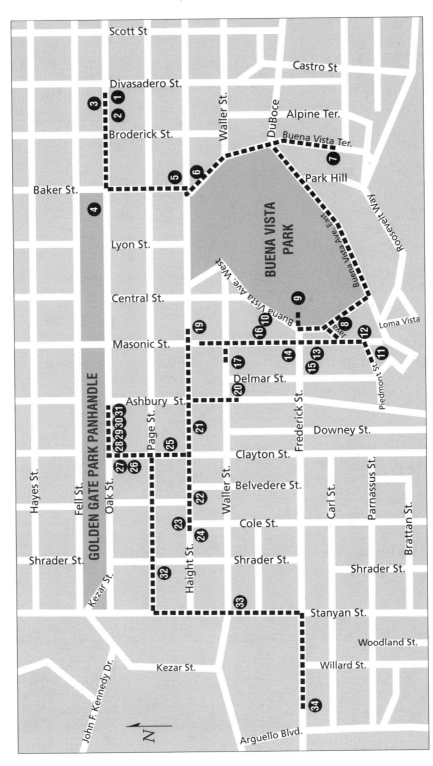

Scott St.

Castro St.

Divasadero St.

Waller St.

DuBoce

Alpine Ter.

Broderick St.

Buena Vista Ter.

Park Hill

Baker St.

BUENA VISTA
PARK

Lyon St.

Buena Vista Ave. East

Roosevelt Way

Central St.

Buena Vista Ave. West

Loma Vista

Masonic St.

Baker

Piedmont St.

Delmar St.

GOLDEN GATE PARK PANHANDLE

Downey St.

Ashbury St.

Page St.

Frederick St.

Hayes St.

Fell St.

Oak St.

Clayton St.

Waller St.

Belvedere St.

Carl St.

Parnassus St.

Brattan St.

Cole St.

Shrader St.

Shrader St.

Shrader St.

Kezar St.

Haight St.

Stanyan St.

Woodland St.

John F. Kennedy Dr.

Kezar St.

Willard St.

Arguello Blvd.

N

Golden Gate Park, and a Round Table Pizza opened its doors and then closed them when too few customers showed up. Thrifty Drugs tried to open a pharmacy on the site of the Straight Theatre. An arsonist burned the building down before it was completed. Thrifty gave up.

The Haight remains one of the most liberal neighborhoods in the city, but there are signs of conflicting attitudes toward social problems. The liberal Haight-Ashbury Neighborhood Council, which dates from the 1959 freeway fight, found itself in conflict with the Cole Valley Improvement Association, described by Gouse as a group that "generally would like to see the neighborhood gentrified even further."[83] The Cole Valley group was particularly adamant about curtailing the activities of street people, many of whom were living in the park and being fed by a sort of latter-day Digger group called Food Not Bombs.

Start at the corner of Divisadero and Oak. The **Abner Phelps House** (1) (c. 1850) at 1111 Oak may be the oldest house in the city. Abner Phelps was one of the Haight's first settlers; he bought 160 acres near Buena Vista Park, probably in 1850, and built this house. A colonel in the Mexican War, he lived in splendid isolation, riding his horse to his law office on Montgomery Street. The house was moved twice and for a time was hidden in the middle of the block before it was moved for a third time and restored. Right next door at 1153 Oak is the **Mish House** (2) (1885), an exemplary Stick-Eastlake home designed by McDougal and Son. Sarah Mish owned a dressmaking and millinery business while engaging in the wholesale business. Her husband, Phenes, imported drygoods and was president of Temple Sherith Israel for

The Abner Phelps House, 1111 Oak, one of the oldest in the city. *Peter Booth Wiley.*

The Mish House, 1153 Oak.
Peter Booth Wiley.

four years. Across the street is a grand old **fire house** (3) (1893) by Hendrickson and Mahoney.

Continue west on Oak. The **Golden Gate Park Panhandle** (4) begins on the right at Baker Street. Originally a drive for horses and carriages, it became one of the favorite gathering places for the Hippie denizens of the Haight in the 1960s. The Diggers served free food here, and the Grateful Dead, Janis Joplin, Jefferson Airplane, Jimi Hendrix, and many others supplied the music. Turn left on Baker and climb the hill to Haight Street. The **Spencer House** (5) (1895), the stately Queen Anne on the northeast corner of Baker and Haight designed by Frederick Rabin, is typical of the grand houses built between Haight and the Panhandle at the turn of the twentieth century. Fully restored, it is now a bed and breakfast. Across the street at **1081 Haight** (6) (1894) is a delightful flatiron by John Clark with a three-story turret and tower cantilevered out over the sidewalk.

Apartment building, 1081 Haight. *Peter Booth Wiley.*

Walk up Buena Vista Avenue East, bearing to the left on Buena Vista Terrace. The **DeLano House** (7) (c. 1880) at 70 Buena Vista Terrace was built for the family of a metalworker, who manufactured fittings for ships. Appropriately, the Corinthian capitals on the porch columns and some of the colonettes are made of iron, which is unusual in a residential building.

Return to Buena Vista Avenue East and turn left, continuing around the edge of Buena Vista Park to Java Street. The corner apartments at **595-97 Buena Vista West** (8) are by Henry Hill, an architect associated with the Second Bay Tradition.

From the top of the steps that enter Buena Vista near the intersection of Buena Vista West and Frederick, there is **an excellent view of the University of San Francisco** (9) on Lone Mountain to the north. When the city lacked a major park, the Lone Mountain Cemetery was a popular gathering place. A Jesuit institution, USF is the city's oldest university. Many a San Franciscan, particularly public employees, went from Catholic high school at St. Ignatius, Riordan, or Sacred Heart to USF to a downtown office. It was once said that with a degree from USF and a dime for a street-car, one could always get a job downtown. The twin towers to the left belong to **St. Ignatius Church** (1914) designed by Charles Devlin. The single Gothic Revival tower in the background sits atop the university's **Lone Mountain Campus** (1932). Designed by H. A. Minton, it was formerly Lone Mountain College, a Catholic women's school.

Continue down Buena Vista West. The **Richard Spreckels Mansion** (10) (1897) at 737 Buena Vista West is the work of Edward Vogel. Spreckels was a nephew of Claus Spreckels, the sugar baron. Ambrose Pierce and Jack London are said to have lived in apartments on the top floor, London while writing *White Fang*. The house was owned by Graham Nash of Crosby, Stills, Nash, and Young and then by Danny Glover, who performed with the San Francisco Mime Troupe before going to Hollywood.

Return to Java, turn right, left on Masonic, and right on Piedmont. The simple Italianate home suggestive of New England at **11 Piedmont** (11) (1860) was moved here from a dairy farm lower down the hillside. Return to Masonic. The shingled house straight ahead at **1526 Masonic** (12) (1910) is by Bernard Maybeck. Walking down the hill, note the plain Classic Revival façade at 1421 Masonic. This is the *back* of the **Fritz Mansion** (13) (1891). To get a glimpse of the front, look between this building and the one on the left.

Mary Fritz bought up hillside pastureland south of Haight in the 1880s, acquiring half the ground between Masonic, Haight, Stanyan, and Seventeenth. She hired a crew to level homesites and lay out streets, including portions of Frederick, Del Mar, Clifford Terrace, and Ashbury Heights, becoming a major developer. Her son Frederick continued her work, building the **Casa Madrona** (14) (c. 1920), a Spanish Revival complex at 116 Frederick, and the **Crossway Apartments** (15) across the street at 191 Frederick. Frederick Fritz became one of the city's wealthiest developers, eventually buying the Huntington and El Cortez Hotels and the Park Lane and Brocklebank Apartments on Nob Hill. He moved the family mansion 100 feet up Masonic and turned the original Victorian façade toward the interior of the block while adding a new Classic Revival façade on Masonic. Frederick's only child, Dolly Fritz Cope, inherited his fortune, becoming one of the city's most closely watched society belles. She drove her white Jaguar to a prestigious prep school, partied with the jet set, was engaged briefly to a Spanish prince, married twice, and died at the age of 40.

The Wasteland, an Art Nouveau storefront, 1660 Haight. *Peter Booth Wiley.*

Walking down Masonic toward Haight, you will discover six Eastlakes at **1322-42 Masonic** (16) (1891) designed by Robert Dickie Cranston for the developer who also built **1315, 1321-23, 1327, and 1333 Waller Street** (17) (1896), one block north of Frederick. Continue downhill to **Haight Street,** once thronged by the young, the colorful, and the stoned, now a fractious interplay of the upscale and the tawdry. The *San Francisco Oracle* (19), the multicolored voice of psychedelia, was located at 1371 Haight. Walk west on Haight and turn left on Ashbury. The **Grateful Dead House** (20) at 710 Ashbury was, according to *Chronicle* music critic Joel Selvin, the unofficial city hall of Haight-Ashbury. Besides housing various members of the Dead family, it was the office of the Haight-Ashbury Legal Organization. A police raid in October 1967, which led to the arrest of two non-pot-smoking members of the band, marked the beginning of the end

of the idyllic days in the Haight. The Dead House is part of a row of Queen Annes, **704 to 714 Ashbury** (1890) designed by Robert Dickie Cranston.

Return to Haight and turn left. The **Psychedelic Shop** (21) was located at 1535 Haight. Opened in early 1966 by two brothers whose father managed the Woolworth's across the street, it was the first store to sell concert tickets and Hippie paraphernalia, such as posters, tie-dyes, paisley fabrics, books on the occult, incense, pipes, and so forth. The **Red Victorian Bed and Breakfast** (22) at 1665 Haight tries to recapture some of the atmosphere of the Sixties as a peace center and living museum featuring rooms "celebrating the Summer of Love, Golden Gate Park, and the brightest hopes of the '60s." It was originally the Jefferson Hotel, built in 1904. Across the street the **Wasteland** at 1660 Haight (23) (1907) is a fine Art Nouveau storefront. The **Red Vic Movie House** (24) (different owner) at 1727 Haight may be a phenomenon unique to San

Francisco, an art film theater in a store-front, featuring couches and various comfortable chairs rather than standard movie house seats.

Backtrack to Clayton and turn left. The **Haight-Ashbury Free Medical Clinic** (25) is located at 558 Clayton. Founded in 1967 by David Smith, a medical student at San Francisco General Hospital, the clinic attracted 30 doctors, who offered their services part-time and gratis for walk-in patients and concert attendees suffering from bad trips. Soule and Hoadley designed the Queen Annes at **409 and 411 Clayton** (26) (1893), and the four Eastlakes at **401-07 Clayton** (27) (1894–95) are by J. B. Hall. Across the street at **400 Clayton** (28) (1895), Coxhead and Coxhead have made the transition from Queen Anne to Classic Revival. Turn right on Oak. The Queen Anne cottage at **1711 Oak** (29) is by Adolph Lutgens (1896). Joseph Cather Newsom's design at **1709 Oak** (30) (1890), with its shin-gle work and bay gable windows, is one of the most original in the city. Maxwell Bugbee designed **1705 Oak** (31) (1893). Turn right on Ashbury, right on Page, and walk along another street lined with gracious Eastlake and Queen Anne designs, interspersed with an occasional latter-day abomination. One of the finest Queen Annes is **1901 Page** (32) (1906), a design by Edward Vogel.

At the end of Page, turn left on Stanyan and walk south to the **Stanyan Park Hotel** (33) (1904–05) at the corner of Waller. William Hammond Hall, the park's first superintendent, initially barred commercial establishments from the park. So a string of hotels and saloons sprang up along Stanyan Street after the park opened. At one time there were seven on Stanyan Street. These establishments catered to customers who also visited the Chutes, the amusement park on Haight, and the Haight Street Grounds, the home of the city's California League baseball team from

The Stanyan Park Hotel, Stanyan and Waller. *Peter Booth Wiley.*

1887 to 1893. Henry Heagerty, who built the Stanyan Park according to a design by Martens and Coffey, replaced his saloon, which catered to the ballpark crowd until the team moved, with a hotel. The Stanyan Park has been restored and still operates as a hotel.

Turn right on Frederick and pass the former gymnasium for the old Polytechnic High School. The high school was replaced by **Park View Commons** (34) (1990). Architect David Baker describes this complex as contextual postmodernism. Built for owners of modest means, he took the idea of the Victorian flat and, rather than present a solid wall of apartments with gardens behind, which is typical of the Victorian, created openings and walkways between the buildings.

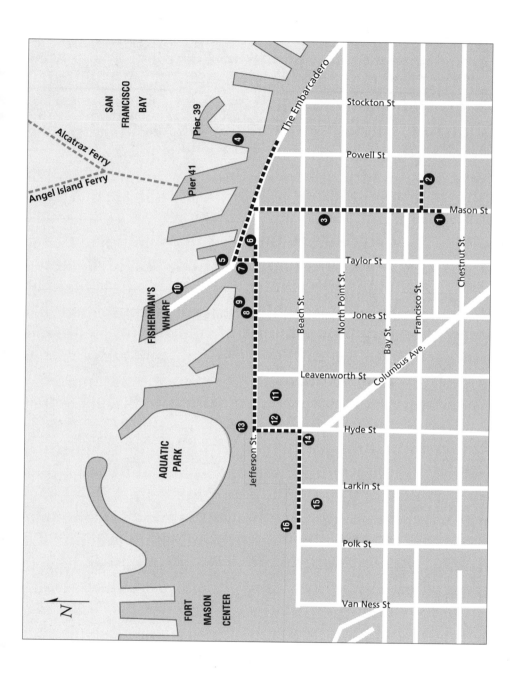

SAN
FRANCISCO
BAY

Alcatraz Ferry

Angel Island Ferry

Pier 39

Pier 41

The Embarcadero

Stockton St

Powell St

Mason St

Taylor St

Beach St.

North Point St.

Jones St

Bay St.

Francisco St.

Chestnut St.

Columbus Ave.

Leavenworth St

Hyde St

Jefferson St.

Larkin St

Polk St

Van Ness St

FISHERMAN'S
WHARF

AQUATIC
PARK

FORT
MASON
CENTER

N

18

Fisherman's Wharf, Aquatic Park Historic District, Angel Island, Alcatraz, and Fort Mason

This tour is on level ground. Its length depends on whether you go to Alcatraz, a three-hour roundtrip, and how much time you spend visiting the historic ships at the Hyde Street pier and the National Maritime Museum in the area. A trip to Angel Island should be a separate undertaking.

In his memoirs San Francisco writer Charles Warren Stoddard describes a boys' Sunday ramble along the northern waterfront in the 1850s. He lived in a brick house on an otherwise empty block on Telegraph Hill. From there, he and his friends would walk down to Meiggs Wharf—which began near Francisco and Mason well inland from Fisherman's Wharf—to watch the locals netting Dungeness crabs by the bushel load. The wharf was the creation of Henry Meiggs, sawmill owner, lumber dealer, and lover of fine music, who took the plunge in Telegraph Hill real estate and then built the wharf, hoping to direct the expansion of downtown toward his pier and undeveloped land. Unfortunately, the Meiggs empire was a house of cards built on questionable financial paper, which he had stolen from the city when he was an alderman. Meiggs and his family were last seen in the autumn of 1854 boarding a ship for Chile.

Near the wharf, Stoddard and his friends would peek into Abe Warner's Cobweb Palace, an odiferous saloon filled with caged birds. Cobwebs as dense as crepe hung like rags from the ceiling, festooning the picture frames on the wall. In front the proprietor kept bears and monkeys in cages. From there the boys walked the beach to Black Point, which today is part of Fort Mason and forms the northern shore of the lagoon at Aquatic Park at the foot of Van Ness Avenue. Scaling a large sand dune, they played in a dense copse of scrub oaks on the point before climbing on top of the wooden flume that brought water to the city from the Presidio. The flume was like an elevated walkway, which the boys could follow almost all the way to Fort Point. They were traversing an enormous sand dune, which ran along the northern shore of the city and left Black Point looking like an island oasis sticking up out of the Sahara (see illustration page 9).

FISHERMAN'S WHARF

Over the next half century the northern waterfront up to the eastern edge of the Presidio became an industrial area with gas works, factories, knitting mills, breweries, distilleries, and a lead smelter. At the foot of Telegraph Hill ships tied up at covered sheds. Nearby there were rows and rows of brick warehouses. One of the first factories along the shore, the Pioneer Woolen Mills, now a part of Ghiradelli Square, opened in 1858. The owners hired Chinese workers, who produced quality blankets, flannels, tweeds, and cash-

The Pioneer Woolen Mill (in perhaps the 1850s) on the shores of Black Point Cove with Russian Hill in the background. Today the main building is part of Ghiradelli Square. Charles Warren Stoddard walked along the wooden flume in the right foreground. *California Historical Society.*

Fisherman's Wharf before 1900, when it was at the foot of Union Street. Note the sail-powered fishing boats with rigging, which could have come from a traditional Egyptian felucca. *San Francisco History Center, San Francisco Public Library.*

mere. Soon a second, larger operation, the Mission Woolen Mills, owned by William Ralston, was built nearby. During the attacks on Chinese labor, both factory owners replaced their Chinese workers with white workers. In 1867, Thomas Selby built a smelter at the corner on Beach between Hyde and Leavenworth. This was the only private smelter refining gold and silver brought from mines in Arizona, California, and Nevada, and later the sole supplier of lead on the West Coast. The sons of Domingo Ghiradelli, who opened a chocolate shop on Jackson Street in 1850 and a factory at the same location five years later, began construction of the Ghiradelli Chocolate Factory on North Point in 1900. Between 1907 and 1909, the California Packing Corporation, later Del Monte, built a cannery and storage warehouse that still stand today.

When Italians from coastal towns near Genoa entered the fishing business in the 1860s, they tied up their feluccas at piers at the foot of Green, Union, and Filbert Streets on the east side of Telegraph Hill. Taking advantage of the anti-Chinese sentiment, the Genoese pushed the Chinese fishermen into outlying camps, like the one at Hunter's Point. In the 1890s, Sicilians, many of them from the town of Santa Flavia near Palermo, tried their hand at fishing, and soon they were at war with the Genoese for control of the fishing grounds. "Boats were sunk, nets have been cut, and sometimes owners too have been cut. Launches have gone to sea and neither launches nor owners have been seen again," reported the *Chronicle* in 1907. Eventually an agreement was reached that left the Genoese in control of tuna and deep-sea fishing and the Sicilians with inshore and crab fishing.

In 1900, toward the end of the construction of the seawall, which had begun in 1878, the fishing fleet was moved to its present location at Fisherman's Wharf. For the first half of the twentieth century, Fisherman's Wharf was both a thriving fishing port and, after the 1906 earthquake, a growing tourist attraction. Gradually, the bay, heavily polluted by mining operations in the Sierra and later by the abundant use of chemicals in California agribusiness, was emptied of its extraordinary bounty of fish, shrimp, oysters, and clams. There have been repeated attempts to revive the wharf's fishing industry, including the construction of new packing facilities at Pier 45, but today fishing has given way to tourism.

THE AQUATIC PARK HISTORIC DISTRICT, THE NATIONAL MARITIME MUSEUM, AND GHIRADELLI SQUARE

Both Frederic Law Olmsted, in 1866, and Daniel Burnham, in 1905, proposed a park at the northern end of Van Ness Avenue. For a time there were a number of bathhouses along the beach at Black Point Cove. From one of them, William Ralston swam to his death in 1876. However, the cove became primarily a dumping ground. Fifteen thousand truckloads of rubble, some of it taken from the ruins of the Palace Hotel, were dumped along the beach after the 1906 earthquake.

In 1923 the city committed itself to the creation of Aquatic Park. Construction did not begin until 1930, however, when gangs of men working with borrowed hand tools used salvage materials to start on a municipal pier. After construction was turned over to the Works Progress Administration (WPA), it began work on the modern shiplike structure that eventually became the headquarters of the National Maritime Museum. Meanwhile, a group of WPA artists, including Hilaire Hiler, Beniamino Bufano, and Sargent Johnson, was working on the interior. Although plans changed constantly, often after work had been completed, the primary function of the structure seemed to be a bathhouse for 5,000 people, complete with showers that were activated by electric eyes, and headquarters for the rowing and swimming clubs located in the area. In 1939 the WPA turned the unfinished project over to the city, which had leased the building to two brothers, who opened a casino. The casino operators and the artists were soon at each other's throats, with the artists charging that the casino operators were interfering with their work and appropriating public space for private use. The white sand brought from Monterey to make a beach washed away, and the cove was too polluted to swim in anyhow.

The military took over the building for barracks during World War II. After the war the building remained locked, until 1951 when the National Maritime

Museum was founded. Alma de Bretteville Spreckels, founder of the Palace of the Legion of Honor, had come up with the idea of a transportation museum as part of a larger plan for a Museum of Science and Industry. Spreckels had retrieved a collection of ship models, which had been displayed at the Treasure Island World's Fair in 1939, and moved them into the Aquatic Park Casino and then into storage after the army took over the building. After the war, Spreckels was visited by Karl Kortum, a farmer's son from Petaluma who was just returning from a long voyage aboard San Francisco's last commercial sailing vessel. Kortum was committed to the idea of a maritime museum. Spreckels offered Kortum a salary and a place to live at her mansion on Washington Street. Kortum wanted to make historic ships the centerpiece of the museum. Spreckels, interested in the larger concept of a transportation museum, opposed the idea of historic ships. Kortum had the backing of *Chronicle* editor Scott Newhall and some of the leaders of the city's shipping industry. Spreckels had a reputation for contentiousness, an appetite for martinis by the pitcherful, an abrasive and dominating personality, and not all that much money to spend. Kortum's ideas prevailed. The Maritime Museum, which acquired the sailing ship *Balclutha* in 1954, eventually became the center of the Aquatic Park Historic District, which includes the Cannery and the Haslett Warehouse, the Hyde Street Pier, and the museum's collection of eight historic ships.

DEVELOPING TOURIST ATTRACTIONS

San Franciscans have taken different approaches to the development of tourist amenities in and around the Wharf. When the Ghiradelli Chocolate Factory was moved to San Mateo in the 1960s, William Matson Roth, an heir to the Matson shipping fortune, bought the abandoned factory on North Point to prevent the construction of apartment towers like the controversial Fontana Towers to the west. Roth hired Wurster, Bernardi & Emmons to design additional buildings to complete the complex. Ghiradelli Square, which incorporates the Pioneer Woolen Mill, is considered one of the first successful transformations of a factory complex into a tourist attraction while maintaining the historical integrity of the buildings.

On the east side of Fisherman's Wharf, Warren Simmons built Pier 39, a characterless collection of used lumber, which houses various shops, restaurants, and an aquarium. When Simmons laid out his plans for a new complex of tourist attractions and a marina on the piers east of Fisherman's Wharf in 1975, there was immediate opposition. Pier 39 opened in 1978 after Simmons made a few well-placed campaign contributions to members of the Board of Supervisors. He had also signed leases for shops in the development with key public figures, including the chief counsel for the Port Commission, a port commissioner who had voted for the project, and Supervisor Dan White. Pier 39's opening was greeted by large crowds and the disdain of the cognoscenti. "Corn. Kitsch. Schlock. Honky-tonk. Dreck. Schmaltz. Merde. Whatever you call the pseudo-Victorian junk with which Warren Simmons has festooned Pier 39, this ersatz San Francisco that never was—a chef d'oeuvre of hallucinatory cliches—is a joke on the port and the planning commission," wrote *Chronicle* architecture critic Allan Temko.

PIER 39, FISHERMAN'S WHARF, THE CANNERY, HYDE STREET PIER MARITIME PARK, GHIRADELLI SQUARE

Start at the **San Remo Hotel** (1) (1906), home to the restaurant **Emma,** at 2237 Mason near Francisco. A. P. Giannini, founder of the Bank of America, built this hotel to replace one that burned in 1906. Its first occupants were Italians who worked at the nearby canneries. The original waterline was here. The foot of Meiggs Wharf began near 444 Francisco, a condominium in the first block to the right as you walk north on Mason. Note the **Bauer-Schweitzer malting factory** (2)—a remnant of the old industrial North Beach—across the street from 444 Francisco. There were ten breweries in this area, and this malting factory helped supply them. It is being remodeled as a residential complex. Continue north on Mason, noting the octagonal structure on the left. This is the **headquarters of International Longshore and Warehouse Local 10** (3), designed by Henry Hill in 1958. It was the site of the first Trips Festival sponsored by Ken Kesey and his Merry Pranksters in 1966.

Turn right on Jefferson. **Pier 39** (4) (1978), designed by Walker and Moody, lies directly in front of you. Note the **Eagle Café** on the second floor to the west. It was once a popular longshoremen's hangout located across the Embarcadero.

Return along Jefferson to **Fisherman's Wharf** (5), the city's most popular tourist attraction, drawing millions of visitors every year. On the right just before Taylor is **Boudin's** (6), named after the historic baker of sourdough bread, one of San Francisco's gustatory treats. French baker Isadore Boudin brought yeast from the mother country, which he used to enhance the quality of the gold miners' sourdough bread—which led to the miners' being called sourdoughs. Boudin's is still using extracts from the original mother dough. The original crab and shrimp stands were put up near the corner of Taylor and Jefferson so that fisherman could grab a quick meal during their working day. Soon after the fishing fleet moved here in 1900, the tourists showed up, leading to the construction of restaurants and various knickknack and trinketry stands. Among the oldest restaurants are **Alioto's** (7) at 8 Fisherman's Wharf, **Castagnola's** (8) at 286 Jefferson, and **Scoma's** (9) at Pier 47, which can be reached by walking west on Jefferson and turning right up the alley marked with a Scoma's sign.

Continue north on Taylor to Pier 45, where the USS *Pampanito* and the SS *Jeremiah P. O'Brien* (10) are tied up and open to the public. Built in 1943 in Portsmouth, New Hampshire, the *Pampanito*, a World War II submarine, saw action in the Pacific. The *O'Brien*, although built in Portland, Maine, in 1943, is typical of the hundreds of fabled Liberty ships built in Bay Area

The Haslett Warehouse, Jefferson and Hyde. *Peter Booth Wiley.*

shipyards during World War II. She saw action in both the Atlantic and the Pacific, notably at the invasion of Normandy to which she returned under her own steam in 1995. The *O'Brien's* location is subject to change.

Continue west on Jefferson. The **Cannery** (11) (1907) is the first of two brick structures joined by a courtyard on Jefferson between Leavenworth and Hyde. Built by the California Fruit Packers Association, the Cannery housed an assembly line where fruit and vegetables brought from the Central Valley by riverboat and ferry were packed before being moved across the courtyard into the **Haslett Warehouse** (12). The Cannery was a principal source of employment for Italian-American immigrants. Through a series of mergers, the Fruit Packers Association, later the Del Monte Corporation, eventually became for a time the largest packer of fruit and vegetables in the world. The original buildings were designed by Philip Bush. The restored Cannery is actually a building within a building. The brick walls surround an interior structure housing shops and restaurants,

designed by Joseph Esherick and Associates in a 1968 conversion.

Turn right on Hyde Street and enter the **Hyde Street Pier Maritime Park** (13) where a number of historical ships are tied up. The pier was originally built to provide ferry service to Sausalito and Tiburon. The **Maritime Store** on the left includes an excellent bookstore where you can obtain (free) a good map of the Golden Gate National Recreation Area. The **Lewis Ark** (1906), which sits on blocks on the pier on the right, was a floating summer cottage owned by a rear admiral in the Navy. The paddle-wheel ferry *Eureka* (originally the *Ukiah*), powered by a walking beam engine, was built in 1890 to carry railroad cars and passengers. It is a reminder that the city was once served by a huge fleet of ferryboats. Opposite the *Eureka* is the *C. A. Thayer,* a three-masted schooner. The *Thayer* was one of dozens of ships that worked the coast, picking up lumber at tiny dog-hole harbors, such as Elk and Mendocino, which were little more than deep, surf-periled indentations in the coastline. The *Thayer* was built in the

Hans D. Bendixsen yard in Humboldt Bay in 1895. In 1912 it became a salmon packet. Don't miss the home movie shown on the *Thayer* or the *Balclutha,* made by one of the ship's last skippers, about salmon fishing off Alaska.

Typical of hundreds of ships that called at San Francisco in the late nineteenth-century, the **Balclutha,** built in Glasgow in 1886 for the California grain trade, is one of the last of the full-rigged ships. On her maiden voyage, the *Balclutha* arrived in San Francisco with a load of coal and returned to Europe via Cape Horn with wheat. When the grain trade declined, she carried lumber from Washington to Australia, returning with coal, and then went into the Alaska salmon trade. The scow-schooner **Alma** is tied up at the end of the pier. This type of vessel was one of the workhorses of the Bay carrying hay, lumber, or produce. The *Alma* was built in 1891 by F. Seimer, a local shipwright. Nearby is the steam-powered tugboat **Hercules,** a rare example of the finest in American shipbuilding technology from the early years of the twentieth century. Built of steel by John H. Dialogue & Son in Camden, New Jersey, in 1907 for a San Francisco company, the *Hercules* was an oceangoing tug. She hauled her sister ship to San

Francisco via Cape Horn on their maiden voyage, helped with the construction of the Panama Canal, towed the first caisson for the naval piers at Pearl Harbor to Hawaii, and was once owned by Mayor James "Sunny Jim" Rolph. On the west side of the pier is another tug, the side-wheeler *Eppleton Hall.*

Walk south on Hyde Street when you leave the pier to Beach. The **Buena Vista Café** (14), the place where Irish coffee was purportedly invented, is on the southwest corner. Turn right on Beach. **Ghiradelli Square** (15) is on your left just past Larkin. The Ghiradelli Chocolate Factory, the brick structure along North Point with its beautiful clock tower, was designed by William Mooser II and built by the sons of Domingo Ghiradelli, who opened his first chocolate factory on Jackson Street. The younger Ghiradellis bought the abandoned **Pioneer Woolen Mill,** which was designed by Mooser's father, William Mooser, in 1856, and then asked the son to design a factory complex that included the mill. The woolen mill, now the site of some shops and the **Mandarin Restaurant,** appears to have been built at a strange angle because it was oriented to the original shoreline of Black Point Cove. The Ghiradelli's instructed Mooser the Younger to build a

The full-rigged ship *Balclutha,* the Hyde Street Pier Maritime Park. *Peter Booth Wiley.*

model factory, an effort that continued from 1900 to 1922, when the clock tower modeled after a French château at Blois was completed. The landmark sign dates from 1923. Ruth Asawa designed *Andrea,* the fountain, which serves as a centerpiece of the courtyard and is surrounded by brick pavilions designed by John Matthias. Lawrence Halprin & Associates did the landscape design. **Builders Booksource,** an excellent architectural bookstore, is located south of the fountain.

Across Beach Street to the north of Ghiradelli Square is the **National Maritime Museum** (16), the Moderne structure designed in 1939 to look like a luxury liner by William Mooser III of the third generation of the family of architects. Before becoming the museum and a senior center, this building served as a casino and barracks for an antiaircraft corps during World War II. Without

clearly defining how the building would be used, the WPA hired artists Hilaire Hiler, Sargent Johnson, Richard Ayer, and John Glut, who worked with the architect to design and decorate the interior. Gay, half Jewish, half Native American, Hiler was a jazz pianist, a psychoanalyst, and an early student of the psychological meaning of color. Choosing for a theme the submerged cities of Atlantis and Mu, Hiler painted the murals in the main lounge and the ladies' lounge on the west end of the second floor. Richard Ayer decorated the third floor, and Sargent Johnson, an African-American artist hired by the WPA, carved the entrance portico and supervised the laying of the mosaic tile on the outside balcony on the second floor. John Glut designed the light fixtures, and Beniamino Bufano contributed two sculptures, also on the second-floor balcony.

ANGEL ISLAND AND ALCATRAZ

Ferries depart from Pier 41 between Pier 39 and Fisherman's Wharf. The trip to Angel Island requires a half day, with steep climbs if you are going to walk around the island. The Alcatraz trip takes three hours pier to pier. There is a steep climb to the top of the island.

Angel Island State Park is a premier walking, biking, camping, and picnicking area with excellent views of San Francisco. When Lieutenant Juan Manuel Ayala, the first European to enter the Bay by ship, surveyed the bay in 1775, he anchored in the cove where ferries now drop off passengers. His activities are described in a small exhibit at park headquarters. There are buildings dating from the Civil War and the remains of numerous other military facilities. The **Immigration Station** through which 175,000 Chinese were processed between 1910 and 1940 is now a museum. Waiting to be accepted or sent back home, those incarcerated scrawled poetry on the walls.

Alcatraz. Ayala named the island *Los Alcatraces,* probably after cormorants (alcatraceo) roosting on its barren, rocky outcrops. The name was later corrupted to **Alcatraz,** which some argue refers to brown pelicans, also common in the Bay. In 1850 the military designated Alcatraz as the centerpiece of a triangular system of forts that would protect the entrance to the Bay. The other two would be located at Fort Point and Lime Point on the northern side of the Golden Gate. The Lime Point fort was never built. During the 1850s workers blasted and hacked away at "the Rock," building gun platforms, magazines, and fortifications along the north, west and southern sides of the island, as well as

Alcatraz before 1969. San Francisco History Center, San Francisco Public Library.

barracks, a guardhouse, and a huge barracks-fortress with two drawbridges surrounded by a moat known as the Citadel. Meanwhile, the federal government built the first lighthouse on the Pacific Coast next to the Citadel.

In 1861, when the Civil War broke out, there were 111 cannon on the island manned by a complement of more than 400 men. Military activity on Alcatraz, however, was limited to firing a warning shot at a British warship when it entered the Bay without following the proper protocol. Colonel Albert Sidney Johnston did move 10,000 muskets and 150,000 cartridges from the Benicia Arsenal to the island to keep them out of the hands of Confederate sympathizers. Asbury Harpending, William Ralston's partner, and his pro-rebel cronies were caught leaving the city on a schooner, which they planned to turn into a privateer. Harpending, convicted of treason, was confined to the Rock until pardoned by Abraham Lincoln. When Lincoln was assassinated, 39 more Confederate sympathizers were shipped here after being arrested for

rejoicing over his death.

For the rest of Alcatraz's life as a military post, Army engineers were confronted with a major problem: It was impossible to create fortifications strong enough to withstand the power of modern cannon fire. This fact did not deter the military from spending hundreds of thousands of dollars reshaping the island's terrain for larger weapons while building new batteries and facilities until the post was decommissioned and became a military prison in 1907. Alcatraz's role as a military prison began quite by happenstance when a group of inmates was shipped to the island in 1859. They were confined to the basement of the guardhouse, where there was no running water, no heat, and nothing to sleep on but straw pallets. This dank hole was soon supplemented by wooden prison barracks for a population that numbered 441 by the end of the century. The prisoners did the bulk of the work, building new batteries and structures and filling in various irregularities along the island shore. Among those confined to the island were a number of Native Americans arrested for resisting the forces of Manifest Destiny. This group included two Modocs accused of conspiring, successfully as it turned out, to murder General E. R. S. Canby during the Modoc War; a close associate of Geronimo's; and a Hopi chief and 18 of his followers. The Hopis were locked up "until they shall evince...a desire to cease interference with the plans of the government for the civilization and education of its Indian wards." [84]

After Alcatraz became a military prison, the Citadel was demolished and replaced in 1912 by a huge cell block, at the time the largest reinforced concrete structure in the world. Simultaneously, the lighthouse was replaced by a light tower and a new keeper's house, both in the Mission Revival style. Facing reduced budgets in the early Depression years, the military turned the prison over to the U.S. Bureau of Prisons in 1933. Alcatraz was designated a maximum security facility for the system's most hardened and notorious inmates, such as Al Capone, Alvin "Creepy" Karpis, and George "Machine Gun" Kelly. Because authorities feared negative publicity in San Francisco, the first prisoners arrived in railroad cars, which were secretly shipped from Tiburon to the island on a barge. Kept carefully screened from public scrutiny by the prison bureaucracy, the Rock soon gained a reputation as a hell hole.

In 1963, Alcatraz, always a costly facility to operate, was closed, and the debate began about what to do with this prime piece of real estate. In 1964 a small party of Sioux went ashore briefly, claiming the island under a treaty that permitted nonreservation Indians to claim property occupied by abandoned military posts. The invaders offered to pay the government the 47 cents an acre recently offered to California Indians for lands taken during the gold rush. When Texas billionaire Lamar

Hunt won the Board of Supervisors' approval to develop the island in 1969, a second group of Native Americans invaded, hoping to create a national Indian cultural center and university. In the midst of the Vietnam War, the government eschewed an armed evacuation of the invaders, deciding instead to gradually turn up the pressure on the occupants by blockading the island and confiscating a barge with the island's only source of fresh water while engaging in prolonged negotiations about the island's future. In June 1970 two mysterious fires damaged the lighthouse and destroyed the warden's house and several other buildings. The feds blamed the Indians; the Indians blamed two figures seen running from the scene. Under pressure, the Indian movement fractured. Nineteen months after the invasion, federal marshals removed the remaining occupants from the Rock. Despite this defeat, the occupation of Alcatraz inspired a nationwide Red Power movement that would have a profound impact on the native population. In 1972, Alcatraz became part of the Golden Gate National Recreation Area.

Alcatraz is very much like an archeological site. Layered one on top of the other are the remains of the old military post, then the military prison, and finally the civilian prison, all topped by the ruins left by the 1970 fires. The **stone bulkhead,** beneath the wharf where the ferry docks, was built from the remains of the earliest gun platforms. Directly behind the wharf are the **bomb-proof or casemate barracks,** which were built on the foundation of the original fortifications. The lower floor with the casemate windows was built beginning in 1865 to resist the more destructive ordnance perfected during the Civil War. The building served as a storage facility and a fortified barracks with openings through which guns could be brought to bear upon boats approaching the landing.

The upper floors were added in 1905. Today the building houses a bookstore, a video theater, and some exhibits. The **switchback road** leading from the wharf to the top of the island was built in 1853. Walk to the right up the hill and into the **guardhouse** (1857), the oldest building on the island and the island's second line of defense. On the left side of the passageway note the opening, which reveals the original moat. Next comes a doorway into the **sally port,** which was protected on either side by 24-pound howitzers. Once there was a drawbridge that could be pulled up into the doorway of the sally port to keep invaders out. Confederate sympathizers were imprisoned in the Guardhouse. The Mission Revival building above the guardhouse, known as the **chapel,** was built in the 1920s. It housed guards who were bachelors and may have served as a school and a meeting room. On the right, past the guardhouse, are the remains of the **Post Exchange** and **Officers' Club,** built in 1910. The building served as a general store for military personnel; later, when Alcatraz became a federal prison, it housed a dance hall, gymnasium, bowling alley, and soda fountain. It burned in 1970.

Beyond the Post Exchange, in an area that is currently fenced off, is the **Quartermaster Warehouse and Power Plant.** This structure, built in 1912, sits on top of the remains of the **North Battery** (note the brick wall on the east side of the building) and its combination guardhouse and powder magazine, built originally in the 1850s and in the 1870s. The **Model Industries Building** on the western tip of the island was built during the 1920s, when the military was emphasizing vocational rehabilitation for prisoners.

From the Post Exchange, follow the road as it snakes up to the **cellhouse** on top of the hill, and enter through a side door for a self-guided tour. The brick foundations on the left are all that remain of **Officer's Row,** where a group of Victorian cottages, including the commandant's, provided housing for senior officers. The classical Revival cellhouse was built on top of the remains of the Citadel between 1908 and 1912. The Citadel's granite entranceways were incorporated into the structure.

Exit the cellhouse through the main entrance. To the left are the remains of the sprawling **Mission Revival mansion** that the warden built for himself and his family in the 1920s. It also burned in 1970. To the right, the **lighthouse tower** remains, the keeper's house having been torn down after the fire. Just beyond the lighthouse is the **parade ground,** which was constructed in the 1870s by leveling this part of the island.

FORT MASON

The National Maritime Museum and Black Point mark the eastern edge of the Golden Gate National Recreation area, the most spectacular urban park in America. The Spanish built earthwork batteries and installed five small guns on what they called Punta Medanos (Points Dunes) in 1797. These must have melted away with the rains because there were no signs of them when the U.S. government made the Point a military reservation in 1850. In that year a joint Army-Navy board recommended that Black Point become part of a system of fortifications and gun placements—on opposite sides of the narrowest part of the Golden Gate, Alcatraz, Angel Island, Black Point, and Yerba Buena Island . They would force enemy ships entering the Bay to run a gauntlet of devastating fire. There were no enemies in sight, however. So the point became popular with squatters, including Bear Flag leader John Fremont, who built a house overlooking Black Cove. The military moved in during the Civil War, naming the area Fort Mason. They tore down Fremont's house and moved several others while building the batteries called for in 1850. New structures were built, including barracks, officers' quarters, and a parade ground.

Starting in 1889, Fort Mason became the control center for a submarine minefield, also designed to protect the entrance to the harbor, which could be activated electrically from a command post on the shore. As the U.S. military presence in the Pacific increased during the Spanish-American War and

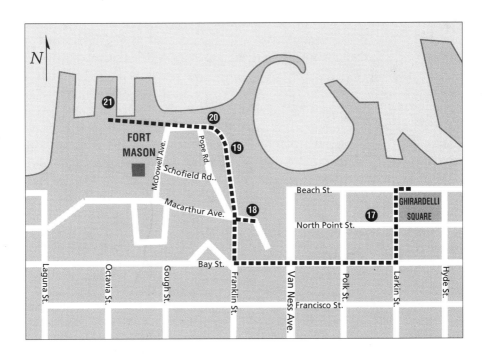

the subjugation of the Philippines, the Army made Fort Mason a center for the shipment of supplies to Hawaii, the Philippines, Guam, and Alaska. For this purpose, land on the western side of the Point was acquired and filled. After the 1906 earthquake, Army forces from Fort Mason and the Presidio played a major role in fighting fires and maintaining order in the city. Between 1912 and 1915 a supply depot, consisting of three large piers, and four warehouses were built, and a railroad tunnel was dug beneath the Point.

In 1939 the supply depot was a sleepy outpost manned by 831 civilians and soldiers, who moved about 48,000 tons of materiel across the piers in a year. By the end of the war 1.6 million soldiers had embarked from the depot accompanied by 23.5 million tons of supplies, making the depot one of the busiest on the West Coast.

Today the Fort Mason Center is a monument to Congressman Phillip Burton. Frustrated by his inability to push a more traditional urban liberal agenda during the Nixon years, Burton became a committed environmentalist and the author of the legislation that created the Golden Gate National Recreation Area (GGNRA) in 1972. The GGNRA, however, was the product of a number of political forces and individuals, some traditionally opposed to each other, who happened to converge around the idea of a great urban park. Among those who first pushed for a new park was renowned photographer Ansel Adams, who grew up on a sandy hillside overlooking the Golden Gate in the Richmond District. Adams and other leaders of the Sierra Club began discussions with the military about ways in which surplus military lands could be used for parks. When Native Americans occupied Alcatraz in 1969, Secretary of the Interior Walter Hickel convinced Nixon that creating a national recreation area was a good way of getting rid of the Indians, who wanted the island for a cultural center. Hickel planted the seed in Burton's fertile mind. Burton was backed by a coalition of environmentalists, Republicans, and neighborhood activists in the Outer Richmond. Burton rammed the GGNRA bill through Congress, accomplishing in three years what normally took ten. In 1977, the National Maritime Museum became part of the GGNRA, and the warehouse and pier complex at Fort Mason was transformed into a nonprofit facility, which houses museums, environmental organizations, and various public service organizations.

To get to Fort Mason from Ghiradelli Square and the National Maritime Museum, walk south on Polk and turn right on Bay. Note the **Fontana Apartments** (17) (1961) on your right at 1000 North Point. This is the apartment tower that triggered an early controversy over height limits. The entrance to **Fort Mason** is on your right at the intersection of Bay and Franklin. Walk north on Franklin, turning right on MacArthur. Through the gates on the left is **McDowell Hall** (18) (1855), the former residence of the commanding general of the Army's western headquarters. Return to Franklin and turn right.

McDowell Hall at Fort Mason, the former residence of the commanding general of the Army's western headquarters. *Peter Booth Wiley.*

Some of the houses lining both sides of Franklin were built in the 1850s by squatters, albeit well-known ones such as John Fremont. On the right are the **Brooks House** (1850s), the **Palmer House** (1855), which was built for a gold rush banker, and the **Haskell House** (19) (1850s), where David Broderick died in 1859 after he was wounded in a duel with Judge David Terry. When the squatters were evicted, these houses became officers' quarters.

Follow the paved pathway at the northern end of Franklin, turning to your left and climbing down a set of stairs to the right to the **Black Point Battery** (20) (1864). Twelve 10-inch Rodman guns were mounted here as part of the defenses of the harbor. Continue west and you will notice the **Fort Mason Center** (21) below you on the right. This was the San Francisco Port of Embarkation, an army supply center designed in the Mission Revival style by

Rankin, Kellogg and Crane, built between 1912 and 1915 to serve U.S. forces in the Pacific. Thousands of American troops and tons of supplies moved through these warehouses and across these piers in World War II. Today the Fort Mason Center is a remarkable assemblage of cultural, media, and environmental organizations. From left to right, Building E houses the **San Francisco Maritime National Historical Park headquarters,** its **Historic Documents Department,** and the **National Maritime Museum Library.** Building D houses the **Mexican Museum** and the **San Francisco Craft and Folk Art Museum.** Building C houses the **Museo ItaloAmericano** and the **San Francisco African American Historical and Cultural Society;** Building A is the home of **Greens,** the vegetarian restaurant owned by the San Francisco Zen Center.

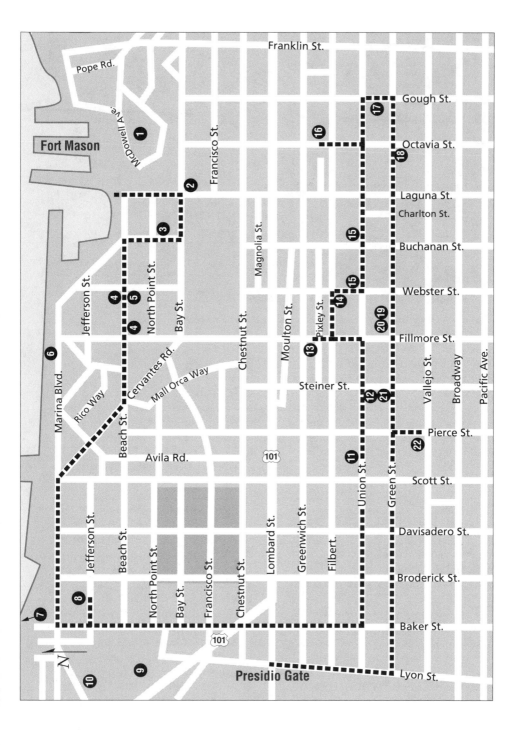

19

Cow Hollow, the Marina, and the Presidio

This is a long walk, with steep climbs in Cow Hollow and the Presidio. It can be divided in two by visiting the Presidio separately. Allow three hours. The tour starts at the western edge of Fort Mason and ends in the Presidio. To return downtown, take the 28 or 29 Muni bus from the end of the Golden Gate Bridge and transfer to the 1 California.

COW HOLLOW

The dunes along the beach were originally a barrier to development along the waterfront west of Van Ness. On the southern edge of the dune was Washerwoman's Lagoon, a two-block body of fresh water, which attracted laundries and, later, tanneries. Nearby was Cow Hollow, roughly defined as the level ground between Union and Lombard Streets to the north of Pacific Heights, west of Van Ness, and east of the Presidio. Dairy and produce farming sprang up on either side of the Presidio Road, which ran from the beach at the Spanish village of Yerba Buena over Russian Hill and roughly along Union and Filbert Streets, entering the Presidio at Lyon (see the illustration on page 9). The practice of feeding cows with the slops from the local distilleries and breweries and the generally wretched condition of many of the dairies attracted the attention of health officials. They found tubercular cows, cows with abscesses and ulcers on their udders, and food contaminated with worms and bacteria. Attributing a sudden increase in deaths from typhoid fever in 1889 to the filthy conditions on Cow Hollow dairy farms, the Health Department began to close them down. By 1897 the number of dairies had declined to three. A photograph at the California Historical Society provides evidence that Chinese farmers were growing vegetables in the area circa 1885. Below Pacific Heights, which looks like little more than a dune with a handful houses on it, there were extensive gardens, some shacks, and crude sheds.

The demise of produce farming and dairies was inevitable, given the unrelenting westward movement of real estate development in the city. A number of the dairy farmers turned to real estate and home building. James Cudworth, a Vermont dairy farmer whose wife was the local schoolteacher, built more than a dozen houses in Cow Hollow between 1877 and 1899, a number of which still stand.

The Panama Pacific International Exposition: A Fantasy City

In 1891, Silver King James Fair bought a huge expanse of land covered with sand north of Lombard, had it graded, extending the shoreline northward, and developed it as an industrial site. Reclamation, as well as the destruction of homes and factories that had been built on earlier fill, commenced in 1911 as the city prepared for the Panama Pacific International Exposition (PPIE), which opened in February 1915 and closed ten months later. The PPIE, meant to celebrate the opening of the Panama Canal, was the city's leaders' way of saying to the world that San Francisco had recovered from the earthquake. A Disneyland before Disney, the PPIE was the city's most significant commitment to its future as a tourist attraction since the arrival of the forty-niners. Construction would pump an estimated $80 million into the local economy, and 19 million visitors would leave bundles of cash behind as they strolled through the 635 acres of shops, carnival attractions, rides, gardens, restaurants, and exhibition halls featuring everything from livestock to the new diesel engine and an assembly line that produced a Ford every ten minutes.

The PPIE was meant to be San Francisco's version—bigger and better, of course—of Chicago's Columbian Exposition of 1893, which had inspired the City Beautiful movement and launched Daniel Burnham's career as an urban planner. Willis Polk, Burnham's former associate, was appointed to the preliminary architectural commission for the PPIE. This was a difficult period for a difficult man. Burnham, Polk's mentor, had recently withdrawn from a partnership with Polk in a San Francisco office after Polk could not drum up enough work and proved to be a poor manager. Further, Polk was a contentious publicity seeker, and often critical of his colleagues. When he was appointed director of the permanent architectural commission, three of his colleagues, including John Galen Howard and Albert Pissis, refused to serve. Polk was soon replaced by George Kelham.

Like the Chicago Exposition, the PPIE was intended to be an expression of the best work of contemporary architects, in this case particularly California architects. The grounds were organized, according to a design by Edward Bennett, Burnham's former protégé, into ten exhibition spaces facing eight great courts, each with buildings designed by a different architect. The architectural centerpiece of the exposition was the Tower of Jewels, designed by the New York firm of Carrere and Hastings. The 43-story building was hung with 100,000 pieces of colored glass, which danced in the wind and provided a spectacular show when illuminated with spotlights at night. Other buildings were done by Arthur Brown Jr.; Kelham; McKim, Mead & White; Louis Mulgardt; and a handful of lesser-known architects. Only two buildings were considered significant enough to keep, the Mission style California Building and Bernard Maybeck's Palace of Fine Arts. Only Maybeck's was saved.

Maybeck wrote that the PPIE "expressed the life of the people of California." He went on to say, "It has its geographic stamp just as the architecture of Thibet [sic] has its geographic reason for being. . . . The future city of California will have the same feeling; because it will be a California city." The PPIE was instead an expression of San Francisco's avoidance of urban planning when confronted by powerful real estate interests and a measure of its healthy fantasy life. As a source of original ideas, neoclassicism, always more mimetic than original, was in its twilight years. Ironically, Maybeck was simultaneously designing buildings that were true examples of an indigenous California architecture. But none of Maybeck's originality nor anyone else's, including Polk's, was expressed at the PPIE. The PPIE, as historian Kevin Starr put it, functioned "as a symbolic substitute for the Burnham Plan."[85] It was a compensatory experience, the planning of a fantasy metropolis in a remote part of the city that could be torn down, like a Hollywood set, leaving the Marina ready for real estate developers.

THE MARINA

After the PPIE buildings, many of them of plaster made to look like travertine marble, were torn down, the area remained a wasteland into the early 1920s. Foreseeing eventual development, city parks chief John McLaren persuaded the city to turn over four blocks along the waterfront for a park, which became Marina Green. Silver King James Fair's daughter, Mrs. Virginia Vanderbilt, retained title to her father's land and sold it to real estate developers, who drew up plans for a development they called Marina Gardens. Their plan called for houses on half-acre and one-acre lots with a central boulevard running to the doorstep of the Palace of Fine Arts. The boulevard was never built. It was more remunerative to build apartment buildings, which are predominant, rather than single-family homes, such as those that line Marina Boulevard. A few streets, such as Cervantes Boulevard, which differ from the traditional orthogonal grid, are all that remain of the original development plan. The Marina became a classic city-suburb where upwardly mobile San Franciscans, including the DiMaggio and Moscone families, moved when they left their more urbanized ethnic enclaves.

The Marina District was the site of some of the most harrowing damage during the 1989 earthquake. It became a case study of what happens to areas built on landfill. The shock waves from the quake were amplified in magnitude by the sandy soil, and six apartment buildings, those with long spans of garages on the first floor, collapsed, and dozens more were damaged. Three people burned to death in a collapsed building.

From Fort Mason's western gate at the corner of Laguna and Beach, take a left on Laguna. Joe Jones's **statue of Representative Phillip Burton** (1), the man who pushed the legislation for the Golden Gate Bridge National Recreation Area through Congress, stands in the open meadow to the left. The large brick building on the southeast corner of Laguna and Bay is the **Heritage Retirement Community** (2) (1925) by Julia Morgan. Turn right on Bay and right on Buchanan. You are now in the **Marina District,** which was developed after the area was filled and leveled for the Panama Pacific International Exposition in 1915. Some of the worst damage in the 1989 Loma Prieta earthquake was concentrated here because the residences were built on fill. The **San Francisco Light and Gas Company** (3) (1893) at 3636 Buchanan was once part of a gasworks and is the sole reminder that this was an industrial area before the PPIE. Continue north on Buchanan and turn left on Beach. The apartment houses along Beach are typical of the variety of styles—though Mediterranean Revival and Deco dominate—employed by architects when the Marina was developed in the 1920s and

1930s. Richard Irvine designed the apartment houses at **1600 and 1695 Beach** (4) (1936 and 1931), one Deco and one Mediterranean Revival, and S. A. Colton did the double house at **1627-29 Beach** (5) (1935) in a French style.

Follow Beach west as it jogs slightly to the south. **Cervantes Boulevard,** a street that cuts across the orthogonal layout of the neighborhood, is a reminder that the first plans for Marina Gardens called for a neighborhood of single-family homes with a less conventional street plan. Turn right on Cervantes and continue to Marina Boulevard, which is lined with large single-family homes. **Marina Green** (6), the lovely bayside park on the north side of the boulevard, was built by John McClaren in the 1920s. To the left on Marina Boulevard is a yacht basin. Across the basin is the **St. Francis Yacht Club** (7), one of the city's elite private gathering places, designed by Willis Polk in 1928 in the Mediterranean Revival style. Turn left on Baker and left on Jefferson. Richard Neutra and Otto Winkler designed the glass-curtain-wall row house at **2056-58 Jefferson** (8) (1937). Neutra, an Austrian immigrant and a renowned practitioner of the International Style, made his mark in Los

Angeles rather than in San Francisco. Built for a German immigrant couple with a collection of Bauhaus furniture, the house was recently restored.

Return to Baker and turn left for a full view of Bernard Maybeck's **Palace of Fine Arts** (9) (1915), all that remains of the Panama Pacific International Exposition. Maybeck described his plan for a domed rotunda and colonnade sitting on the shores of a reflecting pool in front of a long, curved

San Francisco Light and Gas Company at 3636 Buchanan, a remnant of this nineteenth-century industrial area. *Peter Booth Wiley.*

The Palace of Fine Arts during the Panama Pacific International Exposition (1915). *San Francisco History Center, San Francisco Public Library.*

exhibition hall, as looking like a Victorian cloisonné brooch. He wanted visitors to experience a gradual transition from the exciting influences of the fair to the quiet serenity of the galleries. To do this, he tried to recreate what he called the romantic atmosphere of the period after the Renaissance, which he described as "sadness modified by the feeling that beauty has a soothing influence."[86] Accordingly, he placed the rotunda and landscaped colonnade so that they would look like an old Roman ruin standing alone on an island in the middle of a lake. Because they were constructed with plaster, the rotunda and colonnade have had to be restored twice. The PPIE exhibition hall now houses the **Exploratorium** (10) to the west, the city's world-class science museum, known for its innovative, hands-on exhibits. Founded in 1969 by physicist Frank Oppenheimer, the Exploratorium, which describes itself as a museum of science, art, and human perception, has influenced the direction of science museums around the world.

COW HOLLOW–UNION STREET

Continue south on Baker and cross Lombard, turning left on Union. You are now in **Cow Hollow,** once known for its dairy farms. The Presidio Road built by the Spanish to connect the village of Yerba Buena to the Presidio ran roughly along union and Filbert. **Union Street,** with its collection of fancy boutiques and restaurants, is Cow Hollow's main thoroughfare. The house at **2460 Union** (11) (c. 1872) was originally Italianate but was later remodeled by Mooser and Cutherbertson, who added a mansard roof and a gambrel roof over the double-arched windows on the second floor. In the courtyard of **St. Mary the Virgin Episcopal Church** (12) (1891) at 2301 Union is a fountain fed by a spring that once provided water for the dairy farms. Continue east on Union and turn left on Fillmore. The **Six Gallery** (13), where

the San Francisco Renaissance was born in 1955, was located at 3119 Fillmore (see pages 240–241). Turn right on Filbert. The **Vedanta Society** (14) (1905) on the southwest corner of Webster and Filbert is one of the city's great fantasy structures and a testament to California's ongoing infatuation with exotic forms of spiritualism. Swami Trigunatitananda worked with architect Joseph Leonard to capture the essence of Vedanta, a form of Hinduism, which to the Swami meant blending Islamic, medieval, Queen Anne, and colonial features in one building.

Return to Union Street and turn left. The houses at **2040 and 1980 Union** (15) (1874) were built by James Cudworth, a dairy farmer and one of the city's first supervisors. Cudsworth's barn is in the back of his residence at 2040 Union. Continue east on Union and turn left on Octavia. The house at **2940 Octavia** (16) (1870) was the farmhouse for another dairy operation. This property backed up to Washerwoman's Lagoon. Return to Union and turn left, and then right on Gough. The **Octagon House** (17) at 2645 Gough was built by William McElroy, a miller, in 1861 on the east side of Gough facing Union, which was then known as Presidio Road. It is the second surviving structure of a type designed according to the ideas of Orson Fowler. Fowler argued that octagonal houses provided a healthful living environment. The house was bought by the National Society of Colonial Dames in 1951, moved to this lot from across the street, and restored by Warren Perry, the dean of the University of California-Berkeley School of Architecture. It is now a museum of the decorative arts from the Colonial and Federal periods.

Continue South on Gough, turning right on Green. The **Golden Gateway Branch** of the public library (18) (1927) on the southwest corner of Green and Octavia is one of five funded by Andrew Carnegie. The **Sherman House** (19)

The Vedanta Society at Webster and Filbert. *Peter Booth Wiley.*

The Sherman House, 2160 Green. *Sherman House.*

The Casebolt Mansion, 2727 Pierce. *Jan Cigliano.*

(1879), by James Merritt Reid, at 2160 Green was built for the owner of the city's largest music store and is now a beautifully restored luxury hotel with Second Empire furnishings. The west wing of the house is a skylighted, three-story music room where Paderewski, Enrico Caruso, and Lotta Crabtree performed. Crabtree lived in the house on the left at **2170 Green Street** (20). Continue west on Green to the corner of Steiner, where stands the lavishly

detailed **St. Vincent de Paul** (21) (1916) by Shea and Lofquist. Continue on Green, turning left on Pierce. The **Casebolt Mansion** (22) (1866) at 2727 Pierce is the grand manor house of Cow Hollow. Henry Casebolt, a Virginia blacksmith, used massive ships' timbers to build the house with its elaborate Italianate façade. Return to Green, turn left, continue west to the Presidio Wall at Lyon, and turn right. The Presidio Gate is at Lyon and Lombard.

THE PRESIDIO

After Fremont's opera buffa seizure of the abandoned Presidio on July 1, 1846, squatters joined the handful of residents whose houses were scattered through the sandy hills. (For the early history of the Presidio, see Chapter 2). In 1850, President Millard Fillmore decided that it was time for the military to assert its claim to the area. Fillmore called initially for a military reservation that would occupy all the land from Fisherman's Wharf to Land's End. In the face of protests by land speculators, he reduced the boundaries to include the 2,500 acres that surrounded the Spanish-Mexican Presidio.

With no enemies on the horizon, the government actually reduced the number of soldiers stationed at the Presidio until 1854, when construction began to provide quarters for soldiers who were dispatched to Virginia City and Washington Territory to subdue Indians who were resisting the encroachments of miners and settlers. When a joint Army-Navy board recommended fortifying the Golden Gate in 1850, it called for three major fortifications: on the site of Spanish-Mexican Castillo de San Joaquin, at Lime Point directly across the Golden Gate, and on Alcatraz Island, plus a series of smaller fortifications at Black Point, Angel Island, and Yerba Buena Island. With this arrangement, warships trying to enter the Bay would come under continuous fire for a distance of 7 miles. When the military's survey crews deserted for the mines, their officers sailed to Hawaii where they recruited Hawaiians to do the job. The fort at Lime Point was never built.

Fort Point

At Fort Point in 1853, the military began construction in 1853 of a three-fort system that would protect the entrance to the Bay. Although the complex was designed to guard the Bay against invasion from the sea, the first weapons installed at Fort Point were directed instead toward the land south of the fort to forestall a possible attack by Confederate sympathizers. The orders were given by Brigadier General Albert Sydney Johnston, the Army commander of the Department of the Pacific, who would soon resign to join the Confederate army and be killed at Shiloh. Southerners played an important role in the early history of the city, controlling what was known as the "chiv" or chivalry element of the Democratic Party, and were prominent in the city's social life. Johnston was asked to join the conspiracy by Asbury Harpending, William Ralston's sometime partner, but replied that he would defend his post "with the last drop of [his] blood."

Fort Point did not receive its full complement of weapons until 1868. By that time it was militarily obsolete. Massive brick fortifications could no longer withstand modern, rifled cannons. Fort Point would remain a facility without military justification for years. When the military declared the fort, now abandoned and decaying, surplus property after World War II, a citizens group arranged to reopen the fort for intermittent tours and campaigned to turn it into a National Historic Site—which was accomplished in 1970.

Indian Wars

After the Civil War, the military turned its attention to the further subjugation of the native population in the West. The discovery of gold in California was a tragic turning point for Native American Westerners. It marked a rapid increase in the number of immigrants moving through and into Indian territory and in the number of armed confrontations, which often led to the indiscriminate killing of numerous native men, women, and children and their relocation to more remote areas of the country. In 1868, General William Tecumseh Sherman, the former San Francisco banker and Civil War hero renowned for his ruthlessness, became general of the Army. Sherman was convinced that a general Indian war in the West was inevitable. "If it results in the utter annihilation of these Indians [those who refused to accept the loss of their lands]," Sherman said, "it is but the result of what they have been warned again and again, and for which they seem fully prepared."[87] Artillery units from the Presidio were dispatched to participate in some of the most important campaigns against the Sioux after General George Armstrong Custer was killed at Little Big Horn; there were encounters with Chief Joseph and his Nez Perce followers, Captain Jack and the Modocs at the battle of the Lava Beds in northern California, and the Apaches in Arizona.

Beautification

During the period of the Indian wars, the Presidio changed significantly. In 1878 the headquarters for the Military Division of the Pacific were moved from a downtown office to the Presidio, and officers and their families for the first time joined the enlisted men who lived on the base. The Presidio was now the army's most important administrative center on the West Coast. Ambitious plans for remodeling were drawn up. The Presidio was an open base, popular among San Franciscans as a recreational area, and the military seemed eager to enhance its beauty and accessibility to the public. Twelve officers' quarters built in 1862, facing the parade ground with their backs toward the eastern gate of the Presidio, were turned around to enhance their appearance as one entered the Presidio. Pine, acacia, and eucalyptus trees were planted, and the dunes were seeded with lupine, barley, and grass to hold them in place. A trolley line was built to connect the Presidio to the city's streetcar system.

Tens of thousands of trees of a dozen different varieties were planted during a second phase of beautification launched by Major William Albert Jones in 1883. Jones wanted to cover the dunes and marshes with a forest "to make the contrast from the city as great as possible, and indirectly accentuate the ideas of the power of the Government."[88] In 1905, Daniel Burnham, after meeting with the commanding officer of the Presidio, recommended that the army build a new drill ground, reorient its headquarters along the main axis of the original parade ground, and build a large plaza with a view of the Pacific on the hillside above Baker Beach. Burnham's drawing of his Presidio plan shows his characteristic angular boulevards meeting at circular plazas.

Projecting Military Power into the Pacific

In 1898, when the U.S. declared war on Spain, the Presidio served as a recruiting center, from which 80,000 troops were dispatched to the Philippines, starting with soldiers from California and Oregon. After defeating the Spanish, the Americans went on to crush the Filipinos' attempt to establish their independence. The United States had joined the ranks of the Asian colonial powers, and the Presidio would take on a central role in the wars that would convulse the Pacific until the fall of Saigon in 1975. The war against the Filipino insurrectionists evoked Sherman's campaign to annihilate Indian resistance and foreshadowed the United States' disastrous intervention in Vietnam. "Utilizing the lessons of the Indian wars," Secretary of War Elihu Root said at a ceremony to mark the official end of fighting, the U.S. army has "relentlessly followed the guerrilla bands to their fastnesses in the mountains and jungle and crushed them." Faced with widespread popular support for the Filipino insurrectionists, one officer told U.S. Senate investigators, he was instructed to kill and burn, to take no prisoners, and to regard everyone over ten years of age as the enemy.[89] Estimates of the number of Filipino dead ranged from 600,000 to 1 million. Colonel Frederick Funston, who captured the Filipino leader Emilio Aguinaldo, later became a local hero when he and his troops at the Presidio played a major role in the area's recovery in the aftermath of the 1906 earthquake.

With the growing U.S. presence in the Pacific, in 1908 the Army began construction of a second complex of buildings within the Presidio. Up until this time the architectural style for military buildings, which was established in Washington, was predominantly Colonial Revival or Queen Anne. Major William Harts, an Army engineer in charge of planning at the Presidio, noted, "The architecture of government buildings on military posts has in the past always been of a needlessly plain character." Referring to the presence of three original adobe buildings on the base, Harts suggested that the Army take advantage of the Presidio's magnificent location and hire competent civilian architects to design new structures in the Mission Revival style, with cream-colored stucco and tiled roofs. After some initial resistance in Washington, Harts was allowed to proceed with his plans, which resulted in the construction of a new cluster of buildings, known as Fort Winfield Scott, just south of Fort Point.

In 1919, Colonel Henry H. "Hap" Arnold, one of the Army's first pilots, became the Presidio's first air officer. When he arrived, military planes were using an area of landfill near the Bay, which had been a tidal marsh, as an airfield. Arnold extended the landfill onto what would become Crissy Field and covered the new sand runways with a thin layer of clay. The field was soon found to be too small, and military aircraft were transferred to other bases around the Bay Area.

Activity at the Presidio increased during World War II. Fort Winfield Scott became the headquarters for the Bay Area's coastal defenses. A hangar at Crissy Field was converted into a foreign language training school for second-generation Japanese-American soldiers, who were to serve as translators and interrogators in the Pacific. Letterman General Hospital became the nation's largest debarkation hospital. The city's harbor defense system, which included minefields and an antisubmarine net strung across the Golden Gate, was reactivated. And as we have seen, Major John DeWitt, head of the Western Defense Command based at the Presidio, played a major role in persuading Franklin Roosevelt to incarcerate much of the West Coast's Japanese-American population. "But despite these important support services, the Presidio played only a minor military role in the Second World War," historian Lisa M. Benton concluded. "It did not even serve as a training ground as it had during the First World War. It became clear that the post was no longer critical to the U.S. military, although it was still considered an important administrative headquarters" [90] — and a particularly popular post among officers, given its beautiful location, spacious quarters, and golf courses.

"Idle Acres"

After the war, President Harry Truman was rebuffed by the Soviets when he offered the Presidio as headquarters for the United Nations. Soon the local newspapers, inspired by real estate developers, began referring to the Presidio as "Idle Acres." One developer proposed construction of 12,000 units of housing along the waterfront between the St. Francis Yacht Club and Fort Point. As early as 1957, San Franciscans began to organize to preserve and protect the base, which resulted in its designation as a National Historic Landmark in 1963. When the Golden Gate National Recreation Area was created in 1972, the law stated that the Presidio would be included once the government decided that the base was no longer needed for military purposes. Despite repeated discussions about base closures in Washington during the 1980s, Congress was unwilling to accept those recommended by the Pentagon. Instead, power to recommend closures was turned over to a commission, which put the Presidio near the top of the list. In 1989 the closure of the Presidio was signed into law, the Army announced plans to vacate by 1994, and the Presidio became part of the Golden Gate National Recreation Area (GGNRA).

A Great Urban Park

Now the question was what to do with the finest piece of real estate in the city. For a time, Senator Barbara Boxer and Representative Nancy Pelosi, both opponents of the war in Vietnam and large military budgets, argued *against* the closure. Once this effort proved futile, it became apparent that—in an era of declining federal funding for parks—the National Park Service lacked the funding and expertise to plan for the future of a major urban park. The park's citizen support group, the Golden Gate National Park Association (GGNPA), formed the Presidio Council and raised funds for the planning process.

Along with the Mission Bay Project, the planning for the Presidio was the most significant urban development event since the Redevelopment Agency had launched its plans for San Francisco in the 1950s. The activities of the GGNPA suggest an interesting comparison with the Burnham Plan of almost a century earlier. In both instances, private interests seized the planning initiative when public planning was not available. But in contrast to the Burnham Plan, there was extensive public input to this plan after a draft was prepared by the Presidio Council, a private group of corporate leaders, academics, artists, planners, architects, and heads of nonprofits, including environmental organizations.

The plan announced in 1993 called for "a global center for exchanging ideas on critical environmental and societal challenges…an environmental laboratory, a major focus of research and learning, and a demonstration area for ways to improve the quality of life."[91] Equally important, the Presidio would become a model of sustainability. The problem was how to fund such a venture at a time when Congressional advocates of budget-cutting and privatization were a force to be reckoned with. The solution offered by Pelosi and the Presidio Council was the establishment of a nonprofit organization, the Presidio Trust, whose board would be appointed by the president. The Presidio Trust promised that it would make the park financially self-sufficient by replacing government funding with money raised by the lease of Presidio facilities. Facing a hostile House of Representatives under the leadership of speaker Newt Gingrich, Pelosi was forced to make some significant concessions. The final legislation included provisions calling for the reversion of the Presidio to the Defense Department for possible sale if the park is not self-sufficient by 2013, the transfer of the management of open space from the Park Service to the Presidio Trust, and consultation between the chair of the Presidio Trust and House and Senate leaders.

Hailed as a model public-private partnership, the new Presidio park proved to be both politically vulnerable and under enormous pressure to generate sufficient income to remain in existence. Commercial development would become a central part of the first plan announced by the Presidio Trust, and indeed the Presidio Trust's first executive director is a former real estate executive. The Trust's plan called for the establishment of "a city within a city," with the rental of 1,600 units of housing, jobs for 4,800 people, and the lease of 3 million square feet of office space—equivalent to nearly six office buildings the size of the Transamerica Pyramid, as the *Chronicle* pointed out. The Presidio's two major hospitals, one to be torn down and replaced with new commercial structures, the other to be remodeled, were expected to generate the bulk of the Presidio's income.

In August 1999, the Presidio Trust announced that filmmaker George Lucas of *Star Wars* fame was the winner of a competition for the first major commercial lease. The Presidio Trust chose Lucas's proposal—to build 800,000 square feet of office space, an educational foundation, and a visual effects archive on 23 acres of Presidio land now occupied by Letterman Hospital—over an even more ambitious proposal by real estate mogul Walter Shorenstein. Lucas's victory proved to be a rude wake-up call for both the National Park Service and the environmental and preservation organizations which had supported the original plans for a public-private partnership. They found that there was an inherent contradiction between the Presidio Council's plan, which emphasized nonprofit and educational activity, and the Presidio Trust's plan, which called for "a city within a city." It suddenly dawned on its supporters that visitors to this extraordinary park would someday enter the main gate only to pass through a huge commercial operation designed, according to the *Chronicle,* to make San Francisco "a serious center in the glitzy entertainment world." For Lucas, the prospect of signing a deal with the Presidio Trust was a significant coup. He was being offered prime real estate, millions in subsidies, and a free ride around the city's planning process.

Even before the Presidio Trust embraced Lucas, a group of civic organizations, including the National Trust for Historic Preservation, informed the Trust that they could not support the process by which the Trust intended to select a developer for the Letterman site. After the selection, the National Park Service noted that Lucas's proposal was not consistent with the original plan for the Presidio. Given the high stakes involved, it appeared in early 2000 that it might take many years and many lawyers to determine whether the Presidio Trust would be permitted to seriously compromise the Presidio's future as a great urban park.

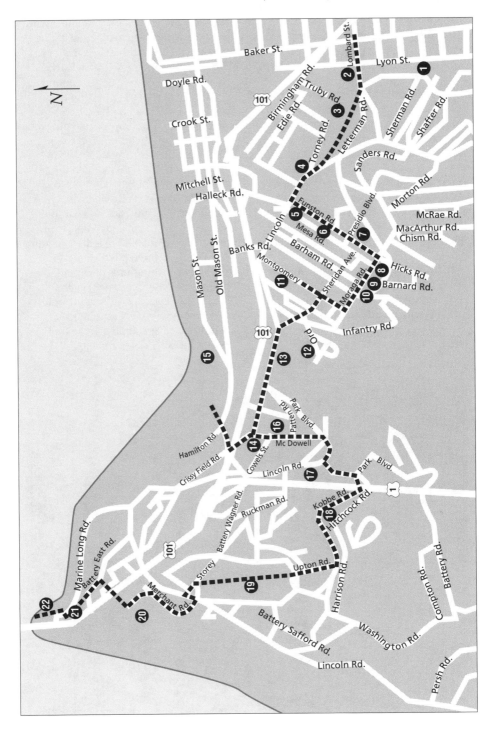

Begin at the Presidio at Lyon and Lombard. The **Presidio boundary wall** (1) (1897) was designed by J. B. Whittlemore to clearly mark the eastern boundary of the military post. Enter the **Presidio** via the **Lombard Street gate** (2), built in 1896. The blocks just outside the gate once offered numerous bars catering to servicemen. African-Americans Lew Purcell and Sam King opened a saloon called the Headquarters at the corner of Broderick and Greenwich to cater to black troops stationed at the Presidio in 1898, before Purcell opened his famous club on the Barbary coast (for more information on the Barbary Coast see page 237–238, 251). Two **cannons** at the gate were cast in 1783.

The modern building on the right, which is part of **Letterman Hospital** (3), will be demolished if George Lucas's film production company becomes the Presidio's anchor tenant. Continue along the walkway, bearing to the right, to the corner of Lincoln and Torney. The **Thoreau Center for Sustainability** (4), which describes itself as "a community of organizations working for a healthy environment and a just society," encompasses 12 buildings, including the Classical Revival building on the right and the Mediterranean building to the right of it. The Army constructed the Classical Revival building in 1899 to replace the Old Post Hospital when it was overwhelmed by sick and wounded soldiers during the Spanish-American War. The far right building is the work of W. H. Wilcox in the 1930s. Letterman treated tens of thousands of wounded until it closed after the war in Vietnam. These buildings and others in the complex were restored and retrofitted according to a "green plan" by Tanner Leddy Maytum Stacy, Architects.

The Old Post Hospital, now the Presidio Museum. *TASC Photo Collection, Golden Gate Recreation Area, National Park Service.*

The Commandante's Headquarters built on the remains of the original Presidio. *TASC Photo Collection, Golden Gate Recreation Area, National Park Service.*

The contractors used lumber from sustained yield forests managed by Native Americans, recycled aluminum, tiles made from recycled car windows, natural fiber insulation, and nontoxic paints. The Thoreau Center epitomizes the original vision of the Presidio as a center for educational and environmental organizations, whereas the Lucas deal marks the Presidio Trust's more aggressively commercial approach to development in the park.

Continue on Lincoln, making a left on Funston. The Old Post Hospital (1864) on the corner is now the **Presidio Museum** (5). In front of the museum is one of the six Spanish guns made in Peru that were spiked and seized by Captain John Fremont in 1846. Behind the museum are two **relief shacks,** examples of the structures built to house people whose homes were burned or demolished in 1906. Continue along Funston. The 12 Victorian cottages on the right were built as **Officers' Quarters** (6) (1862) and originally faced toward the Parade Ground behind them. They were turned around in 1878 to present a more wel-

coming front to civilians entering through the Presidio Gate, which was then located nearby. To the left on Presidio are **four Stick Style cottages** (7) (1885) designed by Captain Daniel Wheeler.

At the end of Funston, turn right on Moraga. **Pershing Hall** (8), the three-story brick structure on the left, was built in 1903 to house unmarried officers. Continue on Moraga to the **Old Protestant Chapel** (9) (later the Roman Catholic Chapel). The original frame building dating from 1864 looked as though it had come right out of New England. It was extensively remodeled by Hewlitt Wells in 1952, giving it a California modern look. Farther on, on the left, is the **Commandante's Quarters** (10). The original Presidio dating from 1776 and the commandante's quarters were in this area. An adobe structure built in the 1820s was rebuilt by the Americans in 1847, remodeled in the Spanish Revival style according to plans by Barney Meeden and using Works Progress Administration (WPA) funds in 1934, and then added to again in 1973 from

Enlisted Men's Barracks on the west side of the Parade Ground in 1895. *TASC Photo Collection, Golden Gate Recreation Area, National Park Service.*

plans by Robert Wong. Part of the original adobe walls were found inside the existing walls. There are two more of the Peruvian cannons spiked by Fremont out front.

Continue west on Moraga and turn right on Montgomery. The long row of **Enlisted Men's Barracks** (11) along Montgomery street on the west side of the Parade ground were built between 1895 and 1897. **The William Penn Mott, Jr., Visitors Center** and a small bookstore are located in the middle of the row. Return to Sheridan Street and turn right, bearing left up the hill on Ord Street to the **Post Chapel** (12), which was built in 1932 with WPA funds in the Spanish Revival style. Inside there is a **mural by Victor Arnautoff,** also funded by the WPA. A student of Diego Rivera and one of the controversial Coit tower muralists, Arnautoff was a Yiddish-speaking Marxist from the Ukraine, who served as an officer in both the Red and White Armies after the Russian Revolution. Returning to Sheridan, turn left to the entrance of the **San Francisco National Cemetery** (13), which was established in 1884. One of the most beautiful cemeteries in the

country, it is the final resting place of those killed during wars, beginning with the Indian wars and ending with Vietnam. Exit the cemetery on Lincoln and turn left, bearing right on Crissy Field Avenue. On the left is the **Presidio Pet Cemetery** (14), a fascinating testament to owners' attachment to their feathered and furry friends. Continue down Crissy Field and turn right on Mason Street. In front of you is the **Crissy Field Restoration Project** (15). Once a tidal inlet, the area was filled for the Panama Pacific International Exposition and then turned into an air-field. It is being restored to an approximation of its original state.

Returning up the hill, turn right on McDowell and pass through the **Presidio Stables** (16) — built in 1914, restored in 1997 — where various cavalry units stationed at the Presidio kept their horses. Besides fighting Indians, cavalry units from the Presidio patrolled and built trails in Yosemite and Sequoia National Parks from 1890 to 1916. The Presidio Archives is located in the first building on the left. Sequoia National Park was the responsibility of the Ninth Cavalry Regiment, an all-black unit known as the Buffalo Soldiers. Continue up the hill on McDowell, cross Lincoln onto Park, and then turn right on Schofield. The **Cavalry Barracks** (17) (1902) on the right, now the Presidio Native Plant Nursery, housed the Ninth Cavalry Regiment. The unit was commanded by Captain Charles Young, the third African-American to graduate from West Point. His unit saw action against Native Americans and in Cuba during the Spanish-American War.

Return to Schofield, make a right on Park and a right on Kobbe. On the left side of Kobbe there is a fine row of **Officers' Houses** (18) (1912) built in the Classical Revival style. Continue on Kobbe, turning right on Upton and crossing Ralston into **Fort Winfield Scott** (19) (1908), a major addition to the Presidio designed by Major William Harts. At Fort Scott, Harts built the first large-scale Spanish Revival complex in the Presidio, adding a second housing complex and parade ground. At the north end of the parade ground, turn left on Storey, left on Lincoln, and right on Merchant Road. On the left are **Battery Godfrey** (20) (1895), **Battery Boutelle** (1900), **Battery Marcus Miller** (1891), and **Battery Cranston** (1897), which were built to protect the entrance to San Francisco Bay once Fort Point became obsolete. Fort Scott was headquarters for the area's coastal artillery.

Follow Merchant, turning left into the tunnel that passes beneath the Golden Gate toll plaza. On the left is a **garden and statue of Joseph Strauss** (21) (1941), the chief engineer for the Golden Gate Bridge, by Frederick Schweigardt (see pages 68–69 for information on the bridge). Don't miss a stroll across the bridge. Behind the statue is a walkway down to **Fort Point** (22). Begun in 1853 and completed in 1861, Fort Point is a third-system fort — the third generation of coastal defense forts built by the U.S. government — with many similarities to Fort Sumter. It is the only one of its kind built west of the Mississippi. The foundation was constructed with granite imported from China and topped by massive brick walls. The fort was obsolete as soon as it was built, owing to the greater destructive power of modern weaponry. The fort contains a museum, a collection of weapons, and a small bookstore. Engineer Strauss was so enamored of the fort's brickwork that he redesigned the bridge with a massive arch over the fort so it would not have to be pulled down.

20

Golden Gate Park, Sutro Heights, and the California Palace of the Legion of Honor

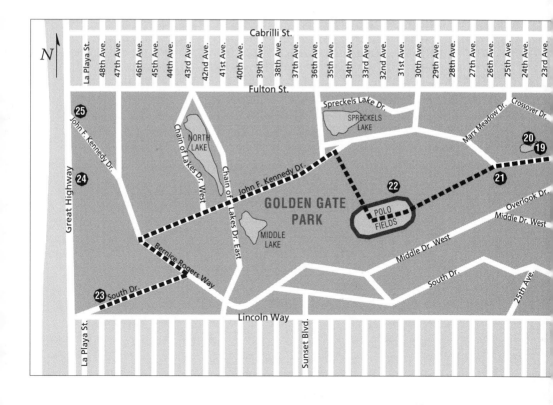

This tour entails a long walk, with gentle ups and downs until you get to the western end of Golden Gate Park and climb Sutro Heights, which is a short, moderately steep climb. Allow three hours minimum, more if you plan to spend time at the Academy of Science, the de Young Museum, and/or the Palace of the Legion of Honor. The Beach Chalet at the west end of the park is a good place for lunch or refreshment. Start at the east end of the park and end at the California Palace of the Legion of Honor.

I n 1865, Frederick Law Olmsted, not yet known as the first great American landscape architect, was in San Francisco on his way to New York City to resume work on Central Park. He had been hired by San Francisco to prepare a plan for the creation of a major park at a time when there were only three small parks in the city (Portsmouth Square, Washington Park, and Union Square). Olmsted noted that San Franciscans had done nothing to compete with Eastern cities to make theirs "a place of permanent residence." Nor did it have those features that Olmsted described as "beauty of green sward" and "great umbrageous trees," common in New York. In fact,

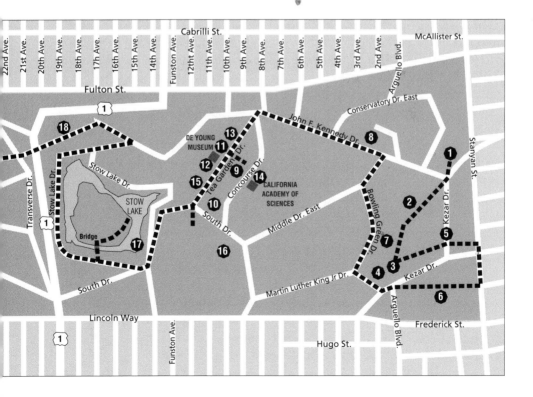

Olmsted could not find "a full grown tree of beautiful proportions" anywhere near San Francisco. For these reasons, San Francisco needed "a pleasure ground peculiar to itself."[92]

Olmsted proposed a system of parks beginning with an anchorage, pier, and ceremonial plaza at the north end of Van Ness and then an artificial excavation like a creek bed running south along Van Ness to Eddy Street, where it would branch off toward Market Street and Hayes Valley. This sunken park would protect people and plantings from the strong prevailing northwest winds.

Olmsted's plan was rejected, but in 1866 Congress finally put a halt to the federal government's attempt to deny San Francisco title to much of its territory. This gave the city access to the so-called Outside Lands, which stretched westward from the Western Addition, and 1,013 acres were set aside for a park. Critics of the proposal were appalled that the commission had chosen what a Santa Rosa reporter described as "a dreary waste of shifting sandhills where a blade of grass cannot be raised without four posts to keep it from blowing away." William Hammond Hall disagreed. Hall was a 24-year-old surveyor working for the army, investigating ways to build coastal batteries along the beach. To do so meant keeping the dunes in place, the prerequisite for a park as well.

In 1870, when the city bought the land for the park, Hall was hired to survey it and then as park superintendent. Without any previous experience in park planning, Hall drew up a plan that called for the park's "pleasure grounds" to be concentrated in its eastern third while the western two thirds would be developed into a natural woodland. Hall laid out east-west roads that were curved rather than straight to cut down on the wind tunnel effect and control the blowing of sand. To keep the sand in place, park workers planted a mixture of barley and lupine seed soaked in water. The barley grew quickly, providing protection for the lupine to become well enough established to keep the sand from drifting. Then Hall organized massive plantings of trees and shrubs—almost 60,000 in his first five years—while a series buildings, most of them concentrated in a picnic area in the northeast corner of the park, were constructed.

Hall resigned in 1876 after he opposed a scheme organized by Mayor Frank McCoppin to level the park dunes and sell the sand as landfill for tidelands in the Mission. For the next ten years little was done to advance work on the park except for the construction of a casino, which catered to the city's demimonde, and the conservatory, which was assembled by park workers after a number of wealthy San Franciscans bought it from the estate of James Lick. The park, meanwhile, began to deteriorate as sand filtered into the park from the beach. The park was immensely popular despite the lack of access via public transportation and the lack of city funding.

Pixley's March to the Sea

The park was so popular that Leland Stanford and his associates made a move to monopolize transportation to the area. Stanford arranged to have himself and his loyal apologist, Frank Pixley, editor of the *Argonaut,* appointed commissioners. With Pixley's help, Stanford secured an illegal lease allowing him to build a railroad line that crossed the southeast corner of the park, ran along its southern border, and then cut across park property again near the beach to a station at the foot of Sutro Heights. Service commenced in 1883. Inspired by Stanford's disdain for the law, Denis Kearney, the sandlot orator and bête noire of the Big Four, and his associates responded in kind, laying claim to beachfront property that ran south from Sutro Heights. They built a kind of amusement park called Mooneysville featuring numerous drinking establishments in the form of crude structures and tent platforms, which had a habit of disappearing at high tide. Soon Mooneysville was a small shantytown with a police officer, 15 saloons, and a lumberyard. Adolph Sutro, who was pouring money into the Cliff House and the gardens around his new home on Sutro Heights, was incensed. He instructed his employees to build a high fence, blocking the approach to the Cliff House, and then blasted away at the south side of Sutro Heights, hoping that the bombardment would drive the squatters away.

The *Chronicle* charged that Kearny and company were setting up their own government while the Board of Supervisors was reluctant to do anything. If the squatters were charged with illegal activities, it might raise questions about Stanford's use of park property. Finally the Board decided to act, giving the squatters 20 days to vacate. The squatters replied with a proclamation noting that most of the men of Mooneysville had served in the military and were ready to build fortifications to defend themselves "should a foreign enemy invade our shores." The newspapers were having a field day with the story. Reporters described park employees under "General" Pixley standing at "Present Shovels" before their "March to the Sea." When they reached the first shack, its owner was in the process of tearing it down.

Pixley, having conquered Mooneysville, retired from the commission, leaving the park with an $800 deficit. William Hammond Hall was asked to return as consulting engineer charged with getting and finding his replacement. Hall recommended John McLaren, who became superintendent in 1890. Raised on a small farm in Scotland, McLaren became a professional gardener on a local estate and then moved to the Royal Botanic Garden in Edinburgh. He subsequently took a job that landed him in San Mateo County, where the city's wealthy elite were building their estates. "Depending on your source," wrote a park historian. "John McLaren was considered either a martinet or a benevolent dictator. Politicians hated him because he did not take orders."[93] One longtime employee said that the best way to get along with McLaren, who habitually swore at park employees, was to swear right back.

McLaren dedicated the rest of his long career—he died at ninety-six after running the park system for fifty-seven years—to completing Hall's plan. He also played a formidable role in shaping not only Golden Gate Park, but the city's entire park system. Like Olmsted, McLaren was an advocate of the "natural look" in horticulture. "Why must people change beautiful things?" he asked, ignoring the total artificiality of Golden Gate Park.

The park was becoming a collection of buildings and attractions, of competing interests and visions of what a great urban park should be. The owners of fancy horses, invariably members of the city's wealthy families, campaigned for a speed track. Bicyclists, champions of a new fad, fought the horsey set over access to roads. San Franciscans donated animals, both dead and alive, to start a museum and a zoo. A donor gave a collection of stuffed birds to Sharon House at the children's playground, making it the park's first museum. Others gave seals, peacocks, ostriches, deer, elk, and three buffalo named Ben Harrison, Bill Bunker, and Sarah Bernhardt. William Randolph Hearst donated a grizzly captured in the wild, and there was an aviary with a walkway at tree-top level.

In 1893, Michael de Young conceived the idea of emulating Chicago's Columbian Exposition by organizing the Midwinter Fair as an antidote to a steep downturn in the economy. Despite protests about inappropriate use of the park and the growing hostility of McLaren, de Young and his associates quickly threw together a wondrous melange of exotic architecture on 200 acres of park property. Among the architects responsible were A. Page Brown, Edward Swain, and Samuel Newsom, all of whom would produce work of greater note. In contrast to the Chicago Exposition, which had produced the City Beautiful movement, the Midwinter Fair produced "a curiously gawky version of near-eastern architecture" and "a rather pathetic but typical carnival of commerce," which was "amusingly provincial, but bereft of any great architectural distinction or influence."[94]

Despite its transience, the Midwinter Fair contributed two new features in the park, the Japanese Tea Garden and the de Young Museum. The Tea Garden, originally the Japanese village, was the work of George Turner Marsh, who brought workers from Japan to plant a traditional garden on his estate. Japanese gardens were just becoming fashionable. After the Fair, the Tea Garden was turned over to gardener Makota Hagiwara. In 1900, Hagiwara was fired because of anti-Asian sentiment in the city. Hagiwara opened his own tea garden outside the park, but when the park's Tea Garden began to deteriorate, McLaren asked him to return to manage it in 1907. Management remained in the Hagiwara family, who lived at the Tea Garden, until 1942, when the city bulldozed their home and Japanese-Americans were sent to internment camps.

At the end of the Fair, de Young, a compulsive collector, donated the Fine Arts Building, an Egyptian affair with a pyramid on top, to the city for a museum. De Young's collection of fine arts included a picture gallery, 23,000 stuffed birds, a forestry exhibit, relics from Alaska and the South Seas, 20 suits of armor, soils, cereals, nuts and fruits, and an Egyptian mummy from the Temple of Karnak. De Young hoped that this strange collections of odds and ends would become the nucleus of a great museum. In the next few years enough artwork and other bric-a-brac, such as a German fighter plane (complete with bullet holes) and a two-man tank from World War I, were acquired that de Young commissioned a new structure, a copy of the Court of the Ages from the Panama Pacific International Exposition designed by Louis Mullgardt. What would become known as the M. H. de Young Memorial Museum opened in 1921. Five years later the original museum was torn down. Under the tutelage of its first two directors, the de Young evolved into a fine arts museum with an eclectic collection. In 1966, the Avery Brundage collection of Asian art, one of the foremost of its kind, was moved into the west wing of the de Young where it became the nucleus of the Asian Art Museum. In 1987, the Asian Art Museum, now a separate entity, decided to move to the renovated old main library in the Civic Center. Having lost their co-tenant, the de Young trustees toyed with the idea of moving their museum to a downtown location. After much Sturm und Drang, they hired the Swiss architectural firm of Herzog & de Meuron to design a new museum for Golden Gate Park.

When the earthquake struck in 1906, numerous park structures, including the Children's House, the de Young Museum, and the band shell, were heavily damaged. As many as 200,000 people moved into the park, many without shelter. The U.S. Army provided tents, then built temporary barracks. Some 40,000 people lived in several encampments until January 1907, when they were moved out of the park.

Despite contending views about the park's future, the one constant has been an increase in the pressures of urban population. In 1904 automobiles were admitted to the park on the condition that drivers not exceed 10 miles per hour on straightaways, 8 on curves, and 6 on the Great Highway. Within a year there were protests about speeding drivers. Horse and carriage drivers had prevailed over bicyclists and pedestrians. Now the park would be subject to the needs of the automobile driver, leading eventually to constant weekend traffic jams. In 1936 the park was effectively cut in two by the construction of Highway 1 through the park.

For its commissioners, the park became the logical place to build more recreation facilities, including tennis courts, baseball diamonds, handball courts, a pitch and putt golf course, archery grounds, bowling greens, soccer fields, a lake for sailing model yachts, and a football stadium, which served for a time as the home of the San Francisco Forty-Niners, the city's professional team. And there have been other problems, including dealing with homeless people, who set up camps in remote areas of the park, only to be flushed out by the police.

The other constant in the park's history has been the ebb and flow of governmental financial support, creating regular cycles of investment and deterioration. By 1999 the city had neglected to invest an estimated $350 million to maintain park facilities—a situation that was partially corrected by the passage of a $125 million bond measure for all city parks in 2000. There was talk of public-private partnerships, and many San Franciscans, who were observing what these partnerships meant in the Presidio, expressed concern over what parts of the park might be sold off to raise the needed funds.

To explore **Golden Gate Park,** start at the west end of the panhandle—the park is the frying pan—where Fell Street enters the park, becoming Kennedy and Kezar Drives. **McLaren Lodge** (1) (1896), park headquarters, is on the right. Designed by Edward Swain, this Romanesque Revival building with its sandstone walls and red tile roof originally housed the family of John McLaren, longtime superintendent of the city's park system. This is a good place to pick up a map. Ask to see the Park Commission's meeting room with its pigskin walls.

Cross Kennedy Drive and enter the long, tree-shaded lawn, which opens to the right. This lawn is characteristic of the pastoral look created by William Hammond Hall, the park's first superintendent, once he had tamed the sand dunes. The rise to the right is known as **Hippie Hill** (2), a favorite gathering place for the wayward youth attracted to the nearby Haight-Ashbury District.

Continue along the lawn to the **Sharon Children's Playground** (3) on the left. Designed by Percy and Hamilton, also in the Romanesque style, it was built in 1886 with funds left by Senator William Sharon. (His heirs had pushed unsuccessfully for the construction of a marble main gate on Stanyan

Street with "Sharon–1885" carved in the marble.) As manager of the Bank of California in Virginia City, Sharon headed William Ralston's effort to monopolize the Comstock lode. By selling mining shares that only he knew were worthless, Sharon precipitated Ralson's downfall and then forced Ralston to turn over all of his personal assets to pay the bank's debts when it collapsed. The **carousel** (4) (c. 1892) is a particularly fine one with a beautiful collection of hand-carved animals, which were lovingly restored in the 1980s.

Walk east, passing through a tunnel under the roadway. The Children's Playground was built on land reclaimed by leveling a sand hill and filling a lake. **The bridge** (5) (1880s) was the country's first arched bridge built with reinforced concrete. Turn right on Stanyan and right again just south of Waller. The **Kezar Pavilion and Stadium** (6) on the right were built in the 1920s, purportedly because Mayor Sunny Jim Rolph's son, who was a member of the football team at nearby Polytechnic High School, was eager to play in a new stadium. It was the home of the city's professional football team, the Forty-Niners, from 1946 to 1972, when it was abandoned and then torn down. In its place an attractive amphitheater, with

McLaren Lodge. *Peter Booth Wiley.*

The Children's House at Sharon Children's Playground. *Peter Booth Wiley.*

gates designed by Alan Fleming, incorporates parts of the old stadium.

At the west end of the stadium, cross Kezar Drive, bearing right on Martin Luther King Jr. Boulevard. Make a right at the first stop sign on Bowling Green Drive, noting the **bowling green and clubhouse** (7) (1901) on the left. Bear to the right, passing tennis courts on your right, to Kennedy Drive, where the **Conservatory of Flowers** (8) (1876) stands on the north side of the road.

The Conservatory of Flowers. *Peter Booth Wiley.*

Millionaire James Lick, one of the city's prominent eccentrics, ordered this elegant glass, wood, and iron structure for his estate in San Jose, but then died before it could be removed from its packing cases. It was bought and given to the city by a group of wealthy San Franciscans, including Leland Stanford, who was campaigning for a right of way through park property at the time. The illusion of a curved surface was created by carefully assembling numerous flat panes of glass in redwood framing. The Conservatory was heavily damaged in a winter storm in 1995 and remains closed while being restored. The building must be taken apart completely and then put back together. Listed as one of the 100 most endangered culturally significant structures in the world, the Conservatory houses hundreds of rare and exotic plants and is the largest wood-frame greenhouse in the country.

Continue west on Kennedy Drive, turning left at Hagiwara Tea Garden Drive. City engineer Michael O'Shaughnessy designed the **Concourse** (9) in front of the band shell as the centerpiece of the Midwinter Fair. The **Music Pavilion** (10) (1899), a gift of Claus Spreckels, the sugar baron, was designed by the Reid Brothers in the neoclassical style. The **de Young Museum** (11) (1921) evolved from the Midwinter Fair. The current building, which also houses the **Asian Art Museum** (12), is a much altered version of Louis Mullgardt's structure. First the exterior ornamentation was stripped away. In 1965, Gardner Daily designed the west wing to house the Asian Art Museum. After the 1989 earthquake the steel buttresses and reinforcing girders were added to keep the building from collapsing. The de Young concentrates on the arts of the Americas, Africa, and Oceania. To the right are two bronze **statues of sphinxes** (13) (1903) by Arthur Putnam. They marked the entrance of the Fine Arts Building from Michael de Young's Midwinter Fair of 1893, later the first de Young Museum.

On the other side of the Concourse are the **Academy of Sciences** and the **Steinhart Museum** (14). The Academy of Sciences was founded in 1853 to promote the study of what its founders called "a virgin soil with new characteristics and attributes, which have not been subjected to a critical scientific examination." The first museum, which was backed by Charles Crocker and Leland Stanford, was housed in the First Congregational Church at the corner of Grant and California and later moved to a building on a property given by James Lick at Fourth and Market. It was destroyed in 1906. This neoclassical building was designed in 1914 by Lewis Hobart, who was married to a cousin of Crocker's son William. Hobart also designed the Aquarium, whose principal donor was Ignatz Steinhart, a San Francisco banker who funded the museum with money left by his brother Sigmund. When the Aquarium opened in 1923, it was the largest and most advanced in the country. A year 2000 bond measure provided funds to remodel the Academy and Aquarium. Renzo Piano, codesigner of the Pompidou Center in Paris, is the architect.

To the left of the de Young as you leave the Concourse is the **Japanese Tea Garden** (15), originally the Japanese Village, another remnant of

the Midwinter Fair. The eastern half of the Garden was built for George Turner Marsh, an Australian art dealer and real estate speculator who had spent time in Japan, by skilled craftsmen he imported from Japan. Marsh owned land and built a home north of the Park, naming the district "Richmond" after the suburb where he was born near Melbourne. A Japanese carpenter built the two-story main gate for Marsh's summer home in Marin County. The gate farther south came from the Japanese pavilion at the Panama Pacific International Expansion. The lake in front of the teahouse was built by Turner's Japanese employees as part of the original Japanese Village. Starting in 1895, Makoto Hagiara managed the garden during two different periods, expanding the landscaping from 1 to 5 acres. He also built a large family home here where he boarded Japanese immigrants, who worked as gardeners while learning English. The Garden is decorated with art objects and bonsai trees, originally owned by the Hagiwaras and restored to the garden by Japanese gar-

Gate at the Japanese Tea Garden brought from the Panama Pacific International Exposition. *Peter Booth Wiley.*

den designer Sam Newsom in the 1960s.

When you leave the Garden, turn right and cross Martin Luther King Jr. Drive, where you can enter the **Strybing Arboretum and Botanical Gardens** (16), one of the loveliest features in the park. Begun in 1937, the Arboretum was a Works Progress Administration (WPA) project. It was redesigned by Robert Tetlow of the University of California-Berkeley Department of Landscape Architecture in 1959. Notice the **Garden of Fragrance,** where plants are described in braille. The limestone walls were fashioned from stone taken from a Spanish monastery bought by William Randolph Hearst. Hearst, a compulsive collector of European art treasures, planned to reassemble the monastery in the Park, but never did. Gardner Dailey designed the modern brick **Helen Crocker Russell Library of Horticulture** (1967), which is located by the main gate.

Exit the Arboretum and walk west on Martin Luther King Jr. Drive, bearing into Stow Lake Drive. Railroad baron Collis Huntington gave the city $15 million for the construction of **Stow Lake** (17) (1895), a circular reservoir built around an island known as **Strawberry Hill.** Ernest Coxhead designed the bridge that connects the mainland to Strawberry Hill island on its south side. Cross the bridge. Man-made **Huntington Falls** flows from the top of Strawberry Hill on the east down to a small **Chinese Pavilion** given to the city by the city of Taipei in 1981.

Return across the bridge and turn right, following the lakeshore past the boathouse, bearing left to Kennedy Drive. Turn left on Kennedy and you will pass another artificial waterfall known as **Rainbow Falls** (18). Continue west on Kennedy under Highway 1. On the right is **Lloyd Lake** (19), named for

another park commissioner and Southern Pacific executive. Across the lake are the **Portals of the Past** (20), once the entranceway to the Towne Mansion on Nob Hill before it was destroyed in 1906. Across from the Portals is **Speedway Meadow** (21), the site of numerous rock concerts in the 1960s. Continue westward along the Meadow to the **Polo Fields** (22), built in 1906 during a moment of aristocratic pretension. The oval dirt track was used by horsemen, early race car drivers, and now by joggers and horse people. Note the stables to the north. The Human Be-In took place here in January 1967, and the largest demonstration ever seen in the city filled this area with 500,000 protesters during the war in Vietnam.

Leave the Polo Fields on the north side, returning to Kennedy Drive and turning left. At the end of Kennedy Drive, go left at Bernice Rodgers Way and right on Martin Luther King Jr. Boulevard. At the end of the boulevard on the right is the **Murphy Windmill** (23) (1905), the second windmill to pump water for the park's irrigation system. The funds for the windmill were donated by Samuel Murphy, a wealthy banker. The windmill is badly in need of restoration. Note the brick mill keeper's cottage. Turn right on the Great Highway. On the right is the **Beach Chalet** (24) (1925). Willis Polk designed this simple, unadorned Spanish Revival structure with handmade roof tiles, which was restored in 1996. Originally built with a lounge and changing rooms for ocean bathers on the ground floor and a municipal restaurant on the second floor, it has also served as a tearoom, headquarters for coastal defense forces during World War II, and a Veterans of Foreign War bar. Funded by the WPA, Lucien Labaudt, the director of a successful school of fashion and design, painted the **murals** in 1935 and then supervised the **mosaic work** of

Willis Polk's Beach Chalet. *Peter Booth Wiley.*

Primo Caredio and the **wood carving** in magnolia on the columns and balustrades by Michael Von Meyer.

Continue north on the Great Highway. The **Dutch Windmill** (25) (1903) was built to pump water for the Park's irrigation system. It was designed by Alpheus Bull Jr., a mechanical engineer who worked for the Union Iron Works. It was restored to working condition in 1981 but no longer pumps water. Continue north on the Great Highway. Just beyond the northern edge of the Park is a site teeming with ghosts: of the squatter-residents of Mooneysville, who were evicted by the police in 1884; of thousands of people who visited Playland, a funky amusement park complete with roller coaster, which was torn down in 1972; and of the last longhairs who patronized Hippie impresario Chet Helms's Family Dog on the Great Highway before it too was torn down soon after.

THE CLIFF HOUSE AND SUTRO HEIGHTS

Point Lobos, with its view of Seal Rocks and the coastline, has been a favorite gathering place for San Franciscans since the city's earliest days. Judging by the size of shell mounds near the point, the area was also popular among the Ohlone, who came here from their inland villages to harvest shellfish. Spaniards under Captain Fernando Rivera y Moncada explored the area in 1774, erecting a cross on the point.

In the 1850s, Charles Butler bought 160 acres around Point Lobos and put in a potato patch. In 1863 he built the Cliff House, a resort connected to the city via a macadamized toll road running along what is now Geary

Boulevard. Instantly popular, the Cliff House gained a reputation as a place where the moneyed elite visited in their fancy carriages and for its high-priced, but poor quality food. Over time the clientele changed with the addition of a second saloon, a card room, and other amenities. The Cliff House soon had a new reputation: for gambling, loose women, and riotous partying.

When Adolph Sutro returned to San Francisco in 1879 with the money he had made from the sale of the Sutro Tunnel, he invested his funds in downtown real estate and 2,200 acres of land along the oceanfront, from near the Presidio to the south side of Golden Gate Park. He bought the Cliff House and a cottage, modest by San Francisco's extravagant standards, on the heights above. With the intention of creating a resort open to the public, Sutro hired a phalanx of workers. They converted the sandy headland into formal gardens and spacious lawns studded with 200 plaster of Paris copies of famous statuary, which he acquired on a trip to Europe in 1883. Visitors entered through a massive Gothic gate guarded by statues of lions and strolled down Palm Avenue to visit the rosarium, a conservatory filled with exotic plants, or the observatory with its telescope. A grand collector in the Victorian style, Sutro planned to build a combined library-museum to house his collections and his books, 250,000 volumes thought to be one of the largest private collections in the world. To bring the public to his gardens, Sutro began work on a railroad running from California Street and Presidio Avenue along the cliffs overlooking the Golden Gate.

In 1887, the schooner *Parallel* ran aground at Point Lobos. The crew abandoned ship and rowed to Sausalito rather than risk landing on the beach in the surf. During the night there was a tremendous explosion, which damaged the Cliff House's foundation, destroyed one wall, and shattered windows there and in Sutro's cottage. The crew had not had time to return to the site of the wreck to inform Sutro that the schooner contained 100,000 pounds of dynamite.

In 1894 the Cliff House burned to the ground in a huge fire. Undaunted, Sutro built a resort hotel designed by Emile Lemme and C. J. Colley in the style of a French château on the site. The new building, five stories on the south side facing the road, featured a large dining room, a bar, numerous private dining rooms, art and photography galleries, and an elevator to take guests up to the observatory in the central tower. When the new Cliff House opened in 1896, it was served by a new electric trolley line constructed by Sutro. In an article in the *Wave* titled "San Francisco's Architectural Monstrosities," Willis Polk included a photo of the Cliff House with the caption "Showing how the beauty of the most picturesque and romantic spot on the Pacific Coast has been heightened by the erection of a wooden bird cage and a half-gross assortment of triangles."

When Sutro opened the new Cliff House, he also opened an even more elaborate structure—an aquarium and bathhouse fed by the tides through a tunnel drilled beneath the headlands just north of the Cliff House. When it was finished, the Sutro Baths and Museum consisted of six saltwater swimming pools and a freshwater pool under a steel and glass structure large enough to accommodate 1,600 bathers. Visitors entered the building through an entranceway in the form of a classical Greek temple and descended a broad staircase, lined with tropical plants and fountains, to the pools. In addition, there were three restaurants, each large enough to accommodate 1,000 people, an amphitheater with seating for 3,700 people, and three floors of balustrades, alcoves, and arcades, which served as galleries for Sutro's collections of shells, natural history specimens, and artifacts from Mexico, Egypt, Syria, Japan, and China. All of this was under a roof made of 100,000 square feet of rainbow-colored stained glass supported by 600 tons of iron girders. Admission: 10 cents, 25 cents for a swim.

Sutro presided over his principality like a gracious sovereign entertaining the rich and famous, hobnobbing with anyone he met. Sadly, he did not live long enough to enjoy and protect his pleasure grounds. He died in 1898, two years after the opening of the Cliff House and the Baths. Sutro never got to build his library. He kept his book collection at his offices in the Montgomery Block. When the fire broke out after the 1906 earthquake, part of the collection was moved to the Mechanics Pavilion opposite City Hall. These books burned, whereas those left in the fireproof Montgomery Block survived to become the core of the Sutro Library, now owned by the state. The second

The Cliff House and Sutro Baths with Sutro's home in the background (1890s). *San Francisco History Center, San Francisco Public Library.*

Cliff House burned in 1907 and was replaced with the central part of the present structure by his daughter Dr. Emma Sutro Merritt.

Unwilling or unable to maintain Sutro's estate, his heirs finally sold it to the city in 1920 on the condition that the facilities would be "forever held and maintained as a free Public Resort or Park." Decay had already started to set in. When Dr. Merritt died in 1938, the city tore down Sutro's home and various outbuildings, leaving only a small gazebo. The gardens were allowed to deteriorate.

The Baths were also doomed. When they no longer drew enough bathers to justify expensive repairs, they were turned into a skating rink and then finally closed. A developer bought the building to tear it down and make way for an apartment tower. During demolition in 1967, the Baths burned, and thousands of San Franciscans lined the cliffs to pay their respects; others sorted through the ruins looking for mementos of a past that could never be recreated. The city did try to protect Point Lobos Drive in front of the Cliff House, facing the cliffs with artificial rocks. In the process they restored the urn that contained Sutro's ashes, moving it to a new hiding place where it was found, only to be hidden again years later.

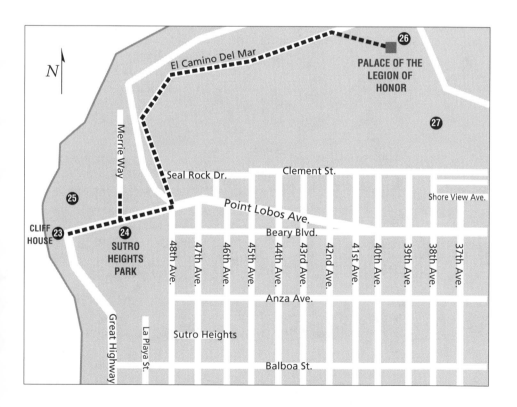

Start at the **Cliff House** (23). This structure was built in 1907 by Adolph Sutro's daughter, Dr. Emma Sutro Merrit, to replace the French château style hotel built by her father, which had burned down. The plain, neoclassical structure designed by the Reid brothers has been obscured by later additions. In a restoration planned by the National Park Service, the building will be pared back to its 1907 dimensions. With its sweeping views of the coast, this is an excellent place for brunch or refreshments. The bar and restaurant on the main floor have just the right atmosphere of tattered Victoriana. Adolph Sutro's ashes repose somewhere in the artifical dribble-castle rocks across from the entrance of the Cliff House. Continue on the Great Highway to a parking lot on the right, where there is a trail leading to **Sutro Heights Park** (24). This is what is left of the elaborate public gardens that surrounded Sutro's home, which stood on the western edge of the heights.

Return to the parking lot and cross the Great Highway to another parking lot, which runs along the cliffs above the remains of the **Sutro Baths** (25). Again you are confronted with only a few broken reminders of the vast glass and steel structure that Sutro opened to the public in 1896. The Baths burned in 1967, leaving remnants of the foundations of the swimming pools, the bathhouses, and the saltwater collecting pools.

Return to the Great Highway and turn left; turn left again on El Camino del Mar. Follow El Camino into a parking lot, which turns into a trail. Sutro's steam railroad ran along these cliffs with their magnificent view of the Golden Gate. Bear to the right up some wooden steps to the California Palace of the Legion of Honor.

THE CALIFORNIA PALACE OF THE LEGION OF HONOR

The California Palace of the Legion of Honor is a monument to San Franciscans' long infatuation with all things French and to the cultural aspirations of Alma de Bretteville Spreckels, one of the city's most colorful social climbers. Big Alma, as she was known, was born to Danish immigrants who owned a farm on the outskirts of San Francisco. Her father was a ne'er-do-well, and her mother, once they had moved to town, brought in a meager income running a bakery and taking in laundry. An educated man who spoke several languages, the elder de Bretteville drew solace from the fact that his family was related to an aristocratic French family that had fled to Denmark during the French revolution.

After school Alma went to work as a stenographer, taking evening classes at the Art Institute in the Hopkins mansion on the top of Nob Hill and earning extra money as an artist's model. Almost 6 feet tall, she was a head-turning beauty. Sketches of her voluptuous body soon graced many a well-known watering hole. Proclaiming that she would "rather be a old man's darling than a young man's slave," she took up with a miner who had struck it rich in the Klondike and then sued him for $50,000 when he refused to marry her. It was at about this time that Alma posed for Robert Aitken's sculpture of Victory, which reposes on top of the Dewey Monument in Union Square. Soon after Alma was seen around town with Adolph Spreckels, son of Claus Spreckels, the sugar baron. Known for his fine horses, his yacht, and his pursuit of beautiful women, Adolph gained notoriety by taking a potshot at Michael de Young, the founder of the *Chronicle*, after de Young ran a series of articles attacking Adolph's father's management of his sugar empire. Adolph pleaded self-defense and innocence by way of insanity and was acquitted.

After a long campaign, Alma finally prevailed upon Spreckels to marry her, finding out only much later that he had hesitated because he had contracted syphilis, which would eventually kill him. Once married, Alma persuaded her husband to build a mansion on Washington Street in the grand style then fashionable in Pacific Heights. On a shopping trip to France in 1914 to buy furnishings for her home, Alma was introduced to Auguste Rodin, the French sculptor, by Loie Fuller, a free-form dancer and lover of beautiful women. Alma and Loie conceived the idea of building a museum

Rodin's *Thinker* in front of the California Palace of the Legion of Honor. *Richard Barnes.*

in San Francisco and filling it with Rodin's work. In 1915, the French government shipped five works of Rodin's, including a copy of the *Thinker*, to San Francisco, where they were displayed in the French Pavilion at the Panama Pacific International Exposition (PPIE). This, Alma convinced her husband, should be the model for a museum that he would give to the city.

When the PPIE closed, Alma removed the five statues, which her husband had acquired, to her home, announcing that it would serve as a temporary museum. As she acquired more and more European works of art, including items donated by the French government in appreciation for relief work she had organized during the war, Alma fixed on the Lincoln Park golf course for a site. The museum opened its doors in 1924. Brash, foul-mouthed Alma de Bretteville Spreckels, who was fond of playing poker with her friends dressed in her bathrobe while quaffing martinis by the pitcher, died a recluse in 1968.

When Alma de Bretteville Spreckels began to work on plans for the California Palace of the Legion of Honor, she was inspired by the bitter rivalry between the de Young and Spreckels families. Her notion of a fine arts museum, she was proud to say, was infinitely more cultured than the de Youngs'. Even after both museums were acquired by the city, they continued to compete against each other for acquisitions until 1971, when they were merged into the Fine Arts Museums of San Francisco. The California Palace of the Legion of Honor concentrates on European arts and works on paper from the extraordinary Achenbach Collection.

Alma Spreckels could not have picked a grander site for her beloved **California Palace of the Legion of Honor** (26). It was originally the city's potters' field; many of the first remains interred here came from Yerba Buena Cemetery, which was dug up to make way for the old main library in the Civic Center. The cemetery became a way station for Chinese who were temporarily buried here before their remains were returned to the mother country. John McLaren built the **Lincoln Park Golf Course** (27) in 1909. For the California Palace of the Legion of Honor (1924), architect George Applegarth copied the design of the French pavilion at the Panama Pacific International Exposition. The pavilion was modeled after the Palais de la Legion d'Honneur in Paris, which Napoleon acquired in 1804 as headquarters for the Legion d'Honneur. The glass pyramid in the museum's courtyard—à la I. M. Pei's pyramid in front of the Louvre—provides light for the underground galleries that were added during a retrofit designed by Edward Larrabee Barnes and John M. Y. Lee & Partners in 1994.

The centerpiece of the collection, which focuses on European art, is Spreckels's fine collection of Rodin sculpture. The museum also houses the **Achenbach Foundation**—an excellent collection of drawings and printed materials covering 500 years and including works by Dürer, Rembrandt, Hogarth, Goya, Whistler, and Picasso—put together by advertising executive Moore Achenbach and his wife before they gave it to the museum in 1951.

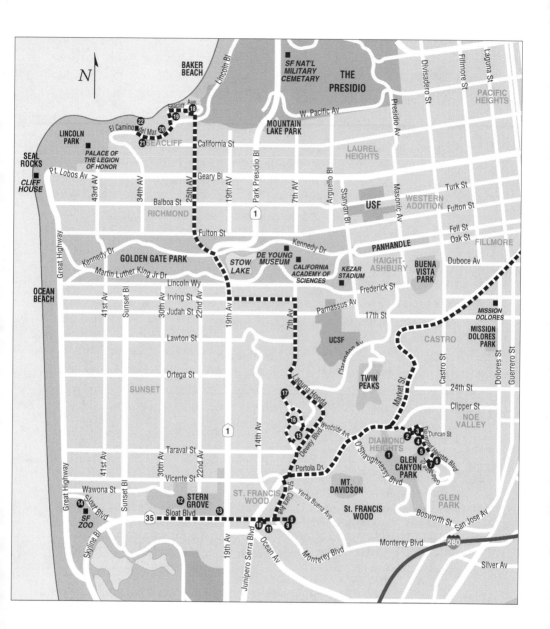

21

The Western Suburbs, Stern Grove, and the Zoo: A Driving Tour

Because this tour covers a large part of the western half of the city, it is not practical to use public transportation or to go on foot. Travel by car is recommended. The tour takes two hours or more, particularly if you choose to spend time at the zoo.

When developers moved westward of the line of hills defined by Mount Davidson, Twin Peaks, and Lone Mountain, the city abandoned the orthagonal grid on which the city had been established for the construction of new streets on the steepest hillsides. In his 1905 report, Daniel Burnham argued that street construction should follow the contours of hillsides. But there is no evidence that the new street pattern was—or was not, for that matter—a result of Burnham's recommendations. Rather, it is likely that it was the developers' interest in building homes for the city's better classes that led to the creation of new neighborhoods that appeared custom-designed. The open spaces in the western half of the city provided developers with an opportunity to engage in planned construction, with an emphasis on such things as uniform architectural styles, landscaped streets, fountains, and gateways. Much of this development took place after 1906. The construction of the Twin Peaks Tunnel in 1918, a pet project of real estate developers, led to a burst of construction in the western half of the city.

Presidio Terrace, the first large, upscale development since South Park, was laid out in 1898 (see pages 279–281 for more on Presidio Terrace). It set the pattern for subsequent developments. In contrast, development on level ground, specifically the sand dunes that would become the Richmond and the Sunset, featured modest homes and apartments, many of them character-less structures built after World War II.

From downtown, drive west on Market Street, which becomes Portola Drive near the top of Twin Peaks. Note the views of the city and the bay. Turn left at Clipper. The **Diamond Heights** (1) redevelopment project begins on your right. The San Francisco Redevelopment Agency (SFRA) chose this area as a redevelopment site in 1953. How it qualified as "a blighted neighborhood" is not entirely clear, inasmuch as it was barely a neighborhood at all. It was, rather, a collection of widely separated houses scattered around the hillsides. So the SFRA described it as "predominantly open blighted lands" when it began to distribute information to other cities about Diamond Heights as an example of a large-scale (9,000 residents on 330 acres) planned development. The street plan was by Vernon DeMars.

After a design competition sponsored by the SFRA and the Northern California Chapter of the American Institute of Architecture, construction was begun on Red Rock Hill in 1961. Property owners were supposed to choose from one of the winning home designs, but much of the initial phase of the project, including some high-rise apartment towers, was not built as originally planned. The SFRA tried to encourage home ownership among moderate-income families by arranging financing at 3⅛ percent. Later, as the controversy over the SFRA's destruction

of low-cost housing accelerated, the agency set aside some lots for the construction of "less than market value housing." The SFRA also selected three sites for nonprofit cooperatives, which could be constructed after a scale model was built to "demonstrate that such construction [would] in no way depreciate the financial investment of the property owners in the area." Notwithstanding the usual insider dealing, Diamond Heights proved to be relatively noncontroversial and became a solid middle-class community. However, the project did little to enhance the reputation of its architects or to recommend this prime location as a desirable place to live. Many of the buildings are looking a bit shabby, owing to the use of cheap materials.

Turn right off of Clipper into Diamond Heights Boulevard. The **Red Rock Hill town houses** (2) (1962) on the right, the first buildings in the project, were designed by Cohen & Leverson. Turn right at Duncan and and then left into Red Rock Way, where Gensler and Associates and Joseph Esherick designed the shingled **Diamond Heights Village** (3) complex (1972). Return to Duncan and turn left. Along Duncan on the right are a number of Eichler homes, constructed between 1962 and 1964 by one of the Bay Area's most successful builders of mass-produced tract homes.

Diamond Heights Village. *Peter Booth Wiley.*

St. Nicholas Antiochian Orthodox Church (4) (1963) at the corner of Duncan and Diamond Heights Boulevard is by William Hempel. Turn right on Diamond Heights Boulevard and pass the **Diamond Heights Shopping Center** (5) (1972) by Morris & Lohrbach, a development that includes a community center and playgrounds. Continuing past the shopping center, turn right on Gold Mine Drive. **St. Aidan's Episcopal Church** (6) (1963) on the corner is by Skidmore Owings Merrill. The shingled **Gold Hill town houses** (7) (1967) on the left at the intersection with Topaz and Ora are by Fisher-Friedman.

Return to Clipper Street along Diamond Heights Boulevard. Note that the houses on the right past Duncan are built on a steep hillside with their garages at street level and living quarters below. Turn left on Clipper and left on Portola. Continue west to Santa Clara Avenue and turn right where you see the Vicente Street sign on the right. The street sign for Santa Clara Avenue is obscured from Portola. You are entering

Mediterranean doorway, 630 St. Francis Boulevard. *Peter Booth Wiley.*

The Trocadero Inn in Stern Grove. *Peter Booth Wiley.*

St. Francis Wood, one of the city's most exclusive neighborhoods, which was developed by Mason McDuffie Company starting in 1912. Continue on Santa Clara to **St. Francis Boulevard,** the development's main thoroughfare. Turn left on St. Francis and drive to the **plaza and fountain** (8) at the top of the street for a full appreciation of the gates, terraces, and fountains, which were designed by John Galen Howard and Henry Gutterson. You may want to park here and walk west on St. Francis. By edict of the local neighborhood organization, the original houses had to be in the Mediterranean Revival style. Note the Hispanic grillwork, tile roofs, and ornamental detail on the houses along St. Francis, notably **630 St. Francis** (9) (1917) by Henry Gutterson and **98 St. Francis** (10) (1927) by Marsten & Hurd. Make a left on San Leandro Way. Julia Morgan designed the scruffy shingled home at **195 San Leandro Way** (11) (1917) at the corner of Monterey.

Drive West on St. Francis through the entrance gate and straight on to Sloat Boulevard. Cross the intersection with Nineteenth Avenue and enter the drive-

way on the right, which goes down the hill into **Sigmund Stern Grove** (12). George Greene, a New England horticulturalist, who arrived in San Francisco in 1847, homesteaded the Grove and later, when his title was in question, erected a fort to keep other claimants away. He planted the original eucalyptus trees in 1871 and built the **Trocadero Inn** (13), the picturesque Victorian cottage with porches, at the bottom of the hill, in 1892. Political boss Abe Ruef used the inn as a hideout when he was fleeing the police after his indictment. Parks superintendent John McLaren pointed out the grove to Rosalie Stern, the widow of Sigmund Stern. Son of Levi Strauss founder David Stern, Sigmund was one of the owners and managers of Levi Strauss after the founders died. Mrs. Stern bought the Grove and gave it to the city, which named it after her husband. The Grove is the site of the Stern Grove Festival, a series of musical events in July and August, which is one of the city's cultural delights.

Return to Sloat and turn right. The **San Francisco Zoological Gardens** (14) are located on the left side of Sloat near where it ends at the beach. The zoo was originally part of a larger recreational complex, which was partially funded in the 1920s by Parks Commissioner Herbert Fleishhacker. A wealthy financier and power broker, Fleishhacker was also the grandson of Lewis Gerstle. For more on the Gerstle-Sloss family, see page 47. The zoo was overshadowed by a 1,000-foot-long saltwater pool, billed as the largest in the world. Fleishhacker Pool "was so huge," recalled San Francisco memoirist Jerry Flamm, "you could not identify your mother if you were at one end and she were at the other." [95] The pool closed in 1971 and was later filled. Little remains beyond the ruins of the elaborate Italian Renaissance bathhouse. Adjacent to the pool were formal gardens, sports facilities, a children's playground, and a small zoo.

The **Mother's House** (1925), designed by George Kelham, was donated by Fleishhacker and his brother Mortimer in memory of their mother, Delia, as a rest facility for mothers. Boys over the age of 6 were banned. The **murals** (1938), scenes from the story of

Noah's Ark, are the collaborative work of Helen Forbes (sketches of animals) and Dorothy Pucinelli (painter) and were funded by the Federal Arts Project. In 1935 the city purchased land for a zoo addition, which was designed by Lewis Hobart using Germany's Hagenbeck Zoo as a model. Construction was funded by the Works Progress Administration (WPA). The **Gorilla House, Wolf House,** and **Tule Elk House** (1980) were designed by Esherick Homsey Dodge & Davis, the **Small Primates House** (1983) by Marquis Associates.

Return east on Sloat Boulevard, bearing left onto Portola to Claremont Boulevard. Turn left and follow Claremont to the circle at the intersection of Dewey and Taraval. Turn right onto Dewey and then left into Pacheco, the entrance to **Forest Hill,** another upscale neighborhood, laid out by Mark Daniel in 1913. Turn left onto Magellan. Bernard Maybeck designed the **Forest Hill Club House** (15) at 381 Magellan. It was built by volunteer labor on weekends. Set in a grove of lovely trees, the adjacent garden with its brick walkway

The Forest Hill Club House, 381 Magellan. *Peter Booth Wiley.*

was built in the 1960s.

Continue on Magellan, turning right on Montalvo. Follow Montalvo up the hill, make a right on Dorantes, a left on San Marcos, and a right on Castenada. Maybeck also designed the **Erlanger House** (16) at 270 Castenada on the left, just past the intersection with Lopez, "to suggest the idea of an English character in California," as he put it. He was referring to then-popular Tudor Revival homes inspired by British architects associated with the Arts and Crafts movement. A masterpiece, the exterior is a collection of gables and dormers with exquisitely detailed windows. Inside is a grand living hall done in redwood. Turn left on Lopez and then left on Sotelo. With the **Young House** (17) (1913) at 51 Sotelo, Maybeck again combined a half timber and shingle exterior with the lavish use of redwood on the rustic interior.

Return on Sotelo to Lopez, make a left on Lopez , a right on Pacheco, and continue to Dewey. Make a left on Dewey, which becomes Laguna Honda Boulevard and then Seventh Avenue. Turn left on Irving, one of the principal shopping streets in the Sunset, follow it west to Nineteenth Avenue, and turn right. Follow Nineteenth Avenue into Golden Gate Park, keeping to the left to follow the signs to Twenty-fifth Avenue. At the northern end of Twenty-fifth Avenue, enter the gates to **Sea Cliff,** two developments with sweeping views of the Golden Gate, Mount Tamalpais, and the coastline. Park your car and walk, following Scenic Way to the left. The original development near this intersection was organized through a home owners association in 1904. A second development to the west was begun in 1916. Willis Polk designed **9, 25, and 45 Scenic Way** (18) (1914). Turn right on Twenty-sixth Avenue and then left on Sea Cliff Avenue. Farr & Ward designed **300 Sea Cliff** (19) (1930), an example of the popular Mediterranean Revival style that is common in the area.

Bear left onto El Camino del Mar. As you walk west, there are more examples of modern designs, such as Wurster, Bernardi & Emmons's house at **850 El Camino** (20) (1958) and Esherick Homsey Dodge and Davis's design at **895 El Camino** (21). Like Pacific Heights, Sea Cliff lends itself to extensive use of glass walls. Continue on El Camino, and just past Thirty-second Avenue on the right is an entrance to the Golden Gate National Recreation Area marked **"Land's End"** (22). Enjoy the sweeping panorama and a good view of Sea Cliff.

Epilogue: The Limits of Preservation

Cities are an immense laboratory of trial and error, failure and success, in city building and city design.[96]

—Jane Jacobs

I believe that cities ought to be magnificent, beautiful places to live. They should be where people can be fulfilled, where they can be what they can be, where there are freedoms, love, ideas, excitement, quiet, and joy. Cities ought to be the ultimate manifestation of a society's collective achievement.[97]

—Allan Jacobs

Welcome tourists, but don't build for them. Build your city for yourselves. If you do it well, people will come to see it. If you build your city for tourists, then the city becomes a stage set.[97]

—Allan Jacobs

At the beginning of the millenium San Francisco remains one of the most beautiful and livable cities in the world, thanks to preservationists and citizens who fought to protect their neighborhoods. With the growth of a preservation ethic it is very unlikely that there will ever be another tragedy such as the widespread destruction of historic buildings during the "Manhattanization" movement and the Redevelopment Agency's attack on "blighted" neighborhoods. However, historic buildings still remain vulnerable to the whims of their owners—witness the destruction of the Shriners Hospital in 1999.

The one serious lack in the city's preservation policy is an appreciation of the need to protect examples of modern architecture. It is shocking to find that one of William Wurster's finest houses, the Coleman House in Pacific Heights, has been completely rebuilt without more than passing reference to Wurster's original design. Docomoca/Noca was founded in 1989 as an affiliate of the international organization based in the Netherlands to stimulate interest in Modernism and to fight for the registration and protection of modern buildings. Members are currently working with the Landmarks Preservation Board to develop criteria for listing modern buildings.

In any livable city, the pressures on the urban environment are enormous, particularly in prosperous times. In 1937 the authors of the New Deal–funded guide to San Francisco noted that "the story of San Francisco is largely the story of its water front." Except for future real estate deals along the southeastern waterfront and plans to construct a cruise ship terminal, this is no longer true. Most of the waterfront has become an urban park devoid of any kind of economic activity except for an occasional bar or restaurant.

Today the story of San Francisco is the story of bankers, brokers, high-tech yuppies, medical researchers, and the thousands of service workers who cater to their needs. San Francisco is still an immigrant community, still remarkably diverse, and will remain so. From the 1960s to the boom years of the 1990s, San Francisco was a welcoming city—and it is still a sanctuary for the dispossessed. But the environment is less hospitable, for the simple reason that there is simply not enough low-cost housing, a fact dramatically symbolized by the presence of thousands of homeless people and by the willingness of nominally liberal politicians to target them as a social problem without offering any real solutions to their plight.

At the same time, San Francisco is where the work is. So it will continue to attract new immigrants, as demonstrated by the presence of hundreds of casual workers waiting along the sidewalks of the Mission for day jobs. In Mission Bay and the Presidio, one witnessed the Redevelopment Agency and the Presidio Trust offering millions in subsidies to huge corporations without bothering to make a real effort to deal with the city's housing crisis. Community-based nonprofits such as the Tenants and Owners Development Corporation (TODCO) and the Mission Housing Development Corporation are struggling valiantly to fill the gap, but the results fall far short of the need. If anything, the preservation movement, despite its good intentions, has contributed unwittingly to the shortage. Victorians, though battered and chopped up into small apartments, once provided housing for low-income families. Restored Victorians are priced well beyond the means of even medium-income professionals. Diversity—economic, racial, and gender—has been the life blood of the city's vibrant cultural life. Without true diversity, the city is faced with the prospect—boring indeed—of becoming a yuppie playground.

Over the decades since the Freeway Revolt, activists have fought their way into the urban design process, but it cannot be said that community groups, despite decades of organizing, demonstrations, and lawsuits, have been able to control the important decisions that shape the city's urban environment. The big decisions—for example, about the nature of the Mission Bay Project and the commercialization of the Presidio—are still made by corporate leaders and their political henchmen. Of course, the developers now take what is known as the soft approach, some of it required by law. There is much consultation with citizens groups. Developers must pay abatement fees for parks, housing, and public art and transportation, and the days of refrigerator-style high rises appear to have been brought to a close by the Downtown Plan. Despite all of this, public transportation and the city's schools are notoriously underfunded and the park system requires a $350 million investment to halt its deterioration.

It is important to remember that after 15 years of organizing, the initiatives that led to restrictions on the construction of high rises and required the payment of abatement fees passed by narrow margins. Further, there are signs of continuing support for both freeways and highrises.

And from an urban design perspective, there is a definite logic to the idea of revisiting the construction of high rises. Despite the open space along the southeastern waterfront, the city occupies a peninsula and cannot sprawl forever. Nor, given the daily traffic jams, which can only grow worse, can the city accommodate many more automobile commuters. In *New Architecture San Francisco*, Skidmore Owings Merrrill (SOM) architects Marc Goldstein and John Kriken acknowledge that high rises cast shadows and pose problems of scale. "But there is another side of the highrise issue," they argue. "Their real value stems from the human dimension of the areas in cities that we call downtown. Highrises stand for the importance and desirability we place on close face-to-face associations. They come from the very basic need of people to come together with some kind of reasonable transportation to and from their homes to work."[98]

Aaron Betsky, the Museum of Modern Art's curator of architecture and design, took this argument one step further. "San Francisco needs more tall buildings," he wrote in a Feburary 1999 article in *San Francisco* magazine calling for the construction of slim, 300-foot-high residential towers, not to exceed 120 feet in width, along the waterfront and even along the borders of Golden Gate Park. "Proponents of slow growth," Betsky argued, "remain fixated on the problem of big buildings without addressing the city's real needs."

Both Betsky and the SOM architects make only passing reference to one of the city's most important "real needs"—an effective public transportation system. There is talk about a massive revival of the ferry system, which would be wonderful, but no one appears ready to bite the bullet and restrict automobile traffic downtown as is done in cities like Singapore. Instead, as South of Market (SOMA) becomes the scene of new attractions, such as the Metreon and the new baseball stadium, the mayor is calling for the construction of more parking garages.

Finally, given the city's contentious environment, what will the new architecture of San Francisco look like? There is already a fascinating creative tension between the Contextualists and the neomodernists—witness Robert Stern's contextual Gap Building and Gensler Associates' neomodernist addition to the Moscone Convention Center. Architectural critics, such as Allan Temko, have argued that San Francisco, because of its preservation ethic, is a hostile environment when it comes to new design ideas. "I think Frank Gehry is right," he told an interviewer, "in saying that he could never do anything good in San Francisco."[99] As we have seen, there have been new design ideas—for example, Fisher Friedman Associates' construction of a modern building within the crumbling walls of the old brick Oriental Warehouse. Further, the scales appear to be tipping toward the neomodernists, at least when judged in the context of designs for new buildings, such as the de Young and Jewish Museums and Rem Koolhas' plans for a downtown luxury store. Only time will tell whether San Francisco, a city known for experimentation, becomes an incubator for new trends in architecture.

Footnotes

1. Randall Milliken, *A Time of Little Choice: The Disintegration of Tribal Culture in the San Francisco Bay Area, 1769–1810*. (Menlo Park, Calif.: Ballena Press, 1995), 220.
2. John Phillip Langellier and Daniel B. Rosen, *El Presidio de San Francisco: A History Under Spain and Mexico, 1776–1846*. (Spokane, Wash.: Arthur H. Clark, 1996), 70.
3. Richard Henry Dana, *Two Years Before the Mast*, quoted in Malcolm E. Barker, ed., *San Francisco Memoirs, 1835–1851*. (San Francisco: Londonborn Publications, 1994), 55.
4. İbid., 67.
5. Malcolm E. Barker, *San Francisco Memoirs, 1852–1899*. (San Francisco: Londonborn Publications, 1996), 117.
6. Albert Shumate, *A San Francisco Scandal: The California of George Gordon* (San Francisco and Spokane, Wash.: California Historical Society and Arthur H. Clarke, 1994), 121.
7. Mark Twain, *Roughing It* (New York: Penguin Books, 1981), 310.
8. Dan de Quille, *A History of the Comstock Silver Lode and Mines* reprint, (New York: Promontory Press, 1974), 39–40.
9. Henry George, "What the Railroad Will Bring Us," *Overland Monthly*, October, 1868.
10. Ronald Delehanty, *In the Victorian Style*. (San Francisco: Chronicle Books, 1997), xi.
11. Frank Soulé et al., *The Annals of San Francisco*. (1855; reprint, Berkeley, Calif.: Berkeley Hills Books, 1998), 160.
12. Franklin Walker, *San Francisco's Literary Frontier* (Seattle: University of Washington Press, 1969), 146.
13. Stanley P. Hirshson, *The White Tecumseh: A Biography of William T. Sherman* (New York: John Wiley & Sons, 1997), 50.
14. Bill Pickelhaupt, *Shanghaied in San Francisco* (San Francisco: Flyblister Press, 1996), 117, 120.
15. William A. Bullough, *The Blind Boss and His City: Christopher Augustine Buckley & Nineteenth Century San Francisco*. (Berkeley: University of California Press, 1979), 138.
16. Robert E. Stewart Jr. and M. F. Stewart, *Adolph Sutro: A Biography*. (Berkeley, Calif.: Howell-North Books, 1962), 207.

17. Mel Scott, *The San Francisco Bay Area: A Metropolis in Perspective* (Berkeley: University of California Press, 1959), 97.
18. Arnold Genthe, *As I Remember.* (New York: Reynal & Hitchcock, 1936), 56.
19. Ibid., 89.
20. Jerry Flamm, *Hometown San Francisco: Sunny Jim, Phat Willie, and Dave* (San Francisco: Scottwall Associates, 1994), 33.
21. Charles P. Larrowe, *Harry Bridges: The Rise and Fall of Radical Labor in the US.* (New York: Lawrence Hill, 1972), 8.
22. Marc Treib, ed., *An Everyday Modernism: The Houses of William Wurster.* (Berkeley: University of California Press, 1995), 189.
23. Kenneth Rexroth, *An Autobiographical Novel.* (New York: New Directions, 1991), 182.
24. Dennis P. Kelly, "Mayor Roger D. Lapham, the Recall Election of 1946, and Neighborhood", *California History LXXVI* (Winter 1997/98), 129.
25. Joyce Jansen, *San Francisco's Cable Cars.* (San Francisco: Woodford Press, 1995), 89, 92.
26. Chester Hartman, *The Transformation of San Francisco.* (Totowa, NJ: Rowman and Allanheld, 1984), 8–9.
27. Ibid., 18.
28. James Richardson, *Willie Brown, A Biography.* (Berkeley: University of California Press, 1996), 46.
29. John Jacobs, *A Rage for Justice: The Passion and Politics of Phillip Burton* (Berkeley: University of California Press, 1995), xxii.
30. Allan B. Jacobs, *Making City Planning Work* (Chicago: American Society of Planning Officials, 1978), 69.
31. Roger Olmsted and T.H. Watkins, *Here Today: San Francisco's Architectural Heritage.* (San Francisco: Chronicle Books, 1968), 5.
32. Interview with author, 1998.
33. Bruce B. Brugmann et al., *The Ultimate Highrise: San Francisco's Rush Toward the Sky.* (San Francisco: San Francisco Bay Guardian Books, 1971), 115.
34. Hartman, *The Transformation of San Francisco,* 227.
35. Ibid., 270.
36. Interview with author, 1998.
37. Hartman, *The Transformation of San Francisco,* 7.
38. Ibid., 32.
39. Ibid., 67.
40. Ibid., 106.
41. Interview with author, 1999.
42. Richard DeLeon, *Left Coast Politics: Progressive Politics in San Francisco, 1975-1991.* (Lawrence: University of Kansas Press,, 1992), 117.
43. Interview with author, 1999.
44. Harold Kirker, *California 's Architectural Frontier: Style and Tradition in the Nineteenth Century,* (Salt Lake City: Peregrine Smith Books, 1986), xxvii.
45. Richard Longstreth, *On the Edge of the World: Four Architects in San Francisco at the Turn of the Century.* (New York: The Architectural History Foundation and Cambridge, Mass.: MIT Press, 1983), 262.
46. Ibid., 78–79.
47. Thomas Hines, *Burnham of Chicago: Architect and Planner* (Chicago: University of Chicago Press, 1979), 74.
48. *Domestic Architecture of the San Francisco Bay Region.* (San Francisco: San Francisco Museum of Art, 1949), n.p.

49. Ibid., n.p.
50. Michael R. Corbett and Charles Page Hall & Associates, *Splendid Survivors: San Francisco's Downtown Architectural Heritage.* (San Francisco: California Living Books, 1979), 23.
51. Spiro Kostof, *The City Shaped: Urban Patterns and Meaning Through History* (Boston: Little, Brown & Co., 1991), 331.
52. Sally Woodbridge, ed., *Bay Area Houses* (Salt Lake City: Peregrine Smith Books, 1988), 20, 22.
53. James Shay, *New Architecture San Francisco.* (San Francisco: Chronicle Books, 1989), 28.
54. Michael R. Corbett et al., *Splendid Survivors*, 169.
55. Daniel Gregory and Karin Nelson, "Designing the City Club: An Interview with Michael Goodman," *A Report from the San Francisco Craft and Folk Art Museum*, Winter, 1988/1989, n.p.
56. Thomas W. Chinn, *Bridging the Pacific: San Francisco Chinatown and Its People.* (San Francisco: Chinese Historical Society of America, 1989), 141.
57. Corbett et al., *Splendid Survivors*, 89.
58. Soule et al., *The Annals of San Francisco*, 594.
59. San Francisco Department of City Planning, *An Introductory Plan for the Civic Center*, 1953, 6.
60. *Mario Botta, Public Buildings.* (Milan: Skira editore, 1999), 35.
61. Dino Cinel, *From Italy to San Francisco: The Immigrant Experience.* (Stanford, Calif.: Stanford University Press, 1982), 126.
62. Felice A. Bonadio, *A.P. Giannini: Banker of America.* (Berkeley: University of California Press, 1994), 21.
63. Cinel, *From Italy to San Francisco*, 126.
64. Lawrence Ferlinghetti and Nancy J. Peters, *Literary San Francisco: A Pictorial History from Its Beginnings to the Present Day.* (San Francisco: City Lights Books and Harper & Row, 1980), 153.
65. David F. Myrick, *San Francisco's Telegraph Hill.* (Berkeley, Calif.: Howell-North Books, 1972), 183.
66. Ibid., 139.
67. Tom Stoddard, *Jazz on the Barbary Coast.* (Berkeley, Calif.: Heyday Books, 1998), 193.
68. Ibid., 190.
69. William Kostura, *Russian Hill: The Summit, 1853–1906.* (San Francisco: Aerie Publications, 1997).
70. Kostura, *Russian Hill*, 51.
71. Ann Bloomfield, "The Real Estate Associates: A Land and Housing Developer of the 1870s in San Francisco," in Thomas Carter, ed., *Images of an American Land: Vernacular Architecture in the Western United States.* (Albuquerque: University of New Mexico Press, 1997), 205.
72. Ibid., 218.
73. Irena Narell, *Our City: The Jews of San Francisco.* (San Diego: Howell-North Books, 1981), 50.
74. Scott, *The San Francisco Bay Area*, 43.
75. Longstreth, *On the Edge of the World*, 78.
76. John H. Mollenkopf, *The Contested City*, (Princeton, N.J.: Princeton University Press, 1983), 146–47.
77. Olmsted and Watkins, *Here Today*, 5.
78. Interview with the author, 1998.

79. Shay, *New Architecture San Francisco,* 127.

80. Interview with the author, 1999.

81. For more information, see Timothy Drescher, *San Francisco Murals.* (St. Paul: Pogo Press, 1994).

82. Charles Perry, *The Haight-Ashbury: A History.* (New York: Vintage Books, 1985), 245.

83. Donna Gouse, "History of the Haight-Ashbury: From 1870 to the Present," www.haight-ashbury.com.

84. John A. Martini, *Fortress Alcatraz: Guardian of the Golden Gates.* (Kailua, Hawaii: Pacific Monograph, 1990), 81.

85. Kevin Starr, *Americans and the California Dream, 1850–1915* (New York: Oxford University Press, 1973), 396.

86. Sally B. Woodbridge, *Bernard Maybeck, Visionary Architect.* (New York: Abbeville Press, 1996), 104.

87. Hirshon, *The White Tecumseh,* 352.

88. Lisa M. Benton, *The Presidio: From Army Post to National Park* (Boston: Northeastern University Press, 1998), 51.

89. William J. Pomeroy, *American Neo-colonialism: Its Emergence in the Philippines and Asia,* (New York: International Publishers, 1970), 92.

90. Benton, *The Presidio,* 50.

91. Ibid., 101.

92. Excerpt from *Civilizing American Cities: Writings on City Landscapes* by Frederic Law Olmsted, *San Francisco Examiner Magazine,* July 27, 1997.

93. Raymond H. Clary, *The Making of Golden Gate Park: The Early Years. 1865–1906* (New York: A California Living Book, 1980), 76–77.

94. Joseph Armstrong Baird Jr., *Times Wondrous Change: San Francisco's Architecture, 1776–1915.* (San Francisco: California Historical Society, 1962), 41.

95. Jerry Flamm, *Good Life in Hard Times: San Francisco's 20s and 30s.* (San Francisco: Chronicle Books), 104.

96. Jane Jacobs, *The Death and Life of American Cities,* (New York: Modern Library, 1993), 9.

97. Jacobs, *Making City Planning Work,* xxiv.

98. Shay, *New Architecture San Francisco,* 115.

99. Sharon Tucker, "Interview with Allan Temko," *Line,* American Institute of Architects, San Francisco Chapter, Spring, 1998.

Bibliography

Asbury, Herbert. *The Barbary Coast: Seventy Years of San Francisco's Underworld.* New York: Ballantine Books, 1973.

Barker, Malcolm E., ed. *Three Fearful Days: San Francisco Memoirs of the 1906 Earthquake and Fire.* San Francisco: Londonborn Publications, 1998.

Bean, Walter. *Boss Ruef's San Francisco: The Story of the Union Labor Party, Big Business, and the Graft Prosecution.* Berkeley: University of California Press, 1972.

Brechin, Gray. *Imperial San Francisco: Urban Power, Earthly Ruin.* Berkeley: University of California Press, 1999.

Brook, James et al., eds. *Reclaiming San Francisco, History, Politics, Culture.* San Francisco: City Lights Books, 1998.

Boutelle, Sara Holmes. *Julia Morgan, Architect.* New York: Abbeville Press, 1995.

Crowe, Michael F. *Deco by the Bay: Art Deco Architecture in the San Francisco Bay Area.* New York: Viking Studio Books, 1995.

Dillon, Richard. *High Steel: Building the Bridges Across the San Francisco Bay.* Berkeley: Celestial Arts, 1979.

Ethington, Phillip J. *The Public City: The Political Construction of Urban Life in San Francisco, 1850–1900.* Cambridge: Cambridge University Press, 1994.

Freudenheim, Leslie Mandelson and Elisabeth Sacks Sussman. *Building with Nature: Roots of the San Francisco Bay Region Tradition.* Santa Barbara: Peregrine Smith, 1974.

Gebhard, David, et al. *Samuel and Joseph Cather Newsom, Victorian Architectural Imagery in California, 1878–1908.* Oakland and Santa Barbara: The Oakland Museum and The University of California Santa Barbara Museum, 1979.

Gentry, Curt. *The Madams of San Francisco.* Sausalito: Comstock Editions, 1964.

Issel, William and Robert W. Cherny. *San Francisco, 1865–1932: Politics, Power, and Urban Development.* Berkeley: University of California Press, 1986.

Kahn, Judd. *Imperial San Francisco: Politics and Planning in an American City, 1897–1906.* Lincoln: University of Nebraska Press, 1979.

Lewis, Oscar. *The Big Four: The First Railroad to the Pacific Coast.* New York: Ballantine Books, 1971.

395

Lotchin, Roger W. *San Francisco from Hamlet to City, 1846–1856.* Urbana: University of Illinois Press, 1997.

Margolin, Malcolm. *The Ohlone Way: Indian Life in the San Francisco-Monterey Bay Area.* Berkeley: Heyday Books, 1978.

Martin, Mildred Crowl. *Chinatown's Angry Angel: The Story of Donaldina Cameron.* Palo Alto: Pacific Books, 1977.

McGrew, Patrick. *The Historic Houses of Presidio Terrace.* San Francisco: Friends of Presidio Terrace, 1995.

Olmsted, Nancy. *The Ferry Building: Witness to a Century of Change 1898–1998.* Berkeley: Heyday Books, 1998.

Pflueger, Milton T. *Time and Tim Remembered.* San Francisco: Pflueger Architects, 1985.

Scharlach, Bernice. *Big Alma: San Francisco's Alma Spreckels.* San Francisco: Scottwall Associates, 1995.

Shilts, Randy. *The Mayor of Castro Street: The Life and Times of Harvey Milk.* New York: St. Martin's Press, 1982.

Stanford, Sally. *The Lady of the House.* New York: G. P. Putnam's Sons, 1966.

Stryker, Susan and Jim Van Buskirk. *Gay by the Bay: A History of Queer Culture in the San Francisco Bay Area.* San Francisco: Chronicle Books, 1996.

Temko, Allen. *No Way to Build a Ballpark and Other Irreverent Essays on Architecture.* San Francisco: Chronicle Books, 1993.

Watkins, T. H. and R. R. Olmsted. *Mirror of the Dream: An Illustrated History of San Francisco.* San Francisco: Scrimshaw Press, 1976.

Weiss, Mike. *Double Play: The San Francisco City Hall Killings.* Reading: Addison-Wesley, 1984.

Willard, Ruth Hendricks and Carol Green Wilson. *Sacred Places of San Francisco.* Novato: Presidio Press, 1985.

Yung, Judy. *Unbound Feet: A Social History of Chinese Women in San Francisco.* Berkeley: University of California Press, 1995.

Index